Houghton Mifflin

Reading

Teacher's Edition

Grade 3

Horizons

Senior Authors J. David Cooper, John J. Pikulski

Authors Kathryn H. Au, David J. Chard, Gilbert G. Garcia, Claude N. Goldenberg, Phyllis C. Hunter, Marjorie Y. Lipson, Shane Templeton, Sheila W. Valencia, MaryEllen Vogt

Consultants Linda H. Butler, Linnea C. Ehri, Carla B. Ford

 HOUGHTON MIFFLIN BOSTON

LITERATURE REVIEWERS

Consultants: Dr. Adela Artola Allen, Associate Dean, Graduate College, Associate Vice President for Inter-American Relations, University of Arizona, Tucson, AZ; **Dr. Manley Begay,** Co-director of the Harvard Project on American Indian Economic Development, Director of the National Executive Education Program for Native Americans, Harvard University, John F. Kennedy School of Government, Cambridge, MA; **Dr. Nicholas Kannellos,** Director, Arte Publico Press, Director, Recovering the U.S. Hispanic Literacy Heritage Project, University of Houston, TX; **Mildred Lee,** author and former head of Library Services for Sonoma County, Santa Rosa, CA; **Dr. Barbara Moy,** Director of the Office of Communication Arts, Detroit Public Schools, MI; **Norma Naranjo,** Clark County School District, Las Vegas, NV; **Dr. Arlette Ingram Willis,** Associate Professor, Department of Curriculum and Instruction, Division of Language and Literacy, University of Illinois at Urbana-Champaign, IL

Teachers: Suzanne Clark, Burlington, VT; **Leola J. Burton,** Vallejo, CA; **Kathleen Gousha,** Camden, NJ; **Angie Pink,** Independence, IA; **Anita Pohlman,** Memphis, TN

PROGRAM REVIEWERS

Linda Bayer, Jonesboro, GA; **Sheri Blair,** Warner Robins, GA; **Faye Blake,** Jacksonville, FL; **Suzi Boyett,** Sarasota, FL; **Carol Brockhouse,** Madison Schools, Wayne Westland Schools, MI; **Patti Brustad,** Sarasota, FL; **Jan Buckelew,** Venice, FL; **Maureen Carlton,** Barstow, CA; **Karen Cedar,** Gold River, CA; **Karen Ciraulo,** Folsom, CA; **Marcia M. Clark,** Griffin, GA; **Kim S. Coady,** Covington, GA; **Eva Jean Conway,** Valley View School District, IL; **Marilyn Crownover,** Tustin, CA; **Carol Daley,** Sioux Falls, SD; **Jennifer Davison,** West Palm Beach, FL; **Lynne M. DiNardo,** Covington, GA; **Kathy Dover,** Lake City, GA; **Cheryl Dultz,** Citrus Heights, CA; **Debbie Friedman,** Fort Lauderdale, FL; **Anne Gaitor,** Lakeland, GA; **Rebecca S. Gillette,** Saint Marys, GA; **Buffy C. Gray,** Peachtree City, GA; **Merry Guest,** Homestead, FL; **Jo Nan Holbrook,** Lakeland, GA; **Beth Holguin,** San Jose, CA; **Coleen Howard-Whals,** St. Petersburg, FL; **Beverly Hurst,** Jacksonville, FL; **Debra Jackson,** St. Petersburg, FL; **Vickie Jordan,** Centerville, GA; **Cheryl Kellogg,** Panama City, FL; **Karen Landers,** Talladega County, AL; **Barb LeFerrier,** Port Orchard, WA; **Sandi Maness,** Modesto, CA; **Ileana Masud,** Miami, FL; **David Miller,** Cooper City, FL; **Muriel Miller,** Simi Valley, CA; **Walsetta W. Miller,** Macon, GA; **Jean Nielson,** Simi Valley, CA; **Sue Patton,** Brea, CA; **Debbie Peale,** Miami, FL; **Loretta Piggee,** Gary, IN; **Jennifer Rader,** Huntington, CA; **April Raiford,** Columbus, GA; **Cheryl Remash,** Manchester, NH; **Francis Rivera,** Orlando, FL; **Marina Rodriguez,** Hialeah, FL; **Marilynn Rose,** MI; **Kathy Scholtz,** Amesbury, MA; **Kimberly Moulton Schorr,** Columbus, GA; **Linda Schrum,** Orlando, FL; **Sharon Searcy,** Mandarin, FL; **Melba Sims,** Orlando, FL; **Judy Smith,** Titusville, FL; **Bea Tamo,** Huntington, CA; **Dottie Thompson,** Jefferson County, AL; **Dana Vassar,** Winston-Salem, NC; **Beverly Wakefield,** Tarpon Springs, FL; **Joy Walls,** Winston-Salem, NC; **Elaine Warwick,** Williamson County, TN; **Audrey N. Watkins,** Atlanta, GA; **Marti Watson,** Sarasota, FL

Supervisors: Judy Artz, Butler County, OH; **James Bennett,** Elkhart, IN; **Kay Buckner-Seal,** Wayne County, MI; **Charlotte Carr,** Seattle, WA; **Sister Marion Christi,** Archdiocese of Philadelphia, PA; **Alvina Crouse,** Denver, CO; **Peggy DeLapp,** Minneapolis, MN; **Carol Erlandson,** Wayne Township Schools, IN; **Brenda Feeney,** North Kansas City School District, MO; **Winnie Huebsch,** Sheboygan, WI; **Brenda Mickey,** Winston-Salem, NC; **Audrey Miller,** Camden, NJ; **JoAnne Piccolo,** Westminster, CO; **Sarah Rentz,** Baton Rouge, LA; **Kathy Sullivan,** Omaha, NE; **Rosie Washington,** Gary, IN; **Theresa Wishart,** Knox County Public Schools, TN

English Language Learners Reviewers: Maria Arevalos, Pomona, CA; **Lucy Blood,** NV; **Manuel Brenes,** Kalamazoo, MI; **Delight Diehn,** AZ; **Susan Dunlap,** Richmond, CA; **Tim Fornier,** Grand Rapids, MI; **Connie Jimenez,** Los Angeles, CA; **Diane Bonilla Lether,** Pasadena, CA; **Anna Lugo,** Chicago, IL; **Marcos Martel,** Hayward, CA; **Carolyn Mason,** Yakima, WA; **Jackie Pinson,** Moorpark, CA; **Jenaro Rivas,** NJ; **Jerilyn Smith,** Salinas, CA; **Noemi Velazquez,** Jersey City, NJ; **JoAnna Veloz,** NJ; **Dr. Santiago Veve,** Las Vegas, NV

CREDITS

Cover

Cover photography © Eric Meola/The Image Bank/Getty Images.

Title page photography © Chase Swift/CORBIS.

Photography

Theme Opener © Kelly Harriger/CORBIS. **152B** © Burstein Collection/CORBIS. **174** Hemera Technologies, Inc. **213BB** Guillarme Dargaud. **213CC** (cover) North Wind Picture Archive. **251Z** © Getty Images.

Illustration

All kid art by Morgan-Cain & Associates.

ACKNOWLEDGMENTS

Grateful acknowledgment is made for permission to reprint copyrighted material as follows:

Theme 5

From *Alice Ramsey's Grand Adventure,* by Don Brown. Copyright © 1997 by Don Brown. Reprinted by permission of Houghton Mifflin Company.

"Going West: Children on the Oregon Trail," by Helen Wieman Bledsoe from *Appleseeds* Magazine, September 1999 issue: "Growing Up on the Oregon Trail." Copyright © 1999 by Cobblestone Publishing, 30 Grove Street, Suite C, Peterborough, NH 03458. All rights reserved. Reprinted by permission of Carus Publishing Company.

From *Pedro's Journal,* by Pam Conrad. Text copyright © 1991 by Pam Conrad. Published by Caroline House, Boyds Mills Press, Inc. Reprinted by permission.

STUDENT WRITING MODEL FEATURE

Special thanks to the following teachers whose students' compositions appear as Student Writing Models: **Cindy Cheatwood,** FL; **Diana Davis,** NC; **Kathy Driscoll,** MA; **Linda Evers,** FL; **Heidi Harrison,** MI; **Eileen Hoffman,** MA; **Julia Kraftsow,** FL; **Bonnie Lewison,** FL; **Kanetha McCord,** MI

Voyagers

Theme 5

Reading Strategies question; predict/infer; monitor/clarify; phonics/decoding

Comprehension making inferences; predicting outcomes; text organization

Decoding Longer Words suffixes *-less,* and *-ness;* possessives, VCCV pattern, vowel sounds in *tooth* and *cook;* vowel sound in *bought;* double consonants

Vocabulary dictionary: syllables; analogies; homophones

Spelling vowel sounds in *tooth* and *cook;* vowel sound in *bought;* VCCV pattern

Grammar subject pronouns; sentence combining with subject pronouns; object pronouns; using the correct verb form; possessive pronouns; proofreading for *its* and *it's*

Writing writing a play; using exclamations; writing a message; writing complete information; write a learning log entry; writing dates and times; process writing: description

Listening/Speaking/Viewing oral book report; nonverbal communication skills; group problem solving

Information and Study Skills multimedia report; graphic organizers; time lines

Theme 5

Voyagers

CONTENTS

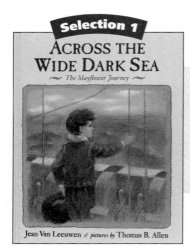

Selection 1

ACROSS THE WIDE DARK SEA
The Mayflower Journey

Jean Van Leeuwen & *pictures by* Thomas B. Allen

Historical Fiction

Below Level   *On Level*   *Above Level*   *Language Support*

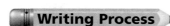

Writing Process ▶

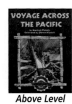

Theme Wrap-Up
Monitoring Student Progress

Fiction

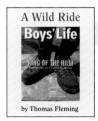

Nonfiction

Focus on Genre — FAIRY TALES

Fiction

Fiction

Below Level   *On Level*   *Above Level*   *Language Support*

Leveled Theme Paperbacks

Leveled Bibliography

BOOKS FOR INDEPENDENT READING AND FLUENCY BUILDING

 To build vocabulary and fluency, choose books from this list for students to read outside class. Suggest that students read for at least thirty minutes a day, either independently or with an adult who provides modeling and guidance.

Key

 Science

 Social Studies

 Multicultural

 Music

 Math

 Classic

 Art

Career

Classroom Bookshelf

WELL BELOW LEVEL

 Take Off!
by Ryan Ann Hunter
Holiday 2000 (32p)
Takes the reader from the days of the Wright brothers to today's jumbo jets.

Tattered Sails
by Verla Kay
Putnam 2001 (32p)
Brief, rhyming text captures the excitement and hardship of a family's voyage from London to the Mass Bay Colony in 1635.

 My Father's Boat
by Sherry Garland
Scholastic 1998 (40p)
This is a story of three generations of Vietnamese American fishermen.

The Relatives Came
by Cynthia Rylant
Simon 1985 (32p) also paper
When the relatives from Virginia arrive for a summer visit, everyone has a boisterous, affectionate good time.

BELOW LEVEL

 Old Crump: The True Story of a Trip West
by Laurie Lawlor
Holiday 2002 (32p)
A faithful ox helps his pioneer family survive a trip across Death Valley.

 Sacajawea
by Joyce Milton
Grosset 2001 (48p) also paper
Sacajawea helps Lewis and Clark find their way across unmapped territory west of the Mississippi.

Edna
by Robert Burleigh
Orchard 2000 (32p)
Living in Greenwich Village, Edna St. Vincent Millay enjoys riding the Staten Island ferry.

Tulip Sees America
by Cynthia Rylant
Scholastic 1998 (32p)
A young man and his dog, Tulip, marvel at the beauty of the country.

Stringbean's Trip to the Shining Sea
by Vera B. Williams
Scholastic 1990 (48p) also paper
Stringbean Coe describes his trip to the West Coast with his big brother, Fred, and their dog, Potato.

ON LEVEL

 A Picture Book of Lewis and Clark
by David A. Adler
Holiday 2003 (32p)
In 1803, Meriwether Lewis and William Clark journey west to find a water route across America.

 The Glorious Flight
by Alice and Martin Provensen
Penguin 1987 (40p)
paper
Louis Blériot is determined to fly across the English Channel.

Annushka's Voyage
by Edith Tarbescu
Clarion 1998 (32p)
Annushka and Tanya sail to America to join their father.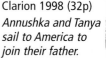

 My Diary From Here to There
by Amada Irma Perez
Children's Press 2002 (32p)
As her family makes its way from Mexico to California, a girl confides her hopes and fears to her diary.

The Journey
by Sarah Stewart
Farrar 2001 (32p)
An Amish girl writes in her diary about the experiences she has on her first trip to Chicago.

***Henry Hikes to Fitchburg**
by D.B. Johnson
Houghton 2000 (32p)
Henry and his friend set out to find the best way to get to Fitchburg.

The Amazing Air Balloon
by Jean Van Leeuwen
Fogelman 2003 (32p)
A boy tells of becoming the first person in America to go up in a hot air balloon.

Duncan's Way
by Ian Wallace
DK 2000 (32p)
When his father can no longer work as a cod fisherman, Duncan tries to find a solution.

---

*Included in Classroom Bookshelf, Level 3

Mae Jemison
by Corinne J. Naden and
[R]ose Blue
[M]illbrook 2003 (48p)

[T]his biography relates the story
[o]f the first African American
[w]oman to make a space flight.

[G]ood-bye for today
[b]y Peter and Connie Roop
[A]theneum 2000 (48p)

[A] young girl keeps a journal as
[s]he sails with her family from
[J]apan to the Arctic.

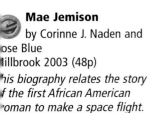

ABOVE LEVEL

Traveling Man
by James Rumford
[H]oughton 2001 (32p)

[I]n the 14th century, Moroccan Ibn
[B]attuta traveled an extraordinary
[7]5,000 miles over the course of
[t]hirty years.

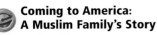
**Coming to America:
A Muslim Family's Story**
[b]y Bernard Wolf
[L]ee & Low 2003 (32p)

[A] Muslim family emigrates from
[E]gypt to New York City in the
[h]ope of making a better life for
[t]hemselves.

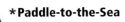
***Paddle-to-the-Sea**
by Holling C. Holling
[H]oughton 1976 (64p)

[A] young Indian boy carves a
[s]mall canoe with a figure he calls
[P]addle-to-the-Sea and sends it on
[a] voyage from the Great Lakes to
[t]he Atlantic Ocean.

The Key Collection
by Andrea Cheng
Holt 2003 (112p)

When Jimmy learns his beloved
grandma Ni Ni must move to
California, he feels he's losing
his best friend.

BOOKS FOR TEACHER READ ALOUD

The Fool of the World and the Flying Ship
by Arthur Ransome
Farrar 1976 (48p)

When the Czar promises his
daughter to whoever brings him
a flying ship, the Fool of the World
sets out to do that, meeting many
unusual people along the way.
**Available in Spanish as
Tontimundo y el barco volador.**

Take Command, Captain Farragut!
by Peter and Connie Roop
Atheneum 2002 (48p)

A thirteen-year-old naval officer
writes his father a series of letters
describing his adventures at sea.

Talkin' About Bessie
By Nikki Grimes
Orchard 2002 (32p)

In a series of monologues, Bessie
Coleman's friends and relatives
tell how she became the first
female African
American aviator.

Technology

Computer Software Resources

- **Get Set for Reading CD-ROM Voyagers**
  Provides background building, vocabulary support, and selection summaries in English and Spanish.

- **CD-ROM for Voyagers.** *Houghton Mifflin Company*

Video Cassettes

- **The Glorious Flight** *by Alice and Martin Provensen. Live Oak Media*

- **The Fool of the World and the Flying Ship** *by Arthur Ransome. BMG Kidz*

Audio

- **The Relatives Came** *by Cynthia Rylant. Live Oak Media*

- **The Glorious Flight** *by Alice and Martin Provensen. Live Oak Media*

- **Lily's Crossing** *by Patricia Reilly Giff. Bantam*

- **The Fool and the Flying Ship.** *Rabbit Ears*

Technology Resources addresses are on page R29.

Education Place®

www.eduplace.com *Log on to Education Place for more activities relating to* Voyagers.
- *e •* **Glossary**
- *e •* **WordGame**

Book Adventure®

www.bookadventure.org *This Internet reading incentive program provides thousands of titles for students to read.*

Accelerated Reader® Universal CD-ROM

This popular CD-ROM provides practice quizzes for Anthology selections and for many popular children's books.

---

[*] Included in Classroom Bookshelf, Level 3

Theme 5

Theme Skills Overview

	Selection 1	Selection 2	Selection 3
	Across the Wide Dark Sea Historical Fiction pp. 149A–183R 	**Yunmi and Halmoni's Trip** Realistic Fiction pp. 185I–213R 	**Trapped by the Ice!** Narrative Nonfiction pp. 213S–251R 

Pacing
Approximately 5–6 weeks

Reading
Comprehension

Information and Study Skills

Leveled Readers
• Fluency Practice
• Independent Reading

| **Guiding Comprehension**
 ⊙ **Making Inferences** T
 ⊙ **Question**

 Social Studies Link
 How to Read a Diagram
 Multimedia Report

 Leveled Readers
 The Golden Land
 Chasing the Train
 Faith's Journey
 Going to America

 Lessons and Leveled Practice | **Guiding Comprehension**
 ⊙ **Predicting Outcomes** T
 ⊙ **Predict/Infer** T

 Art Link
 How to Look at Fine Art
 Using Graphic Organizers 

 Leveled Readers
 Brothers are Forever
 South Pole Bound
 The Same, But Different
 Max Visits London

 Lessons and Leveled Practice | **Guiding Comprehension**
 ⊙ **Text Organization** T
 ⊙ **Monitor/Clarify**

 Media Link
 How to Read a Photo Essay
 Using a Time Line T 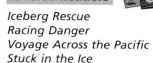

 Leveled Readers
 Iceberg Rescue
 Racing Danger
 Voyage Across the Pacific
 Stuck in the Ice

 Lessons and Leveled Practice |

Word Work
Decoding
Phonics Review

Vocabulary

Spelling

| ⊙ **Suffixes -less and -ness** T

 The Vowel Sounds in *tooth* and *cook*

 ⊙ **Syllables in a Dictionary** T

 Vowel Sounds in *tooth/cook* T | ⊙ **Possessives** T

 The Vowel Sound in *bought*

 ⊙ **Analogies** T

 Vowel Sound in *bought* T | ⊙ **VCCV Pattern** T

 Double Consonants

 ⊙ **Homophones** T

 VCCV Pattern T |

Writing and Oral Language
Writing
Grammar
Listening/Speaking/Viewing

| ✏ **Writing a Play**
 Using Exclamations

 Subject Pronouns T
 Present an Oral Book Report | ✏ **Writing a Message**
 Complete Information

 Object Pronouns T
 Say It Without Words | ✏ **Writing a Learning Log Entry**
 Dates and Times T

 Possessive Pronouns T
 Practice Group Problem Solving |

Cross-Curricular Activities

| Responding: Math, Vocabulary, Internet

 Classroom Management Activities | Responding: Social Studies, Listening and Speaking, Internet

 Classroom Management Activities | Responding: Science, Social Studies, Internet

 Classroom Management Activities |

T Skill tested on Theme Skills Test and/or Integrated Theme Test

Monitoring Student Progress

Check Your Progress
The Island-below-the-Star
Fiction

A Wild Ride
Nonfiction

pp. 251S–267R

Guiding Comprehension

Theme Connections

 Comprehension Skills Review T

 Predict/Infer T

Taking Tests: Writing an Answer to a Question

Connecting Leveled Readers

 Structural Analysis Skills Review T

 Vocabulary Skills Review T

Spelling Skills Review T

Writing Skills Review T

Grammar Skills Review T

Cross-Curricular Activities

Classroom Management Activities

Focus on Genre

Fairy Tales
pp. 267S–295R

Guiding Comprehension

 Understanding Fairy Tales

 Monitor/Clarify

Using an Almanac

Leveled Readers

Smudge-Face
The Little Sparrow
Rella's Wish
To Tell the Truth

Lessons and Leveled Practice

 Prefixes and Suffixes

Two Sounds of c

 Connotations

The /s/ Sound in *face*

Writing a Fairy Tale
Using Similes

Using Pronouns

Comparing Stories in Print and Movies

Responding: Internet

Classroom Management Activities

Combination Classrooms

See the **Combination Classroom Planning Guide** for lesson planning and management support.

 Writing Process

Reading-Writing Workshop: Description
• Student Writing Model
• Writing Process Instruction
• Writing Traits Focus

Additional Theme Resources

• Leveled Theme Paperbacks Lessons
• Reteaching Lessons
• Challenge/Extension Activities

Technology

Education Place
www.eduplace.com

Log on to Education Place® for more activities relating to *Voyagers*.

Lesson Planner CD-ROM
Customize your planning for *Voyagers* with the Lesson Planner CD-ROM.

Cross-Curricular Activities

Independent Activities

Assign these activities at any time during the theme while you work with small groups.

Additional Independent Activities

- Challenge/Extension Activities, Theme Resources, pp. R9, R11, R13, R15, R17, R19
- Theme 5 Assignment Cards 1–9, Teacher's Resource Blackline Masters, pp. 79–84
- Classroom Management Activities, pp. 152A–152B, 185Q–185R, 213AA–213BB, 251Y–251Z
- Language Center, pp. 183M–183N, 213M–213N, 251M–251N
- **Classroom Management Handbook,** Activity Masters CM5-1–CM5-12
- **Challenge Handbook,** Challenge Masters CH5-1–CH5-6

Look for more activities in the Classroom Management Kit.

Math

Create a Budget

Groups	30 minutes
Objective	Plan a trip for four people.
Materials	Travel magazines or guidebooks, brochures, newspaper travel sections

With your group, select a destination. Then write a budget for one week's stay at this destination for four people. Include the cost of the following items in your budget:

Travel Budget

- transportation to and from destination
- lodging for six nights
- 3 meals per day for 4 people
- fees for recreational activities
- spending money for souvenirs

Art

Design a Vehicle

Pairs	30 minutes
Objective	Design an improved vehicle.

With your partner, brainstorm type of transportation. Then think of wa these vehicles could be improved. Consider how they could be

- faster
- more comfortable
- quieter
- more fuel efficient

Work together to design an improv vehicle. Label your vehicle with the improvements you have made. Sha your design with your classmates.

Consider copying and laminating these activities for use in centers.

Science

Perform an Experiment

Pairs	🕐 30 minutes	
Objective	Observe and record data for an experiment.	
Materials	Basin of water, common objects for testing	

...oats are made to float on the water. ...hat are some other things that will ...oat? What are some things that ...ll sink? Experiment and find out!

Choose an object to test.

Each partner makes a prediction about whether it will sink or float. Record your predictions in a chart.

Perform the experiment by placing the object in the water. Observe whether it sinks or floats. Record your observations and check them against your predictions.

Write a paragraph describing your experiment and results.

Material	Prediction	Observation
paper clip	Jenna: float Troy: sink	The paper clip sinks.

Social Studies

Research a Destination

👥 Groups	🕐 45 minutes	
Objective	Research a city and its attractions.	
Materials	Reference sources	

As a group, choose a city that you would like to visit.

- Use newspapers, travel guides, magazines, and encyclopedias to find information about the city.
- List the things that you would like to see and do in the city.

Once your group has completed its research, share your information. Then use your collective research to write a group report. Include pictures of your city as part of your report.

Language Arts

Write a Persuasive Paragraph

🧍 Singles	🕐 30 minutes	
Objective	Write a persuasive paragraph.	

Imagine that a contest has just been announced to take people on a voyage to a space station. Write a paragraph to convince the judges why you would be the best person to go into space and to manage the activities at the space station. Remember to give your reasons and to support them with convincing facts and examples.

> I believe I am the best person for this mission. First of all, I have always wanted to be an astronaut.

Planning for Assessment

During instruction in Theme 5 . . .

1 SCREENING AND DIAGNOSIS

Screening
- Baseline Group Test

Diagnosis
- Leveled Reading Passages Assessment Kit
- Phonics/Decoding Screening Test
- Lexia Quick Phonics Assessment CD-ROM

2 MONITORING PROGRESS

ONGOING INFORMAL ASSESSMENT
- Guiding Comprehension questions
- Literature Discussion groups
- Comprehension Checks
- Fluency Practice
- Monitoring Student Progress boxes
- Writing Samples
- Observation Checklists
- Skill lesson applications

END-OF-THEME REVIEW AND TEST PREPARATION

Monitoring Student Progress
- emphasizes use of comparing and contrasting critical thinking skills, teaches test-taking strategies as preparation for formal assessments, and reviews tested theme skills and reading strategies.

Assessing Student Progress
- provides suggestions for administering formal assessments, identifies areas of difficulty, and lists program resources for differentiating further instruction.

FORMAL ASSESSMENT
- Selection Tests
- Integrated Theme Tests
- Theme Skills Tests
- Fluency Assessment
- Reading-Writing Workshop

3 MANAGING AND REPORTING

 Technology Record each student's performance on the **Learner Profile®** CD-ROM.

National Test Correlation
Documenting Adequate Yearly Progress

SKILLS for *Voyagers*	ITBS	Terra Nova (CTBS)	CAT	SAT	MAT
Comprehension Strategies and Skills					
• Strategies: Predict/Infer, Monitor/Clarify, Question*	O	O	O	O	O
• Skills: Making Inferences, Predicting Outcomes, Text Organization*, Making Judgments*, Cause and Effect*, Sequence of Events*, Story Structure*, Making Generalizations*, Topic/Main Idea/Details*	O	O	O	O	
Structural Analysis					
• Suffixes *-less, -ness*	O	O	O		
• Possessives, including *s'*	O	O		O	
• VCCV Pattern	O	O	O	O	
Vocabulary/Dictionary					
• Syllables					
• Analogies					
• Homophones					O
Information and Study Skills					
• Timelines/Schedules		O	O		
Spelling					
• VCCV Pattern	O	O	O	O	O
• Vowel Sounds in *tooth* and *cook*	O	O	O	O	O
• Vowel Sound in *bought*	O	O	O	O	O
Grammar					
• Pronouns: Subject, Object, Possessive	O	O			
Writing					
• Formats: Writing a Play, Taking Messages, Learning-log Entry	O	O			O
• Writing Dates and Times	O	O		O	O
• Reading-Writing Workshop: Description	O	O		O	O

*These skills are taught, but not tested, in this theme.

KEY

ITBS Iowa Tests of Basic Skills

Terra Nova (CTBS)
Comprehensive Tests of Basic Skills

CAT California Achievement Tests

SAT Stanford Achievement Tests

MAT Metropolitan Achievement Tests

Launching the Theme

Theme **5**

Voyagers

Travellers

Come, let us go a-roaming!
The world is all our own,
And half its paths are still untrod,
And half its joys unknown.

from the poem
by Arthur St. John Adcock

148

149

Introducing the Theme: Discussion Options

Read aloud the theme title and poem on Anthology page 149. Ask:

1 What makes someone a *voyager*?
(taking a long journey to a distant place)

2 What does the poem "Travellers" make you think about?
(Sample answer: that there is a lot of the world that I do not know about yet)

3 Based on the poem and the photograph, what do you think the stories in the theme will be about?
(Sample answers: long journeys, explorers, learning more about the world)

4 Pretend you are a voyager. Where would you go and why?
(Sample answer: a tropical rain forest so I could swim in a waterfall and see the animals)

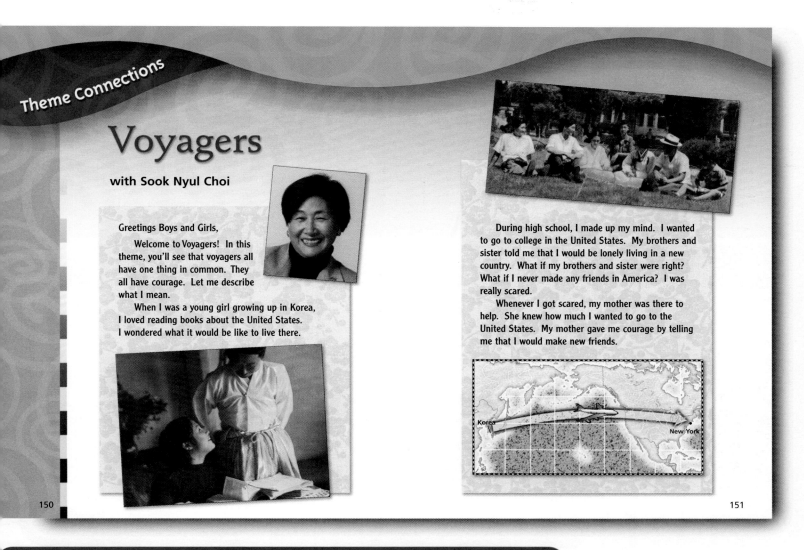

Voyagers

with Sook Nyul Choi

Greetings Boys and Girls,

Welcome to Voyagers! In this theme, you'll see that voyagers all have one thing in common. They all have courage. Let me describe what I mean.

When I was a young girl growing up in Korea, I loved reading books about the United States. I wondered what it would be like to live there.

During high school, I made up my mind. I wanted to go to college in the United States. My brothers and sister told me that I would be lonely living in a new country. What if my brothers and sister were right? What if I never made any friends in America? I was really scared.

Whenever I got scared, my mother was there to help. She knew how much I wanted to go to the United States. My mother gave me courage by telling me that I would make new friends.

Korea   New York

150   151

Building Theme Connections

Ask volunteers to read aloud the author's letter on Anthology pages 150, 151, and 152. Tell students that Sook Nyul Choi wrote *Yunmi and Halmoni's Trip,* a selection they will read in this theme. (See Teacher's Edition page 188 for more information on Sook Nyul Choi.) Use the following questions to prompt discussion.

1 Other than courage, what other things do voyagers have in common?
(Sample answers: sense of adventure, curiosity)

2 Have you read books about other countries and wondered what it would be like to live in them? Tell about it.
(Sample answer: I read a book about a Kenyan boy who ran long distances. I wondered what his hometown looks like because Kenya sounded beautiful.)

3 The author's family and friends helped to give her courage when she was scared. What would help give you courage in a new country? Why?
(Sample answer: reading more books about the place to remind myself of why I wanted to go there in the first place)

Manhattanville College

Wow, was my mother right! I was never lonely, not even on the day I arrived. When I stepped out of the taxi at Manhattanville College in New York, my new roommate and her friends were waiting for me. They rushed over and hugged me. I was so surprised! In Korea, people bow when they greet each other. They don't hug. Best friends in Korea only hold hands. But I loved getting that big hug from my new friends. It was really special.

So you see, all you need to take a voyage is a little courage. Keep that in mind as you read about the voyagers in this theme.

With best wishes to all young voyagers,

Sook Nyul Choi

During her first year at Manhattanville College, Sook Nyul Choi gave a speech to her class.

152

Take a Voyage

Think about the courage Sook Nyul Choi showed by coming to the United States. Was there ever a time in your life when you needed courage? What was that like? As you read the selections in this theme, look for ways the voyagers all show courage.

It's time to go! You'll travel on the *Mayflower*, walk across the South Pole, and discover Hawaii. By the end of this theme, you will all be voyagers!

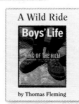

Internet To learn about the authors in this theme, visit Education Place. **www.eduplace.com/kids**

153

Building Theme Connections, *continued*

Read aloud the first paragraph on Anthology page 153.

- Discuss students' experiences with courage. Ask whether they have ever needed courage when they were on a voyage.

- Have students brainstorm ideas, images, and words they associate with taking a voyage. Record their thoughts.

- Discuss how students' ideas compare with Sook Nyul Choi's.

Have students finish reading Anthology page 153.

- Explain that the books pictured on the page are the selections students will read in the theme *Voyagers*.

- Ask students to predict the voyages in each selection. (Answers will vary.)

- Allow students time to look ahead at the selections and illustrations. Have them revise their original predictions as necessary.

Home Connection

Send home the theme letter for *Voyagers* to introduce the theme and suggest home activities. (See the **Teacher's Resource Blackline Masters.**)

For other suggestions relating to *Voyagers*, see **Home/Community Connections.**

Making Selection Connections

Introduce Selection Connections in the Practice Book.

- Have students complete **Practice Book** page 83.
- Preview the **Graphic Organizer** on page 84. Read aloud the directions, selection titles, and boldface questions. Explain that when they finish reading each selection, students will add to the chart to deepen their understanding of the theme *Voyagers*.

Classroom Management

At any time during the theme, you can assign the independent cross-curricular activities on Teacher's Edition pages 148I–148J while you give differentiated instruction to small groups. For additional independent activities related to specific selections, see the Teacher's Edition pages listed below.

- Week 1: pages 152A–152B, 183M–183N
- Week 2: pages 185Q–185R, 213M–213N
- Week 3: pages 213AA–213BB, 251M–251N
- Week 4: pages 251Y–251Z, 265A–265B, 265C–265D, 267N–267O

Monitoring Student Progress

Monitoring Progress

Throughout the theme, monitor your students' progress by using the following program features in the Teacher's Edition:

- Guiding Comprehension questions
- Literature discussion groups
- Skill lesson applications
- Monitoring Student Progress boxes

Wrapping Up and Reviewing the Theme

Use the two selections and support material in **Monitoring Student Progress** on pages 251S–267R to review theme skills, connect and compare theme literature, and prepare students for the Integrated Theme Test and the Theme Skills Test as well as for standardized tests measuring adequate yearly progress.

Practice Book page 83

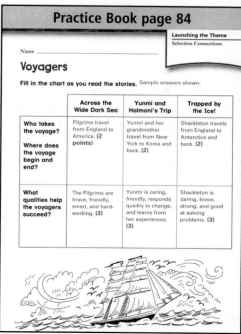

Practice Book page 84

Lesson Overview

Literature

ACROSS THE WIDE DARK SEA
~ The Mayflower Journey ~

Jean Van Leeuwen *& pictures by* Thomas B. Allen

1 Background and Vocabulary

2 Main Selection

Across the Wide Dark Sea
Genre: Historical Fiction

3 Social Studies Link

Selection Summary

A young Pilgrim boy travels with other Pilgrims to an unknown land. After a very difficult voyage, they arrive and build a settlement. With the help of the local Indians, they survive the winter with hope for the future.

Instructional Support

Planning and Practice

- Planning and classroom management
- Reading instruction
- Skill lessons
- Materials for reaching all learners

- Independent practice for skills, Level 3.5

- Newsletters
- Selection Summaries
- Assignment Cards
- Observation Checklists
- Selection Tests

- Transparencies
- Strategy Posters
- Blackline Masters

Reaching All Learners

Coordinated lessons, activities, and projects for additional reading instruction

For
- Classroom teacher
- Extended day
- Pull out
- Resource teacher
- Reading specialist

Technology

Audio Selection
Across the Wide Dark Sea

Get Set for Reading CD-ROM
- Background building
- Vocabulary support
- Selection Summary in English and Spanish

Accelerated Reader®
- Practice quizzes for the selection

www.eduplace.com
Log on to Education Place for more activities related to the selection, including vocabulary support—
  e•Glossary
  e•WordGame

Leveled Books for Reaching All Learners

Leveled Readers and Leveled Practice

- Independent reading for building fluency
- Topic, comprehension strategy, and vocabulary linked to main selection
- Lessons in Teacher's Edition, pages 183O–183R
- Leveled practice for every book

Technology

Leveled Readers
Audio available

Book Adventure®
- Practice quizzes for the Leveled Theme Paperbacks
www.bookadventure.org

● BELOW LEVEL

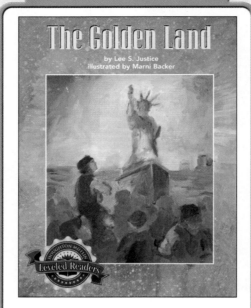

The Golden Land
by Lee S. Justice
illustrated by Marni Backer

▲ ON LEVEL

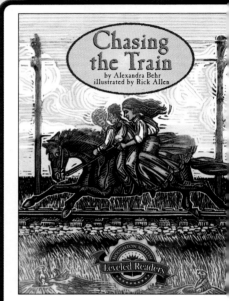

Chasing the Train
by Alexandra Behr
illustrated by Rick Allen

● Below Level Practice

The Golden Land
Key Vocabulary

Name

Vocabulary

Use the words from the box to complete the sentences. Write the answers in the puzzle.

Vocabulary
port
aboard
seasick
gleaming

Across
2. The sun shone on the _____gleaming_____ sea.
4. Many boats went in and out of the _____port_____, or town's harbor.

Down
1. Jenna felt _____seasick_____ when high waves made the boat go up and down.
3. We were happy to be _____aboard_____ the ship when it sailed.

5

▲ On Level Practice

Chasing the Train
Key Vocabulary

Name

Vocabulary

Use the words from the box to complete the sentences in the puzzle.

Vocabulary
journey
settlement
seeping
weary

1. Nan's family took a j o u r n e y to three national parks.
2. The first day, they were w e a r y after a hike up a mountain.
3. That night, rainwater was s e e p i n g through a hole in the tent.
4. The next day, they found a s e t t l e m e n t of houses and stores.

Write the letters above the numbers to answer this question.

What would make cold campers happy?

w a r m t e n t s
1 2 3 4 5 6 7 8 9

5

● Below Level Practice

The Golden Land
Comprehension Skill
Making Inferences

Name

Comprehension

Each list below contains items you might pack for a journey to a certain place. Read each list and think about the items included. Then tell where you might be going on each journey. Possible responses shown.

- swimsuit
- goggles
- flippers
- sunscreen

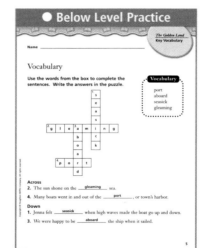

Where you might be going: _____the beach_____

- tent
- sleeping bag
- hiking boots
- sweatshirt

Where you might be going: _____campgrounds, the mountains_____

- camera
- sightseeing books
- walking shoes
- street and subway maps

Where you might be going: _____to the city_____

7

▲ On Level Practice

Chasing the Train
Comprehension Skill
Making Inferences

Name

Comprehension

Reread pages 4–7 of the story and then answer the questions below. Use story clues and what you know to make inferences.
Answers may vary. Possible responses are shown.

1. Why do you think Nathan and Ben want to get off the train?
Nathan and Ben are on a long train ride. It's hard to stay in one place for a long time. They probably want to move around in a bigger space. Also, they might want to explore a new place.

2. Why do you think Nathan and Ben run after the prairie dogs?
The boys may not have seen prairie dogs before. It is probably fun to try to catch the animals, especially because they keep hiding.

3. Why do you think the boys do not hear the train whistle the first time?
They are having fun and playing. They have run far from the train station chasing the prairie dogs, so the sound may not have been very loud to them.

4. How do you think the boys feel when they finally hear the train whistle?
Ben's mother told the boys to listen for the train whistle because it meant that the train is about to leave. They are probably worried that they will miss the train.

7

■ ABOVE LEVEL

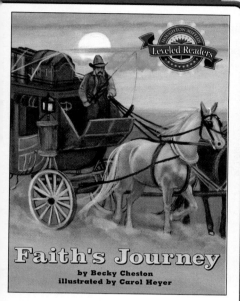

Faith's Journey
by Becky Cheston
illustrated by Carol Heyer

■ Above Level Practice

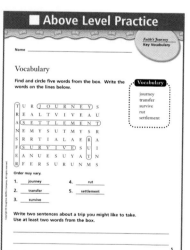

■ Above Level Practice

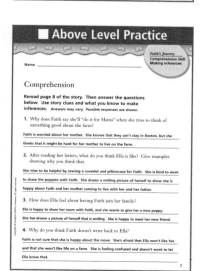

◆ LANGUAGE SUPPORT

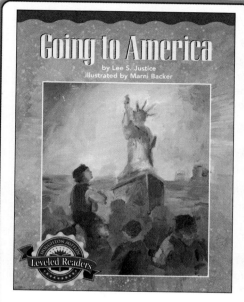

Going to America
by Lee S. Justice
illustrated by Marni Backer

◆ Language Support Practice

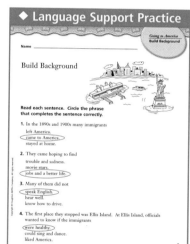

◆ Language Support Practice

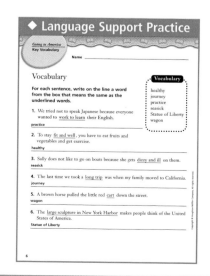

Leveled Theme Paperbacks

- Extended independent reading in Theme-related trade books
- Lessons in Teacher's Edition, pages R2–R7

Below Level

On Level

Challenge

Daily Lesson Plans

 **Technology**
Lesson Planner CD-ROM allows you to customize the chart below to develop your own lesson plans.

T Skill tested on Theme Skills Test and/or Integrated Theme Test

 50–60 minutes

Reading
Comprehension

Leveled Readers
- Fluency Practice
- Independent Reading

 20–30 minutes

Word Work
Phonics/Decoding
Vocabulary
Spelling

 20–30 minutes

Writing and Oral Language
Writing
Grammar
Listening/Speaking/Viewing

DAY 1

 ACROSS THE WIDE DARK SEA

Teacher Read Aloud, 153A–153B
Pedro's Journal

Building Background, 154

Key Vocabulary, 155
anchor   seeping   survive
cramped   settlement   weary
journey

Reading the Selection, 156–177

Comprehension Skill, 156
Making Inferences **T**

Comprehension Strategy, 156
Question

Leveled Readers
The Golden Land
Chasing the Train
Faith's Journey
Going to America

Lessons and Leveled Practice, 183O–183R

Phonics/Decoding, 157
Phonics/Decoding Strategy

Vocabulary, 156–177
Selection Vocabulary

Spelling, 183E
Vowel Sounds in *tooth/cook* **T**

Writing, 183K
Prewriting a Play

Grammar, 183I
Subject Pronouns **T**

Daily Language Practice
1. Us drewed the drowning man out of the water. (We; drew)
2. Him turned bloo with cold (He; blue; cold.)

Listening/Speaking/Viewing,
153A–153B, 165
Teacher Read Aloud, Stop and Think

DAY 2

 ACROSS THE WIDE DARK SEA

Reading the Selection, 156–177

Comprehension Check, 177

Responding, 178
Think About the Selection

Comprehension Skill Preview, 175
Making Inferences **T**

Leveled Readers
The Golden Land
Chasing the Train
Faith's Journey
Going to America

Lessons and Leveled Practice, 183O–183R

Structural Analysis, 183C
Suffixes *-less* and *-ness* **T**

Vocabulary, 156–177
Selection Vocabulary

Spelling, 183E
Vowel Sounds in *tooth/cook* Review and Practice **T**

 Writing, 183K
Drafting a Play

Grammar, 183I
Subject Pronouns Practice **T**

Daily Language Practice
3. The rain felt goode on our faces? (good; faces.)
4. Them soone groo tired of working. (They; soon; grew)

Listening/Speaking/Viewing, 177, 178
Wrapping Up, Responding

Target Skills of the Week

Comprehension	Question; Making Inferences
Vocabulary	Syllables in a Dictionary
Phonics/Decoding	Suffixes -less and -ness
Fluency	Leveled Readers

DAY 3

Rereading the Selection

Rereading for Writer's Craft, 161
Vivid Language

Rereading for Genre, 163
Historical Fiction

Comprehension Skill, 183A–183B
Making Inferences **T**

Leveled Readers

The Golden Land
Chasing the Train
Faith's Journey
Going to America

Lessons and Leveled Practice, 183O–183R

Phonics Review, 183D
Vowel Sounds in *tooth* and *cook*

Vocabulary, 183G
Syllables in a Dictionary **T**

Spelling, 183F
Vocabulary: Exact Words; Vowel Sounds in *tooth/cook* Practice **T**

Writing, 183L
Revising a Play

Grammar, 183J
Pronoun Game **T**

Daily Language Practice
They each losed a boote. (lost; boot)
There was a bird, they floo into the air. (bird.; flew)

DAY 4

Reading the Social Studies Link, 180–183
"Young Voyagers: A Pilgrim Childhood"

Skill: How to Read a Diagram

Comprehension Skill Review, 159
Story Structure

Leveled Readers

The Golden Land
Chasing the Train
Faith's Journey
Going to America

Lessons and Leveled Practice, 183O–183R

Phonics/Decoding, 180–183
Apply Phonics/Decoding Strategy to Link

Vocabulary, 183M
Language Center: Building Vocabulary

Spelling, 183F
Spelling Game, Proofreading **T**

Writing, 183L
Proofreading a Play
Using Exclamations

Grammar, 183J
Subject Pronouns Practice **T**

Daily Language Practice
7. A sailor had a bad problem with a toothe. (tooth)
8. Him couldn't choo his food. (He; chew)

Listening/Speaking/Viewing, 183
Discuss the Link

DAY 5

Rereading for Fluency, 169

Responding Activities, 178–179
Write a Travel Diary
Cross-Curricular Activities

Information and Study Skills, 183H
Multimedia Report

Comprehension Skill Review, 171
Making Judgments

Leveled Readers

The Golden Land
Chasing the Train
Faith's Journey
Going to America

Lessons and Leveled Practice, 183O–183R

Phonics, 183N
Language Center: Sounds Like *tooth* or *cook*

Vocabulary, 183M
Language Center: Vocabulary Game

Spelling, 183F
Test: Vowel Sounds in *tooth/cook* **T**

Writing, 183L, 183M
Publishing a Play
Language Center: Write a Pilgrim Play Scene

Grammar, 183J
Sentence Combining

Daily Language Practice
9. Him and me both wanted to cooke. (He; I; cook)
10. that meat was as tough as an old shoo. (That; shoe)

Listening/Speaking/Viewing, 183N
Language Center: Present an Oral Book Report

Managing Flexible Groups

FLEXIBLE GROUPS

Leveled Instruction and Leveled Practice

	DAY 1	**DAY 2**
WHOLE CLASS	• Teacher Read Aloud (TE pp. 153A–153B) • Building Background, Introducing Vocabulary (TE pp. 154–155) • Comprehension Strategy: Introduce (TE p. 156) • Comprehension Skill: Introduce (TE p. 156) • Purpose Setting (TE p. 157) **After reading first half of** *Across the Wide Dark Sea* • Stop and Think (TE p. 165)	**After reading** *Across the Wide Dark Sea* • Wrapping Up (TE p. 177) • Comprehension Check (Practice Book p. 88) • Responding: Think About the Selection (TE p. 178) • Comprehension Skill: Preview (TE p. 175)
SMALL GROUPS		
Extra Support	**TEACHER-LED** • Preview *Across the Wide Dark Sea* to Stop and Think (TE pp. 156–165). • Support reading with Extra Support/ Intervention notes (TE pp. 157, 161, 164, 167, 168, 169, 176).	**Partner or Individual Work** • Reread first half of *Across the Wide Dark Sea* (TE pp. 156–165). • Preview, read second half (TE pp. 166–177). • Comprehension Check (Practice Book p. 87).
Challenge	**Individual Work** • Begin "A Story About Squanto" (Challenge Handbook p. 38). • Extend reading with Challenge note (TE p. 176).	**Individual Work** • Continue work on activity (Challenge Handbook p. 38).
English Language Learners	**TEACHER-LED** • Preview vocabulary and *Across the Wide Dark Sea* to Stop and Think (TE pp. 155–165). • Support reading with English Language Learners notes (TE pp. 154, 158, 160, 170, 173, 174, 177).	**TEACHER-LED** • Review first half of *Across the Wide Dark Sea* (TE pp. 156–165). ✔ • Preview, read second half (TE pp. 166–177). • Begin Comprehension Check together (Practice Book p. 87).

Independent Activities

• Get Set for Reading CD-ROM
• Journals: selection notes, questions
• Complete, review Practice Book (pp. 85–89) and Leveled Readers Practice Blackline Masters (TE pp. 183O–183R).
• Assignment Cards (Teacher's Resource Blackline Masters pp. 79–80)
• Leveled Readers (TE pp. 183O–183R), Leveled Theme Paperbacks (TE pp. R2–R7), or book from Leveled Bibliography (TE pp. 148E–148F)

✔ Opportunity to informally assess oral reading rate

ereading: Lessons on Writer's Craft, enre (TE pp. 161, 163) omprehension Skill: Main lesson TE pp. 183A–183B)	• Reading the Social Studies Link (TE pp. 180–183): Skill lesson (TE p. 180) • Rereading the Link (TE pp. 180–183) • Comprehension Skill: First Comprehension Review lesson (TE p. 159)	• Responding: Select from Activities (TE pp. 178–179) • Information and Study Skills (TE p. 183H) • Comprehension Skill: Second Comprehension Review lesson (TE p. 171)
EACHER-LED eread, review Comprehension Check Practice Book p. 87). review Leveled Reader: Below Level TE p. 183O), or read book from Leveled ibliography (TE pp. 148E–148F). ✔	**Partner or Individual Work** • Reread the Social Studies Link (TE pp. 180–183). • Complete Leveled Reader: Below Level (TE p. 183O), or read book from Leveled Bibliography (TE pp. 148E–148F).	**TEACHER-LED** • Comprehension Skill: Reteaching lesson (TE p. R8) • Preview, begin Leveled Theme Paperback: Below Level (TE pp. R2–R3), or read book from Leveled Bibliography (TE pp. 148E–148F). ✔
EACHER-LED eacher check-in: Assess progress (Challenge Handbook p. 38). review Leveled Reader: Above Level TE p. 183Q), or read book from Leveled ibliography (TE pp. 148E–148F). ✔	**Individual Work** • Complete activity (Challenge Handbook p. 38). • Complete Leveled Reader: Above Level (TE p. 183Q), or read book from Leveled Bibliography (TE pp. 148E–148F).	**TEACHER-LED** • Evaluate activity and plan format for sharing (Challenge Handbook p. 38). • Read Leveled Theme Paperback: Above Level (TE pp. R6–R7), or read book from Leveled Bibliography (TE pp. 148E–148F). ✔
artner or Individual Work omplete Comprehension Check (Practice ook p. 87). egin Leveled Reader: Language Support TE p. 183R), or read book from Leveled ibliography (TE pp. 148E–148F).	**TEACHER-LED** • Reread the Social Studies Link (TE pp. 180–183) ✔ and review Link Skill (TE p. 180). • Complete Leveled Reader: Language Support (TE p. 183R), or read book from Leveled Bibliography (TE pp. 148E–148F). ✔	**Partner or Individual Work** • Preview, read book from Leveled Bibliography (TE pp. 148E–148F).

Responding activities (TE pp. 178–179)

Language Center activities (TE pp. 183M–183N)

Fluency Practice: Reread *Across the Wide Dark Sea* ✔

Activities relating to *Across the Wide Dark Sea* at Education Place www.eduplace.com

Turn the page for more independent activities.

FLEXIBLE GROUPS

Across the Wide Dark Sea

Classroom Management

Independent Activities

Assign these activities while you work with small groups.

Differentiated Instruction for Small Groups

- **Handbook for English Language Learners,** pp. 166–175

- **Extra Support Handbook,** pp. 162–171

Independent Activities

- Language Center, pp. 183M–183N

- Challenge/Extension Activities, Theme Resources, pp. R9, R15

- **Classroom Management Handbook,** Activity Masters CM5-1–CM5-4

- **Challenge Handbook,** pp. 38–39

Look for more activities in the Classroom Management Kit.

Art

A New Postage Stamp

👤 Singles	🕐 30 minutes
Objective	Design a postage stamp.
Materials	Reference sources, markers

The United States Postal Service creates stamps to honor special people and events. Create your own stamp to honor the people of the *Mayflower*. Choose a person, place, or event. It should represent an important idea or something that the Pilgrims did that should be remembered.

Draw your design for a stamp the size of a piece of paper. Display your stamp design in the classroom.

Science

A Long, Cold Winter

👤 Singles	🕐 45 minutes
Objective	Research winters in Plymouth, Massachusetts.
Materials	Research sources

The Pilgrims' first winter was terrib[le]. They all suffered, and many died. What are the winters like where th[e] Pilgrims landed? Do research in an encyclopedia, an almanac, or on th[e] Internet to find out about the clima[te] around Plymouth, Massachusetts.

Write a paragraph describing the weather and comparing it to wint[er] where you live. Include specific fac[ts] about

- high and low temperatures
- snowfall
- rain

Consider copying and laminating these activities for use in centers.

Primary Sources

The Pilgrims' Point of View

Pairs	⏱ 45 minutes
Objective	Research Pilgrim primary sources.
Materials	A computer with Internet access

We learn much about past events by reading the letters and documents left behind by the people who lived through the events. These first-hand accounts are called primary sources.

With your partner, search the Internet and choose a primary source to read. Summarize in a brief paragraph what you learned about the Pilgrims' journey or lives. Type in one of the following, as your search criteria:

primary sources Pilgrims

primary sources Mayflower

primary sources Plimoth Plantation

primary sources Governor Bradford

If you wish, you may start with this website:

http://www.mayflowerhistory.com/primarySources/primarysources.php

Careers

Help Wanted: Pilgrims

Pairs	⏱ 30 minutes
Objective	Write a help wanted ad.
Materials	Examples of help wanted ads, markers

You are looking for people to go on a voyage to a land across the sea. The ship is the *Mayflower* and the year is 1620. You are looking for people willing to start a new settlement in an unknown place. What kind of people would you want? What skills would be needed?

- Review *Across the Wide Dark Sea*.
- Look at the details and list important qualities the Pilgrims had.
- Then write a help wanted ad describing who you want for your voyage.

Display your ad in the classroom.

Help Wanted
Pilgrim families
Must be in
good health

Poetry

Acrostic Poem

Groups	⏱ 30 minutes
Objective	Write an acrostic poem.

Choose a long word from the story, such as *Mayflower* or *settlement*. Now write a poem about the name or word. Follow these steps:

- Print the word in capital letters down the left side of a sheet of paper.
- Brainstorm several lines or phrases for each letter and then choose the one that works best.
- Next to each letter write a sentence or phrase that begins with that letter. For example, a poem using the word *sea* might read:

Sailing through the stormy ocean,

Every wave pounds the ship.

All eyes look at the endless sea.

Listening Comprehension

Building Background

Tell students that you are going to read aloud part of a story, written in diary form, about what one boy might have experienced during a voyage with Christopher Columbus.

- Discuss with students what they know about Columbus and his voyage from Spain. Point out that at the time of the voyage the sailors believed that no one had ever sailed so far from land.

Fluency Modeling

Explain that as you read aloud, you will be modeling fluent oral reading. Ask students to listen carefully to your phrasing and your expression, or tone of voice and emphasis.

COMPREHENSION SKILL

Making Inferences

Explain that making inferences about things the author has not directly stated involves

- using details from the selection
- using personal experiences

Purpose Setting Read the story aloud, asking students to note details that help them to make inferences as they listen. Then use the Guiding Comprehension questions to assess students' understanding. Reread the story for clarification as needed.

Teacher Read Aloud

Pedro's Journal

A Voyage with
Christopher Columbus
August 3, 1492–February 14, 1493

by Pam Conrad

How would it have felt to have been aboard the *Santa María* when Christopher Columbus set sail to find the New World? In this excerpt from *Pedro's Journal,* a boy keeps a written account of his adventures on the long voyage.

October 10

This has been the worst day of all for the Captain. I am certain of this. We have doubled all previous records of days and leagues at sea, and we've gone way past the point where he originally said we would find land. There is nothing out here. Surely we are lost. And everyone is certain now as well.

This morning the men responded slowly to orders, scowling and slamming down their tools and lines. They whispered in pairs and small groups on deck and below. The air was thick with mutiny and betrayal, until finally everything came to a dead stop. The wind howled through the shrouds, and the men just stood there on deck and did not move aside when Columbus came.

"Enough," one of the men said to his face. "This is enough. Now we turn back."

The other men grumbled their assent and nodded, their fists clenched, their chests broad. And they remained motionless and unmoved while Columbus paced the deck, telling them how close he figured we must be, that land could be right over the next horizon. He told them again of the fame and fortune that would be theirs if they could only last a little longer. And they laughed at him, the cruel laughter of impatient and defeated men.

"All that aside," he added, "with the fresh easterly wind coming at us and the rising sea, we can't turn a course back to Spain right now. We would stand still in the water."

I looked up at the sails, full and straining, taking us farther and farther from Spain. What if a westerly wind never came? What if we were just blown away forever and ever?

"Let me offer you this," Columbus finally said. "Do me this favor. Stay with me this day and night, and if I don't bring you to land before day, cut off my head, and you shall return."

The men glanced at each other. Some nodded. "One day," they said. "One day, and then we turn around."

"That is all I ask," Columbus said.

Later, when I went down to the cabin with the log, the Captain's door was bolted shut, and when I knocked he didn't answer, so I sat outside the door with the heavy journal in my lap and waited.

CRITICAL THINKING
Guiding Comprehension

1 MAKING INFERENCES Why are the men on the ship angry? (The men have been at sea for months with no sign of land. They are tired and feel that Columbus has lied to them. They fear they are lost.)

2 MAKING INFERENCES Why has Columbus bolted his door shut? (He is concerned that the men may change their minds about waiting one more day. He is afraid they will hurt him and take over the ship.)

Discussion Options

Personal Response Ask students to describe how they might have felt if they were sailors on the *Santa María*.

⭐ **Connecting/Comparing** Have students explain how this selection fits in a theme called *Voyagers*.

 English Language Learners

Supporting Comprehension

Explain the words *mutiny* ("open rebellion of sailors against officers in charge") and *betrayal* ("lack of loyalty"). Ask students to think how they would feel if they were crew members on a ship on the ocean for a long time with no land in sight and no maps to tell them where they were. Write words and phrases from their responses. Help students discuss why the men were talking about a mutiny.

Building Background

Key Concept:
Journey of the Pilgrims

Tell students that they will meet a variety of travelers in the theme called Voyagers. The first story, *Across the Wide Dark Sea*, tells about a boy who travels on the *Mayflower*.

Discuss what students know about the Pilgrims' journey on the *Mayflower* in 1620. Use "Journey of the Pilgrims" on pages 154–155 to introduce some of the challenges they faced.

- Have a student read aloud "Journey of the Pilgrims."
- Have students take turns reading the captions and describing the photos.

Get Set to Read

Background and Vocabulary

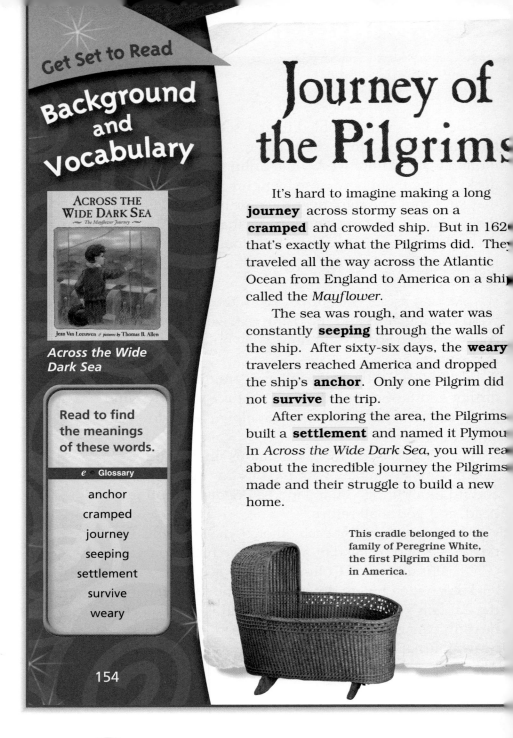

ACROSS THE WIDE DARK SEA
The Mayflower Journey

Jean Van Leeuwen & *pictures by* Thomas B. Allen

Across the Wide Dark Sea

Read to find the meanings of these words.

e Glossary

anchor
cramped
journey
seeping
settlement
survive
weary

Journey of the Pilgrims

It's hard to imagine making a long **journey** across stormy seas on a **cramped** and crowded ship. But in 162[] that's exactly what the Pilgrims did. The[] traveled all the way across the Atlantic Ocean from England to America on a shi[] called the *Mayflower*.

The sea was rough, and water was constantly **seeping** through the walls of the ship. After sixty-six days, the **weary** travelers reached America and dropped the ship's **anchor**. Only one Pilgrim did not **survive** the trip.

After exploring the area, the Pilgrims built a **settlement** and named it Plymou[]. In *Across the Wide Dark Sea*, you will rea[] about the incredible journey the Pilgrims made and their struggle to build a new home.

This cradle belonged to the family of Peregrine White, the first Pilgrim child born in America.

154

English Language Learners

Supporting Comprehension

Beginning/Preproduction Have students listen to the article. Ask them to point out the *Mayflower*. Then ask students to act out hardships the Pilgrims encountered on their journey.

Early Production and Speech Emergence Point out and explain the Key Vocabulary words. Draw an anchor and invite students to explain how it works. Have students mime *cramped* and *weary*.

Intermediate and Advanced Fluency Ask students to state the main idea of each paragraph in their own words. Invite them to explain how each illustration adds to what they know about the Pilgrims.

Mayflower II, a full-size version of what the first *Mayflower* may have looked like, now floats in Plymouth Harbor in Massachusetts.

A cooking pot was one of the most useful things families brought on the *Mayflower*. This one belonged to the Standish family.

155

Introducing Vocabulary

Key Vocabulary

These words support the Key Concept and appear in the selection.

anchor a heavy metal hook attached to a ship and dropped overboard to hold the ship in place

cramped crowded; not enough room to move about

journey a trip from one place to another

seeping slowly leaking; oozing

settlement a small community in a new place

survive to stay alive; to hold up or withstand

weary tired; needing rest

 e • Glossary
e • WordGame

See Vocabulary notes on pages 158, 160, 162, 164, 166, 168, 170, 172, and 176 for additional words to preview.

Display Transparency 5–1.

- Cover the words and their definitions at the bottom of the transparency.

- Model how to figure out the meaning of *anchor*.

- Uncover the first definition, and compare it to the meaning you gave.

- Have students figure out the meaning of each remaining word, following your example.

- Ask students to look for these words as they read and use them while they discuss the Pilgrims' journey.

Practice/Homework Assign **Practice Book** page 85.

Transparency 5–1

Pilgrim Words

iron, weight, <u>anchor</u>
crowded, tight, squishy, <u>cramped</u>
trip, <u>journey</u>, voyage
<u>seeping</u>, oozing, leaking
village, town, <u>settlement</u>
live, hold up, <u>survive</u>, pull through
tired, <u>weary</u>, unrested, worn-out

<u>anchor</u>: a heavy metal hook attached to a ship and dropped overboard to hold the ship in place
<u>cramped</u>: crowded; not enough room to move about
<u>journey</u>: a trip
<u>seeping</u>: slowly leaking; oozing
<u>settlement</u>: a small community in a new place
<u>survive</u>: to stay alive; to hold up or pull through
<u>weary</u>: tired; needing rest

Practice Book page 85

Across the Wide Dark Sea:
The Mayflower Journey
Key Vocabulary

Name _____

Tale of a Sea Voyage

On the line after each sentence, write the correct definition of the underlined word.

Definitions You Will Need:

▶ heavy metal object that keeps a ship in place
▶ crowded
▶ trip from one place to another
▶ passing slowly through small openings
▶ small community in a new place
▶ stay alive
▶ tired

1. In 1620, the Pilgrims made a long <u>journey</u> from England to America. trip from one place to another **(2 points)**

2. With so many people, the ship was <u>cramped</u>. crowded **(2)**

3. Water kept <u>seeping</u> through the wooden walls of the ship.
passing slowly through small openings **(2)**

4. When the ship neared land, the crew dropped the <u>anchor</u>.
heavy metal object that keeps a ship in place **(2)**

5. The many hardships made the Pilgrims <u>weary</u>. tired **(2)**

6. Even though the voyage was very difficult, all but one of the passengers managed to <u>survive</u>. stay alive **(2)**

7. After the Pilgrims landed, they chose a spot and built a <u>settlement</u>.
small community in a new place **(2)**

Introducing Vocabulary 155

COMPREHENSION STRATEGY
Question

Teacher Modeling Ask a student to read the Strategy Focus aloud. Explain that asking questions is a good way to make sure they understand the story. Ask students to read the first three paragraphs on page 159. Then model the strategy.

Think Aloud *On page 159 I learn that a boy and his father are traveling on a sailing ship that is moving out to sea. They are beginning a journey to a new land. One good question I might ask is, Why are the boy and his father traveling to the new land?*

Test Prep Some test questions can pose reading challenges almost as difficult as the passages themselves. Remind students that they can use the Question strategy and other reading strategies to make sure they understand each test question.

COMPREHENSION SKILL
Making Inferences

story pages 159-161 162-165 168-170

Introduce the Graphic Organizer. Tell students that an Inference Chart can help them use story clues and personal knowledge to make inferences, or reasonable guesses. Explain that as they read, students will fill out the Inference Chart found on **Practice Book** page 86.

- Display **Transparency 5–2.** Have students read Anthology page 159.

- Model making the first inference, filling in story clues, personal knowledge, and the inference itself. Monitor students' work as they complete the chart.

MEET THE AUTHOR
Jean Van Leeuwen

For Jean Van Leeuwen, getting lost in a good book is great fun. As a child, she would get so interested in a book that when anyone called her name she would look up wondering where she was! Now Van Leeuwen writes books, too. Sometimes an idea just strikes her like lightning. As she says, "For me, each book begins with a thunderbolt from the sky."

Other books:

A Fourth of July on the Plains, Nothing Here But Trees, The Strange Adventures of Blue Dog

MEET THE ILLUSTRATOR
Thomas B. Allen

Thomas B. Allen likes to mix and match his tools when he draws. For this book he used charcoal, pastels, and colored pencils on rough, bumpy paper to give him just the look he wanted. Allen also illustrated *Going West,* another book by Jean Van Leeuwen.

Other books:

Climbing Kansas Mountains (by George Shannon)

Good-bye, Charles Lindbergh (by Louise Borden)

A Green Horn Blowing (by David F. Birchman)

Internet Visit Education Place to discover more about Jean Van Leeuwen and Thomas B. Allen. **www.eduplace.com/kids**

156

Transparency 5–2

Inference Chart
Responses will vary. Examples are given.

VOYAGERS Across the Wide Dark Sea
Graphic Organizer Inference Chart
ANNOTATED VERSION

1. How does the boy feel when the journey begins?

Story Clues (pages 113–115)	What I Know
He looks ahead at the wide dark sea. He stands close to his father and clings to his father's hand.	Children stay close to their parents and hold their hands when children are afraid.

My Inference The boy is sad and afraid.

2. How does the boy feel after six weeks at sea?

Story Clues (pages 116–119)	What I Know
The ship is crowded, cramped, cold, and wet.	It is uncomfortable to be crowded, cold, and wet.

My Inference He is bored, uncomfortable, and worried about the future.

3. How do the people react to the report of the new land?

Story Clues (pages 122–124)	What I Know
The search party finds fine trees, ponds, and rich black earth.	The materials are good for new homes and growing crops.

My Inference They are relieved and happy to hear the good news.

TRANSPARENCY 5–2
TEACHER'S EDITION PAGES 156 AND 183A

Practice Book page 86

Across the Wide Dark Sea
The Mayflower Journey
Graphic Organizer Inference Chart

Name _____

Inference Chart
Responses will vary. Examples are given.

1. How does the boy feel when the journey begins?

Story Clues (pages 113–115)	What I Know
He looks ahead at the wide dark sea. He stands close to his father and clings to his father's hand. **(1)**	Children stay close to their parents and hold their hands when children are afraid. **(1 point)**

My Inference The boy is sad and afraid. **(2)**

2. How does the boy feel after six weeks at sea?

Story Clues (pages 116–119)	What I Know
The ship is crowded, cramped, cold, and wet. **(1)**	It is uncomfortable to be crowded, cold, and wet. **(1)**

My Inference He is bored, uncomfortable and worried about the future. **(2)**

3. How do the people react to the report of the new land?

Story Clues (pages 122-124)	What I Know
The search party finds fine trees, ponds, and rich black earth. **(1)**	The materials are good for new homes and growing crops **(1)**

My Inference They are relieved and happy to hear the good news. **(2)**

ACROSS THE
WIDE DARK SEA
~ The Mayflower Journey ~

Jean Van Leeuwen & pictures by Thomas B. Allen

Strategy Focus

As you read this story of one boy's journey across the sea, think of **questions** about the Pilgrims and their struggle for survival.

157

REACHING ALL LEARNERS

Extra Support/Intervention

Selection Preview

pages 158–159 A young boy and his family set sail to an unknown land on the *Mayflower*. How do you think they feel as they sail away from England?

pages 160–165 As the journey goes on, storms hit the ship. It begins to leak badly. People are sick and scared. Will they decide to turn back?

pages 166–173 After nine weeks, the travelers reach land. They build homes, but many people get sick and die. Why do you think the boy remembers it as a long, terrible winter?

pages 174–177 In the spring, Indians teach the Pilgrims how to plant and catch fish. How will this help the Pilgrims?

Purpose Setting

- Remind students that this selection tells about the journey of the Pilgrims on the *Mayflower* in 1620.

- Have students preview the selection. Then ask them to predict what the story will tell them about the journey on the *Mayflower*.

- Remind students to use Question and other strategies as they read.

- Ask students to pay attention to the inferences they make while they are reading.

- You may want to preview the Responding questions on Anthology page 178 with students.

Journal ▶ Students can use their journals to record their original predictions and to record questions to ask their classmates. They can also evaluate how well the author describes hardships of the voyage.

STRATEGY REVIEW

Phonics/Decoding

Remind students to use the Phonics/Decoding Strategy as they read.

Modeling Write this sentence from *Across the Wide Dark Sea* on the board: *Pale yellow sand and dark <u>hunched</u> trees were all we saw.* Point to *hunched.*

Think Aloud *The first part of this word reminds me of the word* fun, *except it starts with the letter* h. *It must be* huhn. *Next I see* c-h, *and I know that those two letters make one sound,* ch. *Finally, I see the* -ed *ending. If I blend the sounds, the word is* HUHNCHT. *That means "bent forward." That makes sense in the sentence.*

CRITICAL THINKING

Guiding Comprehension

❶ DRAWING CONCLUSIONS How do you think the boy feels as they begin their journey? How do you know? (anxious, fearful; He clings to his father's hand and looks ahead at the wide dark sea.)

❷ MAKING INFERENCES Why must the travelers bring everything they need with them aboard the ship? (In the land across the sea, there won't be a way of buying what they need.)

158

 English Language Learners

Supporting Comprehension

Review how to take summary notes (answering *who, what, where, when,* and *why*). Read the first page of the story aloud. Then on the board write brief summary notes of what you've read. Read the second page together as a class and ask volunteers to help you write notes on the board.

Vocabulary

anchor a heavy metal hook attached to a ship that is dropped overboard to hold the ship in place

journey a trip

cramped crowded; not enough room to move about

I stood close to my father as the anchor was pulled dripping from the sea. Above us, white sails rose against a bright blue sky. They fluttered, then filled with wind. Our ship began to move.

My father was waving to friends on shore. I looked back at their faces growing smaller and smaller, and ahead at the wide dark sea. And I clung to my father's hand. **❶**

We were off on a journey to an unknown land.

The ship was packed tight with people — near a hundred, my father said. We were crowded below deck in a space so low that my father could barely stand upright, and so cramped that we could scarcely stretch out to sleep.

Packed in tight, too, was everything we would need in the new land: tools for building and planting, goods for trading, guns for hunting. Food, furniture, clothing, books. A few crates of chickens, two dogs, and a striped orange cat. **❷**

Our family was luckier than most. We had a corner out of the damp and cold. Some had to sleep in the ship's small work boat.

159

Story Structure

Review

- Remind students of the main elements of story structure.
  - Characters are the main people (or animals) in a story.
  - Plot is the sequence of story events, which often includes a problem and its solution.
  - Setting is where and when the story takes place.

Practice

- Ask students to identify the main story characters and the setting. (the boy, his father; aboard the *Mayflower*)
- Then ask what the story problem is. (how to survive the journey to a new land)
- Help students use text clues and illustrations to identify the story narrator. (the young boy; from the words *my father* and the illustration of the boy standing next to the man at the rail)

Apply

- Discuss how changing the main character would change parts of the plot. Suggest that students consider how a sailor or the captain might tell the story.

Review Skill Trace	
Teach	Theme 3, p. 419A
Reteach	Theme 3, p. R14
▶ Review	p. 159; Theme 1, p. 25

ASSIGNMENT CARD 1

Decisions, Decisions

Problem Solving

What did the Pilgrims bring on the *Mayflower* to start their lives in the new land? Find out from the list on page 159 and from other parts of the story.

What else do you think the Pilgrims might have needed? Discuss this with a partner. To help you decide, use story details and information you know about living as the Pilgrims did. Then make a more complete list of things the Pilgrims might have needed. Star the items you think are the most important things for the Pilgrims' survival. Share your ideas with the group.

Theme 5: Voyagers

Teacher's Resource BLM page 79

CRITICAL THINKING
Guiding Comprehension

❸ MAKING INFERENCES Why does the boy believe that a sailor's life is a fine one? (The sailors are doing interesting work. They climb and move around, while he can't.)

❹ NOTING DETAILS Why do you think the author uses such vivid words to describe the storm? (to help readers experience what the Pilgrims did)

❺ COMPARE AND CONTRAST Why does the author compare the small, helpless ship to the powerful storm? (Answers will vary. Example: to make the voyagers' fearful reactions seem realistic)

160

Vocabulary

rigging all the ropes, chains, and pulleys used to control the masts and sails of a ship

furl to roll up and fasten

shuddered trembled or shivered suddenly

huddled crowded close together

English Language Learners

Supporting Comprehension

Because this is a long selection, remind students to take a few minutes at the end of each session to write summary notes. Then before they begin reading again, they can review the notes to remind themselves what they know so far.

My summary notes really help me.

The first days were fair, with a stiff wind.

My mother and brother were seasick down below. But I stood on deck and watched the sailors hauling on ropes, climbing in the rigging, and perched at the very top of the mast, looking out to sea.

What a fine life it must be, I thought, to be a sailor. **❸**

One day clouds piled up in the sky. Birds with black wings circled the ship, and the choppy sea seemed angry.

"Storm's coming," I heard a sailor say. We were all sent below as the sailors raced to furl the sails.

Then the storm broke. Wind howled and waves crashed. **❹**
The ship shuddered as it rose and fell in seas as high as mountains. Some people were crying, others praying. I huddled next to my father, afraid in the dark.

How could a ship so small and helpless ever cross the **❺** vast ocean?

161

Vivid Language

Teach

- Remind students that authors use words to help paint pictures in readers' minds and make readers feel as if they were in the story.

- Explain to students that looking for vivid language and visualizing scenes will help them understand what they read.

Practice/Apply

- Read aloud the passage on page 161 that describes the storm.

- Ask students what they pictured in their minds as you read.

- Have students identify the words that created the image. (*broke, howled, crashed, shuddered, rose and fell; high as mountains*)

Extra Support/Intervention

Strategy Modeling: Question

Use this example to model the strategy.

On page 161, I read that people are crying and praying during the storm. Also, the boy is huddling next to his father, afraid in the dark. To help me understand the characters better, a good question to ask might be, Why are the people so afraid during the storm?

CRITICAL THINKING

Guiding Comprehension

6 MAKING INFERENCES What does the boy think about his trip so far? How do you know? (He's tired of it because there is nothing for him to do; from the words *each day like the last*.)

7 NOTING DETAILS Why does the author include the story of the man who is swept overboard? (to add suspense; to show how dangerous the voyage is)

COMPREHENSION STRATEGY

Question

Teacher/Student Modeling Help students identify important story details on page 162. List them on the board. Then model turning a detail into a question. (Examples: trying to stay dry; Why are the people having trouble staying dry?)

Ask students to continue creating questions, including ones that require using personal knowledge as well as story details to form an answer. (Examples: Why do the passengers eat only salt pork, beans, and bread? Why must the boy keep out of the sailors' way?)

Vocabulary

overboard over the side of the boat

desperate driven by a great need

miraculously amazingly, like a miracle

plucked snatched, pulled out

The sun came out. We walked on deck and dried our clothes. But just when my shoes felt dry at last, more clouds gathered.

"Storm's coming," I told my father.

So the days passed, each one like the last. There was nothing to do but eat our meals of salt pork, beans, and bread, tidy up our cramped space, sleep when we could, and try to keep dry. When it was not too stormy, we climbed on deck to stretch our legs. But even then we had to keep out of the sailors' way.

6 How I longed to run and jump and climb!

Once during a storm a man was swept overboard. Reaching out with desperate hands, he caught hold of a rope and clung to it.

Down he went under the raging foaming water.

Then, miraculously, up he came.

Sailors rushed to the side of the ship. Hauling on the rope, they brought him in close and with a boat hook plucked him out

7 of the sea. And his life was saved.

162

163

Historical Fiction

Teach

- Define historical fiction as fiction that weaves historical facts with details made up by the author.

- Explain that in *Across the Wide Dark Sea* the main events are real events; the *Mayflower* journey and the Pilgrims' settlement of Plymouth actually happened.

- Tell students that the author has added many realistic details, such as story characters' words and thoughts, to make the events come alive for readers.

Practice/Apply

- Explain that a man actually did fall overboard on the real *Mayflower* voyage.

- Have students discuss that event, identify facts and fictional details, and complete a chart like this.

Real	Fictional
characters	dialogue
setting	descriptions
events	

- Discuss other parts of the story with students in a similar way.

CRITICAL THINKING

Guiding Comprehension

8 **DRAWING CONCLUSIONS** What does the gathering in the captain's cabin suggest about the way the Pilgrims handle their decisions? (Sample answer: They try to come to an agreement about important decisions.)

9 **MAKING JUDGMENTS** What decision would you have made about turning back or sailing on? Explain. (Example: Turn back; the ship is damaged and the passengers fear for their lives. Sail on; land will be sighted soon.)

10 **DRAWING CONCLUSIONS** Why do you think the passengers left their safe homes to go on this dangerous journey? (They're looking for a better life, for more freedom, for adventure, or for an escape from a troubled past.)

164

Vocabulary

survive to stay alive; to hold up or withstand

jack a mechanical tool used to raise or move heavy objects, such as a car or house

seeping leaking slowly; oozing

 REACHING ALL LEARNERS

Extra Support/Intervention

Review (pages 158–165)

Before students join the whole class for Stop and Think on page 165, have them

- take turns modeling Question and other strategies they used
- add to **Transparency 5–2** with you
- check and revise their Inference Chart on **Practice Book** page 86, and use it to summarize

Storm followed storm. The pounding of wind and waves caused one of the main beams to crack, and our ship began to leak.

Worried, the men gathered in the captain's cabin to talk of what to do. Could our ship survive another storm? Or must we turn back?

They talked for two days, but could not agree.

Then someone thought of the iron jack for raising houses that they were taking to the new land. Using it to lift the cracked beam, the sailors set a new post underneath, tight and firm, and patched all the leaks.

And our ship sailed on.

For six weeks we had traveled, and still there was no land in sight. Now we were always cold and wet. Water seeping in from above put out my mother's cooking fire, and there was nothing to eat but hard dry biscuits and cheese. My brother was sick, and many others too.

And some began to ask why we had left our safe homes to go on this endless journey to an unknown land.

165

Stop and Think

Critical Thinking Questions

1. **NOTING DETAILS** How are the conditions aboard the ship changing? (They're getting worse: the passengers are always cold and wet; the food is worse; more people are sick.)

2. **MAKING INFERENCES** What sights, sounds, and smells might the boy have experienced aboard ship that are not described in the text? (Examples: sights —ocean everywhere, fish and whales, frightened men; sounds—singing, the captain shouting orders, the creaking of the rigging; smells—spoiled food, smoke from the cooking fires, salty air)

Strategies in Action

Have students take turns modeling Question and other strategies they used.

Discussion Options

You may want to bring the entire class together to do one or more of the activities below.

- **Review Predictions/Purpose** Discuss which predictions were accurate and which needed to be revised. Record any changes and new predictions, as well as any new questions students have.

- **Share Group Discussions** Have students share their questions and literature discussions.

- **Summarize** Help students use their Inference Charts to summarize what has happened in the story so far.

Monitoring Student Progress

If . . .	Then . . .
students have successfully completed the Extra Support activities on page 164,	have them read the rest of the selection cooperatively or independently.

ASSIGNMENT CARD 2

Literature Discussion

ith a small group, talk over your questions and ideas about the ry. Also discuss these questions:

- How do you think the sailors might have felt about taking the Pilgrims to settle in a new land?

- The cracked beam was one problem the Pilgrims had to solve. What other problems do you think they might have faced on the voyage?

- Why do you think the Pilgrims were willing to risk their lives and families in order to start a new life?

Theme 5: Voyagers

CRITICAL THINKING

Guiding Comprehension

⑪ MAKING INFERENCES Why do you think the boy has faith that they will find the freedom they seek? (He sees that his father is sure they will find it.)

⑫ NOTING DETAILS How does the author show that land is near? (The sailor says so; seaweed, a tree branch, and a feather from a land bird float by.)

⑪ Why? I also asked the question of my father that night.

"We are searching for a place to live where we can worship God in our own way," he said quietly. "It is this freedom we seek in a new land. And I have faith that we will find it."

Looking at my father, so calm and sure, suddenly I too had faith that we would find it.

⑫ Still the wide dark sea went on and on. Eight weeks. Nine. Then one day a sailor, sniffing the air, said, "Land's ahead." We dared not believe him. But soon bits of seaweed floated by. Then a tree branch. And a feather from a land bird.

Two days later at dawn I heard the lookout shout, "Land ho!" Everyone who was well enough to stand crowded on deck. And there through the gray mist we saw it: a low dark outline between sea and sky. Land!

Tears streamed down my mother's face, yet she was smiling. Then everyone fell to their knees while my father said a prayer of thanksgiving.

Our long journey was over.

166

Vocabulary

worship to take part in a religious ceremony

faith trust or belief, even without proof

167

Extra Support/Intervention

Supporting Comprehension

Pause after reading page 166, and ask: How long have they been at sea? Have a student point to the two references to the period of time: *Eight weeks. Nine.* Then ask: How did they know that land was near? What signs did they see in the water?

Eight or nine weeks is a long voyage!

CRITICAL THINKING

Guiding Comprehension

13 **DRAWING CONCLUSIONS** Why is the small party's report so important to the Pilgrims? (They have to decide whether to look there for a place to build their homes or to sail to a better spot.)

14 **NOTING DETAILS** What are some possible good and bad points to the land features they find? (Examples: good points—firewood for cooking and for building houses, ponds for drinking water, rich soil for crops; bad points —sand hills and swamps where food can't grow and mosquitoes can breed)

15 **MAKING INFERENCES** Why do you think the author includes the detail about finding clams and mussels? (to show that the settlers can find fresh food so they won't starve)

The ship dropped anchor in a quiet bay, circled by land. Pale yellow sand and dark hunched trees were all we saw. And all we heard was silence.

What lurked among those trees? Wild beasts? Wild men? Would there be food and water, a place to take shelter?

What waited for us in this new land?

13 A small party of men in a small boat set off to find out. All day I watched on deck for their return.

14 When at last they rowed into sight, they brought armfuls of firewood and tales of what they had seen: forests of fine trees, rolling hills of sand, swamps and ponds and rich black earth. But no houses or wild beasts or wild men.

So all of us went ashore.

My mother washed the clothes we had worn for weeks beside a shallow pond, while my brother and I raced up and down the beach.

We watched whales spouting in the sparkling blue bay and helped search for firewood. And we found clams and mussels, **15** the first fresh food we had tasted in two months. I ate so many I was sick.

168

Vocabulary

lurked stayed hidden

shelter something that protects or covers

swamps areas of spongy, muddy land that are often filled with water

Extra Support/Intervention

Strategy Modeling: Question

Use this example to model the strategy.

On page 168, I read that a small party of men set out to explore the new land. When they return, they tell what they have seen and everyone goes ashore. So, good questions to ask about this part might be the following: Why does the small party of men set off? What do they find? What do the Pilgrims do because of what the men find?

169

 **Fluency Practice**

Rereading for Fluency Have students choose a favorite part of the story to reread to a partner, or suggest that they read page 168. Encourage students to read with feeling and expression.

 Extra Support/Intervention

Strategy Modeling: Phonics/Decoding

Use this example to model the strategy.

When I look at the word s-p-o-u-t-i-n-g, *I recognize the* s-p *cluster from words such as* spin *and* spell. *Next, I see the shorter word* out *and the* -ing *ending. I blend all the sounds together and say* SPOWT-ihng. *I know a spout is the hole on top of a whale's head. Maybe it's called* spouting *when whales blow water out of that hole. That would make sense in this sentence.*

CRITICAL THINKING
Guiding Comprehension

16 DRAWING CONCLUSIONS Why does the boy's father think that they must find a place before winter comes? (Their survival may depend on having safe homes for the winter; they can't stay on the ship, because it might be wrecked in a storm.)

17 MAKING INFERENCES Why do you think the author includes the detail that half of all the people died? (to show the hardships the people faced)

COMPREHENSION STRATEGY
Question

Student Modeling Have students take turns modeling the Question strategy. If necessary, use the following prompt:

- Why is the place the men find a good place to build a settlement? What does the answer tell you about their future plans?

Vocabulary

settlement a small community in a new place

weary tired

rough built in a hurry; not completely finished

Day after day the small party set out from the ship, looking for just the right place to build our settlement.

The days grew cold. Snowflakes danced in the wind. The cold and damp made many sick again. Drawing his coat tightly around him, my father looked worried.

16 "We must find a place," he said, "before winter comes."

One afternoon the weary men returned with good news. They had found the right spot at last.

When my father saw it, he smiled. It was high on a hill, with a safe harbor and fields cleared for planting and brooks running with sweet water. We named it after the town from which we had sailed, across the sea.

It was December now, icy cold and stormy. The men went ashore to build houses, while the rest of us stayed on board ship. Every fine day they worked. But as the houses of our settlement began to rise, more and more of our people fell sick. And some of them died.

It was a long and terrible winter.

We had houses now, small and rough. Yet the storms and sickness went on. And outside the settlement, Indians waited, seldom seen but watching us.

17 My father and mother nursed the sick, and my father led prayers for them. But more and more died. Of all the people who had sailed for the new land, only half were left.

170

English Language Learners

Supporting Comprehension

Pause after reading page 170 to review the plot. Ask: Why are the Pilgrims coming to a new world? What problems do they have on the voyage? What problems do they have with the new settlement? Do you think they will survive? Why or why not?

171

Making Judgments

Review

- Review the process of making judgments.
  - Ask questions such as, Is this fair? Is this a wise decision?
  - Use story facts and personal experience to think about each side of the issue.
  - Decide whether to agree with what the characters do.

Practice/Apply

- Have students reread the sentence that describes the building site: *It was high on a hill, with a safe harbor and fields cleared for planting and brooks running with sweet water.*

- Ask students to use a chart like the one below to record their ideas about whether the Pilgrims made the right choice for their building site.

Do you think the Pilgrims made a wise choice for their building site?	
Yes	No

Review Skill Trace	
Teach	Theme 4, p. 99A
Reteach	Theme 4, p. R12
▶ Review	p. 171; Theme 1, p. 63; Theme 6, p. 383

ASSIGNMENT CARD 3

Making a Hard Choice

Making Judgments

Picture yourself living in England in 1620. You are offered a chance to sail on the *Mayflower* with the Pilgrims. Is it wise for you to go with them to start a new life in an unknown land?

As a group, discuss the question. Make a list of the good and bad points of going to the new land or of staying behind in England.

Write a paragraph that gives your opinion. Tell whether you think it is wise to go with the Pilgrims. Explain why you think as you do.

Theme 5: Voyagers

Teacher's Resource BLM page 80

CRITICAL THINKING

Guiding Comprehension

18 **MAKING INFERENCES** What does the author mean by *the smell of new-split wood filled the air*? (The settlers are once again at work building their settlement.)

19 **DRAWING CONCLUSIONS** Why do you think the Indians are watching the settlers? (The settlers are unfamiliar people with new ways and tools and may be a threat to the Indians.)

20 **DRAWING CONCLUSIONS** How do you think the Indian knows English? (He may have met English-speaking explorers or pirates and learned English from them.)

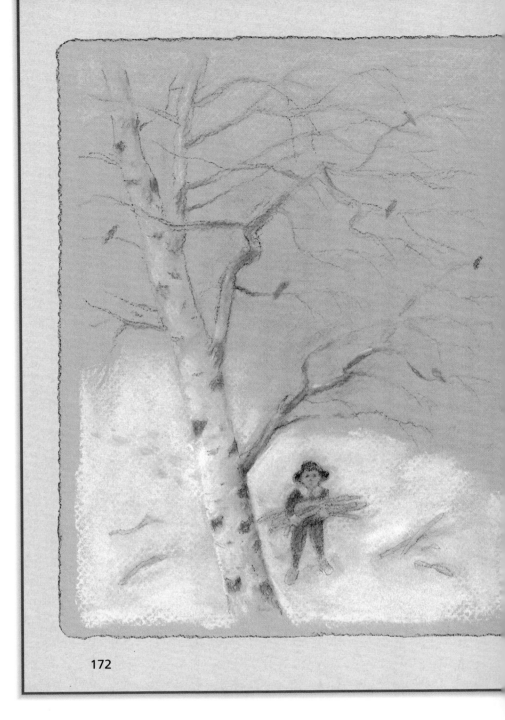

172

Vocabulary

defend to protect from attack

cannons heavy guns set onto wheels

One morning in March, as I was gathering firewood, I heard a strange sweet sound. Looking up, I saw birds singing in a white birch tree.

Could it be that spring had come at last?

All that day the sun shone warm, melting the snow. The sick rose from their beds. And once more the sound of axes and the smell of new-split wood filled the air. **18**

"We have done it," my father said. "We have survived the winter."

But now the Indians came closer. We found their arrows, and traces of their old houses. We caught sight of them among the trees. Our men met to talk of this new danger. How could so small a settlement defend itself? **19**

Cannons were mounted on top of the hill, and the men took turns standing guard. Then one day an Indian walked into the settlement. Speaking to us in our own language, he said, "Welcome." **20**

173

English Language Learners

Supporting Comprehension

Ask students how the boy in the story knows that spring has arrived. Then have them draw one or more of the signs of spring mentioned on page 173.

CRITICAL THINKING
Guiding Comprehension

21 **DRAWING CONCLUSIONS** Why do the Indians help the settlers? (They want peace; they like the settlers; they want to trade with the settlers.)

22 **DRAWING CONCLUSIONS** Why have the Pilgrims brought seeds from England to plant? (so they can grow crops for food and herbs for medicine)

23 **MAKING INFERENCES** What does the scene with the boy's mother reveal about her thoughts? (She's probably been doubting that the settlement can succeed and now feels some hope.)

Our Indian friend came back and brought his chief. We all agreed to live in peace.

21 And one of the Indians stayed with us, teaching us where to find fish in the bubbling brooks, and how to catch them in traps, and how to plant Indian corn so that next winter we would have enough to eat.

My father and I worked side by side, clearing the fields, planting barley and peas and hills of corn.

22 Afterward I dug a garden next to our house. In it we planted the seeds we had brought from home: carrots and cabbages and onions and my mother's favorite herbs, parsley, sage, chamomile, and mint.

Each day I watched, until something green pushed up from the dark earth. My mother laughed when she saw it.

23 "Perhaps we may yet make a home in this new land," she said.

174

English Language Learners

Language Development

Have students find the names of all of the foods mentioned on page 174. Make a list on the board. If possible, show examples of Indian corn.

175

Making Inferences

Teach

drawing a conclusion
making a guess

- Remind students that authors don't always explain everything in a story. Active readers use text clues and their own knowledge to make reasonable guesses, or inferences, about characters and events.

Practice

- Read page 173 with students.

- Guide students to use text clues and personal knowledge to decide why the Indian comes alone. (Text: Cannons show Indians that the settlers are afraid. Personal: One person is less frightening than a group. Inference: Indian is alone so settlers won't be afraid.)

Apply

- Ask groups of students to answer these questions: Why does the Indian bring his chief to meet with the Pilgrim leaders? Why do the Pilgrims want to learn from the Indian?

- Have groups share how they made their inferences.

Target Skill Trace	
Preview; Teach	p. 153A; p. 156; p. 175; p. 183A
Reteach	p. R8
Review	Theme 6, p. 311

CRITICAL THINKING

Guiding Comprehension

24 **COMPARE AND CONTRAST** How does the end of the story compare to the beginning? (Example: The descriptions of the ship are similar as it sails out to sea, but at the end the ship leaves the Pilgrims behind. Both times the Pilgrims' future is uncertain.)

25 **MAKING JUDGMENTS** How has the family's outlook changed since the beginning of the story? (They've survived the journey and first winter and know what to expect, so they feel more sure of their success.)

On a morning early in April our ship sailed back across the sea. We gathered on shore to watch it go. The great white sails filled with wind, then slowly the ship turned and headed out into the wide dark sea.

 I watched it growing smaller and smaller, and suddenly there were tears in my eyes. We were all alone now.

Then I felt a hand on my shoulder.

176

 Extra Support/ Intervention | **On Level** | **Challenge**

Selection Review

Before students join the whole class for Wrapping Up on page 177, have them

- take turns modeling the reading strategies they used
- complete **Transparency 5–2** with you and finish their Inference Charts
- summarize the whole story

Literature Discussion

Have small groups of students discuss the story using their own questions or the questions in Think About the Selection on page 178.

Vocabulary

sprouting beginning to grow as new plants

thatch-roofed a roof covered with straw or reeds

"Look," my father said, pointing up the hill.

Spread out above us in the soft spring sunshine was our settlement: the fields sprouting with green, the thatch-roofed houses and neatly fenced gardens, the streets laid out almost like a town. **25**

"Come," my father said. "We have work to do."

With his hand on my shoulder we walked back up the hill.

177

English Language Learners

Supporting Comprehension

When students have completed reading the story, ask summary questions: How old do you think the narrator is? How can you tell? What problems did the Pilgrims have? How did they survive? Who helped them?

Practice Book page 87

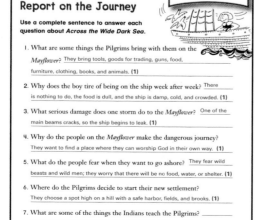

Name _____

Across the Wide Dark Sea:
The Mayflower Journey
Comprehension Check

Report on the Journey

Use a complete sentence to answer each question about *Across the Wide Dark Sea.*

1. What are some things the Pilgrims bring with them on the *Mayflower*? They bring tools, goods for trading, guns, food, furniture, clothing, books, and animals. **(1)**

2. Why does the boy tire of being on the ship week after week? There is nothing to do, the food is dull, and the ship is damp, cold, and crowded. **(1)**

3. What serious damage does one storm do to the *Mayflower*? One of the main beams cracks, so the ship begins to leak. **(1)**

4. Why do the people on the *Mayflower* make the dangerous journey? They want to find a place where they can worship God in their own way. **(1)**

5. What do the people fear when they want to go ashore? They fear wild beasts and wild men; they worry that there will be no food, water, or shelter. **(1)**

6. Where do the Pilgrims decide to start their new settlement? They choose a spot high on a hill with a safe harbor, fields, and brooks. **(1)**

7. What are some of the things the Indians teach the Pilgrims? They teach the Pilgrims where to fish and how to plant corn. **(1)**

8. How do the boy and his father feel about the new settlement in the spring? They feel hopeful. **(1)**

Wrapping Up

Critical Thinking Questions

1. **MAIN IDEA** Why do you think the author has named the story *Across the Wide Dark Sea?* (to describe the Pilgrims' destination and also the uncertain future they faced)

2. **MAKING INFERENCES** What inferences can you make about people's desire to find freedom and a better way of life? (People will endure many hardships to reach their goal.)

Strategies in Action

Ask students to tell how they used the Question strategy and to take turns modeling it. Ask what other strategies they found helpful.

Discussion Options

Bring the entire class together to do one or more of the activities below.

Review Predictions/Purpose Discuss reasons why students' predictions were or were not accurate and how paying attention to story details helped them make inferences about story events.

Share Group Discussions Have students share their reactions to the story.

Summarize Ask students to summarize the story, using their Inference Charts.

Comprehension Check

Use **Practice Book** page 87 to assess students' comprehension of the selection.

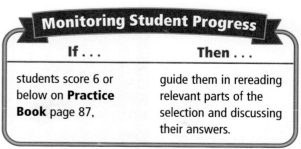

Monitoring Student Progress

If . . .	Then . . .
students score 6 or below on **Practice Book** page 87,	guide them in rereading relevant parts of the selection and discussing their answers.

Reading the Selection **177**

Responding

Think About the Selection

Have students discuss or write their answers. Sample answers are provided; accept reasonable responses.

1. **NOTING DETAILS** They want the freedom to worship the way they wish and hope to find a settlement where their lives will be better.

2. **COMPARE AND CONTRAST** At first he thinks the sailors' lives are exciting. Then he realizes how small and helpless the ship is in storms, and he tires of the cold, dampness, and poor food.

3. **MAKING INFERENCES** They want to think of their new settlement as "home."

4. **MAKING GENERALIZATIONS** enduring the terrible storms and living in damp and crowded conditions; sighting land after nine weeks at sea

5. **PROBLEM SOLVING** Answers will vary. Examples: tractors, plows, chain saws, backhoes

6. **Connecting/Comparing** Answers will vary.

Responding

Think About the Selection

1. Why do the people in this story travel to an unknown land? In what ways do they hope their lives will be different?

2. How do you think the boy's feelings about a sailor's life change during the voyage?

3. Why do you think the settlers name their new town after the one they sailed from?

4. What would you find most difficult and most exciting about the voyage the boy makes?

5. What tools and machines that we have today would have been most useful to the settlers?

6. **Connecting/Comparing** What qualities do the settlers have that help them succeed on their voyage?

Summarizing

Write a Travel Diary

Choose one part of the story, such as the voyage, the first winter in the new land, or the first spring. Write an entry for a travel diary that summarizes the important events during that time.

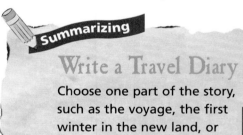
Tips

- To get started, brainstorm a list of events or make a story web.
- Include descriptive details.
- Keep your summary short.

178

English Language Learners

Supporting Comprehension

Beginning/Preproduction Ask students to draw a scene from the journey. Then ask students to label what they have drawn.

Early Production and Speech Emergence Students can make a picture quiz by writing words and drawing pictures. They can ask a partner to match the words and pictures.

Intermediate and Advanced Fluency Ask students to write a five-question quiz. Then have them exchange questions with a classmate and respond.

Math

Calculate Amounts

If a person on the *Mayflower* ate one pound of salt pork, one cup of beans, half a pound of cheese, and three biscuits each day, how much of each of those foods would a person eat in one week? Try drawing a picture to help you find the answer.

Bonus The journey lasted sixty-six days. How much would one traveler have eaten during the entire trip?

Vocabulary

Make a Picture Dictionary

With a partner, write all the words from the story about ships and sailing on separate pieces of paper. Look up each word in a dictionary, write down its meaning, and draw a picture of it. Staple your pages together in alphabetical order to make a book.

Build a Model of the Mayflower

Find instructions on how to build your own paper sailing ship when you connect to Education Place. **www.eduplace.com/kids**

179

Additional Responses

Personal Response Invite students to share their personal responses to the selection with a partner.

Journal ▸ Ask students to write in their journals about a journey they have taken.

Selection Connections Remind students to add to **Practice Book** page 84.

Extra Support/ Intervention

Travel Diary

For the writing activity, help students brainstorm a list of events for each part of the story (voyage, winter, spring). Challenge them to include vivid details as they write their travel diary entries. Suggest they use their Inference Charts to remind them of events and characters' feelings during the voyage.

Practice Book page 84

Launching the Theme
Selection Connections

Name

Voyagers

Fill in the chart as you read the stories. Sample answers shown.

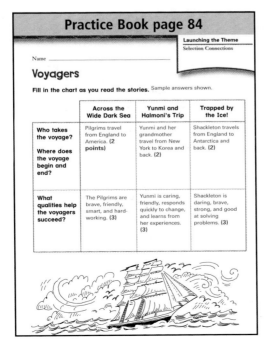

	Across the Wide Dark Sea	Yunmi and Halmoni's Trip	Trapped by the Ice!
Who takes the voyage? / Where does the voyage begin and end?	Pilgrims travel from England to America. (2 points)	Yunmi and her grandmother travel from New York to Korea and back. (2)	Shackleton travels from England to Antarctica and back. (2)
What qualities help the voyagers succeed?	The Pilgrims are brave, friendly, smart, and hardworking. (3)	Yunmi is caring, friendly, responds quickly to change, and learns from her experiences. (3)	Shackleton is daring, brave, strong, and good at solving problems. (3)

Monitoring Student Progress

End-of-Selection Assessment

Selection Test Use the test on pages 135–136 in the **Teacher's Resource Blackline Masters** to assess selection comprehension and vocabulary.

Student Self-Assessment Have students assess their reading with additional questions such as

● Which parts of this selection were difficult? Why?

● Which strategies helped me understand the story better?

● Was this a good adventure story? Why or why not?

Responding 179

Social Studies Link

Skill: How to Read a Diagram

- **Introduce** "Young Voyagers: A Pilgrim Childhood," a nonfiction social-studies article.

- **Discuss** the skill lesson on Anthology page 180. Tell students that a diagram is a graphic with labels and a legend, or key, that describes something.

- **Model** using the diagram to find out about different parts of the ship.

- **Explain** that diagrams can help readers understand the text, and that sometimes diagrams work better than words to convey information. Discuss other criteria that might be useful for categorizing and classifying the ship's layout. (names of decks and masts; rooms for cargo, living, working, recreation)

- **Set a purpose** for reading. Tell students to use the diagram on pages 180–181 to learn more about life on board the *Mayflower*. Remind them to identify the main ideas and supporting details in the paragraphs and use Question and other strategies as they read.

Vocabulary

cargo goods carried by a ship

hardships things that cause suffering

relieved not afraid anymore

Social Studies Link

Skill: How to Read a Diagram

❶ **Identify** what the diagram shows.

❷ **Find** the labels on the diagram. The labels will often be letters or numbers.

❸ **Match** each label with one in the key.

❹ **Read** the description of each labeled part.

❺ As you read, **look back** at the diagram to see how it helps you.

180

Young Voyagers A Pilgrim Childhood

What was life like for the twenty-eight children aboard the *Mayflower*? How did they live once they settled in America? Read on to find out.

On Board the Mayflower

The *Mayflower* was built to carry cargo, not people. Passengers lived in the lower decks — the dark, cramped space between the hold and the main deck.

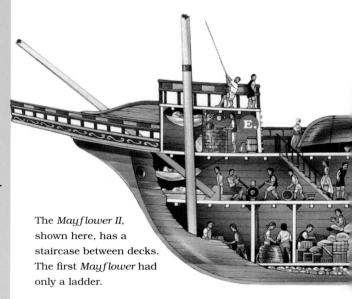

The *Mayflower II*, shown here, has a staircase between decks. The first *Mayflower* had only a ladder.

In good weather, children might have read,
[play]ed games, or exercised on deck. Much of the
[time], however, the passengers had to stay below
[deck] because of stormy weather. They were
[ofte]n seasick, and the ship's motion — up and
[dow]n, side to side — made their cramped living
[spac]e dangerous.

The voyage was filled with hardships, but
[ther]e were joyful events as well. One baby was
[born] during the voyage and named Oceanus.
[Can] you guess why his parents gave him that
[nam]e?) Another child, Peregrine White, was
[born] in Cape Cod Harbor. His first name means
[trave]ler."

After sixty-six days at sea, the Pilgrims
[were] happy and relieved to finally reach their
[new] home.

Parts of the Ship

A. The **Round House** was where the ship's route was planned, using maps and other charts.

B. The **Ship's Bell** was rung during emergencies or to show the passage of time.

C. The **Great Cabin** was where the commander of the ship lived.

D. The **Whipstaff** was a long lever used to steer the ship.

E. The **Cook-room** was where meals were prepared for the crew.

F. The **lower decks** were where the passengers lived.

G. The **Hold** was where most of the food, tools, and supplies were kept.

181

Extra Support/Intervention

[I]nferring the Main Idea

[P]oint out to students that they sometimes have to "read between the lines" to
[u]nderstand the main idea. Have them read the paragraph on page 180 under the
[h]eading "On Board the Mayflower." Explain that what the author doesn't state is
[t]hat the families on the *Mayflower* lived in spaces meant for cargo, not people.
[D]iscuss what the effects might have been.

Living in New Plymouth

What was life like in Plymouth? At Plimoth Plantation in Massachusetts, where these photos were taken, people dress up and show visitors what Pilgrim life may have been like. The facts may surprise you!

Children spent most of the day working! Their chores included fetching water, gathering firewood, herding animals, and gathering berries. They also helped their parents cook, clean, plant and harvest crops, and care for younger children.

Children and adults probably took baths only a few times a year. They thought bathing was unhealthy.

Pilgrim children still had time to play. They probably played marbles, ball games, board games, and running games.

182

English Language Learners

Supporting Comprehension

Before reading, ask students to label the pictures using stick-on tabs (ship, toys, wheelbarrow, etc.). Then read aloud, referring to the pictures frequently. After you have read through once, ask: Where did people stay on the ship? Where did children play? After they arrived in Plymouth, what chores did children do? What games did they play? Who served dinners?

Vocabulary

fetching getting

harvest to gather

At seven years old, children began dressing like their parents. Before that, both boys and girls wore gowns.

There was no school in the early years of New Plymouth. Children learned to read and write from their parents or from neighbors.

ler children were expected
serve meals to their parents.
ldren ate only after their
ents had been served.
ey often ate while standing
he table.

Challenge

Research Skills

Have students research the *Mayflower* voyage and life as a Pilgrim. Provide age-appropriate books, encyclopedias, website URLs, and other materials to help students locate information. Invite them to prepare a short report for the class on the *Mayflower* or the New Plymouth settlement. Challenge students to create a diagram, complete with labels and a legend, that shows the route of the ship, the layout of the settlement, or other relevant information.

Wrapping Up

Critical Thinking Questions

Ask students to read aloud the parts of the selection that support their answers.

1. **MAKING JUDGMENTS** Do you think Pilgrim children had as much fun as children today? Explain. (Answers will vary.)

2. **MAKING INFERENCES/TEXT ORGANIZATION** According to the Parts of the Ship key, where would the most important person on the ship have lived? How is this labeled on the diagram? (The commander, or captain, lived in the Great Cabin, marked as C.)

3. **MAKING GENERALIZATIONS** What things did Pilgrim children learn that would be helpful today? Explain why. (From work, they learned valuable skills and responsibility; by serving their parents and eating last, they learned to respect and honor their parents.)

4. **Connecting/Comparing** What are the differences between the descriptions of the sea voyage in *Across the Wide Dark Sea* and in the article? Why are they different? (The boy describes the voyage in more detail. They differ because the story description is fiction and is from the boy's perspective; the article is nonfiction and includes only known facts.)

Transparency 5–2

Inference Chart
Responses will vary. Examples are given.

1. How does the boy feel when the journey begins?

Story Clues (pages 113–115)	What I Know
He looks ahead at the wide dark sea. He stands close to his father and clings to his father's hand.	Children stay close to their parents and hold their hands when children are afraid.

My Inference The boy is sad and afraid.

2. How does the boy feel after six weeks at sea?

Story Clues (pages 116–119)	What I Know
The ship is crowded, cramped, cold, and wet.	It is uncomfortable to be crowded, cold, and wet.

My Inference He is bored, uncomfortable, and worried about the future.

3. How do the people react to the report of the new land?

Story Clues (pages 122–124)	What I Know
The search party finds fine trees, ponds, and rich black earth.	The materials are good for new homes and growing crops.

My Inference They are relieved and happy to hear the good news.

TRANSPARENCY 5–2 TEACHER'S EDITION PAGES 166 AND 183A
VOYAGERS Across the Wide Dark Sea Graphic Organizer Inference Chart ANNOTATED VERSION

Practice Book page 86

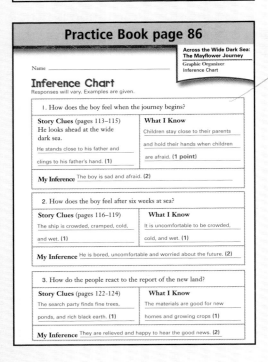

Across the Wide Dark Sea: The Mayflower Journey
Graphic Organizer Inference Chart

Name _____

Inference Chart
Responses will vary. Examples are given.

1. How does the boy feel when the journey begins?

Story Clues (pages 113–115)	What I Know
He looks ahead at the wide dark sea. He stands close to his father and clings to his father's hand. (1)	Children stay close to their parents and hold their hands when children are afraid. (1 point)

My Inference The boy is sad and afraid. (2)

2. How does the boy feel after six weeks at sea?

Story Clues (pages 116–119)	What I Know
The ship is crowded, cramped, cold, and wet. (1)	It is uncomfortable to be crowded, cold, and wet. (1)

My Inference He is bored, uncomfortable and worried about the future. (2)

3. How do the people react to the report of the new land?

Story Clues (pages 122–124)	What I Know
The search party finds fine trees, ponds, and rich black earth. (1)	The materials are good for new homes and growing crops (1)

My Inference They are relieved and happy to hear the good news. (2)

pages wrong

COMPREHENSION: Making Inferences

❶ Teach

Review inferences about *Across the Wide Dark Sea*. Remind students that authors do not always explain in words everything i a story. Sometimes readers must figure out how characters feel or why they do certain things. Complete the Graphic Organizer on **Transparency 5–2** with students. (Sample answers are shown.) Students can refer to the selection and to **Practice Book** page 86 Discuss how readers

- use story clues and their own knowledge to make inferences
- adjust their inferences based on new story information

Model making and adjusting an inference. Have students reread the last four paragraphs of page 166 and the first half of page 168. Then model the skill.

Think Aloud *When I read that the Pilgrims are so happy to find land, I thi. they will rush ashore right away; that is what I would do becau I would want to be off the ship. But on the next page, I learn that just a few me go ashore. I suppose it makes sense that the Pilgrims would be careful and try to find out about the new land before they all go ashore. They want to know that they will be safe there. So that's why they don't all go ashore right away.*

❷ Guided Practice

Have students make inferences. Have students compose ques tions that cannot be answered from the text, similar to the ones below. List the questions. Then have small groups use a chart simi lar to the transparency to record answers to the questions, noting the story details and personal knowledge they used for help.

> How does the sailor know that land is ahead before he sees it?
>
> How does the boy feel when he hears birds singing in the trees?
>
> What do the sprouting seedlings mean to the boy's mother?
>
> How do the Pilgrims feel when the ship sails away?
>
> How do the Pilgrims feel about their new settlement?

Apply

Assign Practice Book pages 88–89. Also have students apply this skill as they read their **Leveled Readers** for this week. You may also select books from the Leveled Bibliography for this theme, pages 148E–148F.

Test Prep Emphasize that many questions on reading tests ask students to make inferences.

- Explain that for these questions students will have to find details in the passage that they can use as clues.

- Point out that they will often have to use their own knowledge and experiences as well as information from the passage.

Leveled Readers and Leveled Practice

Students at all levels apply the comprehension skill as they read their Leveled Readers. See lessons on pages 183O–183R.

● **BELOW LEVEL**   ▲ **ON LEVEL**   ■ **ABOVE LEVEL**   ◆ **LANGUAGE SUPPORT**

Reading Traits

Teaching students how to make inferences is one way of encouraging them to "read between the lines" of a selection. This comprehension skill supports the reading trait **Developing Interpretations.**

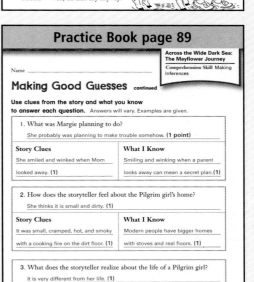

Practice Book page 88

Across the Wide Dark Sea: The Mayflower Journey
Comprehension Skill Making Inferences

Name _____

Making Good Guesses

Read the story. Then answer the questions on the next page.

A Trip Back in Time!

When Dad said we were going to Plymouth to see where the Pilgrims lived, Mom looked at us sharply. She said, "I want you two to behave and learn something today." My sister Margie smiled and winked at me when Mom looked away.

The place was not at all what we expected. Instead of a museum display, we found ourselves walking past full-sized homes with fences and gardens. It looked like New Plymouth might have looked in 1627. People who dressed and talked like Pilgrims answered our questions as they went about their tasks for the day. It seemed as if we had been carried back in time.

The best part of our visit happened by chance. We were looking at the goats when a young Pilgrim girl came by with a bucket of water. She told us how the brown goat had kicked her last week. Then she invited us into her home, which turned out to be a small, cramped, hot, smoky cottage with a cooking fire right on the dirt floor. It was as if we'd made a new friend. We learned all about Mary, how she did chores most of the day, how she hated to milk goats, how she loved to shine the kettle with salt and vinegar. And she was so polite to all the adults! Why, she even curtsied to my parents. Needless to say, we were too busy talking to get into trouble — well, on that day anyway!

Practice Book page 89

Across the Wide Dark Sea: The Mayflower Journey
Comprehension Skill Making Inferences

Name _____

Making Good Guesses *continued*

Use clues from the story and what you know to answer each question. Answers will vary. Examples are given.

1. What was Margie planning to do?

She probably was planning to make trouble somehow. **(1 point)**

Story Clues	What I Know
She smiled and winked when Mom looked away. **(1)**	Smiling and winking when a parent looks away can mean a secret plan. **(1)**

2. How does the storyteller feel about the Pilgrim girl's home?

She thinks it is small and dirty. **(1)**

Story Clues	What I Know
It was small, cramped, hot, and smoky with a cooking fire on the dirt floor. **(1)**	Modern people have bigger homes with stoves and real floors. **(1)**

3. What does the storyteller realize about the life of a Pilgrim girl?

It is very different from her life. **(1)**

Story Clues	What I Know
The Pilgrim girl did chores most of the day; she carried water, milked goats, and polished pots; she curtsied. **(2)**	Modern children go to school, play games, and have spare time; they do not curtsy. **(1)**

Monitoring Student Progress

If . . .	Then . . .
students score 7 or below on **Practice Book** page 89,	use the Reteaching lesson on Teacher's Edition page R8.
students have successfully met the lesson objectives,	have them do the Challenge/ Extension activities on Teacher's Edition page R9.

Target Skill Trace

Teach	p. 183C
Reteach	p. R14
Review	pp. 267F–267G
See	*Handbook for English Language Learners*, p. 167; *Extra Support Handbook*, pp. 162–163; pp. 166–167

Practice Book page 90

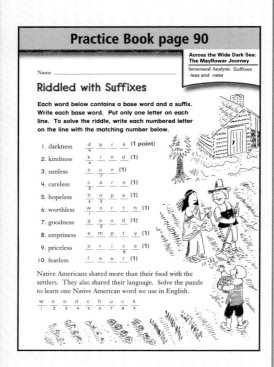

Name _____

Riddled with Suffixes

Each word below contains a base word and a suffix. Write only each base word. Put only one letter on each line. To solve the riddle, write each numbered letter on the line with the matching number below.

1. darkness   d a r k (1 point)
   4
2. kindness   k i n d (1)
   9
3. sunless   s u n (1)
   5
4. careless   c a r e (1)
   3
5. hopeless   h o p e (1)
   6 3
6. worthless   w o r t h (1)
   1
7. goodness   g o o d (1)
   2
8. emptiness   e m p t y (1)
   7
9. priceless   p r i c e (1)
   8
10. fearless   f e a r (1)

Native Americans shared more than their food with the settlers. They also shared their language. Solve the puzzle to learn one Native American word we use in English.

w o o d c h u c k
1 2 3 4 5 6 7 8 9

Monitoring Student Progress

If . . .	Then . . .
students score 7 or below on **Practice Book** page 90,	use the Reteaching lesson on Teacher's Edition page R14.

STRUCTURAL ANALYSIS/ VOCABULARY: Suffixes *-less* and *-ness*

❶ Teach

Define suffixes. Explain that suffixes are word parts that add meaning to a base word.

Explain the suffix *-less*. Write *How could a ship so small and helpless ever cross the vast ocean?*

- In *helpless*, the suffix *-less* adds the meaning "without."
- *Helpless* means "without help."

Explain the suffix *-ness*. Write *Yet the storms and sickness went on*.

- The suffix *-ness* often changes a describing word (an adjective) into a noun.
- The word *sickness* means the "condition of being sick."

List examples of other words with the suffixes *-less* and *-ness*. Have students suggest words with the suffixes *-less* and *-ness*. (Sample answers: *careless, hopeless, worthless; darkness, happiness, fairness, kindness*)

Model the Phonics/Decoding Strategy. Write *And some began to ask why we had left our safe homes to go on this <u>endless</u> journey to an unknown land*. Then model the process of decoding *endless*.

Think Aloud *I see the word* end *and the ending* -less. *When I put these together I say* EHND-lehs. *I know the suffix* -less *means* "without," *so* endless *must mean "without an end." It makes sense that some of the passengers would wonder why they had left their safe homes to go on a long trip that seemed to have no end.*

❷ Guided Practice

Have students decode words with *-less* and *-ness*. Display the sentences below. Ask partners to copy the underlined words, circle the *-ness* and *-less* endings, decode each word, and give its meaning. Have students share their work with the class.

> One big problem on the ship was the dampness.
> After so many days at sea, we began to feel hopeless.
> The Indians showed great kindness toward the settlers.

❸ Apply

Assign Practice Book page 90.

PHONICS REVIEW: The Vowel Sounds in *tooth* and *cook*

❶ Teach

Review the vowel sounds in *tooth* and *cook*. Tell students that understanding the vowel sounds in *tooth* and *cook* can help them decode unfamiliar words.

- The spelling patterns *oo* and *ew* can have the /o͞o/ sound as in *tooth*.
- The spelling pattern *oo* can also have the /o͝o/ sound as in *cook*.

Model the Phonics/Decoding Strategy. Write *One afternoon the weary men returned with good news.* Then model how to decode *afternoon.*

Think Aloud *When I look at this word, I recognize the shorter word* after. *Next I see the letter* n *followed by the* oo *spelling pattern and another* n. *I know the* oo *pattern can make the* u *sound as in* cook, *but* af-tur-NUN *doesn't sound right. I know the* oo *spelling pattern can also have the* oo *sound as in* tooth. *I'll try* af-tur-NOON. *That makes sense.*

❷ Guided Practice

Have students find *oo* vowel sounds. Write:

1. I <u>stood</u> by my father.
2. We <u>grew</u> weary during the long trip.
3. I heard the <u>lookout</u> shout.

- Have students copy the underlined words, circle *oo* vowel sounds in the underlined words, and decode the words.

❸ Apply

Have students decode words with *oo* vowel sounds. Ask students to decode the words below from *Across the Wide Dark Sea* and discuss their meanings.

tools	page 159	firewood	page 168
goods	page 159	brooks	page 170
food	page 159	thatch-roofed	page 177
books	page 159		

OBJECTIVES

- Read words and syllables with the vowel sounds in *tooth* and *cook*.
- Apply the Phonics/Decoding Strategy.

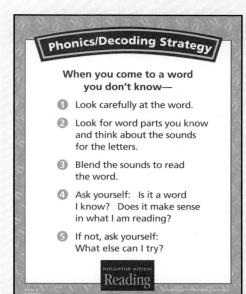

Phonics/Decoding Strategy

When you come to a word you don't know—

1. Look carefully at the word.
2. Look for word parts you know and think about the sounds for the letters.
3. Blend the sounds to read the word.
4. Ask yourself: Is it a word I know? Does it make sense in what I am reading?
5. If not, ask yourself: What else can I try?

HOUGHTON MIFFLIN
Reading

SPELLING: Vowel Sounds in *tooth/cook*

OBJECTIVE

- Write Spelling Words that have the vowel sounds in *tooth* and *cook*.

SPELLING WORDS

Basic

tooth	boot
chew	flew
grew*	shook
cook*	balloon
shoe†	drew
blue†	spoon

Review	**Challenge**
good*	loose
soon*	brook*

*Forms of these words appear in the literature.

†These words are exceptions to the principle.

Extra Support/Intervention

Basic Word List Consider using only the left column of Basic Words with students who need extra support.

Challenge

Challenge Word Practice Students can use the Challenge Words to write sentences about the adventures of the settlers from the story.

DAY 1 — INSTRUCTION

Vowel Sounds in *tooth/cook*

Pretest Use the Day 5 Test sentences.

Teach Write *tooth* and *chew* on the board. Say each word; have students repeat it. Underline *oo* and *ew*, and explain that they are two spelling patterns for the /o͞o/ sound.

- Write *shoe* and *blue* on the board, say them, and have students repeat them. Underline the *oe* and *ue* patterns. Tell students that these are less common ways of spelling the /o͞o/ sound.

- Add *cook* to the board, say it, and have students repeat it. Underline the *oo* pattern; point out that the /o͝o/ sound is often spelled *oo*.

- Write the rest of the Basic Words on the board, and have students say them. Call on students to underline the /o͞o/ and /o͝o/ patterns.

Practice/Homework Assign **Practice Book** page 239.

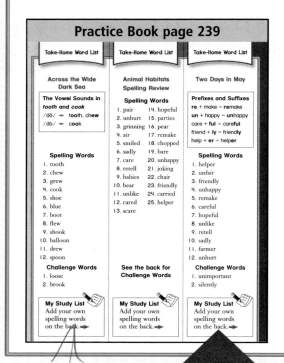

Practice Book page 239

DAY 2 — REVIEW & PRACTICE

Reviewing the Principle

Go over the spelling patterns for the vowel sounds in *tooth* and *cook* with students.

Practice/Homework Assign **Practice Book** page 91.

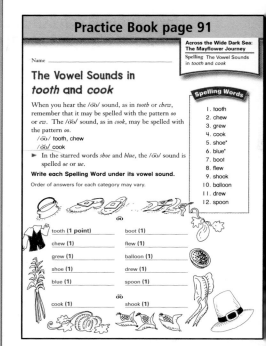

Practice Book page 91

Take-Home Word List

DAY 3 VOCABULARY

Exact Words

Have students work in small groups. Assign one of these words to each group: *cook, flew, shoe.*

Ask each group to brainstorm and list more exact words that could be used in place of their assigned word. Encourage students to use a thesaurus.

Groups can meet to pool their exact words and share the final lists with the class. (Responses will vary.)

List the Basic Words on the board. Have students use each word orally in a sentence. (Sentences will vary.)

Practice/Homework For spelling practice, assign **Practice Book** page 92.

Practice Book page 92

Name ___

Across the Wide Dark Sea: The Mayflower Journey
Spelling The Vowel Sounds in *tooth* and *cook*

Spelling Spree

Puzzle Play Write a Spelling Word to fit each clue.

1. a color b l u e (1 point)
2. a toy you blow up b a l l o o n (1)
3. not a fork or a knife s p o o n (1)
4. past tense of *draw* d r e w (1)
5. a dentist works on it t o o t h (1)
6. to prepare food by heating c o o k (1)

What two words might someone on a ship be glad to hear? To find out, write the boxed letters in order.

l a n d h o i

Name Game Write the Spelling Word hidden in each name. Look for o's and w's to find the words. Use all small letters in your answers.

Example: Dr. Diego O. Delgado good

7. Mr. Jeb O. Otis boot (1)
8. Miss Peg R. Ewing grew (1)
9. Mrs. Peach E. Wild chew (1)
10. Mr. Cash O. O'Krook shook (1)

Spelling Words
1. tooth
2. chew
3. grew
4. cook
5. shoe*
6. blue*
7. boot
8. flew
9. shook
10. balloon
11. drew
12. spoon

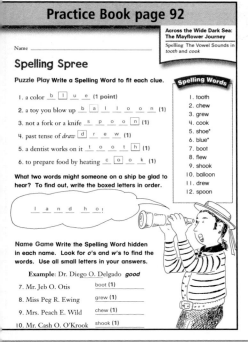

DAY 4 PROOFREADING

Game: Climb the Mast

Ask students to work in groups of 3: 2 players and 1 caller. Give each group a long stick (perhaps a yardstick or broom handle) for a "mast," and give the caller a list of Basic and Review Words. Explain the game rules:

- The caller says a list word.
- If Player 1 spells it correctly, he or she grabs the bottom of the mast with one hand.
- If Player 2 spells the next word correctly, he or she grabs the mast just above Player 1's hand.
- As players spell words, they move their hands one over the other up the mast. If they misspell a word, they cannot move.
- The player who reaches the top of the mast first wins.

Practice/Homework For proofreading and writing practice, assign **Practice Book** page 93.

Practice Book page 93

Name ___

Across the Wide Dark Sea: The Mayflower Journey
Spelling The Vowel Sounds in *tooth* and *cook*

Proofreading and Writing

Proofreading Circle the four misspelled Spelling Words in this diary entry. Then write each word correctly.

This morning, we had fine sailing weather. Never have I seen a sky so clear and blew. Sister and I sat on the deck. We drew pictures of the ship and the sea. Time just floo by! Later, the sails shuk with a sudden wind, and we were sent below. I lost a shue on the stairs as I ran. I will look for it when the storm has passed.

Spelling Words
1. tooth
2. chew
3. grew
4. cook
5. shoe*
6. blue*
7. boot
8. flew
9. shook
10. balloon
11. drew
12. spoon

1. blue (2)
2. flew (2)
3. shook (2)
4. shoe (2)

Write a Travel Poster The Pilgrims traveled from England to America. Have you taken an interesting trip? Did you travel by ship, car, bus, or plane? What did you see and do?

On a separate sheet of paper, write a travel poster. Make readers want to visit the place you are telling about. Use Spelling Words from the list. Responses will vary. (2)

DAY 5 ASSESSMENT

Spelling Test

Say each underlined word, read the sentence, and then repeat the word. Have students write only the underlined word.

Basic Words

1. I lost a baby **tooth**. 6
2. My dog will **chew** this bone. 5
3. The corn **grew** tall. 4
4. The **cook** needed a big pot. 3
5. I have to tie my **shoe**. 2
6. The sky is very **blue**. 1
7. Some snow got inside my **boot**. 12
8. A plane **flew** over my house. 11
9. We **shook** hands when we met. 10
10. I want a green **balloon**. 9
11. Who **drew** this picture? 8
12. There is a **spoon** on the table. 7

Challenge Words

13. The old rope is **loose**. 15
14. Shall we **wade** in the **brook**? 13

Review Words

15. good
16. soon 14

VOCABULARY: Syllables in a Dictionary

OBJECTIVES

- Identify the part of a dictionary entry that shows syllabication.
- Break words into syllables.

Target Skill Trace

Teach	p. 183G
Review	pp. 267H–267I
Extend	Challenge/Extension Activities, p. R15
See	*Handbook for English Language Learners*, p. 171

VOCABULARY SKILLS

❶ Teach

Define syllables. Remind students that a syllable is a word or word part that contains a single vowel sound. If two vowels stand for one sound, they will be part of the same syllable. Knowing how to divide words into syllables can help readers spell words.

Display Transparency 5–3. Cover all but the dictionary entries for *clothing*. Review the features of a dictionary entry. Explain that

- the base, or root, form of a word is shown, along with its part of speech, one or more definitions, and pronunciation,
- the word is divided into syllables in the entry,
- large dots usually show where the syllables break.

Model using the dictionary syllabication feature. Read passage 1 on the transparency aloud. Then use the Think Aloud to model how to divide the word *clothing*.

Think Aloud *If I look at* clothing *and say it out loud, I see that it has two vowel sounds, an* o *and an* i. *So* clothing *must have two syllables. I'll try to find where the syllables break. It sounds as if the break might come after* clo-. *However, when I look in the dictionary, I see that the syllable break comes after* cloth-.

❷ Guided Practice

Give students practice in using the dictionary syllabication feature. Uncover the rest of the transparency. In pairs or small groups, have students answer questions 2 through 6. Ask groups to share their answers with the class.

❸ Apply

Assign Practice Book page 94.

Transparency 5–3

VOYAGERS *Across the Wide Dark Sea*
Vocabulary Skill Dictionary: Syllables
ANNOTATED VERSION

Dictionary: Syllables

clothing *noun* Clothes.
cloth·ing (klō′ thing) · *noun*

1. Packed in tight, too, was everything we would need in the new land: tools for building and planting, goods for trading, guns for hunting. Food, furniture, <u>clothing</u>, books.

furious *adjective* **1.** Full of very great anger. **2.** Fierce; violent: *The furious storm lasted for three days.*
fu·ri·ous (fyŏŏr′ ē as) · *adjective*
furniture *noun* The objects needed to make a room ready for living or working in, such as chairs, tables, and beds.
fur·ni·ture (fûr′ nə chər) · *plural noun*
reliable *adjective* Dependable: *We need a reliable clock.*
re·li·a·ble (rĭ lī′ ə bəl) · *adjective*

2. What symbol is used to show the division between syllables? <u>a big dot</u>
3. How do you know that a word has only one syllable? <u>It isn't shown separated into parts by big dots.</u>
4. How are the words *furious* and *furniture* alike and different? <u>Alike: both words begin with fur. Different: furious does not have r in the first syllable, but furniture does.</u>
5. Which word has a syllable that contains more than one vowel? <u>furious</u>
6. Which word has a syllable with only one letter? <u>reliable</u>

TRANSPARENCY 5-3
TEACHER'S EDITION PAGE 183G

Monitoring Student Progress

If . . .	Then . . .
students score 7 or below on **Practice Book** page 94,	have them work with partners to correct the items they missed.

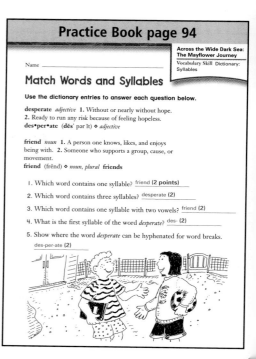

Practice Book page 94

Name _____

Across the Wide Dark Sea: The Mayflower Journey
Vocabulary Skill Dictionary: Syllables

Match Words and Syllables

Use the dictionary entries to answer each question below.

desperate *adjective* **1.** Without or nearly without hope. **2.** Ready to run any risk because of feeling hopeless.
des•per•ate (dĕs′ par ĭt) ◇ *adjective*

friend *noun* **1.** A person one knows, likes, and enjoys being with. **2.** Someone who supports a group, cause, or movement.
friend (frĕnd) ◇ *noun, plural* **friends**

1. Which word contains one syllable? <u>friend</u> **(2 points)**
2. Which word contains three syllables? <u>desperate</u> **(2)**
3. Which word contains one syllable with two vowels? <u>friend</u> **(2)**
4. What is the first syllable of the word *desperate*? <u>des-</u> **(2)**
5. Show where the word *desperate* can be hyphenated for word breaks. <u>des-per-ate</u> **(2)**

STUDY SKILL:
Multimedia Report

OBJECTIVES

- Identify and select appropriate multi-media resources for a given topic.
- Use multimedia resources to give a report.
- Learn academic language: *multimedia*.

❶ Teach

Introduce the multimedia report.

- A multimedia report is a report that contains several kinds of media. Examples of media are:
  - photographs or other art
  - taped interviews (audio or video)
  - music
  - maps
  - CD-ROM or computer displays, such as Internet presentations
  - charts, graphs, or other visual aids

Model how to plan a multimedia report on "Young Voyagers."

- Brainstorm different kinds of media that can be included: a photograph of the *Mayflower* or of Plimoth Plantation; pictures of daily life at the plantation; illustrations of children doing chores; sound effects of the ocean or songs of the sea; filmstrips or videos.

- Ask a librarian what media is available.

- Select the media that best fits the purpose and topic of the report.

- Organize the ideas and write a script that includes what to say and where exactly to use media.

- Practice with small note cards until the presentation is clear.

Planning a Multimedia Report

- Brainstorm kinds of media to use.
- Find the media and then select the best media.
- Organize ideas and write a script.
- Practice the presentation.

❷ Practice/Apply

Give students practice in planning multimedia reports.

- Have small groups select a topic and brainstorm types of media to use for a report. Ask where they might find the media.

- Have groups create and present a brief multimedia report on their topic.

GRAMMAR: Subject Pronouns

OBJECTIVES

- Identify subject pronouns.
- Use subject pronouns.
- Proofread and correct sentences with grammar and spelling errors.
- Combine sentences with subject pronouns to improve writing.
- Learn academic language: *subject pronouns.*

DAY 1 INSTRUCTION

Subject Pronouns

Teach Display the first paragraph on **Transparency 5–5,** and have a volunteer read it aloud.

- Discuss why the paragraph seems monotonous. Students should notice that the repetition of *the storm* is not interesting.

- Display the second paragraph, and have a volunteer read it aloud. Point out that *the storm* is replaced with the pronoun *it.*

- Go over the bulleted definitions and rules below the paragraphs. Use the chart to demonstrate how pronouns can replace nouns.

- Ask volunteers to choose the correct subject pronoun to replace the underlined words in Sentences 1–4.

Daily Language Practice
Have students correct Sentences 1 and 2 on **Transparency 5–4.**

DAY 2 PRACTICE

Independent Work

Practice/Homework Assign **Practice Book** page 95.

Daily Language Practice
Have students correct Sentences 3 and 4 on **Transparency 5–4.**

Transparency 5–4

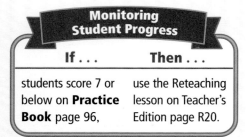

Daily Language Practice

Correct two sentences each day.

1. Us drewed the drowning man out of the water.
   We drew the drowning man out of the water.
2. Him turned bloo with cold
   He turned blue with cold.
3. The rain felt goode on our faces?
   The rain felt good on our faces.
4. Them soone groo tired of working.
   They soon grew tired of working.
5. They each losed a boote.
   They each lost a boot.
6. There was a bird, they floo into the air.
   There was a bird. It flew into the air.
7. A sailor had a bad problem with a toothe.
   A sailor had a bad problem with a tooth.
8. Him couldn't choo his food.
   He couldn't chew his food.
9. Him and me both wanted to cooke.
   He and I both wanted to cook.
10. that meat was as tough as an old shoo.
    That meat was as tough as an old shoe.

TRANSPARENCY 5–4
TEACHER'S EDITION PAGE 183I

Monitoring Student Progress

If . . .	Then . . .
students score 7 or below on **Practice Book** page 96,	use the Reteaching lesson on Teacher's Edition page R20.

Transparency 5–5

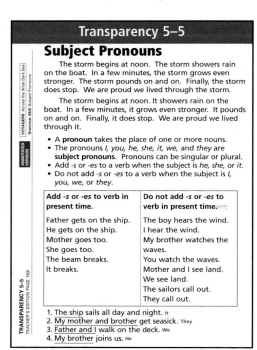

Subject Pronouns

The storm begins at noon. The storm showers rain on the boat. In a few minutes, the storm grows even stronger. The storm pounds on and on. Finally, the storm does stop. We are proud we lived through the storm.

The storm begins at noon. It showers rain on the boat. In a few minutes, it grows even stronger. It pounds on and on. Finally, it does stop. We are proud we lived through it.

- A **pronoun** takes the place of one or more nouns.
- The pronouns *I, you, he, she, it, we,* and *they* are **subject pronouns.** Pronouns can be singular or plural.
- Add *-s* or *-es* to a verb when the subject is *he, she,* or *it.*
- Do not add *-s* or *-es* to a verb when the subject is *I, you, we,* or *they.*

Add *-s* or *-es* to verb in present time.	Do not add *-s* or *-es* to verb in present time.
Father gets on the ship. He gets on the ship. Mother goes too. She goes too. The beam breaks. It breaks.	The boy hears the wind. I hear the wind. My brother watches the waves. You watch the waves. Mother and I see land. We see land. The sailors call out. They call out.

1. The ship sails all day and night. It
2. My mother and brother get seasick. They
3. Father and I walk on the deck. We
4. My brother joins us. He

TRANSPARENCY 5–5
TEACHER'S EDITION PAGE 183I

Practice Book page 95

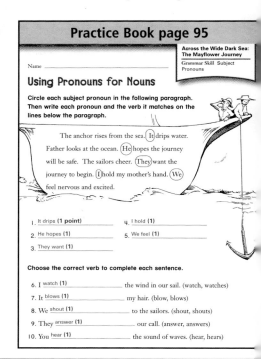

Name _____

Across the Wide Dark Sea:
The Mayflower Journey

Grammar Skill Subject Pronouns

Using Pronouns for Nouns

Circle each subject pronoun in the following paragraph. Then write each pronoun and the verb it matches on the lines below the paragraph.

The anchor rises from the sea. It drips water. Father looks at the ocean. He hopes the journey will be safe. The sailors cheer. They want the journey to begin. I hold my mother's hand. We feel nervous and excited.

1. It drips **(1 point)** _____
2. He hopes **(1)** _____
3. They want **(1)** _____
4. I hold **(1)** _____
5. We feel **(1)** _____

Choose the correct verb to complete each sentence.

6. I watch **(1)** _____ the wind in our sail. (watch, watches)
7. It blows **(1)** _____ my hair. (blow, blows)
8. We shout **(1)** _____ to the sailors. (shout, shouts)
9. They answer **(1)** _____ our call. (answer, answers)
10. You hear **(1)** _____ the sound of waves. (hear, hears)

PRONOUN GAME

Match; It Matches

...ve students write several present-
...ne verbs and the subject pronouns
...ou, he, she, it, we, they on note
...rds. Students should write two
...rds for each verb: one showing the
...rb without -s or -es and one show-
...g it with -s or -es. (Examples: sail,
...ls; watch, watches)

...Students put the pronoun cards in
...one stack, the verb cards in another.
...They take turns drawing one sub-
...ject pronoun and one verb.

...If the verb form matches the pro-
...noun, the student writes a sentence
...using the words and takes the cards.
...If they do not match, the student
...puts the cards in a discard pile.
...(Students should shuffle cards
...before reusing them.)

...The student with the most cards at
...the end of the game is the winner.

...ily Language Practice

...ve students correct Sentences 5
...d 6 on **Transparency 5–4.**

PRACTICE

Independent Work

Practice/Homework Assign **Practice Book** page 96.

Daily Language Practice

Have students correct Sentences 7 and 8 on **Transparency 5–4.**

IMPROVING WRITING

Sentence Combining

Teach Display the first two sentences at the top of **Transparency 5–6.**

- Ask students how the sentences are similar. They should recognize that the action is the same, but the subjects are different. Display the third sentence, and explain how sentences can be combined using *and*.

- Display the next three sentences to model using *or* to combine sentences.

- Ask volunteers to combine the sentence pairs in Items 1–5, using the word in parentheses.

- Have students review a piece of their own writing to see if they can improve it by using subject pronouns.

Practice/Homework Assign **Practice Book** page 97.

Daily Language Practice

Have students correct Sentences 9 and 10 on **Transparency 5–4.**

Practice Book page 96

Name _____

Across the Wide Dark Sea:
The Mayflower Journey

Grammar Skill Subject
Pronouns

Replacing Nouns with Pronouns

Rewrite each sentence. Replace each underlined subject with a subject pronoun.

1. The ship drops anchor.
   It drops anchor. **(1 point)**
2. Father points to our new home.
   He points to our new home. **(1)**
3. The workers build rough houses.
   They build rough houses. **(1)**
4. Mother nurses the sick.
   She nurses the sick. **(1)**
5. The weather is harsh and dangerous.
   It is harsh and dangerous. **(1)**
6. My brother and I take care of the young children.
   We take care of the young children. **(1)**
7. Mother and Father protect our home.
   They protect our home. **(1)**
8. The fields turn green in May.
   They turn green in May. **(1)**
9. The sun shines across the land.
   It shines across the land. **(1)**
10. Mother, Father, my brother, and I watch the sunrise.
    We watch the sunrise. **(1)**

Transparency 5–6

VOYAGERS Across the Wide Dark Sea
Grammar Skill Improving Your Writing

ANNOTATED VERSION

Sentence Combining with Subject Pronouns

He sails on the ship. She sails on the ship.
He and she sail on the ship.

You will see land first. I will see land first.
You or I will see land first.

1. You travel to America. He travels to America. (and)
   You and he travel to America.

2. He plants the crops. She plants the crops. (or)
   He or she plants the crops.

3. They build a house. I build a house. (and)
   They and I build a house.

4. You will be our first guest. She will be our first guest. (or)
   You or she will be our first guest.

5. He cooks dinner. I cook dinner. (and)
   He and I cook dinner.

TRANSPARENCY 5–6
TEACHER'S EDITION PAGE 183J

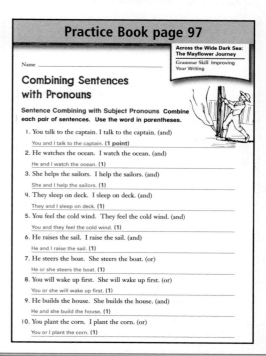

Practice Book page 97

Name _____

Across the Wide Dark Sea:
The Mayflower Journey

Grammar Skill Improving
Your Writing

Combining Sentences with Pronouns

Sentence Combining with Subject Pronouns Combine each pair of sentences. Use the word in parentheses.

1. You talk to the captain. I talk to the captain. (and)
   You and I talk to the captain. **(1 point)**
2. He watches the ocean. I watch the ocean. (and)
   He and I watch the ocean. **(1)**
3. She helps the sailors. I help the sailors. (and)
   She and I help the sailors. **(1)**
4. They sleep on deck. I sleep on deck. (and)
   They and I sleep on deck. **(1)**
5. You feel the cold wind. They feel the cold wind. (and)
   You and they feel the cold wind. **(1)**
6. He raises the sail. I raise the sail. (and)
   He and I raise the sail. **(1)**
7. He steers the boat. She steers the boat. (or)
   He or she steers the boat. **(1)**
8. You will wake up first. She will wake up first. (or)
   You or she will wake up first. **(1)**
9. He builds the house. She builds the house. (and)
   He and she build the house. **(1)**
10. You plant the corn. I plant the corn. (or)
    You or I plant the corn. **(1)**

WRITING: Play

OBJECTIVES

- Identify the characteristics of a play.
- Use a story passage as a basis for writing play dialogue.
- Use exclamation points correctly.

Writing Traits

Conventions As you teach the lesson on Day 2, emphasize that paying attention to conventions makes the play easy to read. Show an example of how to write dialogue.

> **MOTHER:** You can run on the beach while I wash the clothes. Stay close to me.
>
> **BOY:** I'll keep you in sight! *(Runs toward the beach)*

DAY 1 PREWRITING

Introducing the Format

Define a play.

- A play is a story that is written to be acted out for an audience. It has characters, setting, and plot.
- The characters speak to each other in dialogue, or conversation.
- Plays are divided into parts called scenes.
- Stage directions tell how characters sound and move. They are meant to be followed rather than read aloud.

Start students thinking about writing a play.

- Ask students to think about a play they might write based on page 168 of *Across the Wide Dark Sea.*
- Ask students to list the characters and tell how the characters feel. Then they can list some things the characters might do and what they might say.
- Have them save their notes.

DAY 2 DRAFTING

Discussing the Model

Display Transparency 5–7. Ask:

- Where and when does the play take place (on the passenger area of the *Mayflower*, October 1620)
- Who are the characters? (Father, a pilgrim leader, and Son)
- What is happening to them? (They're sailing in a storm.)
- How do they feel about it? (The boy is scared. The father is concerned about the boy.)
- What do the stage directions tell the actors? (how to look and act, for example, *Wakes up with a start. Looks scared.*)

Display Transparency 5–8, and discuss the guidelines.

Have students write play scenes.

- Have students read the last two paragraphs on Anthology page 168.
- Assign **Practice Book** page 98.
- Have them use their notes from Day 1.
- See Writing Traits on this page.
- Provide support as needed.

Transparency 5–7

A Play

Title: The Wide Dark Sea

Scene 1: Time: October 1620
Place: The crowded passenger area on the sailing ship *Mayflower*

Characters
Father — a Pilgrim leader; a strong, calm man about 40 years old
Son — a boy about 8 years old

(Sounds of a storm are heard. Thunder and loud winds)

Son *(Wakes up with a start. Looks scared. Reaches over and shakes his sleeping father awake.)*: Father, Father! Please wake up. I'm so frightened.
Father *(Wakes up. Sees that the boy is trembling.)*: Don't be afraid, son. It's just another storm. We've had several since we sailed from England.
Son: I'm afraid the lightning will hit the ship. Or the waves will pull us under. I'm tired of being cold and wet.
Father: I understand. But we must be brave. We are on a long, hard journey to a new home. We must trust that we will get there safely.
Son: Why are we going to this new land? I wish we had never left England.
Father *(Looks calm and sure of what he says. Speaks quietly but strongly.)*: We are searching for a place to live where we can worship in our own way. It is this freedom we seek in a new land. And I have faith that we will find it.
Son *(Settles back to sleep.)*: I have faith too, Father.

[Curtain]

Transparency 5–8

Guidelines for Writing a Play

- Write the title of the play. Then list the setting and the characters.
- Use the dialogue and the characters' actions to tell the story.
- Each time a different character speaks, write the character's name in bold type or capital letters followed by a colon. Then write the words that the character speaks.
- Write stage directions in parentheses to tell the characters how to speak and move.

Practice Book page 98

Across the Wide Dark Sea
The Mayflower Journey

Writing Skill A Play

Name _____

Writing a Scene from a Play

Title: The Wide Dark Sea

Scene 1: Time — November 1620
Place — a beach in the new land

Characters
Thomas — a boy about 8 years old
William — his brother, a boy about 6 years old

What Happens in This Scene
The two boys race up and down the beach. They find clams and mussels and eat them raw. They eat too many and then feel sick.

How the Boys Feel
They are happy to be off the ship. They are excited about the beach. They also are glad to eat fresh food like the clams and mussels. When they feel sick, they are sorry they ate too much.

Play-act with a partner and pretend to be one of the two boys. Act out the events under **What Happens in This Scene**. Remember to show how the boys feel about each event.

Make notes on this page for dialogue and action ideas. Then write your scene on another sheet of paper.

Scenes will vary. (10 points)

DAY 3 — REVISING

[Eva]luating to Revise

[Disp]lay Transparency 5–8 again.

[As]k students to use the guidelines to [de]cide how to make their writing better. [En]courage students to turn each point [in]to a question: Did I . . . ?

[St]udents may work with a partner in a [w]riting conference.

[As]k students to revise any parts of their [pl]ay scene that still need work.

Transparency 5–9

Using Exclamation Points Correctly

- Use an exclamation point to show strong feeling.
- Use an exclamation point with a command to do something.
- Use an exclamation point at the end of a warning.

Examples

Strong Feelings

Boy (*Talking to himself.*): It is so cramped and crowded on the ship. How I long to run and jump and climb!

Commands and Warnings

(*During a storm, a man has fallen overboard.*)
(*Sound of man's voice shouting "Help!" over and over.*)

Ship Captain (*Throws a rope over the side. Shouts.*): Grab this rope! (*Now the captain speaks to the sailors.*) Haul that rope in! Be careful! And be quick before he drowns!

Find five exclamation points in the scene below. Explain why the exclamation point is used in each of these sentences.

Scene: Place: The deck of the *Mayflower*
Time: November 21, 1620

Sailor (*He stands on the deck, looking through a spyglass. Then he shouts excitedly.*): Land ho! I spy land! strong feeling

Mother (*Tears stream down her face, but she is smiling*): We are saved. Land, at last! strong feeling

Father: Now, we must see what this new land holds for us. (*He speaks to the men.*) Bradford, White, Tompkins. Go ashore in the rowboat. See what awaits us on land. Take your guns! There may be command wild beasts there. I fear for your lives! Be careful! warnings

---

DAY 4 — PROOFREADING

Improving Writing: Using Exclamations

Explain how to use an exclamation point.

- Use it to show strong feeling.
- Use it at the end of a command to do something.
- Use it at the end of a warning.

Display Transparency 5–9.

- Discuss the top of the transparency. Have volunteers read the rules.
- Have a different volunteer read each example using the appropriate tone of voice.
- Have a volunteer read aloud the scene at the bottom of the transparency.
- Ask students to find each exclamation point and explain why it was used.

Assign Practice Book page 99.

- Have students review their plays, adding or deleting exclamation points as needed and proofreading for other errors.

Practice Book page 99

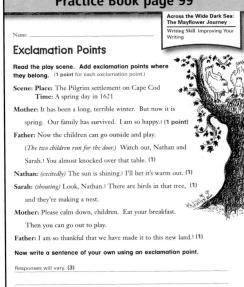

Name _____

Across the Wide Dark Sea:
The Mayflower Journey

Writing Skill Improving Your Writing

Exclamation Points

Read the play scene. Add exclamation points where they belong. (1 point for each exclamation point.)

Scene: Place: The Pilgrim settlement on Cape Cod
Time: A spring day in 1621

Mother: It has been a long, terrible winter. But now it is spring. Our family has survived. I am so happy.! **(1 point)**

Father: Now the children can go outside and play.

(*The two children run for the door.*) Watch out, Nathan and Sarah.! You almost knocked over that table. **(1)**

Nathan: (*excitedly*) The sun is shining.! I'll bet it's warm out. **(1)**

Sarah: (*shouting*) Look, Nathan.! There are birds in that tree, **(1)** and they're making a nest.

Mother: Please calm down, children. Eat your breakfast. Then you can go out to play.

Father: I am so thankful that we have made it to this new land.! **(1)**

Now write a sentence of your own using an exclamation point.

Responses will vary. **(3)**

_____
_____

DAY 5 — PUBLISHING

Sharing Plays

Consider these publishing options.

- Ask students to read their plays from the Author's Chair.
- Encourage students to act out their plays, using simple props and costumes.

Portfolio Opportunity

Save students' plays as samples of their writing development.

Monitoring Student Progress

If . . .	Then . . .
students' writing does not follow the guidelines on **Transparency 5–8,**	work with students to improve specific parts of their writing.

Language Center

VOCABULARY
Building Vocabulary

👤 Singles	🕐 30 minutes
Objective	Create a word cluster for ship parts.
Materials	Reference sources

Across the Wide Dark Sea contains many words that describe what an ocean voyage was like many years ago. Identify as many words as you can from the selection and record them in a word web such as the following:

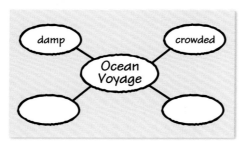

Look through other reference sources, such as encyclopedias and books about the *Mayflower,* to find additional words that describe ocean travel in the seventeenth century. Add these words to the web.

WRITING
Write a Pilgrim Play Scene

👥 Pairs	🕐 45 minutes
Objective	Write a play scene.
Materials	Anthology

Reread page 166 of *Across the Wide Dark Sea.* Imagine that you are on the deck of the *Mayflower* when land is sighted. Write a play scene to show what you said and did just before and just after you hear, "Land ho!" Think about

- what you see, hear, and smell
- how you feel
- how your feelings change after land is sighted
- whom you want to tell first

Tips for Writing a Play Scene

- Give the scene a title. List the setting and the characters.
- Use the dialogue and the characters' actions to tell what happens.
- Each time a different character speaks, write the character's name in capital letters followed by a colon. Then write what the character says.
- Write stage directions in parentheses to tell the characters how to speak and move.

VOCABULARY
Vocabulary Game

👥👥👥 Groups	🕐 30 minutes
Objective	Identify Key Vocabulary words by their individual letters.
Materials	Activity Master 5–1 on page R23

- Cut out the cards, mix them up, and place them face-down in a pile.
- One player takes the top card and, without revealing it, reads the word silently. This player is the cardholder.
- On a sheet of paper, the cardholder draws a short line for each letter of the word.
- The other players take turns asking if the word has a certain letter in it. For example: *Does the word have an e?*
- When someone correctly guesses a letter, the cardholder writes that letter on the line or lines where it appears in the word.
- When a player is ready to guess the word, he or she raises a hand and waits to be called on by the cardholder. If the player is correct, the cardholder gives him or her the card.
- Take turns as the cardholder until the group guesses all seven words.
- The player with the most cards wins.

Consider copying and laminating these activities for use in centers.

LISTENING/SPEAKING

Present an Oral Book Report

👥👥 Groups	🕐 30 minutes
Objective	Present an oral book report.
Materials	Anthology

When you give an oral book report, you are sharing your personal response to a book. Did you like or dislike this book? Why did you feel this way? An oral book report should include

- the title and author of the book
- a brief summary of the story
- your response to the book
- reasons to support your response, such as quotations and details

Prepare and present an oral report about *Across the Wide Dark Sea,* another Anthology selection, or a book that you have recently read.

Tips for Oral Presentations

- Use the book cover, illustrations, or other visuals.
- Read a short passage dramatically.
- Tell enough of the plot to get your audience interested, but don't give away the ending!
- If you liked the book, encourage your audience to read it.
- Tell your audience where to find this book.

PHONICS/SPELLING

Sounds Like tooth or cook

👥 Pairs	🕐 15 minutes
Objective	Sort words with the vowel sounds in *tooth* and *cook*.
Materials	Index cards

With your partner, brainstorm a list of words with the *oo* and *ew* spelling patterns that have the /o͞o/ sound as in *tooth*. Write each word on a separate index card.

Follow the same steps for words with the *oo* spelling pattern that have the /o͝o/ sound as in *cook*.

Mix up the two sets of cards and place them in a pile face-down. Then write *tooth* on one card and *cook* on another card. Place these cards face-up.

- Player 1 takes a card, and without revealing it, reads it out loud.
- Player 2 spells the word.
- Player 1 checks the spelling of the word on the card. If Player 2 spelled the word correctly, Player 1 gives the card to Player 2.
- Player 2 then sorts the card by placing it underneath either the *tooth* card or the *cook* card.
- If Player 2 does not spell the word correctly, the card goes to the bottom of the pile.
- Take turns picking cards, spelling words, and sorting cards.

The Golden Land

Summary *Papa has been in America for three years, earning money so that Mama, Myer, and Samuel can join him. The tickets arrive at last. Though sad to say goodbye to Grandmother, they are happy about going to "the golden land." They travel by wagon, train, and, finally, ship. At the end of their long journey, Mama, Myer, and Samuel are directed toward the place where Papa is waiting—and America.*

Vocabulary

Introduce the Key Vocabulary and ask students to complete the BLM.

port a town or city where people board or leave ships, *p. 7*

aboard being on a ship, *p. 8*

seasick ill from the up-and-down or jerking motions experienced on the water, *p. 10*

gleaming sparkling, *p. 11*

● BELOW LEVEL

Building Background and Vocabulary

Ask students what they know about moving from one country to another. Point out Eastern Europe on a map, and explain that many people from the region moved to the United States in the early 1900s. Preview the story with students, using the story vocabulary when possible.

Comprehension Skill: Making Inferences

Have students read the Strategy Focus on the book flap. Remind students to use the strategy and to use story clues to make inferences about characters and events as they read the book. (See the Leveled Readers Teacher's Guide for **Vocabulary and Comprehension Practice Masters**.)

Responding

Have partners discuss how to answer the questions on the inside back cover.

Think About the Selection Sample answers:

1. The family is traveling to America.
2. Myer thinks that sick people are not allowed to travel to America. He is probably correct, since sick people could get sicker on the long ocean voyage.
3. Responses will vary.

Making Connections Responses will vary.

Building Fluency

Model Read aloud page 5. Pause after reading the first paragraph, and then continue reading. Explain that a reader should pause before beginning the next paragraph.

Practice Have volunteers read aloud other pages, like 7, 8, and 10, pausing appropriately between paragraphs.

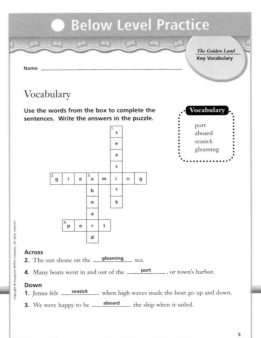

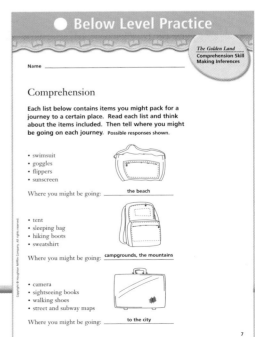

Chasing the Train

Summary *Nathan meets Ben on a train trip from Nebraska to Oregon, where their fathers are both working. The boys get off the train at a stop, but fail to make it back to the train when it leaves the station. Fortunately, a skilled rider named Sheila takes the boys on horseback to meet the train at the next station.*

Building Background and Vocabulary

Show students the state of Oregon on a United States map, and explain that the story is about two boys who are traveling by train to Oregon. Preview the story with students, using the story vocabulary when possible.

Comprehension Skill: Making Inferences

Have students read the Strategy Focus on the book flap. Remind students to use the strategy and to use story clues to make inferences about characters and events as they read the book. (See the Leveled Readers Teacher's Guide for **Vocabulary and Comprehension Practice Masters**.)

Responding

Have partners discuss how to answer the questions on the inside back cover.

Think About the Selection Sample answers:

1. Nathan's father is a wheat farmer there. Nathan and his mother are going there to be with him.

2. They are having fun chasing prairie dogs and don't hear the train whistle.

3. A ticket agent sends a telegram to the station ahead so that the train will wait for them. The agent's sister, Miss Sheila, takes them to the next station on her horse.

4. Possible response: They may try to make the trip seem less difficult than it was.

Making Connections Responses will vary.

Building Fluency

Model Read aloud page 3. Explain to the students that *At the next car* is a transition phrase that indicates a change in place.

Practice Have students look in the book for similar transition phrases that show a change in time or place. If students have trouble, point them to page 15, where they will find the phrase *At the next station*.

Vocabulary

Introduce the Key Vocabulary and ask students to complete the BLM.

journey* a trip from one place to another, *p. 2*

settlement* a small community in a new place, *p. 4*

seeping* slowly leaking, oozing, *p. 11*

weary* tired, needing rest, *p. 11*

*Forms of these words are Anthology Key Vocabulary words.

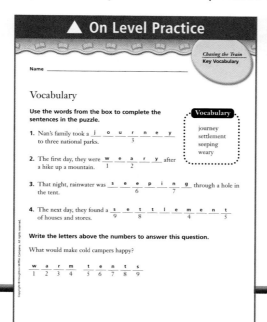

▲ On Level Practice

Name _____

Vocabulary

Use the words from the box to complete the sentences in the puzzle.

Vocabulary
journey
settlement
seeping
weary

1. Nan's family took a j o u r n e y to three national parks.

2. The first day, they were w e a r y after a hike up a mountain.

3. That night, rainwater was s e e p i n g through a hole in the tent.

4. The next day, they found a s e t t l e m e n t of houses and stores.

Write the letters above the numbers to answer this question.

What would make cold campers happy?

w a r m   t e n t s

▲ On Level Practice

Name _____

Comprehension

Reread pages 4–7 of the story and then answer the questions below. Use story clues and what you know to make inferences. Answers may vary. Possible responses are shown.

1. Why do you think Nathan and Ben want to get off the train?
Nathan and Ben are on a long train ride. It's hard to stay in one place for a long time. They probably want to move around in a bigger space. Also, they might want to explore a new place.

2. Why do you think Nathan and Ben run after the prairie dogs?
The boys may not have seen prairie dogs before. It is probably fun to try to catch the animals, especially because they keep hiding.

3. Why do you think the boys do not hear the train whistle the first time?
They are having fun and playing. They have run far from the train station chasing the prairie dogs, so the sound may not have been very loud to them.

4. How do you think the boys feel when they finally hear the train whistle?
Ben's mother told the boys to listen for the train whistle because it meant that the train is about to leave. They are probably worried that they will miss the train.

Leveled Readers

LEVELED READERS

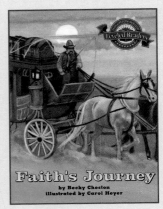

Faith's Journey

Summary *After her father dies, Faith Westfield and her mother must make a new life. Mrs. Westfield corresponds with Lucas Porter, a man in Indiana whose wife has died. The Westfields take a journey from Boston to Indiana to meet Lucas and his daughter, Ella, though Faith worries that she won't be happy in Indiana. When they finally arrive in Indiana, Faith begins to think that her new life might be just fine.*

Vocabulary

Introduce the Key Vocabulary and ask students to complete the BLM.

journey* a trip from one place to another, *p. 5*

transfer to move from one place to another, *p. 9*

survive* to stay alive; to hold up or withstand, *p. 11*

rut a groove made in the ground by the wheels of cars or wagons, *p. 12*

settlement* a small community in a new place, *p. 16*

*Forms of these words are Anthology Key Vocabulary words.

■ ABOVE LEVEL

Building Background and Vocabulary

Point out Indiana on a United States map, and show students the route from Boston to Indiana. Discuss why such a journey would be difficult. Preview the story with students, using the story vocabulary when possible.

⊚ Comprehension Skill: Making Inferences

Have students read the Strategy Focus on the book flap. Remind students to use the strategy and to use story clues to make inferences about characters and events as they read the book. (See the Leveled Readers Teacher's Guide for **Vocabulary and Comprehension Practice Masters**.)

Responding

Have partners discuss how to answer the questions on the inside back cover.

Think About the Selection Sample answers:

1. Faith's father died. Her mother has answered a newspaper ad to join a farmer and his young daughter.

2. She does not want to know what their life will be like there.

3. Possible response: Ella tells Faith in her letters that she is excited about meeting Faith. Faith does not answer Ella's letters, so I think she is not sure she wants to meet Ella.

4. Possible response: Faith's journey helped her realize she could do new things.

Making Connections Responses will vary.

⊚ Building Fluency

Model Read aloud page 2. Explain that characters' thoughts should be read differently from what they actually say. Usually thoughts are read in a softer voice.

Practice Have students find other examples of Faith's thoughts and have them take turns with a partner reading her thoughts in a soft voice.

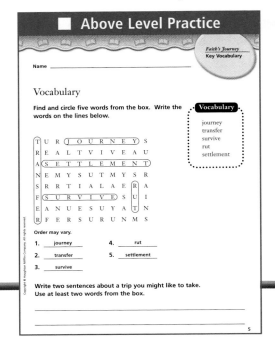

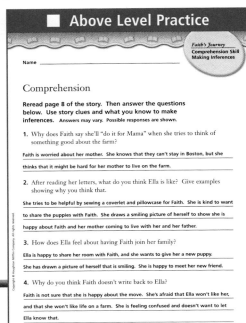

183Q   **THEME 5: Voyagers**

Going to America

Summary *Samuel, his brother, and his mother are journeying from Russia to America, where Samuel's father is working. They ride in a wagon, on a train, and finally in a large ship. They are welcomed to America by the sight of the Statue of Liberty. The family is finally reunited with Papa.*

Vocabulary

Introduce the Key Vocabulary and ask students to complete the BLM.

wagon a four-wheeled vehicle for carrying loads or passengers, *p. 6*

healthy not sick, *p. 8*

seasick dizzy and sick from the motion of the ship, *p. 10*

journey* a trip from one place to another, *p. 11*

Statue of Liberty large sculpture of a lady with a lantern that stands in New York City as a symbol of liberty, *p. 11*

practice to do over and over in order to learn, *p. 15*

*Forms of these words are Anthology Key Vocabulary words.

◆ LANGUAGE SUPPORT

Building Background and Vocabulary

Ask students whether they or anyone they know came to the United States from another country. Discuss how they traveled, how they felt about leaving home, and why they were coming to the United States. Distribute the **Build Background Practice Master,** discuss the picture, and guide students through the activity.

Comprehension Skill: Making Inferences

Have students read the Strategy Focus on the book flap. Remind students to use the strategy and to think about how Samuel might feel as they read the book. (See the Leveled Readers Teacher's Guide for **Build Background, Vocabulary, and Graphic Organizer Masters.**)

Responding

Have partners discuss how to answer the questions on the inside back cover.

Think About the Selection Sample answers:

1. Samuel's father had been in the United States for three years.
2. Possible response: They were sad to have left their country, but happy to be in the United States.
3. Responses will vary.

Making Connections Responses will vary.

Building Fluency

Model Have students follow along in their books as they listen to pages 3–4 on the audio CD.

Practice Have students read aloud with the recording until they are able to read the text on their own accurately and with expression.

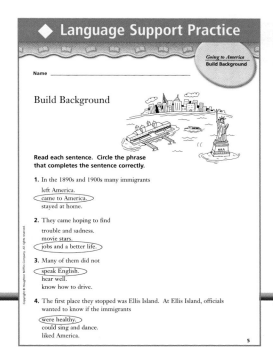

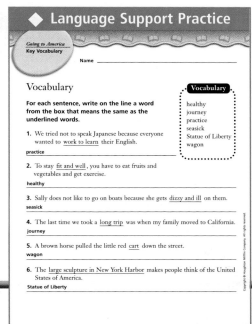

Reading-Writing Workshop

Description

In the Reading-Writing Workshop for Theme 5, *Voyagers*, students read Maurice's description, "A Trip I Have Taken," on Anthology pages 184–185. Then they follow the five steps of the writing process to write a description.

Meet the Author

Maurice B.
Grade: three
State: New York
Hobbies: swimming and biking
What he'd like to be when he grows up: a police officer

Theme Skill Trace

Writing
- Using Exclamations, 183L
- Writing Complete Information, 213L
- Writing Dates and Times, 251L

Grammar
- Sentence Combining with Subject Pronouns, 183J
- Using the Correct Pronoun, 213J
- Proofreading for *its* and *it's*, 251J

Spelling
- Vowel Sounds in *tooth* and *cook*, 183E
- Vowel Sound in *bought*, 213E
- VCCV Pattern, 251E

Pacing the Workshop

Here is a suggestion for how you might pace the workshop within one week or on five separate days across the theme.

DAY 1 — PREWRITING

Students

- read the Student Writing Model, 184–185
- choose a topic for their description, 185A
- explore and plan their description, 185B
- order information for their description, 185C

Spelling Frequently Misspelled Words, 185F; *Practice Book*, 241

DAY 2 — DRAFTING

Students

- learn to use sensory language, 185D
- draft their description, 185D

Spelling *Practice Book*, 102

Focus on Writing Traits: Description

The workshop for this theme focuses on the traits of word choice and sentence fluency. However, students should think about all of the writing traits during the writing process.

WORD CHOICE Your students can make strong word choices without above-grade level vocabularies. Teach them to sort through the words they already know and choose the one that most closely expresses what they mean. When they use an inexact word, try following these steps.

- Ask them to list at least two or three words they might use. Suggest using a thesaurus.
- Then ask them to read over their list and choose the best word.

SENTENCE FLUENCY Many students have difficulty starting a sentence with something other than the subject. Suggest these strategies for varying sentences.

- Start with a word or phrase that tells *where (Next to the car,…)*.
- Start with a word or phrase that tells *when (After we arrived,…)*.

Emphasize that all sentences must have a subject and a predicate.

Tips for Teaching the Writing Traits

- Teach one trait at a time.
- Discuss examples of the traits in the literature the students are reading.
- Encourage students to talk about the traits during a writing conference.
- Encourage students to revise their writing for one trait at a time.

DAY 3 — REVISING

Students

- evaluate their description, 185E
- revise their description, 185E
- have a writing conference, 185E

Spelling *Practice Book*, 103

DAY 4 — PROOFREADING

Students

- proofread their description, 185E
- improve their description by writing complete sentences, 185E
- correct frequently misspelled words in their description, 185F

Spelling *Practice Book*, 104

DAY 5 — PUBLISHING

Students

 publish their description, 185G

- reflect on their writing experience, 185G

Spelling *Assessment*, 185F

Description

Discussing the Guidelines

Display **Transparency RWW5–1,** and discuss what makes a great description.

- Remember that students should think about all the writing traits as they write: ideas, organization, voice, word choice, sentence fluency, conventions, and presentation.

Discussing the Model

Have students read the Student Writing Model on Anthology pages 184–185.

- Discuss with students what the writer did to make his description interesting to read.
- Use the Reading As a Writer questions on the next page.

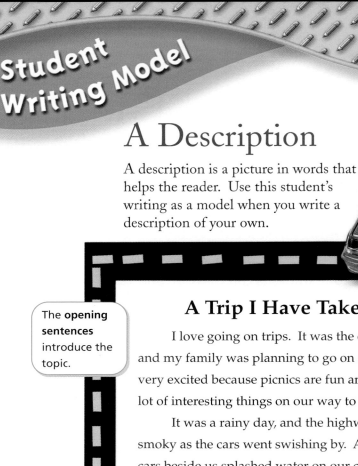

Student Writing Model

A Description

A description is a picture in words that helps the reader. Use this student's writing as a model when you write a description of your own.

A Trip I Have Taken

The **opening sentences** introduce the topic.

I love going on trips. It was the end of summer, and my family was planning to go on a picnic. I was very excited because picnics are fun and I get to see a lot of interesting things on our way to the park.

It was a rainy day, and the highway looked all smoky as the cars went swishing by. At times the cars beside us splashed water on our car, and I would dodge for cover, not remembering that the water could not come inside. We kept hoping there would be sun where the picnic was.

Sense words create pictures in the reader's mind.

It was a very busy highway with a lot of big trucks. I am scared of the trucks, especially when they have to blow their horns. It reminds me of thunder, and I always cover my ears. One special thing I wanted to see was the big bridge that went over the huge river. The water is always blue and

184

Transparency RWW5–1

What Makes a Great Description?

A **description** is a picture in words that helps the reader see, hear, taste, smell, or feel what you are writing about.

Follow these guidelines when you write your description.

- Begin by telling what you are describing.
- Use your five senses to brainstorm details about your topic.
- Include many details to give your reader a clear picture of what you are describing.
- Use vivid, sensory words that tell how something looks, sounds, feels, tastes, or smells.
- Write your details in an order that is easy for your readers to follow.
- Wrap up the description at the end.

looks so beautiful with all the boats with their different colors. Today, even though the water was gray, the boats were still beautiful when we went over the bridge.

Finally we reached the park, and I couldn't wait to get out and have a good stretch. The rain was falling lightly now, and I stuck my tongue out to see if I could taste the rain, but it had no taste. There was a fresh smell in the air, and I took long deep breaths. Then, suddenly, the sun came out! It was time for another fun part of the trip, eating and playing games.

I didn't see much of the journey going back because I was so tired, after a fun day at the picnic, that I fell asleep right away.

> **Comparisons** help the reader create pictures too.

> Good writers present details in the **order** in which they happen.

> A good **ending** wraps up a description.

Meet the Author

Maurice B.
Grade: three
State: New York
Hobbies: swimming and biking
What he'd like to be when he grows up: a police officer

185

Reading As a Writer

1. How does the writer introduce the topic of his description? (In the opening sentences, he says that his family was taking a trip to a picnic.)

2. What does the writer see, hear, and smell? (Sample responses: sees the boats, hears the truck horns, smells the air)

3. What sensory words does the writer use to describe the rain on the highway? (*swishing, splashed, smoky*)

4. How does the ending wrap up the description? (He tells about the end of the trip and that he had fun.)

Choosing a Topic

1 **Explain how to choose a topic for a description.** Tell studen[ts] they are going to write their own description of a place or thing that they know about. Explain that they should choose a topic that they can describe using at least three of five senses: sight, sound, touch, taste, or smell.

2 **Have students list at least three ideas for a description.** Offer the following prompts if students are having trouble getting started.

- What is an exciting place you have been to recently?
- What is your favorite toy or game?
- Do you have a pet?

3 **Have students answer these questions** as they choose their topic, either in a writing journal or on a sheet of paper.

- Who will be your audience: friends? family members? people you don't know?
- What will be your purpose: to tell people about something importa[nt] to you? to entertain?
- How will you publish your description: in a magazine? as an illustrat[ed] booklet?

4 **Have students discuss their ideas with a partner** and decid[e] which topic would be the best one to write about. Then review these tips with students.

Tips for Getting Started with a Topic

- Discuss your topic with a partner. Is your topic too big? If so, how can you make it smaller?
- Tell your partner what your topic looks like. Can you describe what it sounds like? How would you describe it with your sense of touch, taste, or smell?

xploring and Planning

Explain how to brainstorm details for a description. Tell students to think of details about how their topic looks, sounds, tastes, feels, and smells.

- Have students close their eyes and picture what they are describing.
- Have them think about what they see, hear, touch, taste, and smell.
- Tell students that the description should include at least three senses.

Display Transparency RWW5–2, and model using a Five Senses Chart.

- Point out the topic, a ball game, and the places to write details based on the five senses.
- Model adding details about sounds at a ball game.
- Ask students for other sounds at a ball game. Add these to the transparency.
- Repeat with the other four senses. (Sample answers are shown below.)

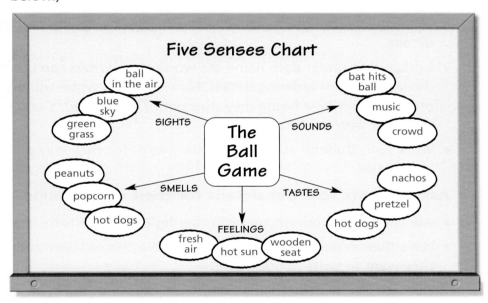

Ask students to explore and plan their description.

- Have them draw a Five Senses Chart similar to the one above.
- Encourage them to fill out as many details as they can. Remind them to brainstorm details for at least three of their five senses.

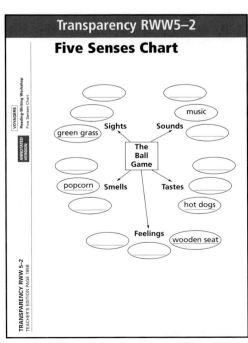

Ordering Information

1 **Emphasize the importance of ordering details.** Remind students that in a good description, details are ordered in a way that is easy for the reader to follow.

2 **Discuss these ways of ordering details.** Tell students that the are many other ways to order details: by size, by quality, by number, and so on. Tell them to choose the type of order that works best for their description.

- **By space or position** A description of a house may order details by the outside of the house, the first floor of the house, the second floor of the house, and the attic.

- **By time** A description of a yard may order details by autumn, winter, spring, and summer.

- **By order of importance** A description of an amusement park may order details first by the rides, then by the games, and finally by the food.

3 **Display Transparency RWW5–3.**

- Tell students that the top row names different ways of ordering details.

- Explain that under each name are words that writers can use to show this way of ordering details. For example, a writer using positi order to describe a house may start with *The top floor...* and later write *The bottom floor...*

- Work with students to think of order words for each way of order- ing details.

4 **Ask students to order details for their descriptions.**

- Ask them to choose the way of ordering that best fits their topic.

- Have them number the details in their Five Senses Chart in the ord they want to write about them.

- Remind them to leave out any details that do not tell more about their topic.

- Encourage them to think of order words to use when they draft.

Transparency RWW5–3

Order Words

VOYAGERS
Reading Writing Workshop: Order Words

ANNOTATED
VERSION

Answers may vary.

Size Order	Position Order	Importance Order	Quality Order	Number Order	Time Order
Biggest	Top/ bottom	Most important	Best	First/ second	First
Large	Front/back	Mainly important	Good	More/less	Next
Medium	Over/ under	Less important	Better	Most/least	Then
Small	In/out	Least important	Worst	Last	Finally

TRANSPARENCY RWW 5–3
TEACHER'S EDITION PAGE 185C

Using Sensory Language

Writing Traits

WORD CHOICE Tell students that good writers use words that are colorful, strong, snappy, and fresh. In a description they use words that tell how something looks, sounds, tastes, feels, and smells. Explain that exact words that use the five senses are called sensory language.

Discuss examples of sensory language from the list below. Then have students brainstorm other words for each sense. Discuss one sense at a time.

Sight sparkling, striped, violet, slim, wrinkled, puffy

Sound roar, squeal, pop, whisper, sputtering, crunchy

Taste stale, buttery, mild, creamy, spicy, peppery

Touch damp, chilly, spongy, tingling, smooth, mushy

Smell rotten, fishy, sweet, faint, sharp, lemony

Display and discuss Transparency RWW5–4.

- Read the first sentence aloud. Ask students for words that describe how it might feel to drive down a road. Read the sample answer.

- Have students work in pairs to complete the rest of the transparency. Invite volunteers to read their sentences to the class.

Have students draft their description. Remind them to do the following.

- Write a beginning that tells what the topic is.

- Describe at least three of five senses, using strong exact words.

- Use order words.

- Use their own voice. Show how they feel about their topic.

- Write an ending that wraps up the description.

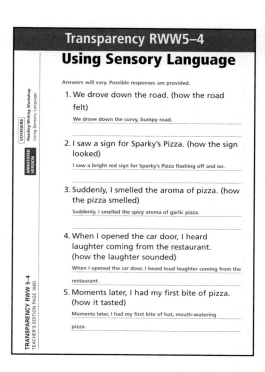

Transparency RWW5–4

Using Sensory Language

Answers will vary. Possible responses are provided.

1. We drove down the road. (how the road felt)

   We drove down the curvy, bumpy road.

2. I saw a sign for Sparky's Pizza. (how the sign looked)

   I saw a bright red sign for Sparky's Pizza flashing off and on.

3. Suddenly, I smelled the aroma of pizza. (how the pizza smelled)

   Suddenly, I smelled the spicy aroma of garlic pizza.

4. When I opened the car door, I heard laughter coming from the restaurant. (how the laughter sounded)

   When I opened the car door, I heard loud laughter coming from the restaurant.

5. Moments later, I had my first bite of pizza. (how it tasted)

   Moments later, I had my first bite of hot, mouth-watering pizza.

Practice Book page 100

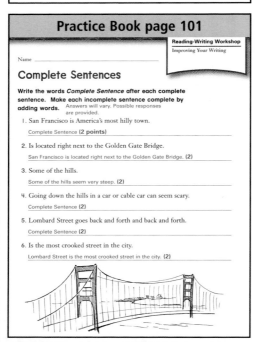

Reading-Writing Workshop
Revising Your Description

Name

Revising Your Description

Reread your description. Put a checkmark in the box for each sentence that describes your paper. Use this page to help you revise.

Rings the Bell

☐ The beginning clearly tells what the description is about.

☐ Details tell what I saw, heard, tasted, smelled, or touched. They are clearly ordered.

☐ I used sensory words for at least three of the five senses.

☐ Readers can easily tell how I feel about the topic.

☐ My sentences start differently. There are few mistakes.

Getting Stronger

☐ The beginning could be clearer about what the topic is.

☐ I need more details. I could order them more clearly.

☐ I need sensory words. I need to write about more senses.

☐ Readers can't always tell how I feel about the topic.

☐ Most sentences sound the same. I made some mistakes.

Try Harder

☐ The beginning doesn't say what the description is about.

☐ There are few details. The order is confusing.

☐ I didn't use any sensory words. I wrote using only one of my senses.

☐ Readers won't have any idea how I feel about the topic.

☐ All sentences sound the same. I made many mistakes.

Practice Book page 101

Reading-Writing Workshop
Improving Your Writing

Name

Complete Sentences

Write the words *Complete Sentence* after each complete sentence. Make each incomplete sentence complete by adding words. Answers will vary. Possible responses are provided.

1. San Francisco is America's most hilly town.
   Complete Sentence **(2 points)**

2. Is located right next to the Golden Gate Bridge.
   San Francisco is located right next to the Golden Gate Bridge. **(2)**

3. Some of the hills.
   Some of the hills seem very steep. **(2)**

4. Going down the hills in a car or cable car can seem scary.
   Complete Sentence **(2)**

5. Lombard Street goes back and forth and back and forth.
   Complete Sentence **(2)**

6. Is the most crooked street in the city.
   Lombard Street is the most crooked street in the city. **(2)**

Transparency RWW5–5

Complete Sentences

Answers will vary. Possible responses are provided.

1. A good player can win thousands of dollars on *High Peril.*
   Complete sentence

2. Likes watching the show.
   Everyone in my family likes watching the show.

3. My cousin Jane appeared on the quiz show.
   Complete sentence

4. She lost the game.
   Complete sentence

5. Scored the most points for much of the game.
   Jane scored the most points for much of the game.

6. The Big Bonus Question.
   The Big Bonus Question was her problem.

7. Jane rang her buzzer too early.
   Complete sentence

8. According to the rules.
   According to the rules, you can't do this.

9. Her chance to answer.
   Jane lost her chance to answer.

10. Lost $24,000!
    My cousin also lost $24,000!

TRANSPARENCY RWW 5-5
TEACHER'S EDITION PAGE 185E

VOYAGERS
Reading-Writing Workshop
Complete Sentences

ANNOTATED VERSION

Revising

Have students use **Practice Book** page 100 to help them evaluate and th revise their description. Students should also discuss their drafts in a writin conference with one or more classmates. (Distribute Conference Master, page R27. Discuss the sample thoughts and questions before students hav their conferences.) Remind students to keep in mind their listeners' commen and questions when they revise.

Writing Traits

SENTENCE FLUENCY Remind students to vary the way their sentences begin. Suggest that they use order words (*after; next to*).

Proofreading

Have students proofread their papers to correct capitalization, punctuatio spelling, and usage. They can use the proofreading checklist and proofrea ing marks on **Practice Book** pages 250 and 251.

Improving Writing: Writing Complete Sentences

Tell students that a complete sentence tells a complete thought and has both a subject and predicate.

- The subject is the person, place, or thing that the sentence is about.

- The predicate tells what the subject does or is. It must contain a verb.

Display and discuss **Transparency RWW5–5.**

- Read Sentence 1. Explain that it is complete because it has both a subje (*player*) and a verb (*can win*).

- Read Sentence 2. Explain that it is not complete because it does not hav a subject. Suggest the subject *Everyone in my family* and read the comple sentence. Have students suggest other answers.

- Work with students to complete the transparency.

Assign **Practice Book** page 101. Then tell students to read their descriptions to make sure they have used complete sentences.

Frequently Misspelled Words

Write the Spelling Words on the board, or distribute the list on **Practice Book** page 241. Help students identify the part of the word likely to be misspelled.

Spelling Pretest/Test

Basic Words

1. Come **down** to Camp Pogo.
2. **How** much fun will you have?
3. Camp Pogo has **its** own lake.
4. I'm **coming** for six weeks.
5. My brother **stopped** coming.
6. I **started** coming last year.
7. I **wrote** a letter from camp.
8. We went **swimming** in the pond.
9. People come **from** far away.
10. Everyone should **write** home.
11. **Writing** is my quiet time.
12. I **brought** some souvenirs home.

Challenge Words

13. Water-skiing is my **favorite** sport.
14. You are **sure** to get wet.
15. Leave your **clothes** in the boat.
16. I've **heard** good camp tales.

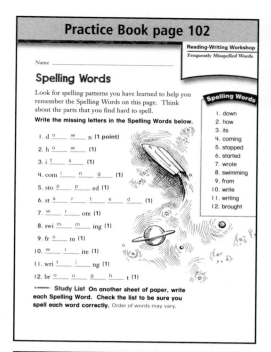

Practice Book page 102

Reading-Writing Workshop
Frequently Misspelled Words

Name _____

Spelling Words

Look for spelling patterns you have learned to help you remember the Spelling Words on this page. Think about the parts that you find hard to spell.

Write the missing letters in the Spelling Words below.

1. d <u>o w</u> n (1 point)
2. h <u>o w</u> (1)
3. i <u>t s</u> (1)
4. com <u>i n g</u> (1)
5. sto <u>p p</u> ed (1)
6. st <u>a r t e d</u> (1)
7. w <u>r</u> ote (1)
8. swi <u>m m</u> ing (1)
9. fr <u>o</u> m (1)
10. w <u>r</u> ite (1)
11. wri <u>t i</u> ng (1)
12. br <u>o u g h</u> t (1)

Study List On another sheet of paper, write each Spelling Word. Check the list to be sure you spell each word correctly. Order of words may vary.

Spelling Words
1. down
2. how
3. its
4. coming
5. stopped
6. started
7. wrote
8. swimming
9. from
10. write
11. writing
12. brought

Words not underlined

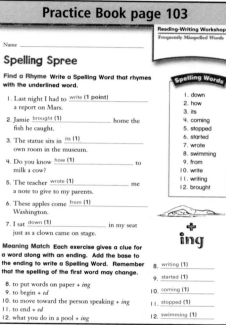

Practice Book page 103

Reading-Writing Workshop
Frequently Misspelled Words

Name _____

Spelling Spree

Find a Rhyme Write a Spelling Word that rhymes with the underlined word.

1. Last night I had to write (1 point) _____ a report on Mars.
2. Jamie brought (1) _____ home the fish he caught.
3. The statue sits in its (1) _____ own room in the museum.
4. Do you know how (1) _____ to milk a cow?
5. The teacher wrote (1) _____ me a note to give to my parents.
6. These apples come from (1) _____ Washington.
7. I sat down (1) _____ in my seat just as a clown came on stage.

Meaning Match Each exercise gives a clue for a word along with an ending. Add the base to the ending to write a Spelling Word. Remember that the spelling of the first word may change.

8. to put words on paper + *ing*
9. to begin + *ed*
10. to move toward the person speaking + *ing*
11. to end + *ed*
12. what you do in a pool + *ing*

Spelling Words
1. down
2. how
3. its
4. coming
5. stopped
6. started
7. wrote
8. swimming
9. from
10. write
11. writing
12. brought

+ ing

8. writing (1)
9. started (1)
10. coming (1)
11. stopped (1)
12. swimming (1)

Practice Book page 104

Reading-Writing Workshop
Frequently Misspelled Words

Name _____

Proofreading and Writing

Proofreading Circle the four misspelled Spelling Words in this diary entry. Then write each word correctly.

May 3rd

Things are going pretty well, except that I'm busy with homework. We have to (rite) a report on an explorer for school. I (startted) writing mine last week. I was going to finish it on Monday, but we went (swiming) instead. Now it's due in two days, and I have to figure out (howe) to finish it on time. I'll be glad when I'm done.

1. write (2 points)
2. started (2)
3. swimming (2)
4. how (2)

Write a Round-Robin Story Get together in a small group with other students. Then write a story about a voyage, with each of you writing one sentence at a time. Use a Spelling Word from the list in each sentence. Responses will vary. (2)

Spelling Words
1. down
2. how
3. its
4. coming
5. stopped
6. started
7. wrote
8. swimming
9. from
10. write
11. writing
12. brought

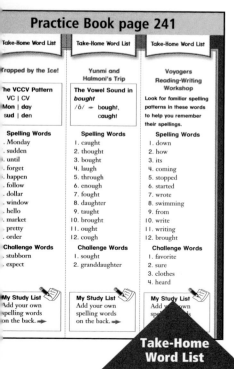

Practice Book page 241

Take-Home Word List

Trapped by the Ice!

The VCCV Pattern
VC | CV
Mon | day
sud | den

Spelling Words
1. Monday
2. sudden
3. until
4. forget
5. happen
6. follow
7. dollar
8. window
9. hello
10. market
11. pretty
12. order

Challenge Words
1. stubborn
2. expect

My Study List
Add your own spelling words on the back.

Take-Home Word List

Yunmi and Halmoni's Trip

The Vowel Sound in *bought*
/ô/ → bought, caught!

Spelling Words
1. caught
2. thought
3. bought
4. laugh
5. through
6. enough
7. fought
8. daughter
9. taught
10. brought
11. ought
12. cough

Challenge Words
1. sought
2. granddaughter

My Study List
Add your own spelling words on the back.

Take-Home Word List

Voyagers
Reading-Writing Workshop

Look for familiar spelling patterns in these words to help you remember their spellings.

Spelling Words
1. down
2. how
3. its
4. coming
5. stopped
6. started
7. wrote
8. swimming
9. from
10. write
11. writing
12. brought

Challenge Words
1. favorite
2. sure
3. clothes
4. heard

My Study List
Add your own spelling words on the back.

Take-Home Word List

Publishing

✔ Portfolio Opportunity

Save students' final copy of their description as an example of the development of their writing skills.

Have students publish their description.

- Ask them to look back at the publishing ideas they noted when they chose a topic. Discuss the Ideas for Sharing box below.
- Then ask students to decide how they want to publish their writing.
- Tell them to make a neat final copy of their description. Remind them use good penmanship and to be sure that they have fixed all mistakes.

Ideas for Sharing

Write It
- Send your description as a letter to family.
- Post your description on the Internet.

Say It
- Read it aloud from the Author's Chair.
- Record your paper on audiotape.

Show It
- Add a drawing of your topic.
- Add a photo of your topic.

Tips for Tape-Recording
- Ask a friend or an adult to help you with the tape recorder.
- Speak clearly and loudly enough to be heard.
- Read with feeling and enthusiasm.
- Add sound effects if they fit the details you are telling in your description.

Monitoring Student Progress

Student Self-Assessment

- What do you think was the best part of your description? Why?
- How well did you use sensory language in your description? What was your best use of sensory language?
- What did you learn about writing from this description? How can you use what you learned the next time you write?

Evaluating

Have students write responses to the Student Self-Assessment questions.

Evaluate students' writing, using the Writing Traits Scoring Rubric. This rubric is based on criteria in this workshop and reflects criteria students used in Revising Your Description on **Practice Book** page 100.

Description

Writing Traits Scoring Rubric

④

IDEAS	The description is clearly focused on a topic. Many details address at least three of the five senses.
ORGANIZATION	The beginning clearly introduces the topic. The writer presented the details in a clear order.
VOICE	The writer's feelings about the subject come through strongly.
WORD CHOICE	Many exact, sensory words help create a vivid picture.
SENTENCE FLUENCY	Sentences start with many different beginnings.
CONVENTIONS	There are almost no errors in spelling, punctuation, capitalization, or usage.
PRESENTATION	The final copy is neat and legible.

③

IDEAS	The description is focused on a topic. The paper needs more details that address at least three of the five senses.
ORGANIZATION	The beginning could be clearer. The order of the details may be unclear or inconsistent in one or two places.
VOICE	The writer doesn't always show his or her feelings about the subject.
WORD CHOICE	The writer could have used more exact, sensory words.
SENTENCE FLUENCY	A few more sentences could start with different beginnings.
CONVENTIONS	There are some mistakes, but they do not affect understanding.
PRESENTATION	The final copy is messy in a few places but still legible.

②

IDEAS	The description may not be clearly focused on a topic. Few details are included.
ORGANIZATION	The beginning doesn't say what the description is about. Details are not ordered clearly.
VOICE	It is often hard to tell what the writer feels about the subject.
WORD CHOICE	The writer used few exact, sensory words.
SENTENCE FLUENCY	Most sentences start with the subject.
CONVENTIONS	Mistakes sometimes make the description hard to understand.
PRESENTATION	The final copy is messy. It may be illegible in a few places.

①

IDEAS	There are almost no details.
ORGANIZATION	There is no beginning. There is no order to the paper.
VOICE	The writer shows no feelings about the subject.
WORD CHOICE	Word choice is vague or uninteresting. It may be confusing.
SENTENCE FLUENCY	All sentences start with the subject.
CONVENTIONS	Many mistakes make the description hard to understand.
PRESENTATION	The final copy is messy. It may be illegible in many places.

Lesson Overview

Literature

Yunmi and Halmoni's Trip

Sook Nyul Choi   *Illustrated by* Karen Dugan

Selection Summary

During their trip to Korea, Yunmi sees how happy Halmoni, her grandmother, is to see her relatives. She worries that Halmoni will not want to return to New York. When Halmoni reassures her, Yunmi learns how lucky she is to have family in two countries.

1 Background and Vocabulary

2 Main Selection

Yunmi and Halmoni's Trip
Genre: Realistic Fiction

3 Art Link

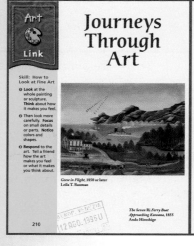

Instructional Support

Planning and Practice

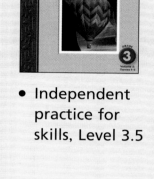

- Planning and classroom management
- Reading instruction
- Skill lessons
- Materials for reaching all learners

- Independent practice for skills, Level 3.5

- Newsletters
- Selection Summaries
- Assignment Cards
- Observation Checklists
- Selection Tests

- Transparencies
- Strategy Posters
- Blackline Masters

Reaching All Learners

Coordinated lessons, activities, and projects for additional reading instruction

For
- Classroom teacher
- Extended day
- Pull out
- Resource teacher
- Reading specialist

Technology

Audio Selection

Yunmi and Halmoni's Trip

Get Set for Reading CD-ROM
- Background building
- Vocabulary support
- Selection Summary in English and Spanish

Accelerated Reader®
- Practice quizzes for the selection

www.eduplace.com

Log on to Education Place for more activities related to the selection, including vocabulary support—
  e • Glossary
  e • WordGame

Leveled Books for Reaching All Learners

Leveled Readers and Leveled Practice

- Independent reading for building fluency

- Topic, comprehension strategy, and vocabulary linked to main selection

- Lessons in Teacher's Edition, pages 213O–213R

- Leveled practice for every book

Technology

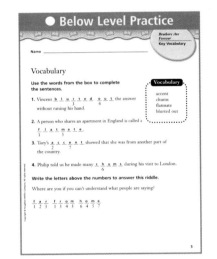

Leveled Readers
Audio available

Book Adventure®

- Practice quizzes for the Leveled Theme Paperbacks
www.bookadventure.org

● BELOW LEVEL

BROTHERS are FOREVER

by Marcy Haber
illustrated by Gail Piazza

Houghton Mifflin Leveled Readers

▲ ON LEVEL

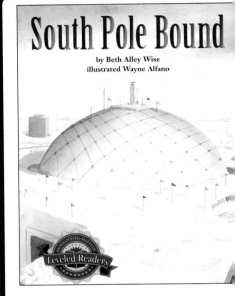

South Pole Bound

by Beth Alley Wise
illustrated Wayne Alfano

Houghton Mifflin Leveled Readers

● Below Level Practice

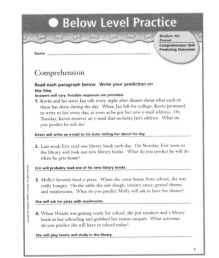

▲ On Level Practice

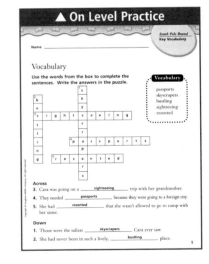

● Below Level Practice

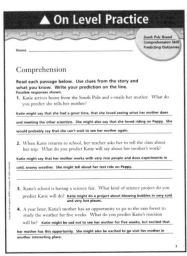

■ ABOVE LEVEL

The Same,
But Different

HOUGHTON MIFFLIN
Leveled Readers

by Perry Hewitt
illustrated by Beth Peck

■ Above Level Practice

The Same,
But Different
Key Vocabulary

Name _____

Vocabulary

Draw a line from each word to its meaning.

Vocabulary
passport
sightseeing
vendor
foreigners
bustling

1. passport — someone who sells things
2. sightseeing — full of activity; busy
3. vendor — people who come from a different country or place
4. foreigners — a government document that allows a person to travel in foreign countries
5. bustling — visiting interesting places; touring

Write a paragraph about a trip you have taken or would like to take. Use at least three words from the box.

_____

5

■ Above Level Practice

The Same,
But Different
Comprehension Skill
Predicting Outcomes

Name _____

Comprehension

Read each passage below. Write your prediction on the line.
Use story clues and what you know.
Answers will vary. Possible responses are provided.

1. Mariah writes a letter to Eleanor, inviting her to come to New York for a visit. What do you predict Eleanor will do? Explain.

Eleanor will probably say yes to the invitation. She had fun when Mariah came to
London, and she might like to go sightseeing in New York and meet Mariah's friends.

2. If Eleanor comes to visit, she will fly from London to New York, and then drive to Mariah's home. What do you predict she will notice on the drive?

Eleanor might notice that in the United States, people don't drive on the same side of
the road as people in London.

3. Eleanor will stay with Mariah, her parents, and her brother Jake. How do you predict Eleanor will feel about spending time with Jake?

Eleanor was friendly with Mariah in London, so she will probably enjoy playing with
Jake and spending time with another cousin.

4. Mariah and Eleanor spend a day with Mariah's friends. What do you predict Eleanor will tell her parents about the day?

Eleanor might say that she likes Mariah's friends and that they are like her friends at
home. She might also say that they use different words for some things, speak with a
different accent, and eat different foods.

7

◆ LANGUAGE SUPPORT

Max Visits **MAX LONDON**

by Marcy Haber
illustrated by
Gail Piazza

HOUGHTON MIFFLIN
Leveled Readers

◆ Language Support Practice

Max Visits London
Build Background

Name _____

Build Background

Look at each picture. Read the British words. Then write in the words an American would use.

Art	🇬🇧	🇺🇸
	chums	friends
	drive on the left	drive on the right
	flat	apartment
	football	soccer
	jolly good!	great

5

◆ Language Support Practice

Max Visits London
Key Vocabulary

Name _____

Vocabulary

Vocabulary
accent
chums
custom
excited
forever
sightseeing

Cathy loves to travel. She gets very
_____excited_____ when she goes someplace new.
Last month, she went to London for the first time. She
went _____sightseeing_____ and shopping. She had
trouble understanding people because they spoke with a
different _____accent_____. But she made friends.
Her new _____chums_____ showed her around. They also told her
about English traditions and the _____custom_____ of driving on the
left side of the road. She felt as if she could stay in England
_____forever_____.

6

Leveled Theme Paperbacks

- Extended independent reading in Theme-related trade books

- Lessons in Teacher's Edition, pages R2–R7

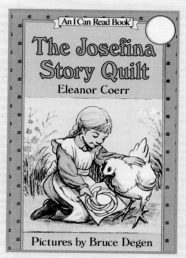

An I Can Read Book
The Josefina Story Quilt
Eleanor Coerr

Pictures by Bruce Degen

Below Level

A Child's Glacier Bay

Text by Kimberly Corral with Hannah Corral
Photographs by Roy Corral

On Level

Balto and the Great Race

Challenge

Daily Lesson Plans

Technology
Lesson Planner CD-ROM allows you to customize the chart below to develop your own lesson plans.

T Skill tested on Theme Skills Test and/or Integrated Theme Test

  50–60 minutes

Reading
Comprehension

Leveled Readers
• Fluency Practice
• Independent Reading

  20–30 minutes

Word Work
Phonics/Decoding
Vocabulary
Spelling

  20–30 minutes

Writing and Oral Language
Writing
Grammar
Listening/Speaking/Viewing

DAY 1

Teacher Read Aloud,
185S–185T
Alice Ramsey's Grand Adventure

Building Background, 186

Key Vocabulary, 187
bustling   passport   skyscrapers
custom   sightseeing   vendor
foreigners

Reading the Selection, 188–207

Comprehension Skill, 188
Predicting Outcomes **T**

Comprehension Strategy, 188
Predict/Infer **T**

Leveled Readers
Brothers Are Forever
South Pole Bound
The Same, but Different
Max Visits London

Lessons and Leveled Practice, 213O–213R

Phonics/Decoding, 189
Phonics/Decoding Strategy

Vocabulary, 188–207
Selection Vocabulary

Spelling, 213E
Vowel Sound in *bought* **T**

Writing, 213K
Introducing a Message

Grammar, 213I
Object Pronouns **T**

Daily Language Practice
1. Yunmi started to laff when she visited we in korea. (laugh; us; Korea)
2. Halmoni thot she would show she the skyscrapers. (thought; her)

Listening/Speaking/Viewing,
185S–185T, 199
Teacher Read Aloud, Stop and Think

DAY 2

Reading the Selection,
188–207

Comprehension Check, 207

Responding, 208
Think About the Selection

Comprehension Skill Preview, 203
Predicting Outcomes **T**

Leveled Readers
Brothers Are Forever
South Pole Bound
The Same, but Different
Max Visits London

Lessons and Leveled Practice, 213O–213R

Structural Analysis, 213C
Possessives **T**

Vocabulary, 188–207
Selection Vocabulary

Spelling, 213E
Vowel Sound in *bought* Review and Practice

Writing, 213K
Writing a Message

Grammar, 213I
Object Pronouns Practice **T**

Daily Language Practice
3. Me and Halmoni soon had enuff sightseeing. (Halmoni and I; enough)
4. I awt to show my passport to he. (ought; him)

Listening/Speaking/Viewing, 207, 208
Wrapping Up, Responding

Target Skills of the Week

Comprehension	Predict/Infer; Predicting Outcomes
Vocabulary	Analogies
Phonics/Decoding	Possessives
Fluency	Leveled Readers

DAY 3

Rereading the Selection
Rereading for Visual
Literacy, 201
Picturing the Scene

Comprehension Skill, 213A–213B
Predicting Outcomes **T**

Leveled Readers
Brothers Are Forever
South Pole Bound
The Same, but Different
Max Visits London

Lessons and Leveled Practice, 213O–213R

Phonics Review, 213D
Vowel Sound in *bought*

Vocabulary, 213G
Analogies **T**

Spelling, 213F
Vocabulary: Word Family for *laugh*; Vowel
Sound in *bought* Practice **T**

Writing, 213L
Complete Information

Grammar, 213J
Pronoun Game **T**

Daily Language Practice
They fot their way into the bustling crowd, it
emed strange to I. (fought; crowd.; It; me)
Yunmi started to coff when the foreigners asked
for our passports. (cough; us)

DAY 4

Reading the Art Link,
210–213
"Journeys Through Art"

Skill: How to Look at Fine Art

Rereading for Visual
Literacy, 212
Cubism

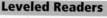

Comprehension Skill Review, 197
Making Generalizations

Leveled Readers
Brothers Are Forever
South Pole Bound
The Same, but Different
Max Visits London

Lessons and Leveled Practice, 213O–213R

Phonics/Decoding, 210–213
Apply Phonics/Decoding Strategy to Link

Vocabulary, 213M
Language Center: Building Vocabulary

Spelling, 213F
Spelling Game, Proofreading **T**

Writing, 213L
Writing Game

Grammar, 213J
Object Pronouns Practice **T**

Daily Language Practice
7. Yunmi feels that her is a true dawter? (she;
daughter.)
8. Halmoni tot they how to make dumplings.
(taught; them)

Listening/Speaking/Viewing, 213
Discuss the Link

DAY 5

Rereading for Fluency,
193

Responding Activities, 208–209
Write a Personal Narrative
Cross-Curricular Activities

**Information and Study
Skills,** 213H
Using Graphic Organizers

Comprehension Skill Review, 205
Cause and Effect

Leveled Readers
Brothers Are Forever
South Pole Bound
The Same, but Different
Max Visits London

Lessons and Leveled Practice, 213O–213R

Structural Analysis, 213N
Language Center: Possessive Matchup

Vocabulary, 213M
Language Center: Vocabulary Game

Spelling, 213F, 213M
Test: Vowel Sound in *bought* **T**
Language Center: Spell My Secret Word

Writing, 213L
Sharing Writing

Grammar, 213J
The Correct Pronoun

Daily Language Practice
9. Yunmi bot a postcard to send to I and Helen.
(bought; Helen and me)
10. She brot It to show Halmoni. (brought; it)

Listening/Speaking/Viewing, 213N
Language Center: Say It Without Words

Managing Flexible Groups

FLEXIBLE GROUPS

Leveled Instruction and Leveled Practice

	DAY 1	**DAY 2**
WHOLE CLASS	• Teacher Read Aloud (TE pp. 185S–185T) • Building Background, Introducing Vocabulary (TE pp. 186–187) • Comprehension Strategy: Introduce (TE p. 188) • Comprehension Skill: Introduce (TE p. 188) • Purpose Setting (TE p. 189) **After reading first half of** *Yunmi and Halmoni's Trip* • Stop and Think (TE p. 199)	**After reading** *Yunmi and Halmoni's Trip* • Wrapping Up (TE p. 207) • Comprehension Check (Practice Book p. 107) • Responding: Think About the Selection (TE p. 208) • Comprehension Skill: Preview (TE p. 203)
SMALL GROUPS **Extra Support**	**TEACHER-LED** • Preview *Yunmi and Halmoni's Trip* to Stop and Think (TE pp. 188–199). • Support reading with Extra Support/Intervention notes (TE pp. 189, 193, 194, 198, 203, 206).	**Partner or Individual Work** • Reread first half of *Yunmi and Halmoni's Trip* (TE pp. 188–199). • Preview, read second half (TE pp. 200–207). • Comprehension Check (Practice Book p. 107)
Challenge	**Individual Work** • Begin "Travel Guide" (Challenge Handbook p. 40). • Extend reading with Challenge note (TE p. 206).	**Individual Work** • Continue work on activity (Challenge Handbook p. 40).
English Language Learners	**TEACHER-LED** • Preview vocabulary and *Yunmi and Halmoni's Trip* to Stop and Think (TE pp. 187–199). • Support reading with English Language Learners notes (TE pp. 186, 191, 193, 196, 198, 204).	**TEACHER-LED** • Review first half of *Yunmi and Halmoni's Trip* (TE pp. 188–199). ✔ • Preview, read second half (TE pp. 200–207). • Begin Comprehension Check together (Practice Book p. 107).

Independent Activities

- Get Set for Reading CD-ROM
- Journals: selection notes, questions
- Complete, review Practice Book (pp. 105–109) and Leveled Readers Practice Blackline Masters (TE pp. 213O–213R).
- Assignment Cards (Teacher's Resource Blackline Masters pp. 81–82)
- Leveled Readers (TE pp. 213O–213R), Leveled Theme Paperbacks (TE pp. R2–R7), or book from Leveled Bibliography (TE pp. 148E–148F)

✔ Opportunity to informally assess oral reading rate

DAY 3

- Rereading: Lessons on Visual Literacy (TE pp. 201, 212)

- Comprehension Skill: Main lesson (TE pp. 213A–213B)

DAY 4

- Reading the Art Link (TE pp. 210–213): Skill lesson (TE p. 210)

- Rereading the Link: Visual Literacy lesson (TE p. 212)

- Comprehension Skill: First Comprehension Review lesson (TE p. 197)

DAY 5

- Responding: Select from Activities (TE pp. 208–209)

- Information and Study Skills (TE p. 213H)

- Comprehension Skill: Second Comprehension Review lesson (TE p. 205)

TEACHER-LED

- Reread, review Comprehension Check (Practice Book p. 107).

- Preview Leveled Reader: Below Level (TE p. 213O), or read book from Leveled Bibliography (TE pp. 148E–148F). ✔

Partner or Individual Work

- Reread the Art Link (TE pp. 210–213).

- Complete Leveled Reader: Below Level (TE p. 213O), or read book from Leveled Bibliography (TE pp. 148E–148F).

TEACHER-LED

- Comprehension Skill: Reteaching lesson (TE p. R10)

- Reread Leveled Theme Paperback: Below Level (TE pp. R2–R3), or read book from Leveled Bibliography (TE pp. 148E–148F). ✔

TEACHER-LED

- Teacher check-in: Assess progress (Challenge Handbook p. 40).

  Preview Leveled Reader: Above Level (TE p. 213Q), or read book from Leveled Bibliography (TE pp. 148E–148F). ✔

Individual Work

- Complete activity (Challenge Handbook p. 40).

- Complete Leveled Reader: Above Level (TE p. 213Q), or read book from Leveled Bibliography (TE pp. 148E–148F).

TEACHER-LED

- Evaluate activity and plan format for sharing (Challenge Handbook p. 40).

- Reread Leveled Theme Paperback: Above Level (TE pp. R6–R7), or read book from Leveled Bibliography (TE pp. 148E–148F). ✔

Partner or Individual Work

Complete Comprehension Check (Practice Book p. 107).

Begin Leveled Reader: Language Support (TE p. 213R), or read book from Leveled Bibliography (TE pp. 148E–148F).

TEACHER-LED

- Reread the Art Link (TE pp. 210–213) ✔ and review Link Skill (TE p. 210).

- Complete Leveled Reader: Language Support (TE p. 213R), or read book from Leveled Bibliography (TE pp. 148E–148F). ✔

Partner or Individual Work

- Reread book from Leveled Bibliography (TE pp. 148E–148F).

Responding activities (TE pp. 208–209)
Language Center activities (TE pp. 213M–213N)
Fluency Practice: Reread *Across the Wide Dark Sea; Yunmi and Halmoni's Trip* ✔
Activities relating to *Yunmi and Halmoni's Trip* at Education Place www.eduplace.com

Turn the page for more independent activities. ➡

Classroom Management

Independent Activities

Assign these activities while you work with small groups.

Differentiated Instruction for Small Groups

- **Handbook for English Language Learners,** pp. 176–185

- **Extra Support Handbook,** pp. 172–181

Independent Activities

- Language Center, pp. 213M–213N

- Challenge/Extension Activities, Theme Resources, pp. R11, R17

- **Classroom Management Handbook,** Activity Masters CM5-5–CM5-8

- **Challenge Handbook,** pp. 40–41

Look for more activities in the Classroom Management Kit.

Art

A Thousand Words

 Singles	⏱ 30 minutes
Objective	Write about an illustration.
Materials	Anthology

There's an old saying that a picture is worth a thousand words. It means that a picture gives a lot of information. Choose one of the pictures in *Yunmi and Halmoni's Trip.* Record what you see in a word web. Then write a paragraph explaining what the picture tells you. Ask yourself:

- What is the setting?
- Who is in this picture?
- What are the people doing?
- What are the people feeling?
- What interesting details are in the picture?
- What does this picture make you think about?

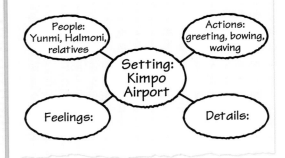

People: Yunmi, Halmoni, relatives

Actions: greeting, bowing, waving

Setting: Kimpo Airport

Feelings:

Details:

Language Arts

A Letter Home

 Singles	⏱ 20 minutes
Objective	Write a letter.

While Yunmi is in Korea, she sends letters home to her friends. Write a letter that Yunmi might have sent.

- Decide whom she is sending the letter to. (You can make up a name and address.)
- Write the letter to the person back home.
- Include a drawing that shows one of the places Yunmi visited or something that she did during her trip.

Consider copying and laminating these activities for use in centers.

Social Studies

Korean Cuisine

 Groups	🕐 45 minutes
Objective	Research food from Korea.
Materials	Korean cookbooks or a computer with Internet access

unhi teaches Yunmi to make *mandoo*. 's a white dumpling filled with eat and vegetables. Find out more bout Korean foods and recipes.

With your group, look through a Korean cookbook or go on the Internet to http://chef2chef.com/dir/Cooking/ World_Cuisines/Asian/Korean and visit one of the websites listed under "links."

Each group member chooses a different dish to research.

Find out what the ingredients are and any other information about the dish—whether it is eaten at a certain time of day or only prepared for special celebrations, for example.

Write a short description of the dish and, if possible, draw a picture of it.

With the other members of your group, combine all the descriptions into a booklet on Korean cuisine.

Kimchi is fermented cabbage mixed with spices.

Math

Calling Across Time Zones

👤 Singles	🕐 30 minutes
Objective	Write and solve time zone problems.

Yunmi is in Korea and she wants to call her parents in New York City. If it is noon in Seoul, what time is it in New York? (Answer: 10 P.M.)

Use the time zone chart below to write other time zone problems. Solve your problems and write the answers on a separate sheet of paper. Post your problems on a bulletin board for other students to solve. Post your answer sheet upside down with your problems.

Seoul	Los Angeles	Denver	Chicago	New York City
12:00 P.M.	7:00 P.M.	8:00 P.M.	9:00 P.M.	10:00 P.M.

Folktale

The Big Idea

👥 Pairs	🕐 45 minutes
Objective	Rewrite the story as a folktale.

Every story has at least one important idea. What's the big idea in *Yunmi and Halmoni's Trip*? Write it at the top of a sheet of paper. Then rewrite the story as a folktale based on this same idea. Remember these characteristics of folktales:

- Folktales are set in the past.

- Story details reflect the country or culture of the people.

- Characters are simple and may stand for traits such as jealousy, greed, or cleverness.

- The story starts with a problem that seems impossible to solve.

- The story has a happy ending in which good is rewarded.

Listening Comprehension

Building Background

Tell students that you are going to read aloud a selection that describes the journey of the first woman to drive a car across the United States.

- Point out New York City and San Francisco on a map. Explain that at the time Alice Ramsey drove cross-country, there were no highways. Have students discuss possible difficulties she might encounter.

Fluency Modeling

Explain that as you read aloud, you will be modeling fluent oral reading. Ask students to listen carefully to your phrasing and your expression, or tone of voice and emphasis.

COMPREHENSION SKILL

Predicting Outcomes

Explain that a prediction tells what may happen in the future. A good prediction is based on

- text clues
- personal knowledge and experiences

Purpose Setting Read the selection aloud, asking students to make and check their predictions as they listen. Then use the Guiding Comprehension questions to assess students' understanding. Reread the selection for clarification as needed.

Teacher Read Aloud

Alice Ramsey's Grand Adventure

by Don Brown

On June 9, 1909, Alice Ramsey drove out of New York City and into a grand adventure. Alice Ramsey wanted to be the first woman to drive across America.

Alice's friend, Hermine, and her sisters-in-law, Nettie and Margaret, traveled with her. They knew nothing about automobiles. The car's good repair would be Alice's job, although the Maxwell company— the maker of the touring car and the sponsor of the trip—promised to help.

1   The Maxwell needed keen attention. Alice used a stick to measure the gasoline in the twenty-gallon tank under the front seat. The headlamps were torches enclosed in brass housings and Alice had to light them with a match! The horn was a rubber bulb.

While Alice steered the car, adjusted the levers, and attended the engine, she also had to find her way. The few roads were narrow and dusty, more accustomed to horses' hooves than automobile tires. There were no road signs. She would have to ask directions or follow instructions from the Blue Book.

The Blue Book was the only guidebook for motorists and it covered just the eastern United States. It told the miles between towns and the turns to make. Turn left at the red barn with the yellow silo, it might say. Excellent directions as long as the farmer hadn't repainted the silo blue.

America slowly revealed itself: New York State, Pennsylvania, Ohio, Indiana. Towns and cities came and went. They passed many, many farms.

Near Toledo, Ohio, Alice raced the Maxwell at top speed—forty-two miles an hour!

Just west of the Mississippi River, the rain started. It rained and rained. The dirt road dissolved into a thick, filthy stew. It was nearly impossible to drive.

"Ship the Maxwell by rail past the difficulties," local residents urged Alice.

"I'll drive every inch of the way if it kills me!" Alice replied.

Eventually, the rain ended but travel remained hard.

The car dropped into a huge pothole. A boy driving a team of horses dragged it out.

The Maxwell's brake pedal broke. Alice slid beneath the car and fixed it with a snip of wire.

The Maxwell's axle snapped and Alice and another mechanic installed a replacement.

A hail storm erupted, and the women sought shelter at a nearby farm owned by a family that spoke only Danish.

Long, hot days of driving passed, sometimes starting before dawn and lasting hours into the night. Once, Alice drove seventeen hours, napped for three hours on a bed made from the Maxwell's seat cushions, then continued driving.

The Sierra Nevada Mountains towered before them: Alice's last great obstacle. She steered the Maxwell up the steep path. The road snaked back and forth up the mountain. The car struggled on the incline and its engine became hot. Alice lifted the hood to cool the motor and rested the Maxwell at each turn. It took eight hours to travel seventy miles.

After the grueling climb, the women were thrilled to be in California and near their goal!

They crested the Sierra Nevadas and followed the road to Oakland.

Alice guided the Maxwell onto a ferry that carried them to San Francisco.

When she rolled off the ferry behind the wheel of her Maxwell, Alice Ramsey became the first woman to have driven across America!

CRITICAL THINKING
Guiding Comprehension

1 **PREDICTING OUTCOMES** Did you think Alice and her companions would have trouble keeping the Maxwell running? Why did you think so? (Yes. They knew very little about how cars run, and the car needed attention.)

2 **PREDICTING OUTCOMES** Did you think Alice would continue driving when she encountered a problem? Why did you think so? (Sample answers: Yes. She had an adventurous spirit and great determination. No. Alice and her companions had traveled almost halfway across the country and may have thought it was too dangerous to continue.)

3 **PREDICTING OUTCOMES** Did you think Alice would be able to drive over the mountains? Why did you think so? (Yes. She continued despite the problems. She had almost reached her goal, and wouldn't want to stop.)

Discussion Options

Personal Response Ask students to tell which part of the cross-country trip they think was the most challenging and why.

⭐ **Connecting/Comparing** Have students compare the difficulties of Alice Ramsey's journey with those faced by the family on the *Mayflower* in *Across the Wide Dark Sea.*

English Language Learners

Supporting Comprehension

Display a map of the United States. Indicate the states Alice and her companions went through. Then ask students to give examples of things that Alice and her friends saw and might have seen along the way. (dirt roads, farms, mountains, ferries, bridges)

Building Background

Key Concept: Visiting a Foreign Country

Point out that *Yunmi and Halmoni's Trip* is a modern-day story about a young girl's visit to Korea. Discuss how traveling to another country can be an adventure. Then use "Visiting Another Country" on Anthology pages 186–187 to build background and discuss what travelers can learn from a new country and culture.

- Have a student read aloud "Visiting Another Country."
- Ask another student to read aloud the captions. Discuss the photos.
- Help students locate Seoul, South Korea, on a globe.

Get Set to Read

Background and Vocabulary

Yunmi and Halmoni's Trip

Read to find the meanings of these words.

e Glossary

- bustling
- customs
- foreigner
- passport
- sightseeing
- skyscrapers
- vendor

186

VISITING ANOTHER COUNTRY

Traveling to another country can be a great adventure. In a big city, it's fun to wander through **bustling** streets full of people and to look up at tall **skyscrapers**. Many visitors go **sightseeing** to look at a country's famous places. Some visitors also learn how a country's **customs**, such as how people greet each other, may be different from their own. In the next story, a girl does many of these things when she travels to Korea with her grandmother.

English Language Learners

Supporting Comprehension

Beginning/Preproduction Have students listen to you read the article. Then ask questions about the photographs: Can you point to some *skyscrapers*? Where is a *vendor*? Show me a *passport*.

Early Production and Speech Emergence Have partners write each key word on an index card. Partners take turns drawing a card and defining the word. They may draw or use pantomime to explain the meaning.

Intermediate and Advanced Fluency Have students choose two Key Vocabulary words and use them in a sentence that restates information in the article.

▲ A **foreigner** must bring a **passport** when visiting other countries. A passport has a photo of a person and information about where that person is from.

[S]eoul is a bustling city [in S]outh Korea.

[M]any people visit the [Gyeon]gbok Royal Palace in [Seo]ul.

[Y]ou can learn a lot [abo]ut a place from the [peo]ple who live and work [the]re, such as a **vendor** [selli]ng items at a market.

187

Introducing Vocabulary

Key Vocabulary

These words support the Key Concept and appear in the selection.

bustling full of activity; busy

custom a tradition; a way of doing something that many people follow

foreigners people who come from another country or place

passport a government document that allows a person to travel in foreign countries

sightseeing visiting interesting places; touring

skyscrapers very tall buildings

vendor someone who sells something

 e • Glossary
e • WordGame

See Vocabulary notes on pages 190, 192, 194, 196, 198, 200, and 204 for more words to preview.

Display Transparency 5–10.

- Model choosing the correct Key Vocabulary word to insert in the first blank. (skyscrapers)

- Ask students to use context clues to answer the remaining questions.

- Have students look for these words as they read and use them as they discuss traveling.

Practice/Homework Assign **Practice Book** page 105.

Transparency 5–10

Sightseeing Words

Every <u>foreign</u> visitor has a <u>passport</u> to show the country he or she is from. And every day tour guides must show many of them around the city. Some guides take visitors <u>sightseeing</u> by foot; others show them the city from buses. They take visitors through the <u>bustling</u> city streets full of hurrying people and up to the top of great, tall <u>skyscrapers</u> for a wonderful view. Some guides will stop at an outside cart where a <u>vendor</u> sells food, drinks, or even postcards. A usual <u>custom</u> is to give each tour guide a tip at the end of the tour.

Which word —

• tells about tall city buildings?	1.	skyscrapers
• names a government document?	2.	passport
• names a person who sells things?	3.	vendor
• describes a busy place?	4.	bustling
• names people from other countries?	5.	foreign
• is a way of doing something that many people follow?	6.	custom
• tells about touring a new city?	7.	sightseeing

Practice Book page 105

Name _____

Yunmi and Halmoni's Trip
Key Vocabulary

Travel Words

Match each word with its definition by writing the letter of the definition on the line beside the word. Then choose a vocabulary word from the list to finish each sentence.

e (1)	bustling	a.	people from outside one's own country
c (1)	custom	b.	person who sells something
a (1)	foreigners	c.	tradition
d (1)	passport	d.	paper allowing someone to visit other countries
f (1)	sightseeing	e.	busy
b (1)	vendor	f.	touring

1. During the summer, many foreigners (1 point) visit the United States.

2. Each traveler needs to bring a passport (1) in order to enter the country.

3. In New York City, the streets are usually bustling (1) with people.

4. Many of the people are tourists going sightseeing (1) .

5. On some streets, they can buy hot dogs and other snacks from a vendor (1) .

6. In America, it is the custom (1) to shake hands with people you meet.

Introducing Vocabulary 187

TARGET SKILL
COMPREHENSION STRATEGY
Predict/Infer

Teacher Modeling Ask a student to read aloud the Strategy Focus. Explain that readers can make predictions based on text clues, illustrations, and personal experience. Have students read the title on page 189 and the first paragraph on page 191. Model the strategy.

Think Aloud *From the title and the first paragraph I know that Yunmi and her grandmother are flying to Korea to visit relatives. I know it can be hard to travel and visit relatives. I think Yunmi will have a challenging visit.*

Test Prep Explain that when answering questions that ask them to make inferences, students must find clues in story details and use their own knowledge and experiences.

TARGET SKILL
COMPREHENSION SKILL
Predicting Outcomes

Introduce the Graphic Organizer. Tell students that a Character Chart can help them list details they can use to predict what characters might do in new situations. Explain that as they read, students should fill out the Character Chart found on **Practice Book** page 106.

- Display **Transparency 5–11.** Have students read Anthology page 191.

- Model how to complete the first row of the chart. Monitor students' work as needed.

Meet the Author
Sook Nyul Choi

As a child in Korea, Sook Nyul Choi loved to read about faraway places. When she was older, Choi moved to one of those places — the United States — to go to college. She now lives in Massachusetts with her two daughters. She loves both the United States and Korea, and her books often tell how these two countries are both the same and different.

Other books: *Halmoni and the Picnic, The Best Older Sister*

Meet the Illustrator
Karen Dugan

Karen Dugan has been making books since she was in first grade. She would fold paper into a book and then draw pictures. She doesn't fold her own pages anymore, but she still draws great pictures. For this book, she based the main character, Yunmi, on the author's daughters.

Other books: *School Spirit* (by Johanna Hurwitz), *Pascual's Magic Pictures* (by Amy Glaser Gage), *Halmoni and the Picnic* (by Sook Nyul Choi)

 **Internet**

To find out more about Sook Nyul Choi and Karen Dugan, visit Education Place.
www.eduplace.com/kids

188

Transparency 5–11
Character Chart
Accept varied responses.

VOYAGERS Yunmi and Halmoni's Trip
Graphic Organizer Character Chart
ANNOTATED VERSION

Yunmi's Feelings	Story Clues
About Her Visit to Korea excited anxious	(See page 145.) from words in the story She held Halmoni's hand.
About Her Korean Cousins fun to be around hard to talk to and understand sometimes jealous	(See pages 150–153 and 158–160.) They take her sightseeing. They show her how to make mandoo. Their English is hard to understand and they giggle when she speaks Korean. Halmoni pays so much attention to her cousins.
About Halmoni misses her attention scared, worried, upset ashamed about being selfish	(See pages 152–153 and 157–159.) Halmoni is busy visiting and overseeing preparations; she gives all her attention to the cousins. She sees how happy Halmoni is with her family in Korea. from words in the story; she'd be lonely without Halmoni.

What do you think Yunmi will do if her cousins come to visit her in New York? Explain why you think as you do.
Accept responses that students can justify.

TRANSPARENCY 5–11
TEACHER'S EDITION PAGES 188 AND 213A

Practice Book page 106

Yunmi and Halmoni
Graphic Organizer Character Chart

Name _____

Character Chart
Accept varied responses.

Yunmi's Feelings	Story Clues
About Her Visit to Korea excited anxious	(See page 145.) from words in the story **(1)** She held Halmoni's hand. **(1)**
About Her Korean Cousins fun to be around **(1 point)** hard to talk to and understand sometimes **(1)** jealous	(See pages 150–153 and 158–160.) They take her sightseeing. They show her how to make mandoo. **(1)** Their English is hard to understand and the giggle when she speaks Korean. **(1)** Halmoni pays so much attention to her cousins. **(1)**
About Halmoni misses her attention **(1)** scared, worried, upset **(1)** ashamed about being selfish	(See pages 152–153 and 157–159.) Halmoni is busy visiting and overseeing preparations; she gives all her attention to cousins. **(1)** She sees how happy Halmoni with her family in Korea. **(1)** from words in story; she'd be lonely without Halmoni. **(1)**

What do you think Yunmi will do if her cousins come to visit her in New York? Explain why you think as you do.
Accept responses that students can justify. **(2)**

---

188   THEME 5: Voyagers

Yūnmi and Hălmŏni's Trip

Sook Nyul Choi   *Illustrated by* Karen Dugan

Strategy Focus

Use your experiences of meeting new people to **predict** what might happen when a girl visits relatives she has never met before.

189

Extra Support/Intervention

Selection Preview

pages 189–195 Yunmi and her grandmother Halmoni fly to South Korea, where Yunmi meets her relatives for the first time. Will Yunmi enjoy her trip?

pages 196–201 Yunmi's cousins take her sightseeing in the city of Seoul. Do you think she's having fun? How can you tell?

pages 202–205 Yunmi sees that Halmoni really loves being with the family. Why do you think Yunmi looks so sad? What do you think Halmoni will do?

pages 206–207 Halmoni talks to Yunmi. What do you think she says? Do you think Yunmi feels better? Why?

Purpose Setting

- Remind students that this selection tells about a girl's visit to Korea.

- Have students preview the selection. Then ask them to predict what might happen when the girl visits relatives she hasn't met before.

- As they read, have students confirm or change their predictions about the girl's visit to Korea.

- Ask students to look for story clues to help them predict outcomes as they read.

- You may want to preview the Responding questions on Anthology page 208 with students.

Journal ▸ Students can record their predictions about the selection and add new ideas as the story unfolds.

STRATEGY REVIEW

Phonics/Decoding

Remind students to use the Phonics/Decoding Strategy as they read.

Modeling Write this sentence from *Yunmi and Halmoni's Trip:* "Everyone <u>embraced</u> Halmoni and then hugged Yunmi too." Point to *embraced*.

Think Aloud *I'll look for word parts I know. The first syllable might sound like ehm. Then I see a b followed by the letters r-a-c-e-d. That should sound like brayst. I'll try saying the word, ehm-BRAYST. I know that word. It means hugged.*

CRITICAL THINKING

Guiding Comprehension

1 **MAKING INFERENCES** Why do you think Yunmi takes Halmoni's hand in the airplane? (Sample answer: She's excited about the trip but is probably anxious too.)

2 **DRAWING CONCLUSIONS** Why do you think the author includes details about plans for Grandfather's birthday celebration? (to describe a Korean custom; to give a reason for the trip)

3 **MAKING INFERENCES** How do you think Halmoni feels about the trip? How do you know? (Sample answers: excited; she talks about the relatives all during the flight.)

190

Vocabulary

passport a government document that allows a person to travel to foreign countries

Seoul (SOHL) the capital city of South Korea

1 Yunmi settled into the airplane seat and took her grandmother's hand. It was Yunmi's first airplane trip. Her Halmoni, or grandmother, had come from Korea to take care of Yunmi while her parents were at work. Now Halmoni was taking Yunmi for a visit to Korea to meet all her aunts and uncles and cousins. Halmoni also wanted Yunmi to join Grandfather's **2** birthday celebration. Yunmi's grandfather had died many years before, but each year the whole family visited his grave and celebrated his birthday.

3 Yunmi was very excited. She had gotten her very first passport for this trip. And she had promised to send lots of postcards to her best friends Helen and Anna Marie. It was a long flight from New York City across the Pacific Ocean to Seoul. It would take fourteen and a half hours. Halmoni, however, had lots of things to talk about during their flight. She pulled out a thick bundle of photos of Yunmi's many relatives, and began to tell her about each of them. Halmoni said, "I think they will all be at Kimpo Airport. They are so excited to meet you and want to show you all around Seoul."

When the airplane landed, they hurried through the airport to have their passports checked.

191

English Language Learners

Supporting Comprehension

Students can gain a lot of information about the characters' lives and feelings from the pictures. As students read, point out different scenes, asking, Who is in this picture? Where do you think he/she is? What do you think he/she is feeling? How can you tell?

CRITICAL THINKING
Guiding Comprehension

4 **DRAWING CONCLUSIONS** Why does the author include the scene in which Yunmi and Halmoni stand in different lines to have their passports checked? (to show that, while they're both part of the same family, Yunmi is an American citizen and her grandmother is a Korean citizen)

5 **MAKING INFERENCES** Why do you think Yunmi feels strange standing in the line for foreigners? (Sample answer: She looks like and identifies with the people in the "Nationals" line, but she isn't a Korean national.)

6 **CAUSE AND EFFECT** Why does Yunmi stop feeling like a foreigner after she talks with the man who checks her passport? (Sample answers: He knows her grandmother and that makes her feel less like a stranger; he welcomes her back to Korea.)

4 Halmoni walked Yunmi over to the long line that said "Foreigners." The line moved slowly as the officer checked each passport. Halmoni got to stand in the fast-moving line that said "Nationals." Yunmi looked like all the Koreans in the nationals line, but she had to stand in the foreigners line.

5 It made her feel strange.

But when it was Yunmi's turn, the man checking passports smiled and said, "Welcome to Seoul. Are you here for a visit with your Halmoni?"

"Yes, how did you know?" asked Yunmi.

"I saw you talking with your Halmoni. She was my favorite high school teacher. I heard she went to America to be with her granddaughter. Please tell her Hojun said 'Welcome back.'"

6 Yunmi nodded happily. She wasn't a foreigner after all. People here already knew who she was. She was proud of Halmoni, too.

192

Vocabulary

foreigners people who come from another country or place

nationals citizens who live in a particular nation or country

193

Fluency Practice

Rereading for Fluency Have students choose a favorite part of the story to reread to a partner, or suggest that they read page 192. Encourage students to read expressively.

Extra Support/ Intervention

trategy Modeling: redict/Infer

Jse this example to model the strategy.

note that Yunmi feels strange as she stands in the foreigners' line. I can infer that she's never thought of herself as being different from other Koreans, or maybe she's not used to thinking of herself as a citizen of the United States. predict that sometimes she'll feel strange when she meets new relatives and has new experiences in Korea.

English Language Learners

Supporting Comprehension

Review making inferences with students. Have them look at the illustrations as they read and guess what the characters are thinking and feeling.

CRITICAL THINKING
Guiding Comprehension

7 **MAKING INFERENCES** How does Yunmi feel when she first meets her relatives? Why? (She's overwhelmed by the crowd of friendly strangers.)

8 **WRITER'S CRAFT** Why do you think the author includes details about Halmoni's Korean house and pets? (Sample answer: to show that Halmoni still has strong ties to Korea)

7 Halmoni was waiting for Yunmi, and they walked toward big sliding doors. Suddenly a huge crowd of people rushed toward them, waving and bowing. Yunmi stood still, her eyes wide. Everyone hugged her. Person after person bowed and embraced Halmoni. Halmoni was so happy, she had to wipe tears from her smiling face. Finally they walked past a long line of green and yellow taxis. An uncle ushered Halmoni and Yunmi into his car, and the rest of the relatives piled into cars and cabs.

194

Vocabulary

embraced hugged

ushered led by someone

skyscrapers very tall buildings

sightseeing visiting interesting places; touring

Kyong Bok Kung (KONG bohk kuhn) the royal palace in Seoul, South Korea

ministers people who are in charge of government departments

REACHING ALL LEARNERS
Extra Support/Intervention

Strategy Modeling: Phonics/Decoding

Use this example to model the strategy. Point out the word *ushered* on page 194.

First I see the word part us. *Then I see either* here *with a* d *or* her *with an* e-d. UHS-heerd, UHS-hur-ehd, UHS-hurd. *I don't recognize any of those. The letters* s-h *can also be pronounced* sh. *I'll try again—*USH-urd. *Oh, I know that word. It means* led by someone. *That makes sense here.*

They sped down broad highways, then through streets crowded with skyscrapers. In the middle of the city at the top of a narrow, winding street was a tall brick wall with a pretty iron gate. Inside was Halmoni's house. Halmoni's older sister, who lived there now, rushed out. A cat and a dog with a fluffy tail ran behind her. Halmoni embraced her sister and bent to pet her dog. "Oh, I missed you, too," she said to him. Then she lifted the cat onto her shoulder and carried her inside. **8**

During the next several days, Yunmi's cousins Jinhi and Sunhi took her sightseeing. They went to the royal palace, called Kyong Bok Kung. Yunmi liked running down the center of the wide steps, where only the kings and queens and ministers had once been allowed to walk.

195

CRITICAL THINKING
Guiding Comprehension

9 **DRAWING CONCLUSIONS** Why do you think the author includes information about the observatory and book printing? (Sample answer: so readers will know more about Korea and Korea's history)

10 **WRITER'S CRAFT** How does the author make the scene at the East Gate Market come alive? (She describes some of the sights and sounds the girls experience there.)

11 **CAUSE AND EFFECT** Why is it a little hard for Yunmi and her cousins to communicate with each other? (Because Yunmi doesn't speak Korean well, and they don't speak English well.)

9 They visited the National Museum. There, Yunmi learned that in the seventh century, Koreans built the Chomsongdae Observatory to study the stars. She also learned that in the thirteenth century, Koreans were the first in the world to invent movable metal type to print books.

10 They went to the bustling East Gate Market. A street vendor there was baking little cakes filled with sweet red beans. Jinhi, Sunhi, and Yunmi each bought one and ate the cakes as they roamed the crowded stalls. "Socks for sale," "Silk shirts here," "Parasols on special," the vendors chanted as the girls walked past. Then Yunmi's cousins took her to their favorite stall.

11 There, Yunmi bought two soft lavender and pink silk purses with shiny black tassels for her friends Anna Marie and Helen. Yunmi was having fun with her cousins, but it was a little hard to understand their English. And when Yunmi spoke Korean, her cousins giggled and said she sounded funny.

196

Vocabulary

Chomsongdae (CHUHM-suhn-day) the Star Observatory, believed to be the oldest observatory in Asia

bustling full of activity; busy

vendor someone who sells something

parasols umbrellas that provide shade from the sun

English Language Learners

Supporting Comprehension

Review making inferences with students. Ask them to look at the illustrations as they read. Instruct students to guess what the characters are thinking and feeling. Ask how they can tell. Explain that this activity can help them find the theme of the story.

I wonder if Yunmi feels at home yet.

197

Making Generalizations

Teach

- Remind students that a generalization is a broad statement that is based on facts or details and is true most of the time.

- Generalizations may include words such as *most, all, often, always,* and *never.*

Practice

- Display the following sentence and read it aloud: *The East Gate Market is usually crowded and bustling.* Note that it tells what the East Gate Market is usually like.

- Ask students to find details in the story that support this generalization. Record their responses in a chart.

Generalization	Supporting Facts
The East Gate Market is usually crowded and bustling.	crowded stalls vendors chanted

Apply

- Have students work in small groups to make generalizations based on story details from pages 198–201.

- Have them record their details and generalizations in a chart.

- Ask students to share and explain their generalizations.

Target Skill Trace	
Preview; Teach	p. 197; Theme 6, pp. 399A–399B
Reteach	Theme 6, p. R12
Review	pp. 413D–413E

Reading the Selection   197

CRITICAL THINKING
Guiding Comprehension

12 **MAKING INFERENCES** Why does Yunmi wish that everyone would disappear? (She wants Halmoni's attention all for herself; she isn't used to sharing Halmoni.)

13 **DRAWING CONCLUSIONS** What do you think Halmoni has in mind when she puts Sunhi in charge of teaching Yunmi to make mandoo? (She wants Yunmi and her cousins to work together and get to know each other better.)

TARGET SKILL

COMPREHENSION STRATEGY
Predict/Infer

Teacher/Student Modeling Discuss clues on pages 198–199 that can help students predict a future problem for Yunmi. Ask what predictions can be made from Yunmi's question, *"What if Halmoni didn't want to leave?"* (When Yunmi returns to New York, Halmoni might stay in Korea.)

Vocabulary

marinated soaked in sauce or spices to add flavor

dumplings pieces of dough, often with a filling, that you cook by steaming or boiling

mandoo Korean dumplings

Yunmi had hardly seen Halmoni since they arrived. Her grandmother was often out, and when she was home, Yunmi's cousins always sat on her lap and got all her attention. "Halmoni, don't ever leave us again," they kept saying. Halmoni just smiled. Yunmi sometimes wished everyone would disappear so she and Halmoni could talk like they did in New York.

For the next few days, Halmoni did stay home. But all Yunmi's aunts and cousins came over to prepare for the big picnic at Grandfather's tomb. They spent two whole days in the kitchen, making marinated beef, vegetables, dumplings, and sweets. Halmoni rushed about, overseeing everything.

"Sunhi," Halmoni said as she gave her a hug, "why don't you be in charge of making the mandoo? You can teach Yunmi. The dumplings are her favorite."

Halmoni rushed back with stacks of thin white dumpling skins, a bowl of water, and a big bowl of meat-and-vegetable filling. Sunhi placed just the right amount of filling on half of a dumpling skin. Then she dipped her pinky in the water and ran it around half the edge of the mandoo skin. She folded it into a half-moon shape and pressed the edge shut. Yunmi tried making them too. Soon they started making funny-shaped mandoo. Some looked like round balls, others like little purses, and some just looked strange. Halmoni smiled as she hurried past.

198

REACHING ALL LEARNERS

Extra Support/ Intervention

Review (pages 189–199)
Before students join the whole class for Stop and Think on page 199, have them

- take turns modeling Predict/Infer and other strategies they used
- add to **Transparency 5–11** with you
- check and revise their Character Charts on **Practice Book** page 106, and use it to predict and infer

English Language Learners

Supporting Comprehension

Pause at the end of page 199 and ask: How has Yunmi changed since the beginning of the story? What is she feeling now? How can you tell? Why do you think she feels this way? If student[s] do not know the word *jealous*, define i[t] and ask whether they think this is wha[t] Yunmi is feeling.

Yunmi saw how happy Halmoni was with all her family, and Yunmi started to worry. What if Halmoni didn't want to leave? In New York, Halmoni had only Yunmi and her parents and Yunmi's friends. She was scared, but tried to think about how much Halmoni loved her.

199

ASSIGNMENT CARD 5

Literature Discussion

With a small group, talk over your questions and ideas about the story. Also discuss these questions:

- How do you think Yunmi feels about her visit to Korea? How can you tell?

- How has Yunmi and Halmoni's relationship changed?

- Compare and contrast Yunmi's trip to a trip you've taken. How were your experiences like Yunmi's? How were they different?

Theme 5: Voyagers

Teacher's Resource BLM page 82

Stop and Think

Critical Thinking Questions

1. **NOTING DETAILS** How would you describe and explain Yunmi's relationship with her grandmother? (They're quite close, probably because her grandmother takes care of her.)

2. **MAKING INFERENCES** Why is Yunmi afraid that Halmoni might enjoy her stay in Korea too much? (Her grandmother may want to stay in Korea, and then their close relationship might end.)

Strategies in Action

Have students take turns modeling Predict/Infer and other strategies they used.

Discussion Options

You may want to bring the entire class together to do one or more of the activities below.

- **Review Predictions/Purpose** Discuss which predictions were accurate and which needed to be revised. Have students record any changes and new predictions. Ask them what they have learned about Yunmi's visit to Korea.

- **Share Group Discussions** Have students share their literature discussions.

- **Summarize** Have students use their Character Charts to summarize what they've learned about Yunmi so far.

Monitoring Student Progress	
If . . .	Then . . .
students have successfully completed the Extra Support activities on page 198,	have them read the rest of the selection cooperatively or independently.

CRITICAL THINKING
Guiding Comprehension

14 **MAKING INFERENCES** How do Yunmi and her cousins feel as they ride in the vans? How can you tell? (They feel relaxed and happy; they play games and sing.)

15 **NOTING DETAILS** How does the author show that the family respects the memory of Grandfather? (The family makes three deep bows to Grandfather, and they eat to celebrate his birthday.)

200

Vocabulary

outskirts areas away from the center of town

cat's cradle a traditional children's game played with string

custom a tradition; a way of doing something that many people follow

tombstone a stone that marks where a dead person is buried

The next day was Grandfather's birthday. They loaded all the food and drink into big vans they had rented. Everyone, all the cousins and uncles and aunts, climbed in, and they sped toward the outskirts of Seoul where Grandfather was buried. As they rode through the big city streets and then the winding country roads, Yunmi and her cousins sang Korean songs, played cat's cradle, and folded paper into the shapes of birds and baskets.

They stopped at the bottom of a small mountain. Everyone got out and climbed all the way to the top, to a small field. In the middle was a little hill covered with soft green grass.

There on the hill was a large, flat stone with Grandfather's name on it. Below that were a lot of other names. Yunmi was surprised to see her parents' names and her name. Then she remembered Halmoni telling her it was a Korean custom to list the names of all the children and grandchildren on a tombstone. Yunmi went up and touched the cool stone and felt the warm sunlight on her hand. Meanwhile, Halmoni gathered the whole family. Together they made three deep bows to Grandfather.

Then Halmoni said, "Grandfather will be happy to see us all having a good time visiting him and each other on his birthday. Let's eat and celebrate this beautiful day." They sat down to a picnic with all the food they had prepared.

201

Picturing the Scene

Teach

- Explain that Karen Dugan, the illustrator, worked with the author to interpret story details. Her pictures help to clarify details that the author provides in the text.

Practice/Apply

- Have a volunteer read aloud the third paragraph on page 201. Ask the following questions.

- **What do you learn from the text?** (Sample answers: Grandfather's grave is on a hill; it is sunny; the whole family is there.)

- **What details mentioned in the text also appear in the illustration on page 200?** (Sample answers: the flat stone; the hill covered with grass; the whole family bowing)

- Ask students to identify details that are not mentioned in the text that the illustrator has included in the picture. (Sample answers: the traditional clothing, the plates of food; the piles of flat rocks by the grave)

ASSIGNMENT CARD 6

Following Directions

..iet Games

..at's cradle is a game that began in Asia. Two people take turns ..oping string over each other's fingers to make different figures. The ..t of paper folding, known as origami in Japan, is practiced in Korea ..d in other Asian countries. Shapes of animals, flowers, and other ..ojects are created by folding paper instead of cutting it.

..earn how to play cat's cradle or fold an origami shape. Then teach it .. others in the group.

Theme 5: Voyagers

Teacher's Resource BLM page 82

CRITICAL THINKING
Guiding Comprehension

16 **DRAWING CONCLUSIONS** What is the author's purpose in contrasting Yunmi's experience visiting an American cemetery with her visit to the Korean one? (to show that people in America and Korea have different customs and different outlooks on death; that her experiences in Korea remind her of her experiences in America)

17 **MAKING INFERENCES** Why do you think Yunmi bursts into tears? (She sees how much Halmoni is enjoying her visit and is afraid her grandmother will stay in Korea.)

COMPREHENSION STRATEGY
Predict/Infer

Student Modeling Have students share their predictions about what they think will happen when Yunmi's visit comes to an end.

202

Yunmi had only been to a cemetery once before. She had seen people place flowers at a grave, say a prayer, and leave quietly. But in Korea, no one cried or looked sad. The cousins ran through the field collecting flowers and smooth stones for Grandfather's hill.

Yunmi wanted to talk with Halmoni, but everyone was crowded around her. Yunmi went and sat under a big tree all by herself to think. As she watched Halmoni, Yunmi grew more and more afraid that Halmoni would not want to go back to New York.

"Yunmi, help us look for more stones," said Sunhi.

"Why are you all by yourself?" Jinhi asked. "What's wrong?"

"Nothing. Nothing's wrong. Why don't you go sit with Halmoni. She's missed you all year," Yunmi said and burst into tears. She jumped up and ran, tears streaming down her cheeks.

203

Extra Support/Intervention

Strategy Modeling: Predict/Infer

Use this example to model the strategy.

When I read that Yunmi goes off by herself, I wonder what what she's feeling. Then, when Jinhi finds her and asks what's wrong, even though Yunmi replies "Nothing," it's clear that she is worried and upset. I see that in the picture on pages 202–203, Halmoni looks happy with her family. I bet Yunmi's afraid that Halmoni won't want to return with her to New York.

Predicting Outcomes

Review

- Remind students that good readers look for clues about story characters as they read. The clues they find will help them predict what might happen.

Practice

- Read page 203 with students, beginning with the second paragraph.

- Help students use text clues to predict what Sunhi and Jinhi would do if they saw another family member looking unhappy. (They would go over to that person, show concern, and ask the person to join them.)

Apply

- Ask students to work in small groups to answer the following questions and list the story clues that helped them predict outcomes.

  – If Halmoni returns to Korea at the same time next year, what will she probably do?

  – If Halmoni asked Sunhi to teach Yunmi how to write Korean words, what do you think would happen?

Review Skill Trace	
Teach	p. 213A
Reteach	p. R10
▶ Review	p. 267D; Theme 1, p. 99; Theme 2, p. 203; Theme 4, p. 93

CRITICAL THINKING
Guiding Comprehension

18 **NOTING DETAILS** How do Yunmi's actions and thoughts show her mixed feelings? (She runs off and cries; she thinks it will be unfair if Halmoni stays in Korea; she also thinks she's being selfish because Halmoni is happy in Korea.)

19 **MAKING INFERENCES** Why do you think Yunmi says *"They just want me to stay so they can keep you here"*? (Sample answers: She's upset, afraid, and confused; she doesn't think her family likes her as much as they like Halmoni.)

20 **MAKING JUDGMENTS** Why does Yunmi feel ashamed and selfish? (She realizes that, in her fear, she hasn't been thinking about what her grandmother might need or want.)

18 When she couldn't run anymore, Yunmi threw herself on the grass and cried and cried. She imagined going back to New York all by herself, and all the lonely afternoons she would spend without Halmoni. She knew Halmoni was happy here, but it all seemed so unfair.

Soon she heard Halmoni's voice. "Yunmi, what's the matter?" She didn't answer.

Halmoni patted her. "Aren't you enjoying your visit? Everyone is so happy you're here. They wish you could stay longer."

19 Yunmi blurted, "They just want me to stay so they can keep you here. I know you want to stay. You're so happy and busy."

204

Vocabulary

blurted said suddenly without thinking

ashamed feeling sorry for doing something wrong or foolish

selfish concerned mainly with oneself and not thinking of others

Halmoni sighed. "Oh, dear! Have I been that bad? I'm sorry. It's just that I want to take care of everything so I'll be ready to spend another year with you."

Yunmi looked up. "Another year with me?"

"Yes, Yunmi. Another year in New York, just as we planned."

Suddenly Yunmi felt ashamed and selfish. She stared down at the grass. "Halmoni, you have your house, your pets, and all your grandchildren and friends here. In New York, you only have my parents and me. If you want to stay, I understand."

205

Cause and Effect

Review

- Remind students that some story events and ideas are related. To figure out these cause-and-effect relationships, students should ask these questions:
  – What happens? *(effect)*
  – Why does it happen? *(cause)*

Practice/Apply

- Point out that Halmoni sees Yunmi crying and thinks she's not enjoying her visit to Korea.

- Ask students to identify the real cause of Yunmi's tears. (She fears that Halmoni plans to stay in Korea.)

- Help students fill in a Cause-and-Effect chart like the one below.

- Have students find other cause-and-effect relationships in the details of the story and add them to the chart. (Sample answer: Halmoni has been taking care of things with her family in Korea so that she can spend another year with Yunmi in New York.)

Cause	Effect
Yunmi fears that Halmoni plans to stay in Korea.	Yunmi starts to cry.

Target Skill Trace	
Teach	Theme 1, p. 121A
Reteach	Theme 1, p. R12
▶ Review	Theme 3, p. 377

Reading the Selection 205

CRITICAL THINKING
Guiding Comprehension

21 **MAKING INFERENCES** Why do you think Yunmi suddenly thinks of inviting her cousins to visit her in New York? (Sample answers: She realizes how important they are to her; she'd like to return their kindness.)

22 **DRAWING CONCLUSIONS** What is the author saying about Yunmi when she says that Yunmi and Halmoni *"walked over to join Yunmi's family"*? (Yunmi now thinks of her relatives as part of her own family.)

Halmoni smiled. "I do miss everyone here, but I have a family I belong to in New York. And you have a family here too. We're lucky because we both have two families."

Yunmi thought of her cousins Sunhi and Jinhi. "Halmoni, I kept wishing all my cousins would disappear. They were so nice to me, and even helped me buy presents for my friends."

Halmoni stroked Yunmi's hair and said, "They like you so much, you are already one of their favorite cousins."

21 "Halmoni, do you think we can invite Jinhi and Sunhi to New York for a visit? I'd like to show them around," said Yunmi.

Halmoni smiled. "Oh, I know they would love to. Why don't you ask them?"

22 Yunmi heard her cousins calling. She took Halmoni's hand and helped her up. Together they walked over to join Yunmi's family.

206

Extra Support/ Intervention | **On Level** **Challenge**

Selection Review

Before students join in Wrapping Up on page 207, have them

- take turns modeling the reading strategies they used
- help you complete **Transparency 5–11** and their Character Charts
- summarize the whole selection

Literature Discussion

Have small groups of students discuss the story, using their own questions or the questions in Think About the Selection on page 208.

Wrapping Up

Critical Thinking Questions

1. **STORY STRUCTURE** How is Grandfather's birthday celebration an important event in the story? (It's the main purpose of the trip; story events build up to it; it's where Yunmi and Halmoni talk about Halmoni's plans.)

2. **MAKING JUDGMENTS** Do you think traveling to a foreign country can change a person's viewpoint? Explain. (Sample answer: Yes; you gain a new understanding of other people's beliefs and customs, and you start to see your own in a different way.)

Strategies in Action

Have students take turns modeling how and where they used the Predict/Infer strategy.

Discussion Options

Bring the entire class together to do one or more of the activities below.

Review Predictions/Purpose Have students discuss how well their predictions matched the story outcome.

Share Group Discussions Have students share their literature discussions.

Summarize Have students use their Character Charts to discuss the characters in the story.

Comprehension Check

Use **Practice Book** page 107 to assess students' comprehension of the selection.

Practice Book page 107

Name _____

Yunmi and Halmoni's Trip
Comprehension Check

Finish the Letter

Suppose Yunmi wrote this letter. Write story details to finish her letter.

Dear Anna Marie,

We've had a wonderful time in Korea! When
Halmoni **(2 points)** _____ and I first arrived

at the airport, I had to stand in the line for
foreigners **(2)** _____ . That made me feel

strange. However, my Korean family made me feel welcome.
I loved sightseeing and shopping, and my cousins Jinhi and
Sunhi helped me buy a silk purse for you **(2)** _____ . For a

time I became sad, because I thought that my grandmother
wanted to stay in Korea **(2)** _____ . Then we went to my

grandfather's gravesite to celebrate his birthday **(2)** _____ .

That's where Halmoni told me that she would be
coming back to New York **(2)** _____ .

Next year I hope that my cousins will come to New York
for a visit. You can help me take them sightseeing! I'll be
home soon, and I can't wait to see you.
Your friend,
Yunmi

Monitoring Student Progress

If . . .	Then . . .
students score 8 or below on **Practice Book** page 107,	guide them in rereading relevant parts of the selection and discussing their answers.

Reading the Selection 207

Responding

Think About the Selection

Have students discuss or write their answers. Sample answers are provided; accept reasonable responses.

1. **MAKING INFERENCES** They're no longer just people in a photo but family members she knows and loves.

2. **DRAWING CONCLUSIONS** They loved him; the custom is an important part of their culture.

3. **CAUSE AND EFFECT** She has a better understanding of Halmoni, of her Korean family, and of who she is.

4. **PREDICTING OUTCOMES** They might be excited to see how their cousin lives; they might feel anxious in another country with a different culture and language.

5. **MAKING JUDGMENTS** Answers will vary.

6. ⭐ **Connecting/Comparing** Both make a journey to a distant land, and both probably feel anxious. The boy travels for over two months on a leaky ship to an unknown wilderness where his family starts a new life. Yunmi travels in fourteen and a half hours in a jet to a modern city where she visits relatives.

Responding

Think About the Selection

1. How does Yunmi feel about her relatives in Korea by the end of the story? Explain your answer.

2. Why do you think that celebrating Grandfather's birthday is so important to Yunmi and Halmoni's family?

3. In what ways does Yunmi change because of her visit to Korea?

4. How do you think Yunmi's cousins would feel about visiting Yunmi in the United States?

5. If someone came to visit you from far away, how would you make them feel welcome?

6. ⭐ **Connecting/Comparing** Both Yunmi and the boy in *Across the Wide Dark Sea* take long voyages. Compare their experiences.

Narrating

Write a Personal Narrative

Have you ever taken a trip to visit relatives or friends? Write about a trip that you have taken. What made the visit exciting or difficult? Tell what was most interesting about your trip.

Tips

- To get started, make a story map of your trip.
- Be sure to keep the events in order.
- Use words that describe sights, sounds, and feelings.

208

English Language Learners

Supporting Comprehension

Beginning/Preproduction Help students make a list of words in the story for Yunmi's different relatives. Then help students add words for other types of family members.

Early Production and Speech Emergence Ask students to tell what things Yunmi learned from her trip and how she learned them.

Intermediate and Advanced Fluency Ask students to describe a visit to relatives or other people they did not know well, especially in another country. Encourage them to tell how they felt and what they learned from their visit.

Social Studies

Find Out Names for Grandparents

In a small group, list all the names you know for *grandmother* and *grandfather*. Include names from other languages if possible. Compare your group's results with the rest of the class.

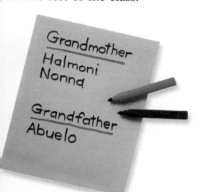

Listening and Speaking

Be a Tour Guide

Yunmi's cousins give her a tour of their town. Plan a tour of your classroom or school. In a small group, decide what places to show and what to tell about each one. Then ask permission to invite visitors to take the tour.

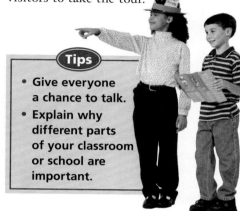

Tips

- Give everyone a chance to talk.
- Explain why different parts of your classroom or school are important.

Solve a Web Crossword Puzzle

What new words did you learn from *Yunmi and Halmoni's Trip*? Go to Education Place and print out a crossword puzzle about the selection. **www.eduplace.com/kids**

209

Additional Responses

Personal Response Invite students to share their personal responses to the selection.

Journal ► Ask students to write about going to visit family members.

Selection Connections Remind students to add to **Practice Book** page 84.

Extra Support/ Intervention

Story Map

Remind students that stories need to have a beginning, middle, and end. Encourage them to write their stories in comic strip form, using pictures and words. You may want all students to begin with the comic strip exercise to help them map out the sequence of events.

Practice Book page 84

Name _____

Launching the Theme
Selection Connections

Voyagers

Fill in the chart as you read the stories. Sample answers shown.

	Across the Wide Dark Sea	Yunmi and Halmoni's Trip	Trapped by the Ice!
Who takes the voyage? Where does the voyage begin and end?	Pilgrims travel from England to America. (2 points)	Yunmi and her grandmother travel from New York to Korea and back. (2)	Shackleton travels from England to Antarctica and back. (2)
What qualities help the voyagers succeed?	The Pilgrims are brave, friendly, smart, and hard-working. (3)	Yunmi is caring, friendly, responds quickly to change, and learns from her experiences. (3)	Shackleton is daring, brave, strong, and good at solving problems. (3)

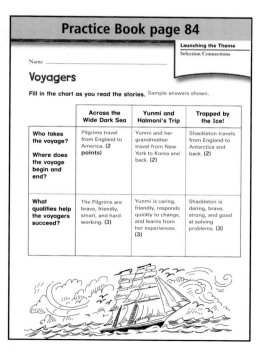

Monitoring Student Progress

End-of-Selection Assessment

Selection Test Use the test on pages 137–138 in the **Teacher's Resource Blackline Masters** to assess selection comprehension and vocabulary.

Student Self-Assessment Have students assess their reading with additional questions such as

- Which parts of this selection were difficult? Why?
- Which strategies helped me understand the story better?
- Would I recommend this story to my friends? Why or why not?

Art Link

Skill: How to Look at Fine Art

- **Introduce** "Journeys Through Art." Explain that students will be examining four paintings and one sculpture, each by a different artist.

- **Discuss** the skill lesson on Anthology page 210. Explain that it can be helpful to follow some guidelines when they are looking at art.

- **Model** how to look at a piece of fine art. Ask students to look at *Geese in Flight,* and then help them follow the steps on Anthology page 210.

- **Set a purpose** for writing. Have students keep track of the details they observe in the artwork and of their own impressions. Have students help you fill in the chart for *Geese in Flight.*

Geese in Flight

Look at the Entire Art Work	Focus on Details	Respond
small town by the sea	geese flying away	I like it because it makes me think of traveling someplace far away.
boats coming and going	train going by	

Journeys Through Art

Skill: How to Look at Fine Art

❶ **Look** at the whole painting or sculpture. **Think** about how it makes you feel.

❷ Then look more carefully. **Focus** on small details or parts. **Notice** colors and shapes.

❸ **Respond** to the art. Tell a friend how the art makes you feel or what it makes you think about.

Geese in Flight, **1850 or later**
Leila T. Bauman

The Seven Ri Ferry Boa
Approaching Kuwana,
Ando Hiroshige

210

至十三次名所圖會
四十三

桑名
七里の
渡口

Extra Support/Intervention

REACHING ALL LEARNERS

Noting Details

Guide students in noting details. Ask them to list the objects they see that suggest motion. (birds, boats, trains, airplanes, cars) Then have them look for other details that give the feeling of motion. (ocean waves, full sails, smoke from the train) Students can then refer to these details as they reflect on what the art expresses.

Cubism

Teach

Explain that *Airplane Over Train* is an example of a modern art form called cubism. Draw a one-dimensional square, and then draw a three-dimensional cube. Explain that a cubist artist often uses shapes with the qualities of a cube, which has many flat sides. Tell students that cubism

- often breaks up a figure
- tries to show hidden or invisible qualities in things
- does not always clearly show the thing it is representing
- can be challenging and require viewers to study the art carefully to understand what it is showing

Practice/Apply

- Ask students to identify the characteristics of cubism in *Airplane Over Train*.
- Have students experiment with cubism by drawing, coloring, or painting an object in the cubist style.

Airplane Over Train, 1913
Natalia Goncharova

212

English Language Learners

Supporting Comprehension

To help students respond to art, look at *Airplane Over Train* on page 212 together and ask, What do you see? List responses in the first two columns of the chart. Then encourage them to give their responses to the art by asking, How does this painting make you feel—happy, sad, afraid? What do you think of when you look at it? Finally, assign one painting from the Art Link to each pair of students and have them answer the same questions about this artwork, filling in a chart.

View of the Pont de Sèvres and the Slopes of Clamart,
St. Cloud, and Bellevue, 1908
Henri Rousseau

Car, 1943
Alexander Calder

213

Wrapping Up

Critical Thinking Questions

Ask students to use their charts and the selection to answer these questions.

1. **MAKING GENERALIZATIONS** Why do you think these pieces of art were chosen for a theme entitled *Voyagers*? (They all feature some form of transportation.)

2. **COMPARE AND CONTRAST** In what ways are the three paintings *Geese in Flight, View of the Pont de Sèvres,* and *Airplane Over Train* different, and how are they similar? (Sample answers: They all show objects in motion; they show methods of transportation; *Geese in Flight* features birds rather than airplanes; *Geese in Flight* and *View of the Pont de Sèvres* are landscapes and are more realistic.)

3. **DRAWING CONCLUSIONS** How can you tell that the works of art on pages 210–213 were all created in the 1900s? (Airplanes and modern cars were not invented until after 1900.)

4. **NOTING DETAILS** What idea or theme do these works of art express that relates to *Yunmi and Halmoni's Trip*? What clue do you find to this relationship on page 210? (traveling; the word *Journeys* in the link title)

REACHING ALL LEARNERS

Challenge

esearch Skills

Have students use encyclopedias, art books, or the Internet to research additional examples of fine art by artists featured in the link. If this is not practical, have them research an artistic style that intrigues them, such as *cubism, impressionism,* or *pop art.* Have students share their findings with the class.

OBJECTIVES

- Use story details and personal knowledge to predict what story characters might do in new situations.
- Learn academic language: *predict outcomes.*

Target Skill Trace

Preview; Teach	pp. 185S; 186; 203; 213A
Reteach	p. R10
Review	pp. 267D–267E; Theme 1, p. 101; Theme 2, p. 201; Theme 4, p. 91
See	*Extra Support Handbook,* pp. 174–175; pp. 180–181

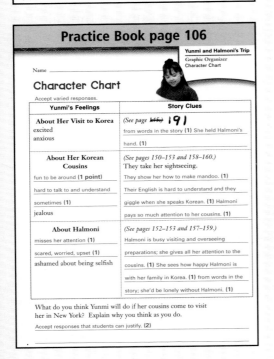

Transparency 5–11

VOYAGERS Yunmi and Halmoni's Trip
Graphic Organizer Character Chart

ANNOTATED VERSION

Character Chart

Accept varied responses.

Yunmi's Feelings	Story Clues
About Her Visit to Korea excited anxious	(See page 145.) from words in the story She held Halmoni's hand.
About Her Korean Cousins fun to be around hard to talk to and understand sometimes jealous	(See pages 150–153 and 158–160.) They take her sightseeing. They show her how to make mandoo. Their English is hard to understand and they giggle when she speaks Korean. Halmoni pays so much attention to her cousins.
About Halmoni misses her attention scared, worried, upset ashamed about being selfish	(See pages 152–153 and 157–159.) Halmoni is busy visiting and overseeing preparations; gives all her attention to the cousins. She sees how happy Halmoni is with her family in Korea. from words in the story; she'd be lonely without Halmoni.

What do you think Yunmi will do if her cousins come to visit her in New York? Explain why you think as you do.
Accept responses that students can justify.

TRANSPARENCY 5–11
TEACHER'S EDITION PAGES 188 AND 213A

Practice Book page 106

Yunmi and Halmoni's Trip
Graphic Organizer
Character Chart

Name _____

Character Chart

Accept varied responses.

Yunmi's Feelings	Story Clues
About Her Visit to Korea excited anxious	(See page 191.) from words in the story (1) She held Halmoni's hand. (1)
About Her Korean Cousins fun to be around (1 point) hard to talk to and understand sometimes (1) jealous	(See pages 150–153 and 158–160.) They take her sightseeing. They show her how to make mandoo. (1) Their English is hard to understand and they giggle when she speaks Korean. (1) Halmoni pays so much attention to her cousins. (1)
About Halmoni misses her attention (1) scared, worried, upset (1) ashamed about being selfish	(See pages 152–153 and 157–159.) Halmoni is busy visiting and overseeing preparations; she gives all her attention to the cousins. (1) She sees how happy Halmoni is with her family in Korea. (1) from words in the story; she'd be lonely without Halmoni. (1)

What do you think Yunmi will do if her cousins come to visit her in New York? Explain why you think as you do.
Accept responses that students can justify. (2)

TARGET SKILL

COMPREHENSION: Predicting Outcomes

1 Teach

Review predicting outcomes for *Yunmi and Halmoni's Trip.*
Remind students that they can use their own knowledge plus story clues to tell what might happen to story characters in new situations. Complete the Graphic Organizer on **Transparency 5–11** with students. (Sample answers are shown.) Students can refer to the selection and to **Practice Book** page 106. Tell students to

- look for story details that tell how Yunmi talks, acts, feels, and makes choices;
- think about how those details can be used to predict her feelings and actions.

Model predicting outcomes. Have students reread pages 204–205 as you think aloud.

Think Aloud
When Yunmi fears that Halmoni will stay in Korea, she thinks how lonely the afternoons will be without her. So I can predict that if Halmoni decides to stay in Korea, Yunmi will miss her and be lonely. But it also says that Yunmi realizes how happy Halmoni is in Korea. I predict that Yunmi will try not to be selfish. She'll want what's best for Halmoni.

2 Guided Practice

Have students predict outcomes. Have pairs or small groups predict what Halmoni might do in the following situation: Halmoni is back in New York and learns that a sick relative in Korea needs help. Ask them to write their predictions and list the story clues that helped them. (Sample answers are shown.)

> **Halmoni**
>
> decides to go to Korea to help the sick relative, but she returns to America when the relative recovers.

Details about Halmoni	Story Clues
helpful	(pages 145–146) She left her home to help Yunmi and her parents.
caring	(pages 158–160) She tells Yunmi that she cares for both families and that she belongs to the family in New York.

Apply

Assign Practice Book pages 108–109. Also have students apply this skill as they read their **Leveled Readers** for this week. You may also select books from the Leveled Bibliography for this theme, pages 148E–148F.

Test Prep Test questions about predicting outcomes often ask about events that actually happen in the story. These questions frequently ask students to identify details from the beginning of a story that helped them predict an event that happens later in the story.

Leveled Readers and Leveled Practice

Students at all levels apply the comprehension skill as they read their Leveled Readers. See lessons on pages 213O–213R.

● BELOW LEVEL   ▲ ON LEVEL   ■ ABOVE LEVEL   ◆ LANGUAGE SUPPORT

Reading Traits

Teaching students how to predict outcomes is one way of encouraging them to "read between the lines" of a selection. This comprehension skill supports the reading trait **Realizing Context.**

Practice Book page 108

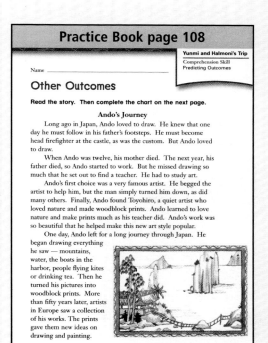

Yunmi and Halmoni's Trip
Comprehension Skill
Predicting Outcomes

Name _____

Other Outcomes

Read the story. Then complete the chart on the next page.

Ando's Journey

Long ago in Japan, Ando loved to draw. He knew that one day he must follow in his father's footsteps. He must become head firefighter at the castle, as was the custom. But Ando loved to draw.

When Ando was twelve, his mother died. The next year, his father died, so Ando started to work. But he missed drawing so much that he set out to find a teacher. He had to study art.

Ando's first choice was a very famous artist. He begged the artist to help him, but the man simply turned him down, as did many others. Finally, Ando found Toyohiro, a quiet artist who loved nature and made woodblock prints. Ando learned to love nature and make prints much as his teacher did. Ando's work was so beautiful that he helped make this new art style popular.

One day, Ando left for a long journey through Japan. He began drawing everything he saw — mountains, water, the boats in the harbor, people flying kites or drinking tea. Then he turned his pictures into woodblock prints. More than fifty years later, artists in Europe saw a collection of his works. The prints gave them new ideas on drawing and painting.

Practice Book page 109

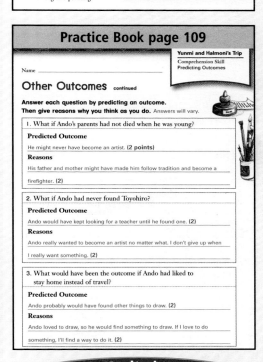

Yunmi and Halmoni's Trip
Comprehension Skill
Predicting Outcomes

Name _____

Other Outcomes continued

Answer each question by predicting an outcome.
Then give reasons why you think as you do. Answers will vary.

1. What if Ando's parents had not died when he was young?

Predicted Outcome
He might never have become an artist. **(2 points)**

Reasons
His father and mother might have made him follow tradition and become a firefighter. **(2)**

2. What if Ando had never found Toyohiro?

Predicted Outcome
Ando would have kept looking for a teacher until he found one. **(2)**

Reasons
Ando really wanted to become an artist no matter what. I don't give up when I really want something. **(2)**

3. What would have been the outcome if Ando had liked to stay home instead of travel?

Predicted Outcome
Ando probably would have found other things to draw. **(2)**

Reasons
Ando loved to draw, so he would find something to draw. If I love to do something, I'll find a way to do it. **(2)**

Monitoring Student Progress

If . . .	Then . . .
students score 8 or below on **Practice Book** page 109,	use the Reteaching lesson on Teacher's Edition page R10.
students have successfully met the lesson objectives,	have them do the Challenge/ Extension activities on Teacher's Edition page R11.

OBJECTIVES

- Read singular and plural possessives.
- Learn academic language: *possessive noun*.

Target Skill Trace

Teach	p. 213C
Reteach	p. R16
Review	pp. 267F–267G
See	*Handbook for English Language Learners,* p. 177; *Extra Support Handbook,* pp. 172–172; pp. 176–177

Practice Book page 110

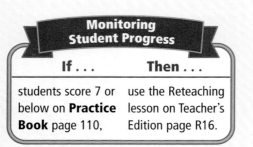

Yunmi and Halmoni's Trip
Structural Analysis
Possessives

Name _____

Who Owns It?

▶ Add an **apostrophe** and *s* (*'s*) to a singular noun to make it show ownership. Add an **apostrophe** (*'*) to a plural noun that already ends with *s* to make it show ownership.

Halmoni's hand   parents' names

Complete each sentence. Add an apostrophe and *s* or just an apostrophe to make each noun in dark type show ownership. The first one is done for you.

Last weekend, my family went to visit my **(mother)** _mother's_ sister. **(Aunt Jenny)** _Aunt Jenny's_ **(1 point)** house is three hours away. I carried my two little **(sisters)** _sisters'_ **(1)** bags out to the car. I couldn't lift my **(parents)** _parents'_ **(1)** suitcases because they were too heavy.

I was very excited to see my cousins. My **(cousins)** _cousins'_ **(1)** names are Ryan and Marie. As soon as my family got there, Ryan and Marie took me to their pet **(rabbits)** _rabbits'_ **(1)** cages behind the house. **(Ryan)** _Ryan's_ **(1)** rabbit is named Flopsy. **(Flopsy)** _Flopsy's_ **(1)** ears hang straight down. **(Marie)** _Marie's_ **(1)** rabbit is named Topsy. **(Topsy)** _Topsy's_ **(1)** ears stick straight up. This time there was a surprise — a rabbit for me! My new **(rabbit)** _rabbit's_ **(1)** name is Mopsy.

Monitoring Student Progress

If . . .	Then . . .
students score 7 or below on **Practice Book** page 110,	use the Reteaching lesson on Teacher's Edition page R16.

STRUCTURAL ANALYSIS/ VOCABULARY: Possessives

❶ Teach

Define possessives. Explain that a possessive noun shows ownership.

Explain singular possessives. Write *Yunmi took* <u>*Grandmother's*</u> *hand.*

- Adding apostrophe plus *s* to a singular noun shows ownership by one person. *Grandmother's* is a possessive noun.
- *Grandmother's hand* is a way of saying "the hand that belongs to Grandmother."

Explain plural possessives. Write *Yunmi was* <u>*surprised*</u> *to see her parents' names on the stone.*

- When a plural noun already ends in *s*, like *parents*, only an apostrophe is added to make it possessive.
- *Parents' names* is a short way of saying "the names that belong to her parents."

Model the Phonics/Decoding Strategy. Write *The next day was* <u>*Grandfather's*</u> *birthday.* Model decoding *Grandfather's.*

> **Think Aloud** *When I read this word I see the shorter words* grand *and* father. *It's a compound word. It ends in* s, *but the apostrophe before the* s *tells me that the word is a possessive. It means "the birthday that belongs to Grandfather."*

❷ Guided Practice

Have students divide words into syllables. Display the phrases below. Ask partners to underline each possessive noun, determine its meaning, and tell whether it is singular or plural. Have students share their work with the class.

Yunmi's relatives	her cousins' favorite stall
the foreigners' line	Grandfather's hill
Halmoni's house	Halmoni's voice

❸ Apply

Assign Practice Book page 110.

PHONICS REVIEW:
The Vowel Sound in *bought*

OBJECTIVES

- Read words and syllables with the vowel sound in *bought*.
- Apply the Phonics/Decoding Strategy.

❶ Teach

Introduce the vowel sound in *bought*. Tell students that understanding the vowel sound in *bought* can help them decode unfamiliar words.

- The spelling patterns *ough* and *augh* can have the /ô/ sound, as in *bought*.

Model the Phonics/Decoding Strategy. Write *She went to America to be with her granddaughter*. Model decoding *granddaughter*.

Think Aloud *When I look at this word, I recognize the shorter word* grand. *Next I see the letter* d *followed by the* augh *spelling pattern. I know this pattern can have the* aw *sound as in* bought, *so I think this part of the word might sound like* daw. *The last part probably sounds like* ter *as in the word* water. *When I try putting it all together, I say* GRAND-daw-tur. *I know that word— it's* granddaughter, *which makes sense in the sentence.*

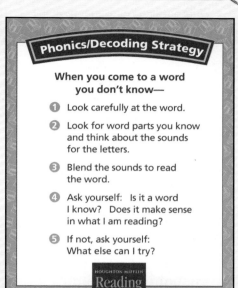

Phonics/Decoding Strategy

When you come to a word you don't know—

❶ Look carefully at the word.

❷ Look for word parts you know and think about the sounds for the letters.

❸ Blend the sounds to read the word.

❹ Ask yourself: Is it a word I know? Does it make sense in what I am reading?

❺ If not, ask yourself: What else can I try?

HOUGHTON MIFFLIN
Reading

❷ Guided Practice

Have students find and decode *ough* and *augh* sounds. Display the sentences below. Have students circle the *ough* or *augh* spelling in each underlined word. Then help them pronounce the word and see if it makes sense. Call on individuals to model their work.

Sunhi <u>taught</u> Yunmi how to make dumplings.

Yunmi <u>thought</u> her grandmother wanted to stay in Korea.

❸ Apply

Have students decode words with *ough* and *augh*. Ask students to decode the following phrases and discuss their meanings.

bought cakes	ought to say thank you
brought home gifts	should not act naughty

SPELLING: Vowel Sound in *bought*

OBJECTIVE

- Write Spelling Words that have the vowel sound in *bought*.

SPELLING WORDS

Basic

caught	fought
thought*	daughter*
bought*	taught
laugh†	brought
through*†	ought
enough†	cough†

Review††	**Challenge**
teeth	sought
was*	granddaughter*

* *Forms of these words appear in the literature.*

† *These words are exceptions to the rule.*

†† *Because this lesson presents these spelling patterns for the first time, the Review Words do not contain the lesson's patterns.*

Extra Support/ Intervention

Basic Word List Consider using only the left column of Basic Words with students who need extra support.

Challenge

Challenge Word Practice Have students use the Challenge Words to write some quotes that Halmoni might say upon her return to New York.

DAY 1 — INSTRUCTION

Vowel Sound in *bought*

Pretest Use the Day 5 Test sentences.

Teach Write *bought* and *caught* on the board.

- Say the words, and have students repeat them. Underline *ough* and *augh*, and explain that they are two spelling patterns for the /ô/ sound.

- Add *laugh, through, enough,* and *cough* to the board. Say each word, and have students repeat it. Explain that these words are special because their *augh* or *ough* patterns do not spell the /ô/ sound. (In *laugh, augh* spells the /ăf/ sounds; in *through, enough,* and *cough, ough* spells the /o͞o/ sound, the /ŭf/ sounds, and the /ôf/ sounds respectively.)

- List the remaining Basic Words, say each word, and have students repeat it. Underline the /ô/ spelling patterns.

Practice/Homework Assign **Practice Book** page 241.

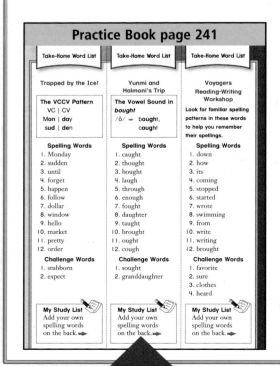

Practice Book page 241

Take-Home Word List	Take-Home Word List	Take-Home Word List
Trapped by the Ice!	**Yunmi and Halmoni's Trip**	**Voyagers Reading-Writing Workshop**
The VCCV Pattern VC | CV Mon | day sud | den	**The Vowel Sound in bought** /ô/ → bought, caught!	Look for familiar spelling patterns in these words to help you remember their spellings.
Spelling Words 1. Monday 2. sudden 3. until 4. forget 5. happen 6. follow 7. dollar 8. window 9. hello 10. market 11. pretty 12. order	**Spelling Words** 1. caught 2. thought 3. bought 4. laugh 5. through 6. enough 7. fought 8. daughter 9. taught 10. brought 11. ought 12. cough	**Spelling Words** 1. down 2. how 3. its 4. coming 5. stopped 6. started 7. wrote 8. swimming 9. from 10. write 11. writing 12. brought
Challenge Words 1. stubborn 2. expect	**Challenge Words** 1. sought 2. granddaughter	**Challenge Words** 1. favorite 2. sure 3. clothes 4. heard
My Study List Add your own spelling words on the back.➡	**My Study List** Add your own spelling words on the back.➡	**My Study List** Add your own spelling words on the back.➡

Take-Home Word List

DAY 2 — REVIEW & PRACTICE

Reviewing the Principle

Go over the spelling patterns for the vowel sound in *bought* with students.

Practice/Homework Assign **Practice Book** page 111.

Practice Book page 111

Yunmi and Halmoni's Trip
Spelling: The Vowel Sound in *bought*

Name _____

The Vowel Sound in *bought*

When you hear the /ô/ sound, remember that it can be spelled with the pattern *ough* or *augh*.
/ô/ bought, caught

► In the starred words *laugh, through, enough,* and *cough,* the *ough* and *augh* patterns spell other sounds.

Write each Spelling Word under its *ough* or *augh* spelling pattern. Order of answers for each category may vary.

Spelling Words
1. caught
2. thought
3. bought
4. laugh*
5. through*
6. enough*
7. fought
8. daughter
9. taught
10. brought
11. ought
12. cough*

ough

thought (1 point)	fought (1)
bought (1)	brought (1)
through (1)	ought (1)
enough (1)	cough (1)

augh

caught (1)	daughter (1)
laugh (1)	taught (1)

Word Family for *laugh*

Write *laugh* and *laughter* on the board, and ask students to say each word after you.

- Tell students that these words are in the same word family because they are related in spelling and in meaning.
- Ask students to suggest other words in the same family. (Some possible answers include *laughs, laughed, laughing, laughingly, laughable.*)
- List the Basic Words on the board. Have students use each word orally in a sentence. (Sentences will vary.)

Practice/Homework For spelling practice, assign **Practice Book** page 112.

Game: Question Relay

Have students form groups of 3 to 5, and ask each group to make a set of word cards for the Basic Words. Tell students to mix up the cards and place them face-down. Explain the rules:

- Player 1 picks a card. Other players take turns asking questions that can be answered with yes or no, such as "Is it the opposite of *cry*?"
- A player can ask a question and make a guess in the same turn. The player must then spell the word correctly to score a point. If the player misspells the word, the next player may try to score a point by spelling it correctly.
- The first player to spell the word correctly draws the next card. The player with the highest score at the end of the game wins.

Practice/Homework For proofreading and writing practice, assign **Practice Book** page 113.

Spelling Test

Say each underlined word, read the sentence, and then repeat the word. Have students write only the underlined word.

Basic Words

1. How many fish were **caught**? 12
2. I **thought** you were home. 11
3. Is that the cat you **bought**? 10
4. The clowns make me **laugh**. 9
5. We walked **through** the park. 8
6. Did you eat **enough** fish? 7
7. We **fought** to change the rules. 6
8. Is that girl your **daughter**? 5
9. My dad **taught** me to swim. 1
10. We **brought** chairs to sit on. 2
11. You **ought** to go before dark. 3
12. The nurse heard him **cough**. 4

Challenge Words

13. I **sought** out Fred to be my friend. 14
14. She made a doll for her **granddaughter**. 13

Practice Book page 112

Yunmi and Halmoni's Trip
Spelling The Vowel Sound in *bought*

Name _____

Spelling Spree

Only Opposites Write the Spelling Word that is the opposite of each clue.

1. not sold, but bought **(1 point)**
2. not learned, but taught **(1)**
3. not dropped, but caught **(1)**
4. not took, but brought **(1)**
5. not son, but daughter **(1)**
6. not cry, but laugh **(1)**

Spelling Words
1. caught
2. thought
3. bought
4. laugh*
5. through*
6. enough*
7. fought
8. daughter
9. taught
10. brought
11. ought
12. cough*

Alphabet Puzzler Write the Spelling Word that goes in ABC order between each pair of words.

7. cool, _____, daze — 7. cough **(1)**
8. open, _____, paste — 8. ought **(1)**
9. thin, _____, thunder — 9. thought **(1)**
10. find, _____, game — 10. fought **(1)**

Practice Book page 113

Yunmi and Halmoni's Trip
Spelling The Vowel Sound in *bought*

Name _____

Proofreading and Writing

Proofreading Suppose Yunmi sent this note. Circle the five misspelled Spelling Words in it. Then write each word correctly.

Dear Mom and Dad,

Halmoni and I are here in Korea! I thoght the plane ride was really neat. Everyone loves the presents we brought. We went throogh a palace today. I hope we have enouf time to see everything. Halmoni has baught some gifts for you. You will laugh when you see them!

Your loving dauter,

Yunmi

Spelling Words
1. caught
2. thought
3. bought
4. laugh*
5. through*
6. enough*
7. fought
8. daughter
9. taught
10. brought
11. ought
12. cough*

1. thought **(2 points)** — 4. bought **(2)**
2. through **(2)** — 5. daughter **(2)**
3. enough **(2)**

Write an Opinion An **opinion** tells what you believe or feel about something. Think of two places you have visited. Did you like one place better than the other? Why?

On a separate sheet of paper, write an opinion. Tell about the places you visited, and explain why you liked one place better than the other. Use Spelling Words from the list.
Responses will vary. **(2)**

OBJECTIVES

- Learn and use a strategy for solving analogies.
- Learn academic language: *analogy.*

Target Skill Trace

Teach	p. 213G
Review	pp. 267H–267I
Extend	Challenge/Extension Activities, p. R17
See	*Handbook for English Language Learners,* p. 33

Transparency 5–12

Analogies

Six Steps to Solve an Analogy

Frog is to **jump** as **worm** is to _____.

1. Take the analogy apart. See it as two pairs of words (one pair will have a blank instead of a word).

   first pair of words   second pair of words

   Frog is to **jump** as **worm** is to _____.

2. Read the first pair of words. In this analogy, they are *frog* and *jump.*

3. Decide how the first pair of words are related to each other.

   Frogs jump to move around.

4. Using the first pair of words, make up a sentence that shows how they are related. For example:

   A frog will jump to move from place to place.

5. Using the same sentence, replace the first pair of words with the second pair:

   A worm will _____ to move from place to place.

6. Now fill in the blank with a word that makes sense in the sentence. Then go back to the analogy and use the same word.

   A worm will (Answers will vary.) wiggle, squirm, crawl to move from place to place.

   Frog is to jump as worm is to (Answers will vary.) wiggle, squirm, crawl _____.

Monitoring Student Progress

If . . .	Then . . .
students score 6 or below on **Practice Book** page 114,	have them work with partners to correct the items they missed.

TARGET SKILL

VOCABULARY: Analogies

❶ Teach

Define analogies. Explain that an analogy is a kind of comparison.

- One pair of words is compared to a second pair.

- Words in the second pair should be related to each other in the same way as the words in the first pair. For example, if the first pair of words are synonyms, then the second pair of words should be synonyms.

Display Transparency 5–12. Read steps 1–6. Emphasize these points:

- Some analogies offer answer choices, while others do not.

- Always begin by focusing on the word pairs.

- If answer choices are given, try not to look at them until step 5 is completed.

Model solving an analogy. Write *Airplane* is to *sky* as *ship* is to _____. Then model how to solve the analogy.

Think Aloud *First, I find the first pair of words,* airplane *and* sky. *Then I ask myself how these words are related. I know that an airplane is a way to travel in the sky. Now I make a sentence: An airplane travels in the sky. Next I replace* airplane *and* sky *with the second set of words,* ship *and a blank: A ship travels in the _____.* Sea, water, *and* ocean *all make sense in the blank. I'll pick the word I like best,* ocean. *So* airplane *is to* sky *as* ship *is to* ocean.

❷ Guided Practice

Give students practice in solving analogies. Have student pairs solve the following analogies:

> <u>Lemon</u> is to <u>sour</u> as honey is to _____ (sweet).

> <u>Hair</u> is to <u>scissors</u> as lawn is to _____ (lawnmower).

Have students share the sentences they made.

❸ Apply

Assign Practice Book page 114.

Practice Book page 114

Name _____

Yunmi and Halmoni's Trip
Vocabulary Skill Analogies

Everything in Its Place

Read the first pair of words in each analogy below. Decide how the words are related. Then write the word that best completes the analogy.

1. **Author** is to **book** as **painter** is to picture **(1 point)** _____
   brush   picture   artist

2. **Breakfast** is to **dinner** as **morning** is to evening **(1)** _____
   sun   toast   evening

3. **Scissors** is to **cut** as **pencil** is to write **(1)** _____
   write   yellow   crayon

4. **Twelve** is to **number** as **green** is to color **(1)** _____
   grass   color   shape

5. **Bee** is to **honey** as **hen** is to egg **(1)** _____
   egg   corn   farm

6. **Rude** is to **polite** as **dishonest** is to honest **(1)** _____
   calm   mean   honest

7. **Television** is to **watch** as **radio** is to listen **(1)** _____
   listen   screen   volume

8. **Frog** is to **tadpole** as **butterfly** is to caterpillar **(1)** _____
   pretty   caterpillar   flying

STUDY SKILL:
Using Graphic Organizers

OBJECTIVES

- Identify the steps in SQRR.
- Use graphic organizers to record information gathered with SQRR.
- Learn academic language: *SQRR.*

❶ Teach

Introduce SQRR.

- SQRR is an abbreviation that stands for the four steps of a method for reading.

  - S survey: Quickly look over the article and get a general idea of what it is about.

  - Q question: Ask questions about each part.

  - R read: Read to find answers to your questions.

  - R review: After reading, review questions and answers.

- Graphic organizers can help to identify and organize information while reading.

Model using SQRR and a graphic organizer. Have students follow along as you model how to identify and organize information in the link "Young Voyagers" on Anthology pages 180–181.

- Survey, or look at the title, the bold type below it, the diagram, and the title and heading on the next page.

- Ask questions. Write the questions on a chart.

- Read to find the answers. Write the answers on the chart.

- Review the chart.

Questions	Answers
Where did the children stay on the ship?	Passengers lived between decks and children played on the deck in good weather.
How was life different for them than it is today?	Children worked more and bathed less than they do today.

❷ Practice/Apply

Give students practice with using SQRR and graphic organizers.

- Have partners use the SQRR technique to reread "I Work in the Ocean" on Anthology pages 66–69. Have students record their questions and answers on a simple question/answer chart.

- Have students use SQRR to find three to five interesting details about a country they have selected. Have them share this information with the class.

GRAMMAR: Object Pronouns

OBJECTIVES

- Identify object pronouns.
- Use object pronouns in sentences.
- Proofread and correct sentences with grammar and spelling errors.
- Use correct pronouns to improve writing.
- Learn academic language: *object pronoun.*

DAY 1 INSTRUCTION

Object Pronouns

Teach Display **Transparency 5–14,** and have a volunteer read aloud the two sentence pairs at the top.

- Remind students that a pronoun takes the place of one or more words. Have students tell what words are replaced in each sentence.
- Go over the bulleted rules and definitions and the chart that shows singular and plural object pronouns.
- Read aloud the examples below the chart, and discuss object pronouns and using *I* and *me* correctly.
- Ask volunteers to choose the correct word or phrase to complete each of Sentences 1–4.

Daily Language Practice
Have students correct Sentences 1 and 2 on **Transparency 5–13.**

DAY 2 PRACTICE

Independent Work

Practice/Homework Assign **Practice Book** page 115.

Daily Language Practice
Have students correct Sentences 3 and 4 on **Transparency 5–13.**

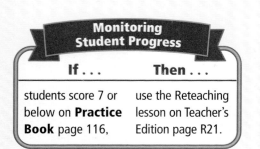

Monitoring Student Progress

If . . .	Then . . .
students score 7 or below on **Practice Book** page 116,	use the Reteaching lesson on Teacher's Edition page R21.

Transparency 5–13

Daily Language Practice

Correct two sentences each day.

1. Yunmi started to laff when she visited we in korea.
   Yunmi started to laugh when she visited us in Korea.
2. Halmoni thot she would show she the skyscrapers.
   Halmoni thought she would show her the skyscrapers.
3. Me and Halmoni soon had enuff sightseeing.
   Halmoni and I soon had enough sightseeing.
4. I awt to show my passport to he.
   I ought to show my passport to him.
5. They fot their way into the bustling crowd, it seemed strange to I.
   They fought their way into the bustling crowd. It seemed strange to me.
6. Yunmi started to coff when the foreigners asked we for our passports.
   Yunmi started to cough when the foreigners asked us for our passports.
7. Yunmi feels that her is a true dawter?
   Yunmi feels that she is a true daughter.
8. Halmoni tot they how to make dumplings.
   Halmoni taught them how to make dumplings.
9. Yunmi bot a postcard to send to I and Helen.
   Yunmi bought a postcard to send to Helen and me.
10. She brot It to show Halmoni.
    She brought it to show Halmoni.

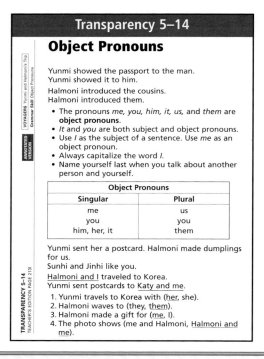

Transparency 5–14

Object Pronouns

Yunmi showed the passport to the man.
Yunmi showed it to him.

Halmoni introduced the cousins.
Halmoni introduced them.

- The pronouns *me, you, him, it, us,* and *them* are **object pronouns.**
- *It* and *you* are both subject and object pronouns.
- Use *I* as the subject of a sentence. Use *me* as an object pronoun.
- Always capitalize the word *I.*
- Name yourself last when you talk about another person and yourself.

Object Pronouns	
Singular	**Plural**
me	us
you	you
him, her, it	them

Yunmi sent her a postcard. Halmoni made dumplings for us.
Sunhi and Jinhi like you.
Halmoni and I traveled to Korea.
Yunmi sent postcards to Katy and me.

1. Yunmi travels to Korea with (her, she).
2. Halmoni waves to (they, them).
3. Halmoni made a gift for (me, I).
4. The photo shows (me and Halmoni, Halmoni and me).

Practice Book page 115

Name _____

Yunmi and Halmoni's Trip
Grammar Skill Object Pronouns

Circling Object Pronouns

Circle each object pronoun in the paragraph below. Then write the object pronouns on the lines below the paragraph.

Sunhi shows Yunmi how to make dumplings. She gives her a thin dumpling skin and some filling. Yunmi rolls it. She places the new dumpling on a tray with the other dumplings. The girls take them to the picnic. They share the dumplings with us. Yunmi gives one to me to taste.

1. her **(1 point)** _____   4. us **(1)** _____
2. it **(1)** _____   5. me **(1)** _____
3. them **(1)** _____

Choose the correct word or phrase in parentheses to complete each sentence.

6. The picnic is a special event for
   us **(1)** _____. (we, us)
7. Yunmi tells them **(1)** _____ about life in New York. (they, them)
8. Halmoni tells her **(1)** _____ a story. (her, she)
9. Her voice makes me **(1)** _____ feel better. (me, I)
10. The picnic made Halmoni and me **(1)** _____ very happy. (me and Halmoni, Halmoni and me)

The Object Comes After

Have students create note cards for each object pronoun: *me, you, him,* *, us, them.* Then have them create a second set of note cards for these words: *gives, shows, helps, teaches,* *anks, to, for, with, of, at.*

Tell students to shuffle the cards and take turns drawing one card from each stack and using the words in a sentence. (Students might write sentences about Yunmi and her grandmother.)

Help students place the verb or preposition before the object pronoun. For example, if students select *us* and *thanks,* have them first arrange the cards to show the phrase *thanks us.* They might then write the sentence *Yunmi thanks us for the gift.*

Daily Language Practice

ave students correct Sentences 5 d 6 on **Transparency 5–13**.

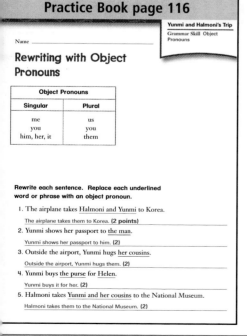

Independent Work

Practice/Homework Assign **Practice Book** page 116.

Daily Language Practice

Have students correct Sentences 7 and 8 on **Transparency 5–13**.

Transparency 5–15

Using the Correct Pronoun

1. Yunmi and me make dumplings.
   Yunmi and I make dumplings.

2. We give them the dumplings.
   Correct

3. Halmoni takes we to the museum.
   Halmoni takes us to the museum.

4. She and him prepare for the picnic.
   She and he prepare for the picnic.

5. Halmoni arrives with Sunhi and I.
   Halmoni arrives with Sunhi and me.

The Correct Pronoun

Teach Tell students that good writers are careful to use correct pronouns. Mention that it is always a good idea to check all pronouns after writing a sentence.

- Display **Transparency 5–15**.
- Have students read the sentences and correct any mistakes in the use of pronouns.
- Have students proofread a piece of their own writing for correct use of subject and object pronouns.

Practice/Homework Assign **Practice Book** page 117.

Daily Language Practice

Have students correct Sentences 9 and 10 on **Transparency 5–13**.

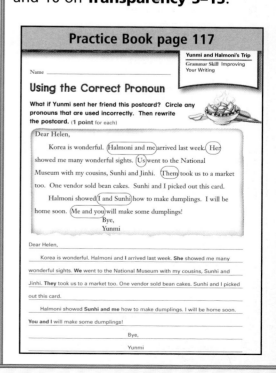

WRITING: Message

OBJECTIVES

- Identify the characteristics of a message.
- Write a message.
- Learn to record exact and complete information when taking a message.

Writing Traits

Presentation Demonstrate the importance of presentation in a message.

- Write these sentences, using unclear handwriting: Phil, your soccer coach called. *Practice is at 10:00 A.M. on Saturday.*

- Write the same sentences again, using clear handwriting.

- Discuss which pair of sentences would be easier to read.

DAY 1 ACTIVITY

Introducing the Format

Introduce taking a message.

- A message is a written summary of a telephone call or other conversation.

- It is usually written for someone else.

- It includes all important information.

- Explain that it is easy to get a message wrong if the writer is not careful.

Play a variation of Telephone.

- Divide the class into groups of eight to ten students.

- Choose one person in each group to think of a message and write it down.

- Have each person in the group whisper the message to the next person.

- Have the last person write the message. Then ask the group to compare the last message with the first message.

DAY 2 INSTRUCTION

Discussing the Model

Display Transparency 5–16. Ask:

- Who is the call for? (Halmoni)

- Who called? (Halmoni's older sister)

- When did she call? (Monday, 4:45)

- What is her telephone number? (011-111-555-1489)

- What is the important information? (Uncle will pick you up at the airport in his car and drive you and Yunmi home.)

Display Transparency 5–17, and discuss the guidelines.

Assign Practice Book page 118.

- Ask one student to pretend to call while the other takes a message.

- Then ask students to switch roles.

- Provide support as needed.

Transparency 5–16

Writing a Message

If Halmoni's older sister had called, she might have left this message.

VOYAGERS *Yunmi and Halmoni's Trip*
Writing Skill Writing a Message

ANNOTATED VERSION

whom the call is for	Hello, Halmoni, my little sister!
the name of the caller	This is your older sister calling all the way from Korea!
when the caller called	It is Monday in New York City, about 4:45 your time.
the message	I am sorry you are not home. I am calling to tell you that we are all looking forward to seeing you and meeting little Yunmi.
Uncle will pick you up at the airport in his car.
He will bring you and Yunmi home.
the caller's telephone number	The telephone number here is 011-111-555-1489.
We love you! See you next week!

This message was taken by the answering machine in Yunmi and Halmoni's home.

TRANSPARENCY 5–16
TEACHER'S EDITION PAGE 213K

Transparency 5–17

Guidelines for Writing a Message

VOYAGERS *Yunmi and Halmoni's Trip*
Writing Skill Message

ANNOTATED VERSION

- Write the name of the person who needs to read the message.
- Write the name of the person who called and left the message.
- Write the caller's phone number.
- Write the time and date of the call.
- Write the message. Include all of the important information the message contains: names, dates, times, places, and other facts.
- Write your name.

TRANSPARENCY 5–17
TEACHER'S EDITION PAGE 213K

Practice Book page 118

Yunmi and Halmoni's Trip
Writing Skill A Message

Name _____

Writing a Message

Use this page to take a message.

Date: _____ (1 point) Time: _____ (1)
For: _____ (1)
From: _____ (1) Telephone number: _____ (1)
Message: _____ (4)

_____
_____
_____
_____
_____

Message taken by: _____ (1)

Improving Writing: Complete Information

Explain how to write messages that are complete and exact.

Messages should be complete. Include all the important information.

Messages should be exact. Names, dates, places, times, and other facts should be precise and free of mistakes.

See Writing Traits on page 213K.

Display and complete Transparency 5–18.

Have students read each voice balloon and each message taken.

Ask students, Is the information complete? Is it exact?

Have students fix incorrect information in the messages and add any missing information from the voice balloons.

Assign Practice Book page 119.

Writing Game

Have partners role-play taking messages.

- Cut out advertisements for various stores from a local newspaper.

- Have a partner read aloud an advertisement, including the store's name and address, its products, and the hours it is open.

- The other partner writes down all the important information.

- Partners compare the message to the advertisement to check that it is accurate and complete. Then they switch roles.

Sharing Writing

Consider these publishing options for sharing students' writing.

- Ask students to read a piece of their writing from the Author's Chair.

- Encourage students to make a bulletin board display of their messages.

Portfolio Opportunity

Save students' messages as samples of their writing development.

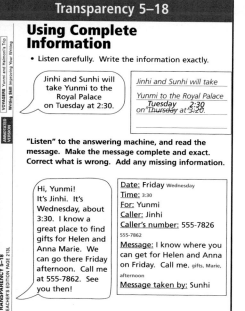

Transparency 5–18

Using Complete Information

- Listen carefully. Write the information exactly.

| Jinhi and Sunhi will take Yunmi to the Royal Palace on Tuesday at 2:30. | Jinhi and Sunhi will take Yunmi to the Royal Palace on ~~Tuesday~~ **Thursday** at ~~2:30~~ **3:20**. |

"Listen" to the answering machine, and read the message. Make the message complete and exact. Correct what is wrong. Add any missing information.

| Hi, Yunmi! It's Jinhi. It's Wednesday, about 3:30. I know a great place to find gifts for Helen and Anna Marie. We can go there Friday afternoon. Call me at 555-7862. See you then! | **Date:** ~~Friday~~ Wednesday **Time:** 3:30 **For:** Yunmi **Caller:** Jinhi **Caller's number:** 555-7826 **555-7862** **Message:** I know where you can get for Helen and Anna on Friday. Call me. gifts, Marie, afternoon **Message taken by:** Sunhi |

TRANSPARENCY 5–18
TEACHER'S EDITION PAGE 213L

VOYAGERS Yunmi and Halmoni's Trip
Writing Skill Improving Your Writing

ANNOTATED VERSION

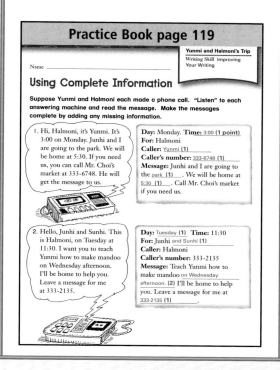

Practice Book page 119

Name _____

Yunmi and Halmoni's Trip
Writing Skill Improving Your Writing

Using Complete Information

Suppose Yunmi and Halmoni each made a phone call. "Listen" to each answering machine and read the message. Make the messages complete by adding any missing information.

1. Hi, Halmoni, it's Yunmi. It's 3:00 on Monday. Junhi and I are going to the park. We will be home at 5:30. If you need us, you can call Mr. Choi's market at 333-6748. He will get the message to us.

Day: Monday. **Time:** 3:00 (1 point)
For: Halmoni
Caller: Yunmi (1)
Caller's number: 333-6748 (1)
Message: Junhi and I are going to the park (1) . We will be home at 5:30 (1) . Call Mr. Choi's market if you need us.

2. Hello, Junhi and Sunhi. This is Halmoni, on Tuesday at 11:30. I want you to teach Yunmi how to make mandoo on Wednesday afternoon. I'll be home to help you. Leave a message for me at 333-2135.

Day: Tuesday (1) **Time:** 11:30
For: Junhi and Sunhi (1)
Caller: Halmoni
Caller's number: 333-2135
Message: Teach Yunmi how to make mandoo on Wednesday afternoon. (2) I'll be home to help you. Leave a message for me at 333-2135 (1)

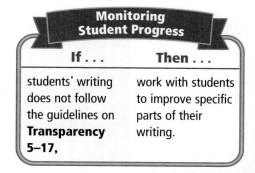

Monitoring Student Progress

If . . .	Then . . .
students' writing does not follow the guidelines on **Transparency 5–17,**	work with students to improve specific parts of their writing.

Language Center

VOCABULARY

Building Vocabulary

👤 Singles	🕐 15 minutes
Objective	Create a family word web.

Yunmi and Halmoni's Trip contains many terms that describe family members. Identify as many of these terms as you can in the story. Record them in a web.

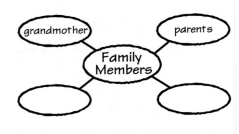

Now think of other words that describe family relationships or special family ties, such as *Nana, Gramps,* or *Sis.*

SPELLING

Spell My Secret Word

👥 Pairs	🕐 30 minutes
Objective	Spell words with vowel sounds.

Play this game with a partner. Take turns.

- The first player secretly chooses one of the spelling words in the list below and writes it down.

- Then the player gives clues to the word to his or her partner. For example, for *brought*, the clue might be: *This word starts like* brother *and rhymes with* caught. *What is my secret word?*

- The second player tries to guess the word. The player must say the word and spell it correctly to get a point. The player who gets five points first wins.

caught	fought
thought	daughter
bought	taught
laugh	brought
through	ought
enough	cough

VOCABULARY

Vocabulary Game

👥 Pairs	🕐 30 minutes
Objective	Use Key Vocabulary words to create a crossword puzzle.
Materials	4 copies of Activity Master 5–2 on page R24 (2 per player)

- Pick four Key Vocabulary words from *Yunmi and Halmoni's Trip.* Don't tell your partner what words you are using.

- With a pencil, write the words on one copy of the grid, either across or down, one letter to a square. Make sure that each word crosses another word where they share a letter. (You might need to erase and move some words around.)

- Put a number in the box that contains the <u>first</u> letter of <u>each</u> word. Start with the number 1. This copy is your answer key.

- On the other grid, make a copy of the puzzle <u>without</u> the words filled in. Outline the boxes for each word. Add the numbers.

- Write the definition of each word next to the numbers below the grid. These are the clues.

- Trade puzzles with your partner and solve.

Consider copying and laminating these activities for use in centers.

LISTENING/SPEAKING

Say It Without Words

👥👥👥 Groups	🕐 30 minutes
Objective	Act out a story scene without words.
Materials	Anthology

Many people visit Korea and other countries without knowing the language. Often they communicate nonverbally, or without words. Here are some examples of nonverbal communication:

- facial expressions
- movements
- gestures
- pantomime
- posture

- Select a scene from the story to act out without words. Look for one that shows strong emotions. The reunion at the airport is a good example.

- Have each group member choose a character to portray.

- Decide what emotion or message you want to communicate and how to convey it without words.

- Practice the scene. Remember to move with confidence and control. Facial expressions and gestures can be very effective.

- Act out the scene for other groups.

- Afterwards, discuss which nonverbal actions were the most successful. Take notes.

> Remember, nonverbal skills such as hand gestures and facial expressions can help with oral presentations, too.

STRUCTURAL ANALYSIS

Possessive Matchup

👥 Pairs	🕐 15 minutes
Objective	Form singular and plural possessives.
Materials	Index cards

Play this game with your partner. To prepare:

- Cut an index card in half. Write an apostrophe (') on one half and an *s* on the other half. Set these cards aside.

- Write these words on separate index cards: *a, two, one, some, many, five.* Write a number *1* on the back of each card.

- On six more cards, write a word that names a person, such as *grandmother, parent,* or *foreigner.* Write the number *2* on the back of each one.

- On six more cards, write a noun, such as *voice, house,* or *relatives.* Write the number *3* on the back of each of these.

- Mix up each set of cards and place each set in a pile, number side up.

To play the game, take turns with your partner.

- Turn over one card from each pile.

- Read the phrase aloud.

- Decide if you need to make the word on card 2 a singular possessive or a plural possessive. Put the apostrophe card and the *s* card in the correct order and write the phrase on a piece of paper.

- Have your partner check your work.

a	parent	'	s	trip

Brothers Are Forever

Summary *Max is excited about seeing his older brother Russ at his college in London. But when he hears Russ's new accent and the new words he's begun to use, he is upset. It takes a heart-to-heart talk for the two brothers to reestablish ties.*

Building Background and Vocabulary

Ask students if they have ever visited a place where people have different customs and ways of talking. Explain that while British people speak English, they use some expressions that are different from those used in U.S. English. Preview the story with students, using the story vocabulary when possible.

Comprehension Skill: Predicting Outcomes

Have students read the Strategy Focus on the book flap. Remind students to use the strategy and to make predictions about what will happen next as they read the book. (See the Leveled Readers Teacher's Guide for **Vocabulary and Comprehension Practice Masters.**)

Responding

Have partners discuss how to answer the questions on the inside back cover.

Think About the Selection Sample answers:

1. They go to visit Max's brother Russ, who is going to school there.
2. Max doesn't like the British words and phrases Russ uses.
3. Accept reasonable responses, such as trying to learn and use the British words and phrases.

Making Connections Responses will vary.

Building Fluency

Model Read aloud page 4. Point out that the fourth sentence is a question and should be read with the correct inflection.

Practice Have students work with partners to find other questions in the story. Partners can take turns reading the questions with inflection. If students have difficulty finding examples, point out the last sentence on page 15.

Vocabulary

Introduce the Key Vocabulary and ask students to complete the BLM.

accent way of speaking typical of a region or country, *p. 6*

chums British term for pals; friends, *p. 6*

flatmate British term for person sharing an apartment with another person, *p. 10*

blurted out said suddenly without thinking, *p. 15*

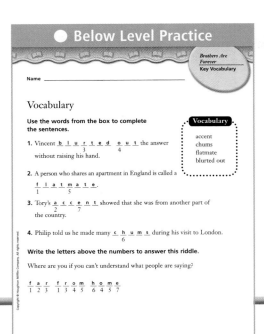

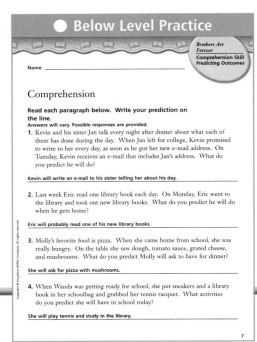

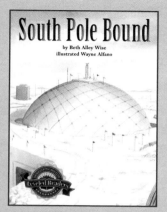

South Pole Bound

Summary *Dr. Chang is a scientist who is temporarily stationed at the South Pole Weather Dome. Katie resents the idea that her mother is working so far from home, until she and her father visit the lab and help with some of the experiments.*

Vocabulary

Introduce the Key Vocabulary and ask students to complete the BLM.

passports* government documents that allow people to travel in foreign countries, *p. 6*

skyscrapers* very tall buildings, *p. 7*

bustling* full of activity, busy, *p. 7*

sightseeing* visiting interesting places; touring, *p. 8*

resented felt hurt and angry, *p. 9*

*Forms of these words are Anthology Key Vocabulary words.

Building Background and Vocabulary

Ask students if they know where the South Pole is located, and discuss what the weather is like in that part of the world. Preview the story with students, using the story vocabulary when possible.

Comprehension Skill: Predicting Outcomes

Have students read the Strategy Focus on the book flap. Remind students to use the strategy and to make predictions about what will happen next as they read the book. (See the Leveled Readers Teacher's Guide for **Vocabulary and Comprehension Practice Masters.**)

Responding

Have partners discuss how to answer the questions on the inside back cover.

Think About the Selection Sample answers:

1. She is studying the weather there.

2. She misses having her mother with her; she doesn't understand why her mother would want to be so far away.

3. Katie was able to help with some experiments and could see why her mother found it interesting.

4. Possible response: I think Katie would like to visit again. I think she is now interested in the work her mother does there.

Making Connections Responses will vary.

Building Fluency

Model Read aloud page 6. Explain that the phrases following dialogue, like *Katie begged her Dad,* can tell how something is said.

Practice Have students work in pairs to find other examples of phrases that tell how a character speaks. Have them read the dialogue to their partners.

▲ On Level Practice

Name _____

South Pole Bound
Key Vocabulary

Vocabulary

Use the words from the box to complete the sentences. Write the answers in the puzzle.

Vocabulary
passports
skyscrapers
bustling
sightseeing
resented

Across

3. Cara was going on a ____sightseeing____ trip with her grandmother.

4. They needed ____passports____ because they were going to a foreign city.

5. She had ____resented____ that she wasn't allowed to go to camp with her sister.

Down

1. Those were the tallest ____skyscrapers____ Cara ever saw.

2. She had never been in such a lively, ____bustling____ place.

5

▲ On Level Practice

Name _____

South Pole Bound
Comprehension Skill
Predicting Outcomes

Comprehension

Read each passage below. Use clues from the story and what you know. Write your prediction on the line.
Possible responses shown.

1. Katie arrives home from the South Pole and e-mails her mother. What do you predict she tells her mother?

Katie might say that she had a great time, that she loved seeing what her mother does and meeting the other scientists. She might also say that she loved riding on Peppy. She would probably say that she can't wait to see her mother again.

2. When Katie returns to school, her teacher asks her to tell the class about her trip. What do you predict Katie will say about her mother's work?

Katie might say that her mother works with very nice people and does experiments in cold, snowy weather. She might tell about her test ride on Peppy.

3. Katie's school is having a science fair. What kind of science project do you predict Katie will do? Katie might do a project about blowing bubbles in very cold and very hot places.

4. A year later, Katie's mother has an opportunity to go to the rain forest to study the weather for five weeks. What do you predict Katie's reaction will be? Katie might be sad not to see her mother for five weeks, but excited that her mother has this opportunity. She might also be excited to go visit her mother in another interesting place.

7

■ ABOVE LEVEL

The Same, But Different

Summary *When Mariah arrives in London with her mother, she isn't sure that she will enjoy spending time with her mother's family in a foreign country. By the time she leaves, however, she appreciates the time she spent with family, sightseeing and reminiscing, and realizes that life in London is "the same, but different."*

Vocabulary

Introduce the Key Vocabulary and ask students to complete the BLM.

passport* a government document that allows a person to travel in foreign countries, *p. 2*

sightseeing* visiting interesting places; touring, *p. 6*

vendor* someone who sells things, *p. 6*

foreigners* people who come from a different country or place, *p. 10*

bustling* full of activity, *p. 11*

*Forms of these words are Anthology Key Vocabulary words.

Building Background and Vocabulary

Ask students if they have ever visited a place where people have different customs and ways of talking. Preview the story with students, using the story vocabulary when possible.

◉ Comprehension Skill: Predicting Outcomes

Have students read the Strategy Focus on the book flap. Remind students to use the strategy and to make predictions about what will happen next as they read the book. (See the Leveled Readers Teacher's Guide for **Vocabulary and Comprehension Practice Masters**.)

Responding

Have partners discuss how to answer the questions on the inside back cover.

Think About the Selection Sample answers:

1. They are going to visit her mother's family.

2. Possible responses: Cars drive on the "wrong" side of the road. Potato chips are called "crisps." French fries are called "chips."

3. Possible response: She feels a little homesick and is confused because things are almost like her life at home, but not quite.

4. Responses will vary.

Making Connections Responses will vary.

◉ Building Fluency

Model Read aloud the final paragraph on page 5. Explain that readers should pause when they reach a dash in a sentence.

Practice Have partners find the other sentence from the book with a dash (page 9) and take turns reading it appropriately.

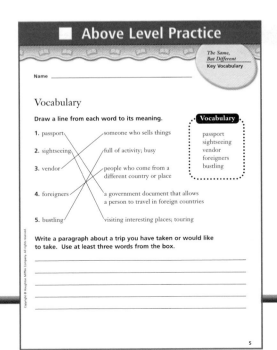

Max Visits London

Summary *Max and his family visit his older brother Russ. Max fears that Russ's new life and interests in London have become more important to him than his little brother. Max acts out his fears by disliking everything British. When Russ reassures Max that brothers are forever, Max feels better. And suddenly, he likes London better, too.*

Vocabulary

Introduce the Key Vocabulary and ask students to complete the BLM.

excited emotionally stirred, *p. 3*

chums close friends, pals, *p. 6*

accent a way of speaking that is typical of a certain group or country, *p. 6*

custom something that members of a group usually do, *p. 8*

sightseeing* visiting interesting places; touring, *p. 14*

forever always, for all times, *p. 16*

*Forms of these words are Anthology Key Vocabulary words.

◆ LANGUAGE SUPPORT

Building Background and Vocabulary

Ask students what might be different in London, England. Explain that, even though they speak English, people in England often use different words than Americans do. Ask students to share any examples. Then distribute the **Build Background Practice Master,** and have partners complete the page.

Comprehension Skill: Predicting Outcomes

Have students read the Strategy Focus on the book flap. Remind students to use the strategy and to predict what might happen as they read the book. (See the Leveled Readers Teacher's Guide for **Build Background, Vocabulary, and Graphic Organizer Masters**.)

Responding

Have partners discuss how to answer the questions on the inside back cover.

Think About the Selection Sample answers:

1. Russ goes to school in London, England.

2. Possible responses: No, he doesn't want Russ to change because he feels like Russ might not come back home; Once Max realizes that Russ still loves him, Max likes some of the ways Russ is changing.

3. Responses will vary.

Making Connections Responses will vary.

Building Fluency

Model Read aloud pages 10–11, as students follow along in their books. Then have students point to the picture of each speaker, as you reread the dialogue.

Practice Have small groups take the roles of Max, Russ, Ian, and the narrator, and act out the scene. Suggest that students rehearse their parts several times before performing for the whole class.

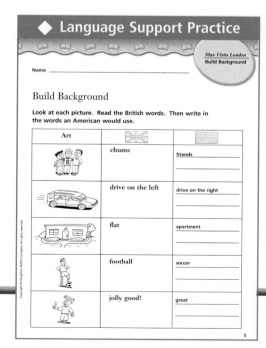

Lesson Overview

Literature

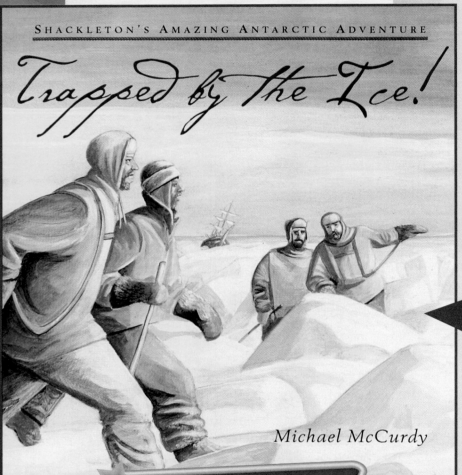

SHACKLETON'S AMAZING ANTARCTIC ADVENTURE

Trapped by the Ice!

Michael McCurdy

Selection Summary

In the middle of Sir Ernest Shackleton's Antarctic expedition, his ship *Endurance* is trapped and crushed in the ice. Shackleton and some of his men then set out on a long and perilous journey across ice, stormy seas, and jagged mountains to get help. They make it, and then go back to save the rest of the crew.

1 Background and Vocabulary

2 Main Selection

Trapped by the Ice!
Genre: Narrative Nonfiction

3 Media Link

Instructional Support

Planning and Practice

- Planning and classroom management
- Reading instruction
- Skill lessons
- Materials for reaching all learners

- Independent practice for skills, Level 3.5

- Newsletters
- Selection Summaries
- Assignment Cards
- Observation Checklists
- Selection Tests

- Transparencies
- Strategy Posters
- Blackline Masters

Reaching All Learners

Coordinated lessons, activities, and projects for additional reading instruction

For
- Classroom teacher
- Extended day
- Pull out
- Resource teacher
- Reading specialist

Technology

Audio Selection

Trapped by the Ice!

Get Set for Reading CD-ROM
- Background building
- Vocabulary support
- Selection Summary in English and Spanish

Accelerated Reader®
- Practice quizzes for the selection

www.eduplace.com

Log on to Education Place for more activities related to the selection, including vocabulary support—

e • Glossary
e • WordGame

Leveled Books for Reaching All Learners

Leveled Readers and Leveled Practice

- Independent reading for building fluency

- Topic, comprehension strategy, and vocabulary linked to main selection

- Lessons in Teacher's Edition, pages 251O–251R

- Leveled practice for every book

Technology

Leveled Readers
Audio available

Book Adventure®

- Practice quizzes for the Leveled Theme Paperbacks
  www.bookadventure.org

● BELOW LEVEL

Iceberg Rescue

by Sarah Amada
illustrated by S. Saelig Gallagher

▲ ON LEVEL

Racing Danger

by Minnie Timenti

illustrated by Tom McNeely

● Below Level Practice

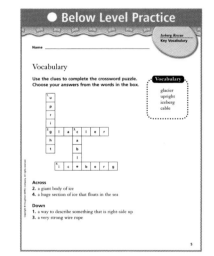

▲ On Level Practice

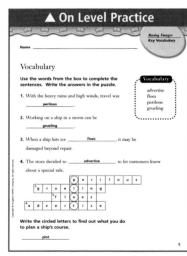

● Below Level Practice

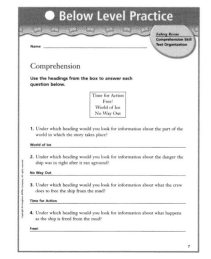

▲ On Level Practice

■ ABOVE LEVEL

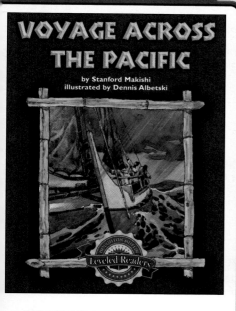

VOYAGE ACROSS THE PACIFIC
by Stanford Makishi
illustrated by Dennis Albetski

Leveled Readers

◆ LANGUAGE SUPPORT

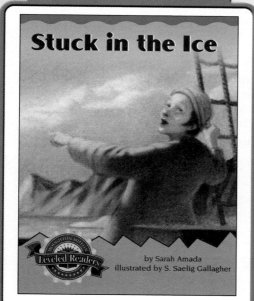

Stuck in the Ice

Leveled Readers

by Sarah Amada
illustrated by S. Saelig Gallagher

Leveled Theme Paperbacks

- Extended independent reading in Theme-related trade books
- Lessons in Teacher's Edition, pages R2–R7

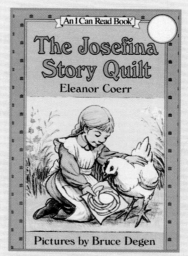

An I Can Read Book

The Josefina Story Quilt
Eleanor Coerr

Pictures by Bruce Degen

Below Level

A Child's Glacier Bay

Text by Kimberly Corral with Hannah Corral
Photographs by Roy Corral

On Level

Balto and the Great Race

by Elizabeth Cody Kimmel
Illustrated by Nora Koerber

Challenge

■ Above Level Practice

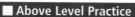

Name _____

Voyage Across the Pacific
Key Vocabulary

Vocabulary

Use the words from the box to complete the sentences.

Vocabulary
navigate
deserted
perilous
grueling

1. We thought we could n a v i g a t e
    ‾3‾   ‾6‾
the canoe through any type of water.

2. We had always wanted to visit the
d e s e r t e d island.
‾7‾   ‾8‾

3. A thunderstorm blew in, making our journey a
p e r i l o u s one.
‾5‾   ‾2‾

4. We were not prepared for the long, g r u e l i n g day we had.
                                        ‾4‾   ‾1‾

Write the letters above the numbers to answer this riddle.

What feels good after a hard week's work?

a l o n g   r e s t
1 2 3 4   5 6 7 8

5

◆ Language Support Practice

Name _____

Stuck in the Ice
Build Background

Build Background
Exploring the World Around Us

Take this paper and a pencil and find a place to stand in the room. Follow the steps below.
Answers will vary.

1. Write down the two most important things you see.

_____

2. Turn one step to your right and write down two more things.

_____

3. Turn another step to your right and add two more things.

_____

4. Now take a final right turn, look carefully and write down two more things you see.

_____

5. Make illustrations of what you wrote down. Use the back of this page.

5

■ Above Level Practice

Name _____

Voyage Across the Pacific
Comprehension Skill
Text Organization

Comprehension

Read each question below. Write your answer on the line.
Answers will vary. Possible responses are provided.

1. What information does the heading *The Voyage Begins* provide?

The heading tells me that the preparation is complete and the canoe and its crew are
ready to start the voyage. I expect that I will read what happens on the journey.

2. What information do the illustrations on pages 4–5 provide?

These illustrations help me understand the design of the boat and see the parts
described in the selection.

3. What information does the illustration on page 11 provide?

The illustration shows crew members cooking a meal on the canoe. I can also see how
there isn't a lot of space on the canoe. The illustration reminds me that they had to go
about their lives very close to everyone else. During those 34 days, the crew members
never had time to be by themselves.

4. In what ways do the dates in the selection help you understand the sequence of events?

The dates tell when the project started, when the boat was ready to be tested, and
when the journey actually began. This information helped me understand that the
group planned and prepared for about three years.

7

◆ Language Support Practice

Stuck in the Ice
Key Vocabulary

Name _____

Vocabulary

Write a word from the box to complete each sentence.

Vocabulary
cable
explorers
glacier
iceberg
stuck
tide

1. If you cannot move, you are ____stuck____

2. People who go to new and unknown places are
____explorers____

3. A ____cable____ is a heavy piece of rope or
metal that is used often on ships and bridges.

4. A large heavy mass of ice that slowly moves along on the ocean is a
____glacier____

5. A piece of a glacier that falls off is called an ____iceberg____

6. The water in the ocean rises and falls. When the water rises, it is high
____tide____

6

Daily Lesson Plans

 **Technology**
Lesson Planner CD-ROM allows you to customize the chart below to develop your own lesson plans.

T Skill tested on Theme Skills Test and/or Integrated Theme Test

 50–60 minutes

Reading
Comprehension

Leveled Readers
- Fluency Practice
- Independent Reading

 20–30 minutes

Word Work
Phonics/Decoding
Vocabulary
Spelling

 20–30 minutes

Writing and Oral Language
Writing
Grammar
Listening/Speaking/Viewing

DAY 1

Teacher Read Aloud, 213CC–213DD
Going West: Children on the Oregon Trail

Building Background, 214

Key Vocabulary, 215

barren	floes	perilous
crevasse	grueling	terrain
deserted	impassable	

Reading the Selection, 216–245

 Comprehension Skill, 216
Text Organization **T**

Comprehension Strategy, 216
Monitor/Clarify

Leveled Readers
Iceberg Rescue
Racing Danger
Voyage Across the Pacific
Stuck in the Ice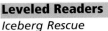

Lessons and Leveled Practice, 251O–251R

Phonics/Decoding, 217
Phonics/Decoding Strategy

Vocabulary, 216–245
Selection Vocabulary

Spelling, 251E
VCCV Pattern **T**

🖊 **Writing,** 251K
Introducing Learning Logs

Grammar, 251I
Possessive Pronouns **T**

Daily Language Practice
1. on mundy, the men watched they ship sink. (On; Monday; their)
2. Shackleton asked his men to folow him on him's journey. (follow; his)

Listening/Speaking/Viewing, 213CC–213DD, 229
Teacher Read Aloud, Stop and Think

DAY 2

Reading the Selection, 216–245

Comprehension Check, 245

Responding, 246
Think About the Selection

 Comprehension Skill Preview, 233
Text Organization **T**

Leveled Readers
Iceberg Rescue
Racing Danger
Voyage Across the Pacific
Stuck in the Ice

Lessons and Leveled Practice, 251O–251R

 Structural Analysis, 251C
VCCV Pattern **T**

Vocabulary, 216–245
Selection Vocabulary

Spelling, 251E
VCCV Pattern Review and Practice **T**

🖊 **Writing,** 251K
Writing a Learning Log Entry

Grammar, 251I
Possessive Pronouns Practice **T**

Daily Language Practice
3. All of a sudn, the men were stranded in they's boat. (sudden; their)
4. There path went through impassable terrain. (Their)

Listening/Speaking/Viewing, 245, 246
Wrapping Up, Responding

Target Skills of the Week

Comprehension	Monitor/Clarify; Text Organization
Vocabulary	Homophones
Phonics/Decoding	VCCV Pattern
Fluency	Leveled Readers

DAY 3

Rereading the Selection

Rereading for Writer's Craft, 239
Setting

Rereading for Genre, 243
Narrative Nonfiction

Comprehension Skill, 251A–251B
Text Organization **T**

Leveled Readers

Iceberg Rescue
Racing Danger
Voyage Across the Pacific
Stuck in the Ice

Lessons and Leveled Practice, 251O–251R

Phonics Review, 251D
Double Consonants

Vocabulary, 251G
Homophones **T**

Spelling, 251F
Vocabulary: Classifying; VCCV Pattern
Practice **T**

Writing, 251L
Dates and Times **T**

Grammar, 251J
Pronoun Game **T**

Daily Language Practice

The deserted island was cold and not at all prity. (pretty)

Tom never foregot his's meeting with the sea leopard? (forgot; his; leopard.)

DAY 4

Reading the Media Link, 248–251
"Shackleton's Real-Life Voyage"

Skill: How to Read a Photo Essay

Rereading for Visual Literacy, 250
Photography

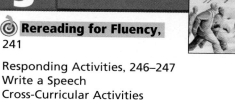

Comprehension Skill Review, 221
Sequence of Events

Leveled Readers

Iceberg Rescue
Racing Danger
Voyage Across the Pacific
Stuck in the Ice

Lessons and Leveled Practice, 251O–251R

Phonics/Decoding, 248–251
Apply Phonics/Decoding Strategy to Link

Vocabulary, 251M
Language Center: Building Vocabulary

Spelling, 251F
VCCV Game, Proofreading **T**

Writing, 2251L
Writing Game

Grammar, 251J
Possessive Pronouns Practice **T**

Daily Language Practice
7. Did one man catch him's foot in an icy crevasse (his; crevasse?)
8. Untill that time, the crew ate they food and saved they water. (Until; their; their)

Listening/Speaking/Viewing, 251
Discuss the Link

DAY 5

Rereading for Fluency, 241

Responding Activities, 246–247
Write a Speech
Cross-Curricular Activities

Information and Study Skills, 251H
Using a Time Line **T**

Comprehension Skill Review, 223
Topic, Main Idea, Supporting Detail

Leveled Readers

Iceberg Rescue
Racing Danger
Voyage Across the Pacific
Stuck in the Ice

Lessons and Leveled Practice, 251O–251R

Phonics, 251N
Language Center: VCCV Match

Vocabulary, 251M
Language Center: Vocabulary Game

Spelling, 251F
Test: VCCV Pattern **T**

Writing, 251L
Sharing Writing

Grammar, 251J, 251M
Proofreading: *its, it's*
Language Center: Possessive Pronouns

Daily Language Practice
9. mine teacher told us about Shackleton and he's crew. (My; his)
10. Affter that, we wrote ours report about hims journey. (After; our; his)

Listening/Speaking/Viewing, 251N
Language Center: Practice Group Problem Solving

Managing Flexible Groups

	DAY 1	**DAY 2**
WHOLE CLASS	• Teacher Read Aloud (TE pp. 213CC–213DD) • Building Background, Introducing Vocabulary (TE pp. 214–215) • Comprehension Strategy: Introduce (TE p. 216) • Comprehension Skill: Introduce (TE p. 216) • Purpose Setting (TE p. 217) **After reading first half of *Trapped by the Ice!*** • Stop and Think (TE p. 229)	**After reading *Trapped by the Ice!*** • Wrapping Up (TE p. 245) • Comprehension Check (Practice Book p. 122) • Responding: Think About the Selection (TE p. 246) • Comprehension Skill: Preview (TE p. 233)
SMALL GROUPS		
Extra Support	**TEACHER-LED** • Preview *Trapped by the Ice!* to Stop and Think (TE pp. 216–229). • Support reading with Extra Support/ Intervention notes (TE pp. 217, 221, 228, 234, 243, 244).	**Partner or Individual Work** • Reread first half of *Trapped by the Ice!* (TE pp. 216–229). • Preview, read second half (TE pp. 230–245). • Comprehension Check (Practice Book p. 122)
Challenge	**Individual Work** • Begin "The Arctic and Antarctica" (Challenge Handbook p. 42). • Extend reading with Challenge note (TE p. 244).	**Individual Work** • Continue work on activity (Challenge Handbook p. 42).
English Language Learners	**TEACHER-LED** • Preview vocabulary and *Trapped by the Ice!* to Stop and Think (TE pp. 215–229). • Support reading with English Language Learners notes (TE pp. 214, 218, 222, 227, 232, 236, 239, 245).	**TEACHER-LED** • Review first half of *Trapped by the Ice!* (TE pp. 216–229). ✔ • Preview, read second half (TE pp. 230–245). • Begin Comprehension Check together (Practice Book p. 122).

Independent Activities

- Get Set for Reading CD-ROM
- Journals: selection notes, questions
- Complete, review Practice Book (pp. 120–124) and Leveled Readers Practice Blackline Masters (TE pp. 251O–251R).
- Assignment Cards (Teacher's Resource Blackline Masters pp. 83–84)
- Leveled Readers (TE pp. 251O–251R), Leveled Theme Paperbacks (TE pp. R2–R7), or book from Leveled Bibliography (TE pp. 148E–148F)

✔ Opportunity to informally assess oral reading rate

FLEXIBLE GROUPS

Leveled Instruction and Leveled Practice

- Rereading: Lessons on Writer's Craft, Genre (TE pp. 239, 243)
- Comprehension Skill: Main lesson (TE pp. 251A–251B)

- Reading the Media Link (TE pp. 248–251): Skill lesson (TE p. 248)
- Rereading the Link: Visual Literacy lesson (TE p. 250)
- Comprehension Skill: First Comprehension Review lesson (TE p. 221)

- Responding: Select from Activities (TE pp. 246–247)
- Information and Study Skills (TE p. 251H)
- Comprehension Skill: Second Comprehension Review lesson (TE p. 223)

TEACHER-LED

Reread, review Comprehension Check (Practice Book p. 122).

Preview Leveled Reader: Below Level (TE p. 251O), or read book from Leveled Bibliography (TE pp. 148E–148F). ✔

Partner or Individual Work

- Reread the Media Link (TE pp. 248–251).
- Complete Leveled Reader: Below Level (TE p. 251O), or read book from Leveled Bibliography (TE pp. 148E–148F).

TEACHER-LED

- Comprehension Skill: Reteaching lesson (TE p. R12)
- Reread Leveled Theme Paperback: Below Level (TE pp. R2–R3), or read book from Leveled Bibliography (TE pp. 148E–148F). ✔

TEACHER-LED

Teacher check-in: Assess progress (Challenge Handbook p. 42).

Preview Leveled Reader: Above Level (TE p. 251Q), or read book from Leveled Bibliography (TE pp. 148E–148F). ✔

Individual Work

- Complete activity (Challenge Handbook p. 42).
- Complete Leveled Reader: Above Level (TE p. 251Q), or read book from Leveled Bibliography (TE pp. 148E–148F).

TEACHER-LED

- Evaluate activity and plan format for sharing (Challenge Handbook p. 42).
- Reread Leveled Theme Paperback: Above Level (TE pp. R6–R7), or read book from Leveled Bibliography (TE pp. 148E–148F). ✔

Partner or Individual Work

Complete Comprehension Check (Practice Book p. 122).

Begin Leveled Reader: Language Support (TE p. 251R), or read book from Leveled Bibliography (TE pp. 148E–148F).

TEACHER-LED

- Reread the Media Link (TE pp. 248–251) ✔ and review Link Skill (TE p. 250).
- Complete Leveled Reader: Language Support (TE p. 251R), or read book from Leveled Bibliography (TE pp. 148E–148F). ✔

Partner or Individual Work

- Reread book from Leveled Bibliography (TE pp. 148E–148F).

Responding activities (TE pp. 246–247)

Language Center activities (TE pp. 251M–251N)

Fluency Practice: Reread *Across the Wide Dark Sea; Yunmi and Halmoni's Trip; Trapped by the Ice!* ✔

Activities relating to *Trapped by the Ice!* at Education Place www.eduplace.com

Turn the page for more independent activities.

Classroom Management

Independent Activities

CLASSROOM MANAGEMENT

Assign these activities while you work with small groups.

Differentiated Instruction for Small Groups

- **Handbook for English Language Learners,** pp. 186–195

- **Extra Support Handbook,** pp. 182–191

Independent Activities

- Language Center, pp. 251M–251N

- Challenge/Extension Activities, Theme Resources, pp. R13, R19

- **Classroom Management Handbook,** Activity Masters CM5-9–CM5-12

- **Challenge Handbook,** pp. 42–43

Look for more activities in the Classroom Management Kit.

Social Studies

Map It!

👥 **Pairs**	🕐 **45 minutes**
Objective	Create a map of Shackleton's route.
Materials	A globe or atlas, Anthology

Work with a partner to make a map that shows Shackleton's route. Trace a map of Antarctica to make an outline map.

- Using a globe or an atlas, locate all the landmarks mentioned in *Trapped by the Ice!*

- Review the selection to recall Shackleton's route. Draw it on your map.

- Mark each place the crew stopped on the route.

- Next to each place, write the date when the men were there.

Science

A Harsh Environment

👤 **Singles**	🕐 **45 minutes**
Objective	Write a description of the Antarctic environment.
Materials	Reference sources

Write a description of the Antarctic environment. For example, tell what the physical features are and what living things can survive there. For your research, use the following steps

- Reread "Exploring Antarctica."

- Review details in *Trapped by the Ice!* and "Shackleton's Real-Life Voyage."

- Use an encyclopedia or other reference source.

Consider copying and laminating these activities for use in centers.

Careers

Explorers Wanted!

👤 Singles	🕐 15 minutes
Objective	Write a job description.

Write a job description for a crew member on an Antarctic expedition. Before writing, ask yourself the following questions:

What qualities would make a good crew member?

What special skills would be most helpful on such an expedition?

What kind of experience is necessary?

Are there rewards other than money?

Science

What's the Weather?

👤 Singles	🕐 30 minutes
Objective	Write a weather report for Antarctica.
Materials	A computer with Internet access

Many scientists and other professionals work in Antarctica. Others study the continent from warmer climates. Write a weather report for a place in Antarctica. Follow these steps:

- Go to a weather site on the Internet for Antarctica such as http://www.wunderground.com/global/AN_ST_Index.html.

- Click on the map or place names to find the current weather conditions there and a forecast.

- Use the data you collect to write a weather report for a place in Antarctica that could be posted on the website.

- Include in your report a weather map with temperature data.

Health

Frostbite

👥 Pairs	🕐 30 minutes
Objective	Research the causes and effects of frostbite.
Materials	Reference sources, art supplies

When Shackleton, Big Tom, and Skipper Worsley arrived at the whaling station, their faces were blackened by frostbite. Frostbite is a serious health hazard faced by people on Antarctica or by anyone exposed to freezing temperatures for a long time.

Use an encyclopedia or another reference source to research frostbite with a partner. Determine the causes and effects of frostbite. Then write a survival guide for people who are exposed to the cold and at risk for frostbite. Think about

- ways to create warmth
- ways to protect the skin
- other outdoor survival tips

Add illustrations and a cover and share your work with your class.

Listening Comprehension

OBJECTIVE
- Listen to identify text organization.

Building Background

Explain to students that you are going to read aloud a nonfiction article that describes what it was like for pioneers to travel west on the Oregon Trail.

- Discuss with students how traveling west in the 1800s would have been different from traveling west today.

Fluency Modeling

Explain that as you read aloud, you will be modeling fluent oral reading. Ask students to listen carefully to your phrasing and your expression, or tone of voice and emphasis.

COMPREHENSION SKILL

Text Organization

Explain that authors of nonfiction use text organization to present information clearly. They may

- use features, such as titles, headings, quotations, introduction, and captions
- organize paragraphs by sequence or by main ideas and supporting details

Purpose Setting Read the selection aloud, asking students to think about how the text is organized as they listen. Then use the Guiding Comprehension questions to assess students' understanding. Reread the selection for clarification as needed.

213CC THEME 5: Voyagers

Teacher Read Aloud

Going West: Children on the Oregon Trail
by Helen Wieman Bledsoe

1

"In the month of April 1844, my father got the Oregon fever and we started west."

Matilda Sager wrote these words from her new home in Oregon. To get there, she traveled for six months in a covered wagon. With her parents, brothers, and sisters, she crossed plains and mountains, deserts and rivers. They traveled along the route called the Oregon Trail. The trail stretched more than 2,000 miles, from Independence, Missouri, all the way to the Pacific Ocean.

The Sagers were pioneers, people who do something new and different. In those days, most Americans lived east of the Mississippi River. Traveling thousands of miles west to Oregon was a new idea. And life in Oregon was very different from anything the pioneers had ever known before!

Like many other pioneers, the Sagers traveled west in a long line of covered wagons. This was called a wagon train. The trip was a hard and dangerous one.

2 What was it like to travel west on the Oregon Trail in 1844? First of all, you had to get ready for a very long and difficult trip. It might take as long as a year to prepare. Families needed to bring everything necessary for months on the trail.

Once you got going, it was a long, long walk. Only babies and toddlers rode in the wagons with their mothers. All other children and adults had to walk. There wasn't room in the wagon for everyone, and the load would have been too heavy for the oxen to pull.

There was a lot to keep you busy along the trail. Everyone had a job to do. Girls cared for younger children. They helped their mothers cook over the campfire. They washed clothes in the rivers. They gathered wood for fires. And they milked the cows.

Boys looked after the animals and got the oxen ready to pull the wagons every morning. They added to the food supply by hunting rabbits and squirrels with their fathers. When families had to cross wide rivers, boys and men had to unload the wagons and put everything into small boats. The oxen swam across the river, pulling the wagon. Then everything had to be put back into the wagons on the other side.

The trip wasn't all work, though. Late every afternoon, the wagon train stopped for the night. Usually, all the wagons pulled together into a circle. The animals were penned inside. Now it was time for games, stories, songs, and lessons. Sometimes adults would read aloud around the campfire, often from the Bible.

There were many dangers along the trail. In the Great Plains, the grass was so tall that small children sometimes got lost in it. Playing near the rolling wagons was dangerous too. Pioneer Amelia Stewart wrote about one day: "Chet had a very narrow escape from being run over. . . . He escaped with only a bad scare." Catherine Sager wasn't so lucky, though. Her leg was badly broken under a wagon wheel.

Illness was always a threat. Diseases like measles, mumps, cholera, malaria, and mountain fever took many lives. When fever struck the Sagers' wagon train, both Mr. and Mrs. Sager died.

Friendly families offered to divide the seven Sager children among the wagons. But the Sagers wanted to stay together. The youngest was only five months old. John, the oldest, was fourteen. With other families to help them, the brave Sager children made it all the way to Oregon.

CRITICAL THINKING
Guiding Comprehension

1 **TEXT ORGANIZATION** What is the topic of this selection? (children going west on the Oregon Trail) What text features tell you this? (title, quotation, introductory paragraphs)

2 **TEXT ORGANIZATION** What kind of information does the opening question of this paragraph, *What was it like to travel west on the Oregon Trail in 1844*, suggest will follow? (Sample answer: details about life on the trail)

3 **TEXT ORGANIZATION** What details support the main idea *There was a lot to keep you busy along the trail?* (information about girls' and boys' chores, such as cooking, cleaning, gathering wood and food, tending animals, loading the wagons; details about what travelers did for fun)

Discussion Options

Personal Response Ask students to discuss qualities they admire in the Sager family and in the other pioneers who traveled west.

⭐ **Connecting/Comparing** Have students compare Yunmi's trip to Korea with the Sager children's trip west, including how long the trips took, what was fun or difficult about them, and how they think Yunmi and the Sager children each felt about their trips.

English Language Learners

Language Development
Display a map of the United States and point out where the Oregon Trail began (Independence, Missouri) and where it ended (Oregon City, on the coast of Oregon). Invite students to describe some of the hardships they heard about traveling the Oregon Trail, and write them down.

Building Background

Key Concept: Shackleton's Antarctic Journey

Remind students that the stories in this theme all deal with voyages. Point out that *Trapped by the Ice!* tells a true story about a perilous voyage to Antarctica, the continent located at the South Pole. Discuss what challenges such a journey might bring. Then use "Exploring Antarctica" on Anthology pages 214–215 to build background and introduce key vocabulary.

- Have a student read aloud "Exploring Antarctica."

- Have students study the map and the photo showing the location of Antarctica and its topographical features.

Background and Vocabulary

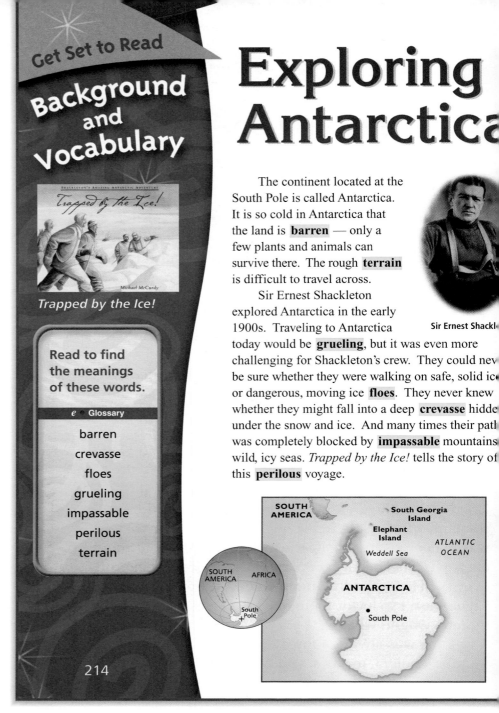

Trapped by the Ice!

Read to find the meanings of these words.

e ▸ Glossary

barren
crevasse
floes
grueling
impassable
perilous
terrain

214

Exploring Antarctica

The continent located at the South Pole is called Antarctica. It is so cold in Antarctica that the land is **barren** — only a few plants and animals can survive there. The rough **terrain** is difficult to travel across.

Sir Ernest Shackleton explored Antarctica in the early 1900s. Traveling to Antarctica today would be **grueling**, but it was even more challenging for Shackleton's crew. They could nev[er] be sure whether they were walking on safe, solid ic[e] or dangerous, moving ice **floes**. They never knew whether they might fall into a deep **crevasse** hidde[n] under the snow and ice. And many times their path was completely blocked by **impassable** mountains [or] wild, icy seas. *Trapped by the Ice!* tells the story of this **perilous** voyage.

Sir Ernest Shackl[eton]

SOUTH AMERICA
South Georgia Island
Elephant Island
ATLANTIC OCEAN
Weddell Sea
SOUTH AMERICA   AFRICA
South Pole
ANTARCTICA
• South Pole

English Language Learners

Supporting Comprehension

Beginning/Preproduction Have students listen to the article. Ask them to draw or act out how a crevasse might be perilous for travelers.

Early Production and Speech Emergence Have students repeat these Key Vocabulary words after you: *barren, grueling, impassable, terrain*. Help students find context clues in the article to define the words.

Intermediate and Advanced Fluency Have partners take turns asking and answering questions about the article. Encourage them to use the boldfaced vocabulary words in their questions and answers.

215

Introducing Vocabulary

Key Vocabulary

These words support the Key Concept and appear in the selection.

barren having little plant or animal life

crevasse deep hole or crack

deserted empty; not lived in, or having few or no people

floes large sheets of floating ice

grueling very tiring

impassable not able to be crossed or traveled through

perilous very dangerous

terrain land, ground, or earth

 e•Glossary
e•WordGame

See Vocabulary notes on pages 218, 220, 222, 224, 226, 230, 232, 234, 236, 238, 240, and 242 for additional words to preview.

Display Transparency 5–19.

- Model how to use context clues to figure out the meaning of *barren* in the first item.

- Have students fill in the remaining blanks, following your example. Have them explain how they figured out each word.

- Ask students to look for these words as they read and to use them as they discuss the Antarctic journey.

Practice/Homework Assign **Practice Book** page 120.

Transparency 5–19

Cold Words!

| barren | deserted | grueling | perilous |
| crevasse | floes | impassable | terrain |

1. Sara hadn't seen any animals or plants on the camping trip.
   "What a ____barren____ land!" she thought.
2. As he hiked along, Patrick stooped to pick up trash from a previous hiker's ____deserted____ camp.
3. It was ____grueling____ to hike while carrying heavy backpacks.
4. The beautiful ____terrain____, which sparkled as sunlight hit the snow, made the challenge worthwhile.
5. Patrick faced a ____perilous____ situation when strong winds blew away his tent.
6. "It could have been worse," Patrick said. "Remember last year's hike, when I fell waist-deep into a hidden ____crevasse____?"
7. The hikers watched penguins sitting on the ice ____floes____ floating in the frozen bay.
8. Sara said, "The mountain will become ____impassable____ if these winds keep up. We'll have to turn around and go back."

Practice Book page 120

Name _____

Trapped by the Ice!
Key Vocabulary

Selection Vocabulary

Cross out the word that doesn't belong.

1. terrain   earth   ~~sky~~   land **(1 point)**
2. grueling   ~~resting~~   tiring   difficult **(1)**
3. perilous   dangerous   ~~safe~~   risky **(1)**
4. deserted   empty   uninhabited   ~~bustling~~ **(1)**

True or False?

5. It is easy to walk across something impassable.
   false **(1)**
6. Ice sheets floating on water are called floes.
   true **(1)**
7. Land that is barren has many plants and animals.
   false **(1)**
8. A crevasse is a deep crack.
   true **(1)**

Introducing Vocabulary 215

COMPREHENSION STRATEGY
Monitor/Clarify

Teacher Modeling Ask a student to read the Strategy Focus aloud. Remind students that to monitor means to pause and check understanding as you read. Explain that rereading, thinking about what you know, and reading ahead can help you clarify, or figure out, anything that is confusing. Then have students read the first paragraph of the story on page 218. Model the strategy.

Think Aloud *The first two sentences tell me that the* Endurance *is trapped in the ice. I guess* Endurance *is the name of a ship. Yes, the next sentence says that Shackleton is standing on the deck. I know that a deck is a part of a ship.*

✔ **Test Prep** Under pressure on a test, some students feel that they can only read a passage in one direction—forward. Emphasize the importance of rereading and reading ahead to clarify understanding.

COMPREHENSION SKILL
Text Organization

Introduce the Graphic Organizer. Tell students that a Text Organization Chart can help them locate specific text features. Explain that, as they read, students will fill out the Text Organization Chart found on **Practice Book** page 121.

- Display **Transparency 5–20.** Have students turn to Anthology page 218.

- Model how to identify and record on the chart the page number (218) with the heading "October 27, 1915."

- Tell students to complete the Text Organization Chart as they read the selection. Monitor students' progress.

MEET THE AUTHOR AND ILLUSTRATOR
Michael McCurdy

Fact File

- Michael McCurdy has illustrated nearly 200 books, including classic stories such as *The Wonderful Wizard of Oz*. He has also written many books himself.

- In art school, McCurdy was a roommate of David McPhail, another children's author and illustrator.

- To create an illustration, McCurdy usually carves a picture on a wood block, covers the carving with ink, and stamps it on paper. But it's never too late to try something new — this story is the first book McCurdy has ever illustrated with paintings.

- McCurdy lives with his family in Massachusetts, where he works on his books in a big red barn. He enjoys playing the piano and hiking.

 Internet

If you'd like to learn more about Michael McCurdy, stop by Education Place.
www.eduplace.com/kids

216

Transparency 5–20
Text Organization Chart

Text Feature	Where It Is	Purpose
heading (date)	pp. 172, 174, 176, 180, 182, 184, 186, 190, 192, 196, 198	helps readers follow the order of events
photograph, caption, illustration	pp. 172–179	help readers understand the text; give more details
definition	p. 190 "Graybeards are monstrous waves that come quietly and quickly, threatening everything in their path."	helps readers understand the meaning of a special term
chronological sequence	Page 172: The first event takes place on October 27, 1915. Page 198: The last event takes place on May 20, 1916.	helps readers understand the order of events

ANNOTATED VERSION

VOYAGERS *Trapped by the Ice!*
Graphic Organizer Text Organization Chart

TRANSPARENCY 5–20
TEACHER'S EDITION PAGE 216

Practice Book page 121

Trapped by the Ice!
Graphic Organizer Text Organization Chart

Name _____

Text Organization Chart

Text Feature	Where It Is	Purpose
heading (date)	pp. 172, 174, 176, 180, 182, 184, 186, 190, 192, 196, 198 **(1 point)**	helps readers follow the order of events **(1)**
photograph, caption, illustration	pp. 172–179 **(1)**	helps readers understand the text; gives more details **(1)**
definition	p. 190 "Graybeards are monstrous waves that come quietly and quickly, threatening everything in their path." **(1)**	helps readers understand the meaning of a special term **(1)**
chronological sequence	Page 172: The first event takes place on October 27, 1915. Page 198: The last event takes place on May 20, 1916. **(1)**	helps readers understand the order of events **(1)**

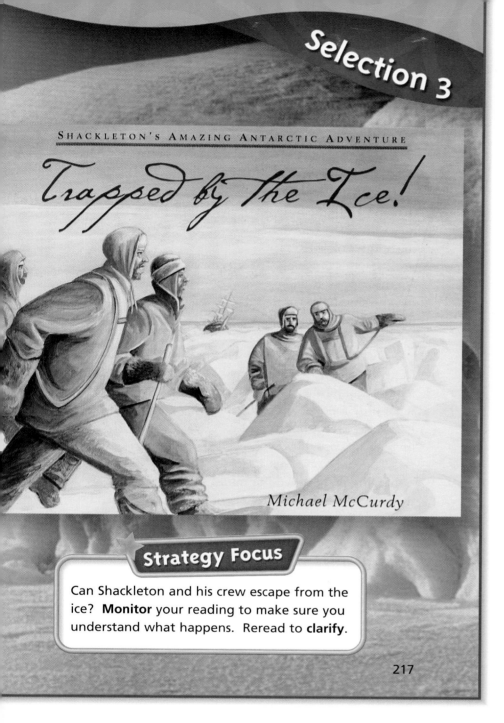

SHACKLETON'S AMAZING ANTARCTIC ADVENTURE

Trapped by the Ice!

Michael McCurdy

Strategy Focus

Can Shackleton and his crew escape from the ice? **Monitor** your reading to make sure you understand what happens. Reread to **clarify**.

217

Extra Support/Intervention

Selection Preview

pages 218–221 Trapped by the ice, the *Endurance* cannot take Shackleton and his crew any farther. How will the voyagers survive in barren, deserted Antarctica?

pages 222–229 The men travel across the ice. They reach open water and decide to try to reach Elephant Island. How important is teamwork to their survival?

pages 230–237 Some must stay at Elephant Island while Shackleton and others go for help. What challenges do they all face?

pages 238–245 Shackleton's group tries to reach a whaling station to get help. Will they rescue the men who were left on Elephant Island?

Purpose Setting

- Remind students that this selection tells about a voyage to Antarctica.

- Have students preview the selection by looking at the illustrations. Ask them to predict what will happen in the story.

- Remind students to revise and add to their predictions as they read.

- Ask students to think about the purpose of text features as they read and add to their Text Organization Charts.

- You may want to preview the Responding questions on Anthology page 246 with students.

Journal ▸ Students can use their journal to record their original predictions and to add new ones.

STRATEGY REVIEW

Phonics/Decoding

Remind students to use the Phonics/Decoding Strategy as they read.

Modeling Write this sentence from *Trapped by the Ice!*: *After an* <u>exhausting</u> *week battling the sea, the men nearly lost all hope.* Point to *exhausting*.

Think Aloud *The beginning probably sounds like ehks as in the word* extra. *Next I see the* a-u *spelling pattern. That makes the* aw *sound, like* August. *I blend it with the letters around it and say* hawst. *I put it together with the* -ing *ending and say* ehks-hawst-ihng. *If I don't pronounce the* h, *it's close to a word I know,* ihg-ZAWST-ihng. *It means "really tiring." That makes sense in the sentence.*

CRITICAL THINKING
Guiding Comprehension

❶ MAKING INFERENCES What can you infer about the fact that even though Shackleton's main goal was to become the first person to cross the South Pole's ice cap, *now his only concern was for his men?* (He's a good, responsible leader who thinks that keeping his men safe is more important than achieving his goal.)

❷ DRAWING CONCLUSIONS Why does the author describe the *Endurance* as *a sad sight?* (The ship has been transformed from the crew's home, which provided warmth, travel, and safety, into a crushed, miserable wreck. The men may feel sad when looking at the ship.)

❸ MAKING INFERENCES How do you think the crew members feel at this point? (scared, sad, worried)

October 27, 1915

The *Endurance* was trapped. Giant blocks of ice were slowly crushing her sides. From the deck, Sir Ernest Shackleton looked at the snow and ice that spread to the horizon. Ten months before, all he had wanted was to be the first person to cross the South Pole's ice cap.

❶ Now his only concern was for his men. What would happen to them — and how much longer did the ship have before it broke apart? The *Endurance* was leaking badly. Shack could not delay.

Shack ordered his crew off the *Endurance* and camp was set up on the frozen Weddell Sea. Tools, tents, scrap lumber for firewood, sleeping bags, and what little food rations and clothing the men had left were saved from their ship, along with three lifeboats in case they ever reached open water.

❷ The *Endurance* was a sad sight now, a useless hulk lying on its side. For months she had been the crew's home. Now they would have to get used **❸** to life on the ice — stranded hundreds of miles from the nearest land.

218

Vocabulary

horizon the line where the earth and the sky meet

delay to wait until later to do something

rations supplies, usually food, that are limited

hulk the body of an old or wrecked ship; something large and clumsy

stranded trapped or stuck in a difficult situation

English Language Learners

Supporting Comprehension
Pause after reading page 218. Ask students to say where the men are and to describe what has happened to the ship. Call on a student to read the date aloud. Discuss what communications and travel were like in 1915. Ask, Do you think anyone can rescue the sailors? Why or why not?

CRITICAL THINKING
Guiding Comprehension

4 MAKING INFERENCES Why do you think the sound of crushing wood startles the men? (Even though they probably knew that the ship might be crushed, it is still shocking to them because they didn't know when it would happen; it is loud.)

5 WRITER'S CRAFT Why do you think the author says that the *Endurance* is swallowed by the Weddell Sea? (to add to the suspense by making the sea seem like something alive; to emphasize that the ship has disappeared forever)

6 DRAWING CONCLUSIONS What kinds of things might Shackleton, Worsley, and Wild have to think about when making a plan for what to do next? (how to travel and carry their supplies; food; water; staying warm; finding shelter; getting off the ice and on land; getting rescued or making it back home)

November 21, 1915

4   Almost one month later, the sound of crushing wood startled the men. It was what they had feared. Turning toward the ship's wreckage, they saw her stern rise slowly in the air, tremble, and slip quickly beneath the ice.

220

Vocabulary

startled surprised, alarmed, or shocked

stern the rear part of a ship or boat

tremble to shake or shiver

skipper captain

Minutes later, the hole had frozen up over the ship. She was gone forever, swallowed by the Weddell Sea. Shack talked with the ship's skipper, Frank Worsley, and his next-in-command, Frankie Wild. Among them, they would have to decide what to do next.

5

6

221

Sequence of Events

Review

- Remind students that the sequence of events is the order in which things happen in a story.

- In *Trapped by the Ice!* events are presented in sequential order (from first to last).

- Show students how to list events in sequential order. Point out that the events do not make sense in the wrong order.

Practice/Apply

- Have students complete a chart like this. (A sample answer is shown.)

And Then What Happened?

1. The Endurance is trapped in the ice.

2. _____

3. _____

Review Skill Trace	
Teach	Theme 1, p. 121A
Reteach	Theme 1, p. R12
▶ Review	p. 221; Theme 1, p. 81; Theme 4, p. 57

Extra Support/Intervention

Strategy Modeling: Monitor/Clarify

Use this example to model the strategy.

I'm a little confused about how the Endurance *sinks. I know that it's been trapped in the ice. Is there water beneath the ice? I reread page 220, and note that the men hear the sound of wood being crushed. Maybe the ice froze around the ship so tightly that it cracked a hole in it and the ship filled up with water. That must be right.*

CRITICAL THINKING
Guiding Comprehension

7 **MAKING INFERENCES** How do you think Shackleton feels when making decisions and giving orders? (great pressure and responsibility)

8 **MAKING INFERENCES** Why does Shackleton decide to try to pull the loads even though it seems impossible? (There's a chance they might succeed and it would have been faster than floating on the ice.)

COMPREHENSION STRATEGY
Monitor/Clarify

Teacher/Student Modeling Help students clarify information on pages 222–223.

- Ask, What details are used to describe the original plan for reaching land? (Lifeboats full of supplies are mounted on sleds and pulled by the men.)

- Then ask students to reread page 223 to clarify why and how the original plan is changed. (The boats are too heavy to move; the men wait for the floating ice to carry them to open water.)

Vocabulary

executing carrying out or doing

barren having few plants or animals

sledge a sled used to carry loads across snow and ice

harnessed wearing straps for pulling a sled or plow

current the path or flow of moving water, such as a river or sea

December 23, 1915

Executing their plan would be difficult. By pulling the lifeboats, loaded with supplies, they would try to cross the barren ice to open water. If they made it, they would use the three boats to reach the nearest land. Shack studied the unending snow and ice ahead of him. Was it possible?

222

English Language Learners

Supporting Comprehension

Encourage students to take summary notes each time they stop reading and to reread their notes before they begin again. Pause at page 222 to model with a Think Aloud:

I know that the boat was crushed by moving ice, so the explorers have to leave. They put everything they need on three boats that they hope will take them out of Antarctica. I will write down these notes.

Each boat was mounted on a sledge. Harnessed like horses, the men pulled, one boat at a time. Pulling 2,000-pound loads was hard work. Soon everybody was so tired and sore that no one could pull anymore. The crew would have to wait for the ice, moved by the sea's current, to carry them north to open water.

223

Topic, Main Idea, Supporting Details

Review

- Remind students that the topic of a selection is what it is about.
- The main idea of a paragraph or paragraphs explains the topic.
- Supporting details are facts, examples, or other small pieces of information that explain (support) each main idea.

Practice

- Help students identify the topic. Ask: What is this selection mainly about? (a journey to Antarctica)
- Have students read page 222. Ask, What is the main idea? (Carrying out the plan would be difficult.) What details support this idea? (The men would have to haul the lifeboats, loaded with supplies, all the way to open water.)

Apply

- Have students read page 223 and complete this chart.

Main Idea	Supporting Detail
Pulling the lifeboats was hard work.	The men got so tired that they couldn't pull anymore.

Review Skill Trace	
Teach	Theme 2, p. 259A
Reteach	Theme 2, p. R14
▶ Review	p. 223; Theme 4, p. 27

Reading the Selection 223

CRITICAL THINKING
Guiding Comprehension

9 **MAKING INFERENCES** How does the author tell you that the men eat penguins and seals? (by writing that the men who provide food have to search farther because penguins and seals were becoming scarce)

10 **COMPARE AND CONTRAST** How is Tom like a penguin to the sea leopard? (Like a penguin, Tom is a creature for the sea leopard to hunt.)

11 **DRAWING CONCLUSIONS** What reversal (a situation that suddenly turns into the opposite) does the author tell about on page 224? (The sea leopard tries to eat humans and is eaten by humans instead.)

9 Over the next few months, food was always a concern, and it was Tom Orde-Lees's job to find it. Penguins and seals were growing scarce. To find meat to eat, hunters had to go farther away.

10 This was dangerous. Once, when Tom was skiing back to camp, a monstrous head burst from the ice. A giant sea leopard lunged at Tom, only to slip quickly back into the dark water, stalking Tom from below, as sea leopards do when they hunt penguins.

Tom tripped and fell. The huge animal lunged again, this time springing out of the water and right onto the ice. Back on his feet, Tom tried to get away. He cried for help, and Frankie Wild rushed over from camp carrying a rifle.

The sea leopard now charged Frankie, who dropped calmly to one knee, took careful aim, and fired three shots. The sea leopard fell dead. There **11** was plenty to eat for days afterward!

224

Vocabulary

scarce not enough

lunged moved forward suddenly

stalking moving secretly while tracking prey

ASSIGNMENT CARD 7

You Were There

Point of View

How would this story be different if a crew member described the dangerous trip? One way is that he'd tell it from the **first-person** point of view, using the words *I, me, we,* and *us.* In a small group, discuss how else the story would change. To help, use these questions

- What details might the crew member feel are important to tell? What details might he leave out?

- How would the crew member's story be affected by his feelings and experiences? How might hearing him tell the story help you understand the dangers the crew faced?

Theme 5: Voyag

Teacher's Resource BLM page 83

225

Guiding Comprehension

12 **WRITER'S CRAFT** In the first paragraph, why do you think the author describes the men in such detail? (to help the reader understand what they look like, how they feel, and how hard their voyage has been)

13 **WRITER'S CRAFT** How does the author remind you that Shackleton continues to observe the men and revise his plan as needed? (by describing how Shackleton revises his plan after seeing that all his men would not survive an 800-mile journey in an open boat)

14 **PREDICTING OUTCOMES** Based on Shackleton's decision, what can you predict about the open boat journey to Elephant Island? (It will be very difficult and possibly deadly, but not as difficult or dangerous as sailing to South Georgia Island.)

April 8, 1916

12 The men smelled terrible. During their five and a half months on the ice they hadn't had a bath. Clothes were greasy and worn thin, and they rubbed against the men's skin, causing painful sores. Hands were cracked from the cold and wind, and hunger sapped everyone's strength.

By now, the ice floes were breaking up into smaller and smaller pieces all around the men as they drifted closer to the edge of the polar sea. Shack thought it was a good time to launch the lifeboats, rigged with small canvas sails. He **13** knew his men could not all survive the grueling 800-mile open-boat journey to the whaling station on South Georgia Island. So he decided to try **14** to reach Elephant Island first.

226

Vocabulary

sapped weakened

floes large sheets of floating ice

grueling very tiring

227

English Language Learners

Supporting Comprehension

Pause at page 226 to ask students to imagine how the men are feeling. Challenge partners to role-play dialogue for the explorers. Instruct them to include "I feel" and "I hope" statements. Have volunteers role-play for the class.

I hope we don't have a storm.

I think we're going to make it.

CRITICAL THINKING
Guiding Comprehension

15 **MAKING INFERENCES** Do you think it is just the noise of the killer whales that keeps the men from sleeping well? (No, it is also the strange, unfamiliar situation and the possibility that the whales might attack them or damage their boats or their ice floe.)

16 **WRITER'S CRAFT** How does the author create suspense by choosing the words *wriggling shape* to describe what Shackleton first observes in the crevasse? (The words *wriggling shape* make you think that either a man has fallen into the crevasse or that an animal is lurking there.)

11 p.m. April 8, 1916

Steering around the blocks of ice was hard. The boats bumped into ice floes — or crashed into icebergs. As night fell, the boats were pulled up onto a big floe and the tents were raised. But sleeping was difficult with damp bags and blankets, and with noisy killer whales circling around.

15

One night, Shack suddenly felt something was wrong. He shook Frankie, and they crawled out of their tent for a look. A huge wave smacked headlong into the floe with a great thud, and the floe began to split into two pieces. The crack was headed straight toward Tent Number 4!

16

Then Shack heard a splash. Looking into the crevasse, he saw a wriggling shape below in the dark water. It was a sleeping bag — with Ernie Holness inside! Shack acted quickly. Reaching down, he pulled the soggy bag out of the water with one mighty jerk. And just in time, too — within seconds the two great blocks of ice crashed back together.

228

Extra Support/Intervention

Review (pages 218–228)

Before students who need support join the whole class for Stop and Think on page 229, have them

- take turns modeling Monitor/Clarify and any other strategies they used
- add to **Transparency 5–20,** check their Text Organization Chart on **Practice Book** page 121, and use it to summarize

Vocabulary

crevasse deep hole or crack

Stop and Think

Critical Thinking Questions

1. **CAUSE AND EFFECT** Why do all the voyagers camp out for five and a half months on the ice? Why do they sail in the boats after this time has passed? (They are stranded with their lifeboats on top of ice floes until the sea's current moves them to open water; they've come to open water and are now trying to reach Elephant Island.)

2. **MAKING JUDGMENTS** Do you think Shackleton is a good leader? Explain your answer. (Yes, because he consults with others, adjusts his plans to changing conditions, and shows concern for his men.)

Strategies in Action

Have students take turns modeling Monitor/Clarify and other strategies they used.

Discussion Options

You may want to bring the entire class together to do one or more of the activities below.

- **Review Predictions/Purpose** Discuss which predictions were accurate and which needed to be revised. Record any changes and new predictions, as well as any new questions students have.

- **Share Group Discussions** Have students share their questions and literature discussions.

- **Summarize** Help students use their Text Organization Charts to summarize what has happened in the story so far.

Monitoring Student Progress

If . . .	Then . . .
students have successfully completed the Extra Support activities on page 228,	have them read the rest of the selection cooperatively or independently.

ASSIGNMENT CARD 8

Literature Discussion

In a small group, talk over your questions and ideas about the selection. Also discuss these questions:

- What challenges do Shackleton and his men face before and after the *Endurance* is trapped by the ice?

- How do you think Shackleton feels after the *Endurance* is trapped? How do you think the crew feels? Why?

- Do you think Shackleton is a good leader? Why do you think as you do?

Theme 5: Voyagers

Guiding Comprehension

⑱ CAUSE AND EFFECT What effects do the rough seas have on the men in the boats? (Most become seasick; they become thirsty because seawater spoiled their drinking water.)

⑲ MAKING INFERENCES How do you think the men feel when they see Elephant Island? (relieved to finally reach land, but worried because it looks so barren)

April 13, 1916

Finally, the men reached open water. The savage sea slammed furiously into the three little boats — called the *James Caird*, the *Dudley Docker*, and the *Stancomb Wills*. Tall waves lifted them up and down like a roller coaster. Blinding sea spray blew into the men's faces. Most of them became seasick.

⑱ Worst of all, they were very thirsty, because seawater had spoiled the fresh water. The men's tongues had swelled so much from dehydration they could hardly swallow. Shack had his men suck on frozen seal meat to quench their thirst. They *had* to make land. They had to get to Elephant Island!

April 15, 1916

After an exhausting week battling the sea, the men nearly lost all hope. Big Tom Crean tried to cheer the men with a song, but nothing worked. Finally, something appeared in the distance. Shack **⑲** called across to Frank Worsley in the *Dudley Docker*, "There she is, Skipper!" It was land. It was Elephant Island at last. It looked terribly barren, with jagged 3,500-foot peaks rising right up out of the sea, yet it was the only choice the men had.

230

Vocabulary

savage wild

furiously violently

dehydration sickness caused by not having enough water

quench to satisfy

exhausting very tiring

jagged ragged, full of parts sticking up and out

231

Challenge

REACHING ALL LEARNERS

Description

Have students write a description of how they think the barren Elephant Island looks.

Elephant Island

CRITICAL THINKING
Guiding Comprehension

20 **WRITER'S CRAFT** Reread the first sentence on page 232. Why do you think the author uses a dash instead of a comma between the last two items in the series? (to draw special attention to the wind on Elephant Island, which was so strong that it blew the tents away)

21 **MAKING INFERENCES** Most or all of the men probably have frozen fingers. Why do you think the author describes only Chippy's condition? (As the carpenter, Chippy needs his fingers to do his job.)

COMPREHENSION STRATEGY
Monitor/Clarify

Student Modeling Have students model the strategy by clarifying Shackleton's decision to take five men to South Georgia Island, leaving twenty-two men behind on Elephant Island. If necessary, use the following prompt:

- What things must Shackleton consider when deciding the best way to reach safety?

Vocabulary

pitched put up (tents)

deserted empty; not lived in, or having few or no people

April 24, 1916

20 Elephant Island was nothing but rock, ice, snow — and wind. Tents were pitched but quickly blew away. Without resting, Shack planned his departure for South Georgia Island. There he would try to get help. Twenty-two men would stay behind while Shack and a crew braved the 800-mile journey in the worst winter seas on earth.

232

English Language Learners

Supporting Comprehension

Pause after reading page 233 to help students make predictions. Ask, What do you think will happen? Will all the men on Elephant Island survive? Why or why not? Will Shackleton's brave crew make it to the whaling station? What makes you think that?

I wonder how many men will survive.

The five ablest men were picked: Frank Worsley; Big Tom Crean; the carpenter, Chippy McNeish; and two seamen, Tim McCarthy and John Vincent. With frozen fingers and a few tools, Chippy prepared the *Caird* for the rough journey ahead. Only nine days after the men had first sighted the deserted island, Shack and his crew of five were on open water once again.

21

233

ASSIGNMENT CARD 9

Whatever It Takes

eroism and Courage

ith a partner, list ways that Shackleton and his crew showed great urage. Also list examples of brave people you know from your own es. Then get together in a group to share your ideas and to discuss at makes a hero. Use the following questions for help:

• Do you think Shackleton and his crew are heroes? Why?

• Must you do something daring, like traveling to Antarctica, to show how brave you are? Can someone be a hero in his or her everyday life? If so, how?

Theme 5: Voyagers

Teacher's Resource BLM page 84

Comprehension Preview

TARGET SKILL
Text Organization

Teach

• Explain that readers can use text organization to recognize the main ideas in a selection. Features of text organization include title, headings, and illustrations.

Practice

• Write the heading *April 24, 1916*. Guide students to locate the section in their books to which the heading applies. (pages 232–235)

• Give students the main idea *Preparing for the Trip to South Georgia Island*. Have them identify the page number to which the main idea applies. (page 233)

Apply

• Distribute cards or strips of paper with main ideas, headings, and page numbers on them; then have students try to find other students with the appropriate corresponding page numbers, main ideas, or headings.

Target Skill Trace	
Preview; Teach	p. 213CC; p. 216; p. 233; p. 251A
Reteach	p. R12
Review	pp. 267D–267E; Theme 3, p. 333, p. 392

CRITICAL THINKING
Guiding Comprehension

22 **DRAWING CONCLUSIONS** What might have happened if the men on Elephant Island hadn't had materials to build a permanent shelter? (They might have frozen to death.)

23 **MAKING INFERENCES** What do you think are the challenges of living in the dark and cramped hut without knowing when or if Shack will return? (not giving up hope; the cold, the dampness, the darkness, and the smell)

24 **WRITER'S CRAFT** How, in only a few words, does the author show you what life is like for the men left behind on Elephant Island? (by choosing vivid details, such as the smelly bird droppings melting in the heat of the hut)

22 For the men who stayed behind, permanent shelter was now needed or they would freeze to death. Frankie Wild had the men turn the two remaining boats upside down, side by side. Then the boats were covered with canvas and a cookstove was put inside.

23 The hut was dark and cramped, lit only by a burning wick. And something happened that the men had not expected: heat from their bodies and **24** the stove melted the ice under them as well as piles of frozen bird droppings left for years by the frigate birds and penguins. The smell was terrible!

Day after day the men looked toward the sea, wondering if Shack would make it back to rescue them. How long would they be left here? Was Shack all right?

234

Vocabulary

permanent meant to last for a long time

hut small, simple house or shelter

cramped crowded

wick the cord that burns on a candle or a lamp

frigate birds a type of sea bird

Extra Support/Intervention

Strategy Modeling: Monitor/Clarify

How do the boats keep the men on Elephant Island warm? I'll go back and reread. The boats are turned upside down and covered with canvas, and a stove is put inside. The stove keeps the air under the boats warm. Yes, I see. It says that the hut—that's the upside-down boat—was cramped. That's because all the men are under the boat.

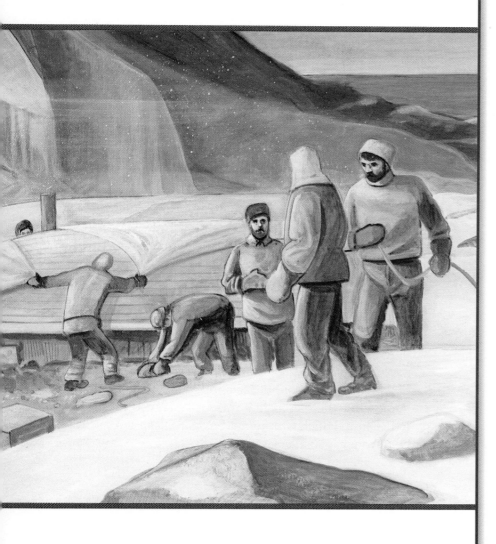

Guiding Comprehension

25 **WRITER'S CRAFT** How and why does the author shift the setting on page 236? (To continue the story of what happens on Shackleton's voyage, the author shifts the scene from the men left behind on Elephant Island to Shackleton's small group sailing on to South Georgia Island.)

26 **WRITER'S CRAFT** How does the author build suspense in his description of the graybeard? (First, the author explains what a graybeard is, making the reader afraid that the men will face one. Then Shackleton screams from the tiller, which makes the reader aware—before the crew knows—that a graybeard is ahead.)

27 **DRAWING CONCLUSIONS** How do you think the jagged rocks in the hull of the Caird *saved the day*? (by holding the boat down, so that it stayed upright as it spun around in the giant wave)

May 5, 1916

25 The *Caird* made her way through the storm-tossed seas, while Shack and his men drank rancid seal oil to prevent seasickness. The ocean swelled and hissed and broke over the small boat as the **26** men worried about the terrible graybeards found in these waters. Graybeards are monstrous waves that come quietly and quickly, threatening everything in their path.

The men had to battle to keep the boat free of ice, because any added weight might sink the *Caird*. Suddenly, Shack screamed from the tiller. The men turned around to face the biggest wave they had ever seen. It was a graybeard!

The boat shuddered on impact as the mountain of water spun it around like a top. Water filled the *Caird* while the men bailed furiously. Jagged rocks **27** in her hull, which Chippy had used to keep the boat from capsizing, saved the day.

236

Vocabulary

rancid having a nasty smell or taste

tiller part used to steer a boat

impact crash

bailed got water out of a boat by filling containers and emptying them, over and over

hull the body or frame of a ship or boat

capsizing turning bottom side up

English Language Learners

Supporting Comprehension

Ask students to choose a scene that they like from the story. Ask them to write a diary entry as if they were a character experiencing that scene. Model writing a diary for your own favorite scene and display it for students.

May 15, 16, 17
I couldn't believe my eyes when I saw the graybeard!

CRITICAL THINKING
Guiding Comprehension

28 **NOTING DETAILS** What new problems do the men have as they finally approach South Georgia Island? (Their fresh water has run out; they are weak; they have to land on the opposite side of the island from the whaling station; they fight a hurricane for nine hours.)

29 **WRITER'S CRAFT** How do you think the author chose which parts of the men's seventeen days at sea to include in the selection? (The author probably chose the parts that are the most dramatic or the most important to the larger story of Shackleton's voyage.)

30 **MAKING JUDGMENTS** Based on the facts in this part of the selection, would you rather have been part of the crew that stayed behind on Elephant Island or part of the crew that traveled with Shackleton to South Georgia Island? Explain your answer. (Answers will vary.)

May 10, 1916

28

29

Finally, after seventeen grueling days at sea, young McCarthy shouted, "Land ho!" South Georgia Island lay dimly ahead. The whaling station was on the other side of the island, but the men had to land *now* or die. Their fresh water was gone, and they were too weak to battle the sea to the other side of the island.

238

Vocabulary

dimly not seen easily or clearly

miraculously amazingly; seemingly impossibly

While the men planned their landing attempt, they were hit by the worst hurricane they had ever encountered. For nine terrible hours they fought to keep afloat. Miraculously, just as things looked hopeless, the sea calmed enough to allow the *Caird* to land safely on the rocky beach of King Haakon Bay.

239

Setting

Teach

- Explain that setting is the time and place of the action or events in a story or non-fiction selection. It is the background in which the fictional or real-life characters live and act.

Practice/Apply

- Guide students to identify the general setting of the selection. (Antarctica)

- Then read aloud page 238. Help students identify specific details that tell about the setting. (the date; the phrase "*Land ho!*")

- Ask students to find a phrase on page 239 that shows a change of setting from sea to land. (*the sea calmed enough to allow the Caird to land safely on the rocky beach of King Haakon Bay*)

English Language Learners

Language Development

The author uses well-chosen adjectives throughout the story. Pair students with English-speaking partners, or work as a group to list the adjectives on pages 238–239. These include: *grueling, weak, worst, terrible,* and *hopeless.* Discuss how these words contribute to the overall feeling of the story.

CRITICAL THINKING
Guiding Comprehension

31 **WRITER'S CRAFT** Why do you think the author shifts the focus of the story on page 240 from the whole group to what each individual man in the group is doing? (to help readers relate more deeply to the story by making a personal connection with the individuals)

32 **MAKING JUDGMENTS** If you were in the party on South Georgia Island, would you rather be in the weaker group left behind to rest in the cave or in the stronger group that attempts the dangerous mountain hike to the whaling station? Explain your answer. (Answers will vary.)

33 **MAKING INFERENCES** How do you think Shackleton, Big Tom, and Skipper Worsley feel when they set out on their hike to the whaling station? (nervous or scared, because of the danger; excited or happy, because they are close to reaching people who might help them rescue the others and return home)

31
32
The men landed near a small cave with a freshwater spring nearby. The cave would become a temporary home for John Vincent and Chippy McNeish. Both had suffered too much on the voyage and could not survive the long hike across the island to the whaling station. Tim McCarthy stayed behind to take care of the two sick men. Fortunately, water for drinking, wood from old shipwrecks for fire, and albatross eggs and seals to eat meant those who stayed behind would be all right while waiting for their resc

240

Vocabulary

temporary lasting for only a short time

albatross a large sea bird

Fluency Practice

Rereading for Fluency Have students choose a favorite part of the story to reread orally in small groups, or suggest that they read pages 240–241. Encourage students to read with feeling and expression.

But Shack, Big Tom, and Skipper Worsley would have to climb over a series of jagged ridges that cut the island in half like a saw blade. All they could carry was a little Primus stove, fuel for six meals, fifty feet of rope, and an ice ax. Their only food consisted of biscuits and light rations that hung in socks around their necks. On their eighth day ashore, May 18, it was time to set off on the most dangerous climb they had ever attempted. **33**

241

Guiding Comprehension

34 **NOTING DETAILS** What are the challenges the men face as they hike across the mountains? (They are exhausted and poorly equipped; they have little food or sleep; they climb and reclimb impassable mountains; they have to slide down the mountain; they have to lower themselves by rope through an icy waterfall.)

35 **MAKING INFERENCES** What are the risks of sliding down the mountain on Shackleton's makeshift toboggan? Why do the men laugh when they hit the snowbank? (They could have been injured or killed; they laugh because they are relieved to have survived unhurt.)

36 **WRITER'S CRAFT** How does the author hold your interest in the last stages of the hike to the whaling station? (by presenting details, such as the men at the whaling station looking like insects from a distance, and stressing, through Shackleton's caution on the descent, that the voyage is perilous up to the very end)

Vocabulary

terrain land, ground, or earth

impassable not able to be crossed or traveled through

summit the highest point

gamble a risky action

makeshift something used as a temporary substitute for something else

perilous very dangerous

reckless not careful or cautious

torrents violent, fast-moving streams of liquid

May 19, 1916

34   Three times the men struggled up mountains, only to find that the terrain was impassable on the other side. The men stopped only to eat a soup called "hoosh," to nibble on stale biscuits, or to nap five minutes, with each man taking a turn awake so that there would be someone to wake the others.

    On and on the exhausted men hiked. From one mountain summit they saw that night was coming fast. Being caught on a peak at night meant certain death. They had to make a dangerous gamble. Shack assembled a makeshift toboggan from the coiled-up rope and the men slid 1,500 feet down the mountain in one big slide. Despite the perilous

35 landing, they couldn't help but laugh with relief after they had crashed, unhurt, into a large snowbank.

    The men had survived the long slide, but danger still lay ahead. They had been hiking for more than thirty hours now without sleep. Finally, all three heard the sound of a far-off whistle. Was it the whaling station?

    They climbed a ridge and looked down. Yes, there it was! Two whale-catchers were docked at the pier. From this distance, the men at the station were the size of insects.

36   Shack fought against being too reckless. The three still had to lower themselves down a thirty-foot waterfall by hanging on to their rope and swinging through the icy torrents. At last, the ragged explorers stumbled toward the station. They had done it!

242

243

Narrative Nonfiction

Teach

Define narrative nonfiction as fiction that

- tells about real people, animals, places, or events

- is told in story form

- gives facts about the subject

- usually describes events in chronological order

- may include photographs, captions, illustrations, and graphic aids to convey information

Practice/Apply

- Guide students in identifying the people and places in the story. (Shack, Big Tom, and Skipper Worsley—real people; and South Georgia Island—a real place)

- Ask students to identify other details from the scene that make *Trapped in the Ice!* a piece of narrative nonfiction. (They actually cross the mountains to reach the whaling station; the events are told in story form and in chronological order.)

Extra Support/Intervention

Strategy Modeling: Phonics/Decoding

Use this example to model the strategy.

When I look at the word t-o-b-o-g-g-a-n, *I notice the shorter word* to. *I think* b-o-g *probably has the short vowel sound because there's a single vowel followed by a consonant,* bahg. *The last part probably has the short vowel sound as in the word* man, gan. *When I put it all together, I say* too-bahg-gan. *I've got it. The word is* tuh-BAHG-uhn. *That's a kind of sled.*

Guiding Comprehension

37 MAKING INFERENCES From the facts in the selection, what can you infer about Thoralf Sørlle? (By Sørlle's concern for the terrible condition of the men and the tears in his eyes when he recognizes Shackleton, it can be inferred that he is a kind, caring person.)

38 DRAWING CONCLUSIONS How can you figure out the meaning of the words *pack ice* on page 244? (The phrase *to break through* and the word *winter* are context clues that show the meaning, "a thick mass of ice.")

39 WRITER'S CRAFT How does the author end the story? (The author summarizes the rescue efforts that end with all of Shackleton's men finally reaching safety.)

4 p.m. May 20, 1916
Torlaf

Thoralf Sørlle, the manager of the whaling station, heard a knock outside his office and opened the door. He looked hard at the ragged clothes and blackened faces of the men who stood before him. "Do I know you?" he asked.

37 "I'm Shackleton," came the reply. Tears welled up in Sørlle's eyes as he recognized his old friend's voice.

The three explorers received a hero's welcome from the whaling crew. The whalers knew that no one had ever done what Shack had accomplished. The next day, Skipper Worsley took a boat and picked up McCarthy, Vincent, and McNeish while Shack began preparations for the Elephant Island rescue.

38 It would take more than three months — and four attempts — to break through the winter pack
39 ice and save the stranded men. But Shack finally did it — and without any loss of life. The men were glad to have a ship's deck once again under their feet. Finally, they were going home!

244

Extra Support/ Intervention	**On Level**	**Challenge**

Selection Review

Before students join the whole class for Wrapping Up on page 245, have them

- take turns modeling the reading strategies they used
- complete **Transparency 5–20** with you and finish their Text Organization Charts
- summarize the whole selection

Literature Discussion

Have small groups of students discuss the story using their own questions or the questions in Think About the Selection on page 246.

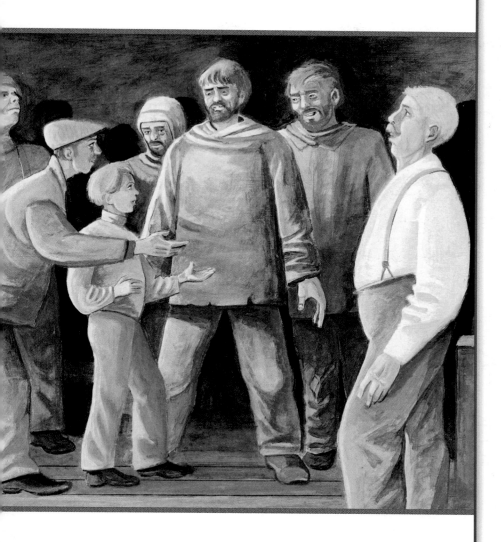

245

Wrapping Up

Critical Thinking Questions

1. **TEXT ORGANIZATION** Why do you think the author uses dates to introduce each section of the story? (to help readers follow events that take place over many months)

2. **MAKING JUDGMENTS** Why do you think the author chooses to refer to Shackleton as "Shack"? Do you think this is a good idea? Use facts from the story to support your answer. (Answers will vary.)

Strategies in Action

Have students take turns modeling the Monitor/Clarify strategy. Ask what other strategies helped.

Discussion Options

Bring the entire class together to do one or more of the activities below.

Review Predictions/Purpose Have students discuss whether their predictions were or were not accurate.

Share Group Discussions Have students share their questions and literature discussions. Invite them to share their opinions of whether Shackleton is a hero.

Summarize Have students use their Text Organization Charts to recall and summarize the main events of the story.

Comprehension Check

Use **Practice Book** page 122 to assess students' comprehension of the selection.

Monitoring Student Progress

If . . .	Then . . .
students score 7 or below on **Practice Book** page 122,	guide them in rereading relevant parts of the selection and discussing their answers.

REACHING ALL LEARNERS

English Language Learners

Supporting Comprehension

As a class or in two groups, rewrite the story as a short skit. Assign tasks to students, including characters, authors, set designers, and costumers. Check the script for accuracy before students begin practicing. Encourage students to memorize their lines. Perform for each other with classroom lights off, to set the mood.

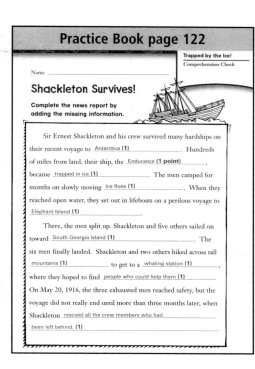

Practice Book page 122

Name _____

Trapped by the Ice!
Comprehension Check

Shackleton Survives!

Complete the news report by adding the missing information.

Sir Ernest Shackleton and his crew survived many hardships on their recent voyage to Antarctica **(1)** _____. Hundreds of miles from land, their ship, the Endurance **(1 point)** _____, became trapped in ice **(1)** _____. The men camped for months on slowly moving ice floes **(1)** _____. When they reached open water, they set out in lifeboats on a perilous voyage to Elephant Island **(1)** _____.

There, the men split up. Shackleton and five others sailed on toward South Georgia Island **(1)** _____. The six men finally landed. Shackleton and two others hiked across tall mountains **(1)** _____ to get to a whaling station **(1)** _____, where they hoped to find people who could help them **(1)** _____. On May 20, 1916, the three exhausted men reached safety, but the voyage did not really end until more than three months later, when Shackleton rescued all the crew members who had been left behind. **(1)** _____.

Responding

Think About the Selection

Have students discuss or write their answers. Sample answers are provided; accept reasonable responses.

1. **MAKING JUDGMENTS** Answers will vary.

2. **MAKING INFERENCES** They were probably grateful to be in a place with shelter, food, and water. They were probably also worried that Shackleton wouldn't be able to find help and rescue them.

3. **MAKING JUDGMENTS** Answers will vary. Possible answers: A person would need to be physically fit, work well in a team, be creative and able to think under pressure, be able to adapt to change, and to remain hopeful.

4. **MAKING JUDGMENTS** Answers will vary.

5. **DRAWING CONCLUSIONS** Shackleton was a hero because of his leadership in surviving incredible hardships without losing any members of his crew.

6. **Connecting/Comparing** The voyages were alike in that the people on both ships were traveling into the unknown. Both voyages were attempting to achieve a goal, and both experienced hardships. The goals were different. The people aboard the *Mayflower* wanted religious freedom, while Shackleton and his crew wanted to be the first to cross the South Pole's ice cap. The *Mayflower* journey took place nearly 300 years earlier and included families, while the *Endurance* journey included only explorers and crew.

Responding

Think About the Selection

1. What do you think would have been the most difficu[lt] part of Shackleton's Antarctic voyage?

2. When Shackleton went to find help, how do you thi[nk] the crew members who were left behind felt?

3. Name some qualities a person would need to surviv[e a] voyage like Shackleton's.

4. Would you have gone back with Shackleton to rescu[e] the men on Elephant Island? Explain your answer.

5. Why do people call Shackleton a hero even though [he] didn't succeed in crossing the South Pole's ice cap?

6. **Connecting/Comparing** How is Shackleton's sea voyag[e] like the *Mayflower* voyage? How is it different?

Write a Speech

Shackleton gave speeches telling people about his adventures. Choose a group Shackleton might have spoken to, such as reporters, other explorers, or students. Write a short speech Shackleton might have given to this group.

Tips
- Say *hello* and *good-bye* to the group. At the end, thank them for listening.
- Choose only a few parts of the voyage. Describe them in detail.
- Read your speech aloud to hear how it sounds.

246

English Language Learners

Supporting Comprehension

Beginning/Preproduction Have students draw a scene from the journey. Then help them write a caption for the drawing.

Early Production and Speech Emergence Ask students to retell the story based on the illustrations. Have each student take a turn.

Intermediate and Advanced Fluency Ask, What qualities do you think an explorer needs to have? How has exploration changed?

Science

Investigate Ice

In a small group, talk about the way water freezes into ice and melts back into water. Then discuss the following questions.

- Why doesn't the stove melt the ice at the men's first camp? (pages 220–221)

- How can the ice carry Shackleton's crew north? (page 223)

- Why do the ice floes break up at the edge of the polar sea? (page 226)

Social Studies

Make a Timeline

Record Shackleton's journey on a timeline. On paper, draw a straight line. For each date, draw and label a dot on the line. Below each dot, write what happened on that date. Keep the events in order from left to right.

Bonus Figure out when Shackleton began his journey and when he rescued the men on Elephant Island. Add these events to your timeline.

Oct. 27, 1915

🌐 **Take a Web Field Trip**

You've read about three exciting voyages — now do some exploring of your own! Visit Education Place and link to Web sites for young travelers. **www.eduplace.com/kids**

247

Additional Responses

Personal Response Invite students to share their personal responses to the selection with a partner.

Journal ▶ Ask students to write reviews of the selection in their journals.

Selection Connections Remind students to add to **Practice Book** page 84.

Extra Support/ Intervention

Strong Adjectives

For the writing activity, prepare the questions that reporters and other listeners may have asked. Challenge them to use strong adjectives in Shackleton's descriptions of his adventures. Suggest that they use their Text Organization charts to remind them of the events of the voyage.

Practice Book page 84

Launching the Theme
Selection Connections

Name _____

Voyagers

Fill in the chart as you read the stories. Sample answers shown.

	Across the Wide Dark Sea	Yunmi and Halmoni's Trip	Trapped by the Ice!
Who takes the voyage? Where does the voyage begin and end?	Pilgrims travel from England to America. (2 points)	Yunmi and her grandmother travel from New York to Korea and back. (2)	Shackleton travels from England to Antarctica and back. (2)
What qualities help the voyagers succeed?	The Pilgrims are brave, friendly, smart, and hard-working. (3)	Yunmi is caring, friendly, responds quickly to change, and learns from her experiences. (3)	Shackleton is daring, brave, strong, and good at solving problems. (3)

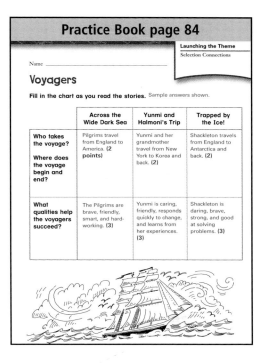

Monitoring Student Progress

End-of-Selection Assessment

Selection Test Use the test on pages 139–140 in the **Teacher's Resource Blackline Masters** to assess selection comprehension and vocabulary.

Student Self-Assessment Have students assess their reading with additional questions such as

- Which parts of this selection were difficult? Why?

- Which strategies helped me understand the story better?

- Would I recommend this story to my friends? Why or why not?

Responding 247

Media Link

Skill: How to Read a Photo Essay

- **Introduce** the photo essay, "Shackleton's Real-Life Voyage."

- **Discuss** the Skill Lesson on Anthology page 248. Tell students that when they read a photo essay they should focus equally on the words and the photos to help them understand the topic.

- **Model** reading the photo essay. Read the title and captions first.

- **Explain** that using a Visual Details Chart can help students make inferences about photographs. Have students help you complete the chart shown below for the photograph of the *Endurance* crew.

- **Set a purpose** for reading. Tell students to read "Shackleton's Real-Life Voyage" to add to their understanding of the crew's perilous situation and how the voyagers overcame it. Encourage them to pay attention to text organization and remind them to use Evaluate and other strategies as they read.

Visual Details Chart

Photo: Endurance crew

Details:

- clothing suggests bitter cold conditions
- men look strong and rugged
- men's calm, neat appearance shows photo was taken early on in adventure

READ & COMPREHEND

Media Link

Skill: How to Read a Photo Essay

❶ **Read** the title and introduction. **Scan** the photos.

❷ **View** the photos one at a time.

❸ **Read** the caption that describes each photo.

❹ **Note details** in the photos. Ask yourself what each photo shows you and how it helps you understand the topic.

Shackleton's Real-Life Voyage

The story of Shackleton's Antarctic journey is so amazing, it's hard to believe it really happened. But it did, and everyone survived. One crew member, Frank Hurley, even took photos during the voyage.

Hurley didn't know if he would return home. He wasn't sure if anyone would ever see his photos. However, he never gave up hope. He worked hard to protect the photos from ice, snow, water, wind, and freezing cold. Today, his photos still help people understand what this incredible adventure was like.

Frank Hurley

Hurley photographed the entire crew soon after the ship was caught in the ice.

The *Endurance* was slowly crushed by the powerful ice.

249

Extra Support/Intervention

Primary Sources

Emphasize that Hurley's photographs are especially valuable. They form an eyewitness report that supports the stories the voyagers told after their ordeal and brings their experience to viewers today. Explain that such eyewitness accounts, called primary sources, help historians and writers tell readers what *really* happened.

Photography

Teach

- Explain that when these photographs were taken, photography required far more effort and preparation. Instead of negatives, the photographer developed the photographs from heavy glass plates.

- Point out that a photographer's choice of subject, lighting, and camera angle can strongly influence what people learn about an event.

Practice/Apply

- Have students discuss what, specifically, makes these photos so dramatic and important.

- Ask students to identify their favorite photo from the essay and to explain their choice. Ask them to list as many descriptive adjectives as they can.

The crew tried to chop a path out of the ice. But the ice was too solid and thick, and there was too much of it.

As the ice destroyed their ship, the crew had to camp in the freezing cold.

The crew pulled lifeboats and supplies across the icy terrain. It was grueling work.

250

English Language Learners

Supporting Comprehension

As a group, look at the photographs. Ask students to note small details. Assign groups one photograph each, which they will describe in detail and write an alternate caption for. Encourage them to use quotations, dates, and narrative descriptions. Have a class sharing in which one member of each group reads the photo description and another reads the caption.

Vocabulary

grueling tiring and difficult

The smashed wreck sank slowly into the ice. One sad day, it disappeared forever.

Rescued! Shackleton used a rowboat to carry the twenty-two men from Elephant Island to the *Yelcho*, the ship in the background. Finally, after nearly two years on the ice, the crew traveled home.

251

Compare / Contrast

pairs

Visual Literacy

"Picture = 1000 words"

2. **TEXT ORGANIZATION** How do the photograph and caption on page 249 work together to give information? (The photo shows how the *Endurance* was crushed by ice; the text tells that it happened slowly.)

3. **DRAWING CONCLUSIONS** How does the photograph of the crew pulling the lifeboat sum up the men's situation? (It shows how difficult their daily struggle for survival really was.)

4. **Connecting/Comparing** How does the photo essay add to what you learned about the voyage in the selection? (It deepens appreciation of what the voyagers went through.)

Challenge

A Photo Essay

Have selected students use family photographs to create a photo essay of a voyage (trip) that they may have taken. Alternatively, if resources permit, have volunteers create a photo essay to document a class field trip or other class activity.

I have good photos from our field trip.

OBJECTIVES

- Identify where specific text features are located in the selection.
- Identify the function of each text feature.
- Learn academic language: *text organization.*

Target Skill Trace

Preview; Teach	p. 213CC; p. 214; p. 233; 251A
Reteach	p. R12
Review	pp. 267D–267E; Theme 3, pp. 333, 392
See	*Extra Support Handbook,* pp. 184–185; pp. 190–191

Transparency 5–20

Text Organization Chart

Text Feature	Where It Is	Purpose
heading (date)	pp. 172, 174, 176, 180, 182, 184, 186, 190, 192, 196, 198	helps readers follow the order of events
photograph, caption, illustration	pp. 172–179	help readers understand the text; give more details
definition	p. 190 "Graybeards are monstrous waves that come quietly and quickly, threatening everything in their path."	helps readers understand the meaning of a special term
chronological sequence	Page 172: The first event takes place on October 27, 1915. Page 198: The last event takes place on May 20, 1916.	helps readers understand the order of events

TRANSPARENCY 5–20
TEACHER'S EDITION PAGE 251A

Practice Book page 121

Trapped by the Ice!
Graphic Organizer Text Organization Chart

Name _____

Text Organization Chart

Text Feature	Where It Is	Purpose
heading (date)	pp. 172, 174, 176, 180, 182, 184, 186, 190, 192, 196, 198 (1 point)	helps readers follow the order of events (1)
photograph, caption, illustration	pp. 172–179 (1)	helps readers understand the text; gives more details (1)
definition	p. 190 "Graybeards are monstrous waves that come quietly and quickly, threatening everything in their path." (1)	helps readers understand the meaning of a special term (1)
chronological sequence	Page 172: The first event takes place on October 27, 1915. Page 198: The last event takes place on May 20, 1916. (1)	helps readers understand the order of events (1)

TARGET SKILL COMPREHENSION: Text Organization

❶ Teach

Review the text organization of *Trapped by the Ice!* Remind students that authors use text organization to

- help readers learn new information
- present information so that it is easy to understand

Complete the Graphic Organizer on **Transparency 5–20** with students. (Sample answers are shown.) Students can refer to the selection and to **Practice Book** page 121.

Model identifying text features and their functions. Have students examine the selection to identify the type of headings (dates) that the author primarily uses to organize information. Ask students to look at page 190 as you think aloud.

Think Aloud *I read the heading* May 5, 1916, *on page 236. The heading helps me locate story events in time. On May 5, a graybeard* the Caird, *spinning the lifeboat around and around and almost causing it to caps*

❷ Guided Practice

Have students record text features. Ask students to identify other information the author might have included in the heading and tell how it might help readers. Have students record their answers on a chart similar to the one below.

Additional Information That Could Appear in Headings	How This Information Could Help
_____ (Location) _____	Knowing where the events take place might help a reader follow and understand the selection.

③ Apply

Assign Practice Book pages 123–124. Also have students apply this skill as they read their **Leveled Readers** for this week. You may also select books from the Leveled Bibliography for this theme, pages 148E–148F.

Test Prep Tell students that thinking about text organization will help them find details to answer test questions. They can scan the title, the byline, the headings, and the captions.

Leveled Readers and Leveled Practice

Students at all levels apply the comprehension skill as they read their Leveled Readers. See lessons on pages 183O–183R.

● BELOW LEVEL ▲ ON LEVEL ■ ABOVE LEVEL ◆ LANGUAGE SUPPORT

Reading Traits

Teaching students how to recognize text organization is one way of encouraging them to "read between the lines" of a selection. This comprehension skill supports the reading trait **Decoding Conventions.**

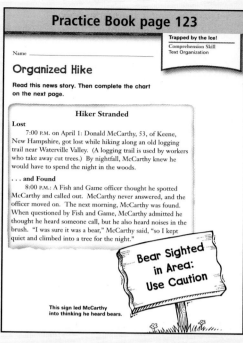

Practice Book page 123

Name _____

Trapped by the Ice!
Comprehension Skill
Text Organization

Organized Hike

Read this news story. Then complete the chart on the next page.

Hiker Stranded

Lost
   7:00 P.M. on April 1: Donald McCarthy, 53, of Keene, New Hampshire, got lost while hiking along an old logging trail near Waterville Valley. (A logging trail is used by workers who take away cut trees.) By nightfall, McCarthy knew he would have to spend the night in the woods.

. . . and Found
   8:00 P.M.: A Fish and Game officer thought he spotted McCarthy and called out. McCarthy never answered, and the officer moved on. The next morning, McCarthy was found. When questioned by Fish and Game, McCarthy admitted he thought he heard someone call, but he also heard noises in the brush. "I was sure it was a bear," McCarthy said, "so I kept quiet and climbed into a tree for the night."

Bear Sighted in Area: Use Caution

This sign led McCarthy into thinking he heard bears.

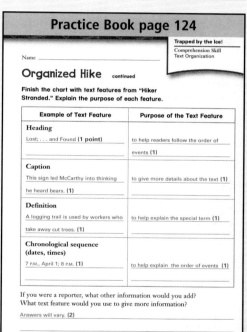

Practice Book page 124

Name _____

Trapped by the Ice!
Comprehension Skill
Text Organization

Organized Hike   continued

Finish the chart with text features from "Hiker Stranded." Explain the purpose of each feature.

Example of Text Feature	Purpose of the Text Feature
Heading Lost; . . . and Found **(1 point)**	to help readers follow the order of events **(1)**
Caption This sign led McCarthy into thinking he heard bears. **(1)**	to give more details about the text **(1)**
Definition A logging trail is used by workers who take away cut trees. **(1)**	to help explain the special term **(1)**
Chronological sequence (dates, times) 7 P.M., April 1; 8 P.M. **(1)**	to help explain the order of events **(1)**

If you were a reporter, what other information would you add? What text feature would you use to give more information?

Answers will vary. **(2)**

Monitoring Student Progress

If . . .	Then . . .
students score 7 or below on **Practice Book** page 124,	use the Reteaching lesson on Teacher's Edition page R8.
students have successfully met the lesson objectives,	have them do the Challenge/ Extension activities on Teacher's Edition page R9.

Practice Book page 125

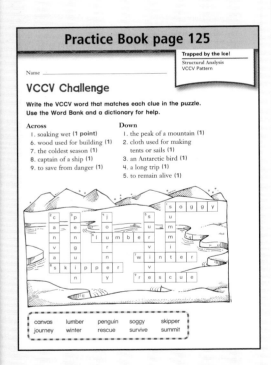

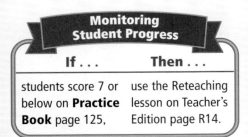

Monitoring Student Progress

If . . .	Then . . .
students score 7 or below on **Practice Book** page 125,	use the Reteaching lesson on Teacher's Edition page R14.

STRUCTURAL ANALYSIS/ VOCABULARY: VCCV Pattern

❶ Teach

Introduce the VCCV pattern. Tell students that when they encounter unfamiliar words, one good strategy for decoding is to look for the VCCV syllable pattern.

- Write *cus/tom*. Explain that a word with the VCCV pattern can often be divided into syllables between the two consonants.

Define open syllables. Write the word *go* and pronounce it. Explain that this is an open syllable. It ends in a vowel, so the vowel has a long sound.

Define closed syllables. Now place a *t* at the end of *go* and pronounce it. Tell students that this is a closed syllable because it ends in a consonant and has a short vowel sound.

Model the Phonics/Decoding Strategy. Write *That doesn't* <u>*concern*</u> *me.* Model decoding *concern*.

Think Aloud *I know that each syllable has only one vowel sound. I see two vowels, o and e, so I'll mark each with a V. Next, I'll label the consonants n and c between these vowels with C. Now I see that this word has the VCCV syllable pattern. I'll divide the word into syllables between the consonants. I know that con is a closed syllable because it ends with a consonant. So it has a short vowel sound. The second syllable has an er spelling which is pronounced ur. I blend the syllables and read the word: kuhn-SURN.*

❷ Guided Practice

Have students decode words with the VCCV pattern. Display the phrases below. Ask partners to copy the underlined words, underline the VCCV pattern in each word, draw a line between the syllables, and pronounce the word. Have students share their work with the class.

wanted to be the first <u>person</u>   icy <u>torrents</u>

scrap <u>lumber</u> for firewood   <u>ragged</u> explorers

in the <u>distance</u>   their <u>landing</u> attempt

a hero's <u>welcome</u>

❸ Apply

Assign Practice Book page 125.

PHONICS REVIEW: Double Consonants

OBJECTIVES

- Read words that have double consonants.
- Apply the Phonics/Decoding Strategy.

❶ Teach

Review double consonants. Tell students that understanding double consonants can help them decode unfamiliar words.

- A VCCV word may have a double consonant. Divide between the consonants to find the syllables.

Model the Phonics/Decoding Strategy. Write *The ship's <u>skipper</u> was Frank Worsley.* Model decoding *skipper*.

Think Aloud *When I look at this word, I see double consonants in the middle. I also see the* VCCV *pattern. I'll try splitting it into syllables between the two* p's: skihp-pur. *Oh, it's* SKIHP-ur. *I know that word. A* skipper *is a person who is in charge of a ship. That makes sense.*

❷ Guided Practice

Have students find double consonants. Display the following sentences.

1. The ice was moved by the sea's <u>current</u>.
2. He pulled the <u>soggy</u> bag out of the water.
3. The boat <u>shuddered</u> on impact.

- Have students copy the underlined words. Then help them circle the double consonants and decode the words.
- Call on individuals to model their work at the board.

❸ Apply

Have students decode words with double consonants. Ask students to decode the words below from *Trapped by the Ice!* and discuss their meanings.

terrible	page 180	jagged	page 184
difficult	page 182	suffered	page 194
swallow	page 184	nibble	page 196

Phonics/Decoding Strategy

When you come to a word you don't know—

1. Look carefully at the word.
2. Look for word parts you know and think about the sounds for the letters.
3. Blend the sounds to read the word.
4. Ask yourself: Is it a word I know? Does it make sense in what I am reading?
5. If not, ask yourself: What else can I try?

HOUGHTON MIFFLIN
Reading

SPELLING: VCCV Pattern

OBJECTIVES

- Write Spelling Words that have the VCCV pattern.

SPELLING WORDS

Basic

Monday	dollar
sudden*	window
until	hello
forget	market
happen*	pretty
follow	order*

Review	**Challenge**
after*	stubborn
funny	expect*

Forms of these words appear in the literature.

Extra Support/ Intervention

Basic Word List Consider using only the left column of Basic Words with students who need extra support.

Challenge

Challenge Word Practice Students can use the Challenge Words to write sentences from a speech given to honor the crew of the *Endurance*.

DAY 1 INSTRUCTION

VCCV Pattern

Pretest Use the Day 5 Test sentences.

Teach Write *Monday* and *sudden* on the board, say the words, and have students repeat them.

- Point out each word's vowel-consonant-consonant-vowel pattern. Explain that finding the syllables of VCCV words will help students to spell the words.

- Draw lines to syllabicate the examples. Tell students that words with the VCCV pattern are divided between the two consonants, whether the consonants are different or the same.

- List the remaining Basic Words, and have students say them. Call on students to identify each word's VCCV pattern and tell you where to divide the word into syllables.

Practice/Homework Assign **Practice Book** page 241.

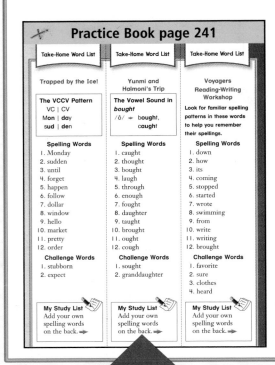

Practice Book page 241

DAY 2 REVIEW & PRACTICE

Reviewing the Principle

Go over the VCCV pattern with students.

Practice/Homework Assign **Practice Book** page 126.

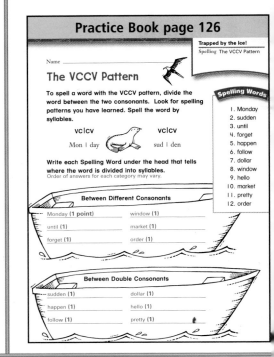

Practice Book page 126

Take-Home Word List

Classifying

Write the Basic Words on the board.

Dictate the following word groups and ask students to write the Basic Word that fits in each group.

nickel, quarter, (dollar)

store, shop, (market)

door, porch, (window)

Sunday, Thursday, (Monday)

Have students use each Basic Word from the board orally in a sentence. (Sentences will vary.)

Practice/Homework For spelling practice, assign **Practice Book** page 127.

Game: Match It!

Ask pairs of students to make a set of 24 syllable cards, one for each syllable of the 12 Basic Words. Have the pairs shuffle the cards and arrange them face-down in 4 rows of 6 cards each.

- Players take turns flipping over 2 cards at a time, hoping to make a match of the 2 syllables in a Basic Word.
- If the cards match, the player may keep the cards after using the word correctly in a sentence. If the cards do not match, they are turned face-down again.
- The player with more cards at the end wins.

Practice/Homework For proofreading and writing practice, assign **Practice Book** page 128.

Spelling Test

Say each underlined word, read the sentence, and then repeat the word. Have students write only the underlined word.

Basic Words

1. School starts on **Monday**.
2. The car came to a **sudden** stop.
3. We can play outside **until** dark.
4. Did you **forget** your lunch?
5. What will **happen** next?
6. We will **follow** the trail.
7. What can I buy with a **dollar**?
8. Did you shut the **window**?
9. The friendly clown said **hello**.
10. We can buy jam at the **market**.
11. This pond looks so **pretty**!
12. Write the numbers in **order**.

Challenge Words

13. Your brother is very **stubborn**.   *14*
14. I do not know what to **expect** next.   *13*

Review:
after
funny

12
7
1

Practice Book page 127

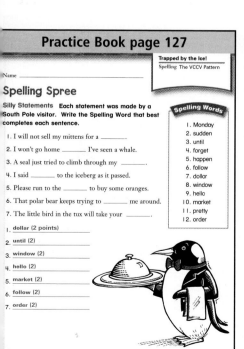

Trapped by the Ice!
Spelling The VCCV Pattern

Name _____

Spelling Spree

Silly Statements Each statement was made by a South Pole visitor. Write the Spelling Word that best completes each sentence.

1. I will not sell my mittens for a _____.
2. I won't go home _____ I've seen a whale.
3. A seal just tried to climb through my _____.
4. I said _____ to the iceberg as it passed.
5. Please run to the _____ to buy some oranges.
6. That polar bear keeps trying to _____ me around.
7. The little bird in the tux will take your _____.

Spelling Words
1. Monday
2. sudden
3. until
4. forget
5. happen
6. follow
7. dollar
8. window
9. hello
10. market
11. pretty
12. order

1. **dollar** (2 points)
2. **until** (2)
3. **window** (2)
4. **hello** (2)
5. **market** (2)
6. **follow** (2)
7. **order** (2)

Practice Book page 128

Trapped by the Ice!
Spelling The VCCV Pattern

Name _____

Proofreading and Writing

Proofreading Circle the five misspelled Spelling Words in this script. Then write each word correctly.

> **Sam:**   We are leaving (Mondy) for a trip to the South Pole.
> **Emma:** Wow! I didn't know that. Is this a (suddin) trip?
> **Sam:**   No, we've been planning it for ages. I hear it's a really (pritty) place.
> **Emma:** If you (hapen) to see any penguins, say hello for me.
> **Sam:**   Sure. If you want me to say hi to a killer whale, though, you can (ferget) it!

Spelling Words
1. Monday
2. sudden
3. until
4. forget
5. happen
6. follow
7. dollar
8. window
9. hello
10. market
11. pretty
12. order

1. **Monday** (2 points)
2. **sudden** (2)
3. **pretty** (2)
4. **happen** (2)
5. **forget** (2)

Write a List How would you prepare for a trip to the South Pole? Would you need to buy things? If so, what? Where would you buy the goods?

On a separate sheet of paper, write a list of things to do to get ready for a trip to the South Pole. Use Spelling Words from the list. Responses will vary. (2)

OBJECTIVES

- Read and understand words that are homophones.
- Use sentence context to identify the appropriate homophone.
- Learn academic language: *homophone.*

Target Skill Trace

Teach	p. 251G
Review	pp. 267H–267I
Extend	Challenge/Extension Activities, p. R15
See	*Handbook for English Language Learners*, p. 171

Transparency 5–21

Homophones

Example sentences:
The sound of crushing <u>wood</u> startled the men.
They <u>would</u> have to decide what to do next.

1. Using the example sentences above, figure out which word is correct in the following sentence.
   The men piled more (<u>wood</u>/would) on the fire.

   wood

2. Example sentences:
   Snowflakes <u>blew</u> into the men's faces.
   The ice in the crevasse looked <u>blue</u>.

   The wind on Elephant Island (<u>blew</u>/blue) the tents away.

   blew

3. Example sentences:
   The men hunted for <u>meat</u> to eat.
   They never knew what dangers they would <u>meet</u>.

   The men didn't know if they would ever (<u>meat</u>/meet) again.

   meet

TRANSPARENCY 5–21
TEACHER'S EDITION PAGE 251G

VOYAGERS *Trapped by the Ice!*
Vocabulary Skill Homophones
ANNOTATED VERSION

Monitoring Student Progress

If . . .	Then . . .
students score 7 or below on **Practice Book** page 129,	have them work with partners to correct the items they missed.

VOCABULARY: Homophones

❶ Teach

Define homophones. Tell students that words that sound alike but have different meanings and spellings are called homophones.

Display Transparency 5–21. Cover all but the example sentences. Read the two sentences aloud. Point out the underlined words, *wood* and *would*. Tell students that since the words sound alike, they are homophones.

Model how to determine the correct homophone. Uncover practice Sentence 1 and read it aloud. Then use the Think Aloud to model how to use sentence context to determine which homophone correctly completes the sentence.

Think Aloud
In the first example sentence the word wood *is a noun. It names something that makes a sound when it is crushed. In the second example,* would *is a verb. To fill in the blank in Sentence 1, I need a word that names something the men piled on a fire, so it must be a noun.* Wood *is used to build ships and can be used to start a fire. The word* wood *makes sense in Sentence 1.*

❷ Guided Practice

Give students practice in using homophones. Uncover the rest of the transparency. Read aloud the examples and practice sentences. Ask students which homophone correctly completes each practice sentence. Have students explain why their choice is correct.

❸ Apply

Assign Practice Book page 129.

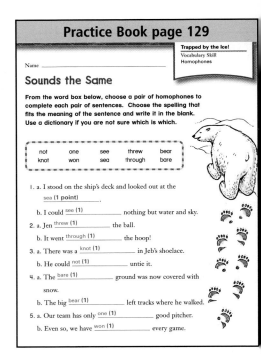

Practice Book page 129

Name _____

Trapped by the Ice!
Vocabulary Skill
Homophones

Sounds the Same

From the word box below, choose a pair of homophones to complete each pair of sentences. Choose the spelling that fits the meaning of the sentence and write it in the blank. Use a dictionary if you are not sure which is which.

not	one	see	threw	bear
knot	won	sea	through	bare

1. a. I stood on the ship's deck and looked out at the sea **(1 point)** .
   b. I could see **(1)** nothing but water and sky.
2. a. Jen threw **(1)** the ball.
   b. It went through **(1)** the hoop!
3. a. There was a knot **(1)** in Jeb's shoelace.
   b. He could not **(1)** untie it.
4. a. The bare **(1)** ground was now covered with snow.
   b. The big bear **(1)** left tracks where he walked.
5. a. Our team has only one **(1)** good pitcher.
   b. Even so, we have won **(1)** every game.

STUDY SKILL: Using a Time Line

OBJECTIVES

- Use a time line to locate information.
- Summarize information from a nonfiction selection by creating a time line.
- Learn academic language: *time line*.

❶ Teach

Introduce time lines.

- A time line is a quick, efficient way to picture the order in which important, related events took place.
- A time line shows at a glance whether a short time or a long time passed from one event to the next.

Display Transparency 5–22.

- Read aloud the time line title and the events.
- Point out that the time line uses the present tense.

Model how to find information on a time line. Point to labels and information on the time line as you explain how it is organized.

Think Aloud *The first event in the selection about Shackleton's Antarctic adventure was dated October 27, 1915. This time line starts with October and shows what happened in the months that followed. I can clearly see what was happening during each month. I can see that the* Endurance *sank in November. This shows that the men set out to cross the ice in December. The bracket on the time line shows that for these three months, they were on the ice traveling north. The selection does not include any dates for those months, so this helps me understand how long it took.*

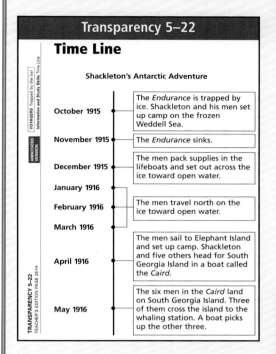

Transparency 5–22

Time Line

Shackleton's Antarctic Adventure

October 1915	The *Endurance* is trapped by ice. Shackleton and his men set up camp on the frozen Weddell Sea.
November 1915	The *Endurance* sinks.
December 1915	The men pack supplies in the lifeboats and set out across the ice toward open water.
January 1916	
February 1916	The men travel north on the ice toward open water.
March 1916	
April 1916	The men sail to Elephant Island and set up camp. Shackleton and five others head for South Georgia Island in a boat called the *Caird*.
May 1916	The six men in the *Caird* land on South Georgia Island. Three of them cross the island to the whaling station. A boat picks up the other three.

❷ Practice/Apply

Give students practice in using a time line.

- Have partners use the time line to answer these questions:
    - In what month did the men reach Elephant Island? (April)
    - In what month did Shackleton reach the whaling station? (May)
    - After the *Endurance* sank, about how long did it take Shackleton to reach the whaling station? (about six months)
- Draw a time line like the one on the transparency and label four points as follows: *April 8, April 24, May 10, May 20.* Have pairs of students write summaries of what happened on those dates and attach them to the appropriate points along the time line.
- Have students share their work.

GRAMMAR: Possessive Pronouns

OBJECTIVES

- Identify possessive pronouns.
- Use possessive pronouns in sentences.
- Proofread and correct sentences with grammar and spelling errors.
- Proofread for *its* and *it's* to improve writing.
- Learn academic language: *possessive pronoun.*

DAY 1 INSTRUCTION

Possessive Pronouns

Teach Remind students that pronouns replace one or more words.

- Display **Transparency 5–24,** and have students identify the words replaced by pronouns in the two sets of sentences at the top. Help students recognize that the pronouns *his* and *Its* replace possessive nouns.
- Go over the bulleted definitions and the chart that shows singular and plural possessive pronouns.
- Ask volunteers to read aloud the sentences below the chart and replace the underlined word or words with a possessive pronoun.
- Ask other volunteers to complete Sentences 1–4 by choosing the correct pronoun from the choices at the end of each sentence.

Daily Language Practice
Have students correct Sentences 1 and 2 on **Transparency 5–23.**

DAY 2 PRACTICE

Independent Work

Practice/Homework Assign **Practice Book** page 130.

Daily Language Practice
Have students correct Sentences 3 and 4 on **Transparency 5–23.**

Transparency 5–23

Daily Language Practice

Correct two sentences each day.

1. on mundy, the men watched they ship sink.
   On Monday, the men watched their ship sink.
2. Shackleton asked his men to folow him on him's journey.
   Shackleton asked his men to follow him on his journey.
3. All of a sudn, the men were stranded in they's boat.
   All of a sudden, the men were stranded in their boat.
4. There path went through impassable terrain.
   Their path went through impassable terrain.
5. The deserted island was cold and not at all prity.
   The deserted island was cold and not at all pretty.
6. Tom never foregot his's meeting with the sea leopard?
   Tom never forgot his meeting with the sea leopard.
7. Did one man catch him's foot in an icy crevasse
   Did one man catch his foot in an icy crevasse?
8. Untill that time, the crew ate they food and saved they water.
   Until that time, the crew ate their food and saved their water.
9. mine teacher told us about Shackleton and he's crew.
   My teacher told us about Shackleton and his crew.
10. Affter that, we wrote ours report about hims journey.
    After that, we wrote our report about his journey.

TRANSPARENCY 5-23
TEACHER'S EDITION PAGE 2511

Monitoring Student Progress

If . . .	Then . . .
students score 7 or below on **Practice Book** page 131,	use the Reteaching lesson on Teacher's Edition page R22.

Transparency 5–24

Possessive Pronouns

The men followed Shackleton's plan.
The men followed his plan.

The storm's winds were fierce.
Its winds were fierce.

- A **possessive pronoun** shows ownership.
- The pronouns *my, your, her, his, its, our,* and *their* are possessive pronouns.

Possessive Pronouns	
Singular	**Plural**
my	our
your	your
his, her, its	their

Shackleton's crew faced a dangerous journey.
Shackleton wanted to save the men's lives.
The tired men felt the fire's warmth.
The sea leopard jumped at Tom's feet.

1. The men carried _____their_____ food. (their, they)
2. My friend shared _____her_____ map of the journey. (she, her)
3. ____My____ report is about Shackleton's voyage. (Me, My)
4. May I read ____your____ report? (you, your)

TRANSPARENCY 5-24
TEACHER'S EDITION PAGE 2511

Practice Book page 130

Trapped by the Ice!
Grammar Skill Possessive Pronouns

Name _____

Writing Possessively

Write the possessive pronoun in each sentence.

1. The men began their voyage in 1915. their **(1 point)**
2. Shackleton and his crew were very brave. his **(1)**
3. Our class read about the amazing adventure. our **(1)**
4. I asked my teacher about ice floes. my **(1)**
5. Her explanation was clear and helpful. her **(1)**

Write the possessive pronoun that could take the place of the underlined word or words.

6. I think that Shackleton's story is remarkable. his **(1)**
7. I admire the men's courage. their **(1)**
8. The station's light was a marvelous sight. Its **(1)**
9. Shackleton returned to John, Chippy, and Tim's camp. their **(1)**
10. Thoralf was happy to see Thoralf's old friend. his **(1)**

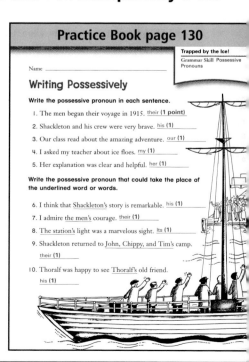

THEME 5: Voyagers

~~O~~ur Perilous Journey

~~Ha~~ve students imagine that they ~~we~~re members of Shackleton's crew.

~~A~~sk them to write sentences from ~~t~~heir diaries. Each sentence should ~~i~~nclude a possessive pronoun. ~~(~~Examples: *Today our bark sank ~~u~~nder the ice. The men have ~~f~~inished their fresh water. My legs ~~a~~che. Shackleton described his plan.*)

~~H~~ave students exchange sentences ~~a~~nd check each other's use of ~~p~~ossessive pronouns.

~~S~~tudents may wish to add illustra~~t~~ions or use their sentences as the ~~b~~asis for a longer writing project.

Independent Work

Practice/Homework Assign **Practice Book** page 131.

Proofreading: *its, it's*

Teach Tell students that *its* and *it's* are two commonly confused words. Point out that good writers always check these words when they proofread.

- Display **Transparency 5–25,** and have students compare *its* and *it's* in the two sentences at the top. Help them understand that *its* is a possessive pronoun meaning "belonging to it," whereas *it's* is a contraction for *it is.*

- Ask students to read Items 1–5 and decide whether or not *its* and *it's* are used correctly.

- Have students proofread a piece of their own writing for correct use of *its* and *it's.*

Practice/Homework Assign **Practice Book** page 132.

~~Dai~~ly Language Practice
~~Ha~~ve students correct Sentences 5 ~~an~~d 6 on **Transparency 5–23.**

Daily Language Practice
Have students correct Sentences 7 and 8 on **Transparency 5–23.**

Daily Language Practice
Have students correct Sentences 9 and 10 on **Transparency 5–23.**

Practice Book page 131

Trapped by the Ice!
Grammar Skill Possessive Pronouns

~~Name~~ _____

~~C~~hoosing Possessives

~~C~~hoose the correct word in parentheses to complete ~~e~~ach sentence.

1. Shackleton led his **(1 point)** crew to Antarctica. (him, his)

2. The *Endurance* was a useless hulk, lying on its **(1)** side. (it's, its)

3. The men carried their **(1)** food with them. (they, their)

4. Their **(1)** journey was just beginning. (Their, There)

5. Shackleton described his **(1)** plan. (he's, his)

6. The lifeboats were their **(1)** only hope. (their, they're)

7. Each boat had its **(1)** own sled. (its, its')

8. Our **(1)** class studied the perilous trip. (Our, Ours)

9. I decided to write my **(1)** story about Antarctica. (me, my)

~~1~~0. Is your **(1)** story about Shackleton? (your, you)

Transparency 5–25

VOYAGERS: Trapped by the Ice!
Grammar Skill Improving Your Writing
ANNOTATED VERSION

Proofreading for *Its* and *It's*

The crew is ready to leave on <u>its</u> journey.
The men know <u>it's</u> going to be a dangerous trip.

Read each example. Decide whether or not *its* or *it's* is used correctly in each. Rewrite any incorrect sentences.

1. The boat is weak. It's wood is cracked.

   The boat is weak. Its wood is cracked.

2. The boat is sinking. Its filled with ice.

   The boat is sinking. It's filled with ice.

3. The storm is fierce. Its winds are powerful.

   Correct

4. What is that? Its ice from the storm.

   What is that? It's ice from the storm.

5. Shackleton sees the whaling station. It's light shines across the barren landscape.

   Shackleton sees the whaling station. Its light shines across the
   barren landscape.

TRANSPARENCY 5–25
TEACHER'S EDITION PAGE 251J

Practice Book page 132

Trapped by the Ice!
Grammar Skill Improving Your Writing

Name _____

Writing a Story

Alana wrote a story about Shackleton's crew. Proofread Alana's writing. Check that *its* and *it's* are used correctly. Then rewrite the letter on the lines below. (1 point each)

May 19, 1916

Its very cold again today. John and Chippy are still very ill. The sun is bright, but it's light brings no heat. This barren land is deserted and lonely.

I explored the terrain yesterday. Its difficult to follow a trail. At last, I killed a seal. It's meat will feed us for several days. The food is so cold it has lost it's taste.

I hope that Shackleton and the others can survive their journey. Its hard to imagine a more grueling adventure.

May 19, 1916

It's very cold again today. John and Chippy are still very ill. The sun is bright, but **its** light brings no heat. This barren land is deserted and lonely.

I explored the terrain yesterday. **It's** difficult to follow a trail. At last, I killed a seal. **Its** meat will feed us for several days. The food is so cold it has lost **its** taste.

I hope that Shackleton and the others can survive their perilous journey. **It's** hard to imagine a more grueling adventure.

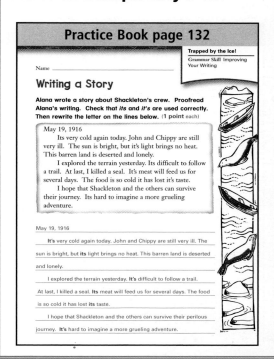

WRITING: Learning Log Entry

OBJECTIVES

- Identify the characteristics of a learning log entry.
- Write a learning log entry.
- Write dates and times.
- Learn academic language: *learning log.*

Writing Traits

Organization As students write their learning log entries, encourage them to use connecting words. You might work with them to brainstorm a chart of these words and phrases.

Connecting Words
also, too, another, in addition
however, although, in contrast, similarly
also, too, another, in addition

DAY 1 ACTIVITY

Introducing the Format

Introduce learning logs.

- A learning log is a set of notes.
- A learning log keeps track of what you have learned in different subjects.
- A learning log entry can be about books you have read, writing you have done, and math or science projects.
- It also records goals for future learning or improvement.

Start students thinking about writing a learning log entry.

- Ask students to reread something they have written.
- Have students jot down notes about why they wrote the piece and how they feel about it.
- Then ask how they might change or improve the writing.
- Have students save their notes.

DAY 2 INSTRUCTION

Discussing the Model

Display and discuss Transparency 5–26.

- What subject is the learning log entry about? (writing)
- What kinds of writing is it about? (a poem and a report)
- What does the writer do well? (connects own experience to writing, relates topics to personal likes)
- What does the writer not do very well? (spelling, proofreading)
- What are the writer's future goals? (Proof read more carefully; add to research repo

Display Transparency 5–27 and discuss the guidelines.

Have students draft a learning log ent

- They can base it on recent examples of their own writing assignments.
- Have them use their notes from Day 1.
- Assign **Practice Book** page 133.
- See Writing Traits on this page.

Transparency 5–26

A Learning Log Entry

Writing Samples

For my learning log, I will use a poem about ice and a report about sea lions. I wrote the poem for the story *Trapped by the Ice!* The story made me shiver. I really hate the cold. That's why I wrote the poem.

connects own experiences to reading

I like my poem because it makes me shiver, just like the story. I think I used interesting words and ideas to describe ice. I see three spelling mistakes. I need to

goal

proofread more carefully. The report is about sea lion families.

relates topics to personal likes

I think sea mammals are really interesting. If I could be an animal, I would be a sea lion.

Reading my report, I can think of a few more questions to research. Rereading something long after it is written is different.

goal

I would like to add to my report to include answers to my new questions.

Transparency 5–27

Guidelines for Writing a Learning Log Entry

- Decide what subject you will write about.
- Decide what particular part of that subject you will write about. Will you write about a poem or research report? a math activity? a social studies project?
- List what you have learned under the heading *What I Learned.*
- List the areas that need improvement under *My Goals.*

Practice Book page 133

Trapped by the Ice!
Writing Skill Improving Your Writing

Name _____

A Learning Log Entry

Pick two examples of your own writing. Carefully reread your work. Complete the Learning Log entry. List what you have learned under *What I Learned.* List what needs more work under *My Goals.*

LEARNING LOG		
Writing sample 1: _____		Date: _____
Writing sample 2: _____		Date: _____
What I Learned: (5 points)		**My Goals:** (5)

DAY 3 · INSTRUCTION

Improving Writing: Dates and Times

Explain writing dates.

Dates can be written using the name of the month or just using numerals.

Dates begin with the month, followed by the number of the day, and then the year.

Write today's date, including the year, using the name of the month. Note the comma.

Write today's date, including the year, using numerals. Note the slash marks.

Explain writing times.

P.M. stands for the Latin phrase *post meridiem,* which means "after noon."

A.M. stands for the Latin phrase *ante meridiem,* which means "before noon."

Write the time now, using A.M. or P.M.

Note the colon between the hour and the minute.

Display Transparency 5–28.

Show only the top. Discuss each bullet.

Uncover Exercises 1–5. Work with students to write each date or time.

Assign Practice Book page 134.

Transparency 5–28

Writing Dates and Times

- Dates are written this way: month, day, year. A comma separates the day and year.
  The thirty-first of January in 2004:
  January 31, 2004
- Dates can also be written in numerals separated by slash marks.
  The thirty-first of January in 2004: 1/31/04
- A.M. stands for morning, from one minute after midnight until noon.
  Nine o'clock in the morning: 9:00 A.M.
- P.M. stands for after noon, from one minute after noon until midnight.
  Three o'clock in the afternoon: 3:00 P.M.

1. The eighteenth of March in the year 2005
   March 18, 2005   3/18/05

2. The fifth of August in 2008
   August 5, 2008   8/5/08

3. In 2012, the twenty-first of February:
   February 21, 2012   2/21/12

4. Seven o'clock in the morning.   7:00 A.M.

5. Eight thirty at night.   8:30 P.M.

DAY 4 · ACTIVITY

Writing Game

Have students write a learning log entry about a sport or other activity.

- Ask students to name a hobby or activity they do often, such as swimming, camping, participating in team sports, or playing a musical instrument.

- Ask them to think of one important learning experience they had while doing this hobby or activity. It could be a formal lesson, a practice, game, or some other performance.

- Have them write a learning log entry for this experience.

- Remind them to use the heads *What I Learned* and *My Goals.*

Practice Book page 134

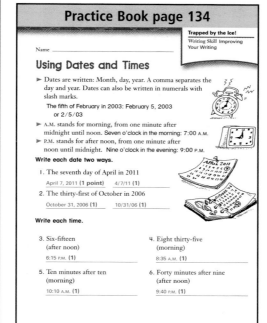

Name _____

Trapped by the Ice!
Writing Skill Improving Your Writing

Using Dates and Times

▶ Dates are written: Month, day, year. A comma separates the day and year. Dates can also be written in numerals with slash marks.
  The fifth of February in 2003: February 5, 2003 or 2/5/03

▶ A.M. stands for morning, from one minute after midnight until noon. Seven o'clock in the morning: 7:00 A.M.

▶ P.M. stands for after noon, from one minute after noon until midnight. Nine o'clock in the evening: 9:00 P.M.

Write each date two ways.

1. The seventh day of April in 2011
   April 7, 2011 **(1 point)**   4/7/11 **(1)**

2. The thirty-first of October in 2006
   October 31, 2006 **(1)**   10/31/06 **(1)**

Write each time.

3. Six-fifteen (after noon)
   6:15 P.M. **(1)**

4. Eight thirty-five (morning)
   8:35 A.M. **(1)**

5. Ten minutes after ten (morning)
   10:10 A.M. **(1)**

6. Forty minutes after nine (after noon)
   9:40 P.M. **(1)**

DAY 5 · ACTIVITY

Sharing Writing

Consider these options for sharing students' writing.

- Ask students to read a piece of their writing from the Author's Chair.

- Encourage students to make a class book of learning log entries.

Portfolio Opportunity

Save students' learning log entries as samples of their writing development.

Monitoring Student Progress

If . . .	Then . . .
students' writing does not follow the guidelines on **Transparency 5–27,**	work with students to improve specific parts of their writing.

Language Center

VOCABULARY

Building Vocabulary

👥 Pairs	🕐 15 minutes
Objective	Create a word web of ship terms.

The selection *Trapped by the Ice!* includes many terms that are used aboard a ship. With your partner, look through the selection for as many words relating to ships as you can. Record the words in a web such as the following.

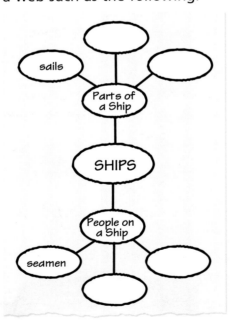

Work with your partner to write a definition of each word in your web. Then brainstorm other words that tell about ships and the people who work on ships. Add these words to your web.

GRAMMAR

Possessive Pronouns

👥 Pairs	🕐 30 minutes
Objective	Play a matching game with possessive pronouns.
Materials	Index cards

Write on separate cards: **my, your, her, his, its, our, their.** Mix them up and place them face-down in a pile. Write the words and phrases below on separate cards, mix them up, and place them face-down in another pile:

I	Ken and Lisa
you	the crewman
Ken	and you
Lisa	the lifeboat
Lisa and I	the waves

- Now, turn over one card from each pile. If the possessive pronoun can stand for the word or phrase on the other card, call out **"Match!"**

- Then say a sentence, using the words on both cards. For example, if you turned over *our* and *Lisa and I,* one sentence would be, ***Lisa and I** went on **our** aunt's boat.*

- If your sentence is correct, keep the noun/pronoun card and return the possessive card to the bottom of the pile. Now it's your partner's turn.

VOCABULARY

Vocabulary Game

👥 Pairs	🕐 30 minutes
Objective	Play a game of concentration with Key Vocabulary words.
Materials	Activity Master 5–3 on page R25

Cut out the cards, spread them out face-down, and scramble them up.

To play the game:

- The first player picks two cards and turns them over.

- If one of the cards has the definition of the word on the other card, you must say a sentence with the word.

- If you make up a correct sentence, you keep both cards.

- If the cards don't match, or you can't think of a sentence, put the cards back, face-down.

- Take turns picking pairs of cards and using the words in sentences.

- When you've picked up all the cards, the player with the most number of matching pairs wins.

- Now, play again!

Consider copying and laminating these activities for use in centers.

LISTENING/SPEAKING

Practice Group Problem Solving

Groups	🕐 30 minutes
Objective	Create a survival plan.
Materials	Anthology

Shackleton and his crew needed to solve some very serious problems. Shackleton, his skipper, and his next in command met as a group to figure out what to do. Groups are often better at solving problems than individuals. Here's why:

- More ideas are suggested.

- Group members may be experts at different things.

- The group can discuss the strengths and weaknesses of each idea and choose the best ones.

Read the problem below and come up with a survival plan. List the things you will bring. Write the procedures you will follow to survive. Illustrate your plan if you wish. Remember to work as a group. Present your plan to the class.

Problem: Your group must survive for two days and one night on Antarctica. You will have nothing with you except what you can carry for one mile. You cannot go back for more supplies. You will find no people or buildings, only rocks, ice, and wind.

PHONICS/SPELLING

VCCV Match

👥 Pairs	🕐 30 minutes
Objective	Match syllables to form VCCV words.
Materials	Dictionary, 12 index cards

List these VCCV words on a separate piece of paper:

Monday	dollar
sudden	window
until	hello
forget	market
happen	puppy
follow	kitten

- Draw a line to divide each word into syllables. Check a dictionary if necessary.

- Now, cut each index card in half.

- Write the first syllable of each word on a card, shuffle the cards, and set them face-down in a pile.

- Do the same with the second syllables.

To play the game, take turns with your partner.

- Turn over the top card in each pile.

- If the cards placed side by side make a VCCV word, set them aside.

- If they don't, put each one back in its pile, and shuffle each pile again.

- See which player can make the most VCCV words.

Leveled Readers

Iceberg Rescue

by Sarah Amada
illustrated by S. Saelig Gallagher

Iceberg Rescue

Summary *Explorer Louise Arner Boyd and her team are mapping the coast of Greenland, in 1933, when their ship, the* Veslekari, *runs aground. When their first efforts to free the ship fail, Louise tries connecting the* Veslekari *to a nearby iceberg by cable and uses the ship's power to lift the ship out of the mud. As the ship pulls away, Louise is already thinking of her return.*

Vocabulary

Introduce the Key Vocabulary and ask students to complete the BLM.

glacier giant body of ice, *p. 4*

upright right side up, *p. 11*

iceberg large, floating mass of ice that has broken off a glacier, *p. 15*

cable very strong wire rope, *p. 15*

● BELOW LEVEL

Building Background and Vocabulary

Discuss the possible dangers of explorations in the Arctic Ocean, making sure that students understand what an iceberg is. Preview the story with students, using the story vocabulary when possible.

Comprehension Skill: Text Organization

Have students read the Strategy Focus on the book flap. Remind students to use the strategy and to note text features as they read the book. (See the Leveled Readers Teacher's Guide for **Vocabulary and Comprehension Practice Masters.**)

Responding

Have partners discuss how to answer the questions on the inside back cover.

Think About the Selection Sample answers:

1. She is gathering information and making maps of the area.
2. Possible responses: She is not easily frightened. It is not easy to keep her from doing what she wants to do.
3. Responses will vary.

Making Connections Responses will vary.

Building Fluency

Model Read aloud pages 3–4. Point out the heading and explain that headings tell about the paragraphs that follow them.

Practice Have students find and read aloud each heading in the story. Then they can read the paragraphs that follow the heading and explain why the heading is appropriate.

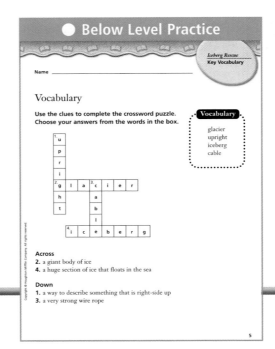

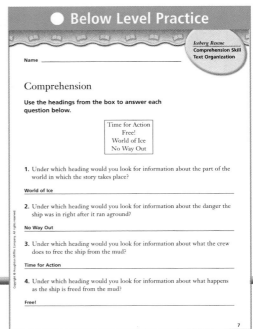

10 THEME 5: Voyagers

Racing Danger

Summary *When Mary Ann Patten joins her husband on a sailing voyage, she helps by cooking and treating the sick. When her husband becomes ill, she is called upon to take command of the ship. With Mary in command, Neptune's Car completes the sailing race to San Francisco, finishing in second place.*

Vocabulary

Introduce the Key Vocabulary and ask students to complete the BLM.

advertise to tell about a product or service so as to make people want to buy or use it, *p. 5*

floes* large sheets of floating ice, *p. 8*

perilous* very dangerous, *p. 9*

grueling* very tiring, *p. 15*

*Forms of these words are Anthology Key Vocabulary words.

▲ ON LEVEL

Building Background and Vocabulary

Show students an illustration of a clipper ship, and explain that these ships were the fastest sailing ships of their time. Ask students to discuss what it would be like to race in such a ship. Preview the story with students, using the story vocabulary when possible.

Comprehension Skill: Text Organization

Have students read the Strategy Focus on the book flap. Remind students to use the strategy and to note text features as they read the book. (See the Leveled Readers Teacher's Guide for **Vocabulary and Comprehension Practice Masters**.)

Responding

Have partners discuss how to answer the questions on the inside back cover.

Think About the Selection Sample answers:

1. The clipper ship is in a race with two other ships to see which ship is the fastest.
2. Captain Patten had become very sick. Only Mary knows how to navigate.
3. Possible response: She is smart and very brave. She had to be very confident.
4. Responses will vary, but might include the captain's illness, the extreme weather and sailing conditions, and being afraid of a disaster at sea.

Making Connections Responses will vary.

Building Fluency

Model Read aloud page 9. Explain to the students that *But after two weeks* is a transition phrase that indicates a change in time.

Practice Have students look in the book for similar transition phrases that show a change in time or place. If students have trouble, point them to page 16, where they will find the phrase *After 136 days at sea.*

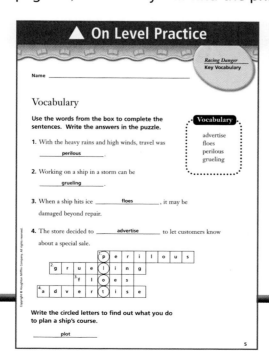

VOYAGE ACROSS THE PACIFIC
by Stanford Makishi
illustrated by Dennis Albetski

Voyage Across the Pacific

Summary *Ben Finney, Herb Kawainui Kane, and Tommy Holmes become intrigued with the idea of how the Polynesians discovered the vast and scattered islands of the Pacific. They set out to prove that the islands were discovered not by accident, but intentionally. After much planning and preparation, the men and others recreate the journey. Their efforts yield valuable information about early exploration and settlement.*

Vocabulary

Introduce the Key Vocabulary and ask students to complete the BLM.

perilous* very dangerous, *p. 4*

navigate steer or control the course of, *p. 7*

deserted* empty; not lived in, or having few or no people, *p. 15*

grueling* very tiring, *p. 16*

*Forms of these words are Anthology Key Vocabulary words.

■ ABOVE LEVEL

Building Background and Vocabulary

On a world map, point out the islands of the central and south Pacific. Discuss the dangers of sailing small boats on the open ocean. Preview the story with students, using the story vocabulary when possible.

Comprehension Skill: Text Organization

Have students read the Strategy Focus on the book flap. Remind students to use the strategy and to note text features as they read the book. (See the Leveled Readers Teacher's Guide for **Vocabulary and Comprehension Practice Masters.**)

Responding

Have partners discuss how to answer the questions on the inside back cover.

Think About the Selection Sample answers:

1. to solve a mystery about how the Polynesians traveled across the ocean

2. Possible responses: They studied drawings of boats from the 1700s. They studied the Pacific Ocean to decide on the size of the canoe.

3. They wanted to use the ancient Polynesian methods of navigation. They asked a man who knew these methods, Mau Pialug, to lead them.

4. Possible response: The voyage showed that their ancestors had been skilled sailors.

Making Connections Responses will vary.

Building Fluency

Model Read aloud page 4 and write the word *double-hulled*. Point out that *double-hulled* is a compound word because it is made up of two smaller words. Explain that *double-hulled* is a hyphenated compound word, but also note that not all compound words have hyphens.

Practice Have volunteers read aloud the compound words they find.

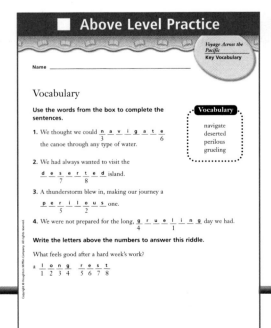

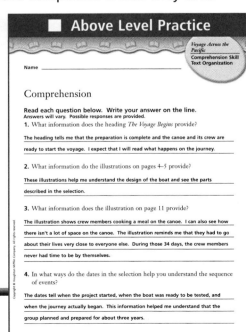

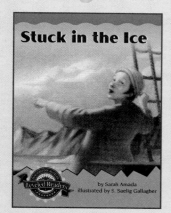

Stuck in the Ice

by Sarah Amada
illustrated by S. Saelig Gallagher

Stuck in the Ice

Summary *Louise Arner Boyd and her team of explorers were on a ship to Greenland in 1933, when they got stuck in the ice. Boyd's suggestion to tie a cable around an iceberg and use it to pull the ship free was a success. Her team had a good trip, taking many photographs before returning home safely.*

Vocabulary

Introduce the Key Vocabulary and ask students to complete the BLM.

explorers people who go to unknown or unfamiliar places, *p. 3*

glacier a large mass of ice that moves very slowly, *p. 4*

stuck attached and unable to move, *p. 7*

tide the rising and falling of the surface of the ocean, *p. 12*

iceberg a large mass of ice floating in the ocean, usually pieces of a glacier that have fallen off, *p. 15*

cable a strong thick rope made of fiber or steel, *p. 15*

◆ LANGUAGE SUPPORT

Building Background and Vocabulary

Display pages 6–7 of the book and ask students to describe what they see. Explain that the people on this ship are here to explore this unknown part of the world. Point out that explorers took photographs and notes and made drawings of places they explored. Distribute the **Build Background Practice Master.** Invite students to be classroom explorers and complete the page.

Comprehension Skill: Text Organization

Have students read the Strategy Focus on the book flap. Remind students to use the strategy and to look for ways the text is organized as they read the book. (See the Leveled Readers Teacher's Guide for **Build Background, Vocabulary, and Graphic Organizer Masters.**)

Responding

Have partners discuss how to answer the questions on the inside back cover.

Think About the Selection Sample answers:

1. She was an explorer who was taking photographs and making maps.
2. Sample response: The iceberg was large, would stay where it was, and could be attached to the ship with a cable.
3. Responses will vary.

Making Connections Responses will vary.

Building Fluency

Model Read aloud pages 16–17 as students follow along. Explain that the exclamation points show that something is exciting or loud. Reread, and have students decide whether each sentence tells about something loud or exciting.

Practice Have partners read the same text to each other three times, or until they can read it accurately and with expression.

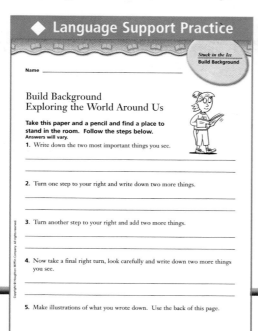

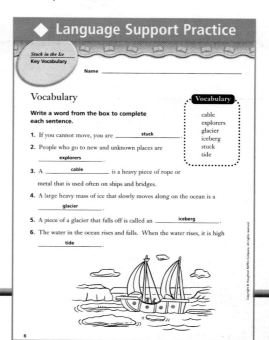

Connecting and Comparing Literature

Check Your Progress

Use these Paired Selections to help students make connections with other theme literature and to wrap up the theme.

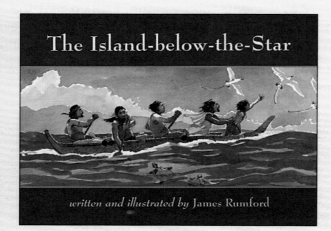

The Island-below-the-Star
Genre: Fiction

Five brothers contribute their unique talents to sail their canoe across the South Pacific to an island below a distant star, today's Hawaii.

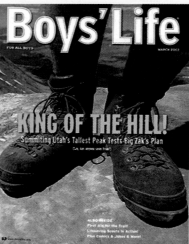

by Thomas Fleming

A Wild Ride
Genre: Nonfiction

This magazine article tells about two young brothers who rode across the United States in 1910—alone and on horseback.

Preparing for Tests

Taking Tests: Strategies

Use this material to prepare for tests, to teach strategies, and to practice test formats.

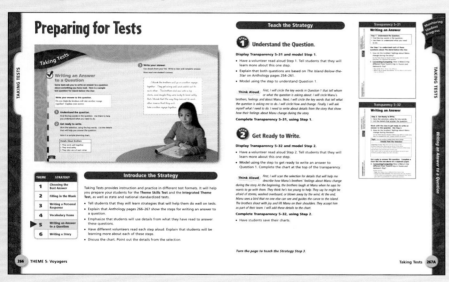

- Independent practice for skills

- Transparencies
- Strategy Posters
- Blackline Masters

Skill Review

Use these lessons and supporting activities to review tested skills in this theme.

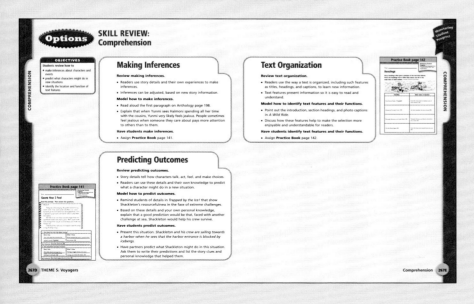

Technology

Audio Selections
The Island-below-the-Star

A Wild Ride

www.eduplace.com
Log on to Education Place for vocabulary support—
e•Glossary
e•WordGame

Theme Connections

Anthology Literature

Activities to help students think critically

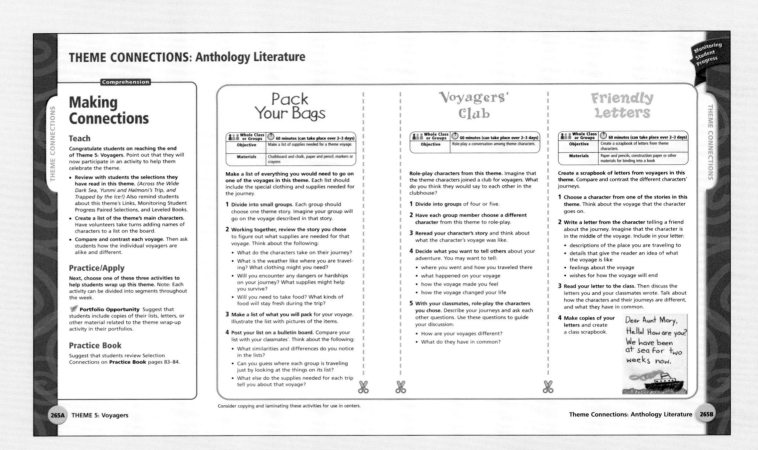

THEME CONNECTIONS: Anthology Literature

Monitoring Student Progress

Comprehension

Making Connections

Teach

Congratulate students on reaching the end of **Theme 5: Voyagers.** Point out that they will now participate in an activity to help them celebrate the theme.

- Review with students the selections they have read in this theme. (*Across the Wide Dark Sea, Yunmi and Halmoni's Trip,* and *Trapped by the Ice!*) Also remind students about this theme's Links, Monitoring Student Progress Paired Selections, and Leveled Books.
- Create a list of the theme's main characters. Have volunteers take turns adding names of characters to a list on the board.
- Compare and contrast each voyage. Then ask students how the individual voyagers are alike and different.

Practice/Apply

Next, choose one of these three activities to help students wrap up this theme. Note: Each activity can be divided into segments throughout the week.

Portfolio Opportunity Suggest that students include copies of their lists, letters, or other material related to the theme wrap-up activity in their portfolios.

Practice Book

Suggest that students review Selection Connections on **Practice Book** pages 83–84.

Pack Your Bags

👥👥👥 Whole Class or Groups	⏱ 60 minutes (can take place over 2–3 days)
Objective	Make a list of supplies needed for a theme voyage.
Materials	Chalkboard and chalk, paper and pencil, markers or crayons

Make a list of everything you would need to go on one of the voyages in this theme. Each list should include the special clothing and supplies needed for the journey.

1 Divide into small groups. Each group should choose one theme story. Imagine your group will go on the voyage described in that story.

2 Working together, review the story you chose to figure out what supplies are needed for that voyage. Think about the following:

- What do the characters take on their journey?
- What is the weather like where you are traveling? What clothing might you need?
- Will you encounter any dangers or hardships on your journey? What supplies might help you survive?
- Will you need to take food? What kinds of food will stay fresh during the trip?

3 Make a list of what you will pack for your voyage. Illustrate the list with pictures of the items.

4 Post your list on a bulletin board. Compare your list with your classmates'. Think about the following:

- What similarities and differences do you notice in the lists?
- Can you guess where each group is traveling just by looking at the things on its list?
- What else do the supplies needed for each trip tell you about that voyage?

Voyagers' Club

👥👥👥 Whole Class or Groups	⏱ 60 minutes (can take place over 2–3 days)
Objective	Role-play a conversation among theme characters.

Role-play characters from this theme. Imagine that the theme characters joined a club for voyagers. What do you think they would say to each other in the clubhouse?

1 Divide into groups of four or five.

2 Have each group member choose a different character from this theme to role-play.

3 Reread your character's story and think about what the character's voyage was like.

4 Decide what you want to tell others about your adventure. You may want to tell:

- where you went and how you traveled there
- what happened on your voyage
- how the voyage made you feel
- how the voyage changed your life

5 With your classmates, role-play the characters you chose. Describe your journeys and ask each other questions. Use these questions to guide your discussion:

- How are your voyages different?
- What do they have in common?

Friendly Letters

👥👥👥 Whole Class or Groups	⏱ 60 minutes (can take place over 2–3 days)
Objective	Create a scrapbook of letters from theme characters.
Materials	Paper and pencils, construction paper or other materials for binding into a book

Create a scrapbook of letters from voyagers in this theme. Compare and contrast the different characters' journeys.

1 Choose a character from one of the stories in this theme. Think about the voyage that the character goes on.

2 Write a letter from the character telling a friend about the journey. Imagine that the character is in the middle of the voyage. Include in your letter:

- descriptions of the place you are traveling to
- details that give the reader an idea of what the voyage is like
- feelings about the voyage
- wishes for how the voyage will end

3 Read your letter to the class. Then discuss the letters you and your classmates wrote. Talk about how the characters and their journeys are different, and what they have in common.

4 Make copies of your letters and create a class scrapbook.

Dear Aunt Mary,
Hello! How are you?
We have been
at sea for two
weeks now.

Consider copying and laminating these activities for use in centers.

Three Main Selections

ACROSS THE WIDE DARK SEA
The Mayflower Journey

Jean Van Leeuwen & pictures by Thomas B. Allen

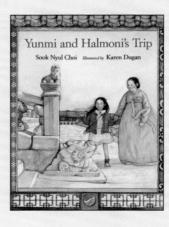

Yunmi and Halmoni's Trip
Sook Nyul Choi *Illustrated by* Karen Dugan

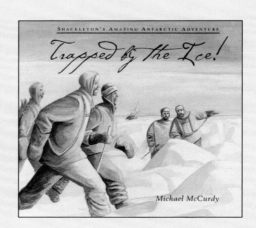

SHACKLETON'S AMAZING ANTARCTIC ADVENTURE
Trapped by the Ice!
Michael McCurdy

OVERVIEW

eveled Books

tivities to help students connect and compare

Independent Activities

While you work with small groups, students can choose from a wealth of books to complete these activities.

Leveled Readers . . .

for *Across the Wide Dark Sea*
The Golden Land
Chasing the Train
Faith's Journey
Going to America

for *Yunmi and Halmoni's Trip*
Brothers are Forever
South Pole Bound
The Same, But Different
Max Visits London

for *Trapped by the Ice!*
Iceberg Rescue
Racing Danger
Voyage Across the Pacific
Stuck in the Ice

Leveled Theme Paperbacks
The Josefina Story Quilt
A Child's Glacier Bay
Balto and the Great Race

Leveled Bibliography
pages 148E–148F

THEME CONNECTIONS:
Leveled Books

Mixed-up Stories

👥 Singles or Pairs	⏱ 30 minutes
Objective	Write a story taking a character from one book on a voyage from a different book.
Materials	Reference materials

Choose a character from any of the books you have read. Then choose a voyage from a different book. Imagine what it would be like if the character went on this new journey. How would the story be different?

Think about

- how the character you chose would react to the sights and events of this new journey
- what the character might do on this new journey
- how this new journey might make the character feel
- how this new journey might change the character

Write a story in which your character sets off on the new voyage. Then trade stories with a partner.

After you finish reading each other's stories, discuss them together. Use these questions to guide your discussion:

- How did different voyagers make the journeys different?
- How did the new journeys change the voyagers?

Create a Picture Album

👥 Pairs	⏱ 30 minutes
Objective	Draw pictures of places and events from a journey.
Materials	Paper, crayons or markers, stapler or other materials for binding pictures into an album, reference materials

Choose a character from any of the books you have read. Create an album of pictures showing what that character did and saw on his or her journey. You might include pictures showing

- what it is like to leave home
- how the character travels
- who travels with the character
- places the character visits
- people the character meets on the journey
- exciting things the character does

Share your picture album with the class or with a small group. Compare your character's journey with the journeys of other characters you have read about.

Use these questions to guide your discussion:

- What makes the journeys exciting?
- What problems do the characters face on their journeys?
- What do the characters learn on their journeys?

Your Own Journey

👤 Singles	⏱ 30 minutes
Objective	Compare and contrast student's own journey (or imaginary journey) with a journey from a Leveled Reader.
Materials	Reference materials

Have you been on a journey to a place you had never visited before? Your journey could be anything from a trip to another country to a visit to a local skating rink.

Think about a journey you have taken. Write some notes about your journey. Think about

- where you went on your journey
- what you did and saw there
- how your journey made you feel

Now choose a journey from any of the books you have read. Write a paragraph comparing and contrasting your own journey with the journey from the book. How were the journeys different? How were they the same?

While you write your paragraph, think about these questions:

- How did you travel on your journey? How did the characters travel in the book?
- Did you travel as far as the characters did? Did your journey last as long?
- How did the characters' journey make them feel? Did you feel the same way on your journey?
- Did you and the characters learn similar things on your journeys?

Consider copying and laminating these activities for use in centers.

velve Leveled Readers

Three Leveled Theme Paperbacks

Daily Lesson Plans

Technology
Lesson Planner CD-ROM allows you to customize the chart below to develop your own lesson plans.

T Skill tested on Theme Skills Test and/or Integrated Theme Test

 50–60 minutes

Connecting and Comparing Literature

CHECK YOUR PROGRESS

 A Wild Ride
Boys' Life
KING OF THE HILL!
by Thomas Fleming

Leveled Readers
- Fluency Practice
- Independent Reading

 40–60 minutes

Preparing for Tests

TAKING TESTS: Strategies

SKILL REVIEW OPTIONS

Comprehension

Structural Analysis

Vocabulary

Spelling

Grammar

Prompts for Writing

DAY 1

Introducing Paired Selections

Key Vocabulary, 253
harpoons	awe
seaworthy	hull
calabashes	roiling

Reading the Selection, 254–261
The Island-below-the-Star

Comprehension Strategy, 254
Predict/Infer **T**

Classroom Management Activities, 251Y–251Z

Leveled Readers
The Golden Land
Chasing the Train
Faith's Journey
Going to America

Introduce the Strategy, 266
Writing an Answer to a Question

Comprehension, 267D–267E
Skill Review Options **T**

Structural Analysis, 267F–267G
Skill Review Options **T**

Vocabulary, 267H–267I
Skill Review Options **T**

Spelling, 267J
Vowel Sounds in *tooth/cook* **T**

Grammar, 267L
Subject Pronouns **T**

Prompts for Writing, 267N
Play Scene/Using Exclamations

DAY 2

Reading the Selection
The Island-below-the-Star

Connecting and Comparing
Making Inferences, 255, 257, 259
Predicting Outcomes, 261

Stop and Think, 261A

Classroom Management Activities, 251Y–251Z

Leveled Readers
Brothers are Forever
South Pole Bound
The Same, But Different
Max Visits London

Step 1: Understand the Question, 267A

Comprehension, 267D–267E
Skill Review Options **T**

Structural Analysis, 267F–267G
Skill Review Options **T**

Vocabulary, 267H–267I
Skill Review Options **T**

Spelling, 267J
Vowel Sound in *bought* **T**

Grammar, 267L
Object Pronouns **T**

Prompts for Writing, 267N
Message/Complete Information

DAILY LESSON PLANS

Target Skills of the Week

Comprehension
Vocabulary
Phonics/Decoding
Fluency

Monitoring Student Progress

DAILY LESSON PLANS

DAY 3

A Wild Ride
Boys' Life
KING OF THE HILL!
by Thomas Fleming

Key Vocabulary, 261B
territory
slogging
newsreel

Reading the Selection, 262–264
A Wild Ride

Comprehension Strategy, 262
Predict/Infer **T**

Classroom Management Activities,
251Y–251Z

Leveled Readers
Iceberg Rescue
Facing Danger
Voyage Across the Pacific
Stuck in the Ice

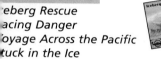

Step 2: Get Ready to Write, 267A

Comprehension, 267D–267E
Skill Review Options **T**

Structural Analysis, 267F–267G
Skill Review Options **T**

Vocabulary, 267H–267I
Skill Review Options **T**

Spelling, 267K
CCV Pattern **T**

Grammar, 267M
Possessive Pronouns **T**

Prompts for Writing, 267O
Learning Log/Writing Dates **T**

DAY 4

A Wild Ride
Boys' Life
KING OF THE HILL!
by Thomas Fleming

Reading the Selection
A Wild Ride

Connecting and Comparing
Text Organization, 263

Think and Compare, 265

**Theme Connections: Anthology
Literature,** 265A–265B

Classroom Management Activities,
251Y–251Z

Leveled Readers
Theme Connections: Leveled Books,
265C–265D

Step 3: Write Your Answer, 267B

Comprehension, 267D–267E
Skill Review Options **T**

Structural Analysis, 267F–267G
Skill Review Options **T**

Vocabulary, 267H–267I
Skill Review Options **T**

Spelling, 267K
Added Endings

Grammar, 267M
The Verb *be*

Prompts for Writing, 267O
News Article/Audience

DAY 5

The Island-below-the-Star

A Wild Ride
Boys' Life
KING OF THE HILL!
by Thomas Fleming

**Theme Connections:
Anthology Literature,** cont.

Rereading for Fluency,
257, 264

Classroom Management Activities,
251Y–251Z

Leveled Readers
Theme Connections: Leveled Books,
265C–265D

Writing an Answer Test Practice, 267C

Comprehension, 267D–267E
Skill Review Options **T**

Structural Analysis, 267F–267G
Skill Review Options **T**

Vocabulary, 267H–267I
Skill Review Options **T**

Spelling Test, 267K

Grammar, 267M
Helping Verbs

Prompts for Writing, 267O
Description **T**/Writing Complete Sentences

Classroom Management

Independent Activities

Assign these activities at any time during the week while you work with small groups.

Suggest that students include copies of their work in their portfolios.

Art

Night Sky

Singles	<image src="clock" /> 30 minutes
Objective	Draw a picture of the night sky.
Materials	Reference sources, dark blue or black paper, chalk

Early sailors often relied on the stars to help them navigate from one place to another. In the Northern Hemisphere, sailors use Polaris, the North Star, as a guide.

Look in an encyclopedia or other reference source to find out about the North Star as well as about groups of stars called constellations.

Draw the night sky, including the North Star and at least one constellation. Label your drawing.

Math

How Far Is It?

Pairs	30 minutes
Objective	Calculate the travel times between cities.
Materials	Calculator

In "A Wild Ride," Bud and Temple make stops at Oklahoma City, St. Louis Washington, D.C., and New York City With your partner, find out how lor it takes to travel to these four cities

- If the boys had the Brush Runabo at the start of their journey, how long would it take—traveling at 30 miles an hour—to go from Oklahoma City to St. Louis? from St. Louis to Washington, D.C.? from Washington, D.C. to New York City?

- Use the mileage chart below to figure out how many hours it would take to drive between ead pair of cities.

FROM	TO	MILEAGE
Oklahoma City	St. Louis	457 miles
St. Louis	Washington, D.C.	714 miles
Washington, D.C.	New York City	204 miles

Look for more activities in the Classroom Management Kit.

Consider copying and laminating these activities for use in centers.

Social Studies

Sailing into the Unknown

Pairs	🕐 30 minutes
Objective	Compare and contrast two sea voyages.
Materials	Anthology

When the Pilgrims set off on the Mayflower, they had no idea what crossing the Atlantic Ocean would be like. When the brothers sailed to find the island below the star, they, too, were voyagers facing unknown dangers.

Look through Across the Wide Dark Sea and The Island-below-the-Star to find ways in which these voyages are the same and different. Record your findings in a Venn diagram like the one begun below.

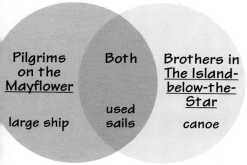

Pilgrims on the <u>Mayflower</u>

large ship

Both

used sails

Brothers in <u>The Island-below-the-Star</u>

canoe

Technology

Staying on Course

👥 Pairs	🕐 45 minutes
Objective	Research navigation.
Materials	Reference sources

When the brothers in The Island-below-the-Star and the crew of the Endurance sailed across the seas, they had none of today's modern navigation equipment. They used the stars, charts, and their experience to find their way.

Today's voyagers have radar and the GPS (Global Positioning System) to keep them on course. Research and write a paragraph about technology that modern sailors, pilots, or astronauts use to help them know exactly where they are. Think about

- what this technology does
- why this technology is helpful
- who uses this technology

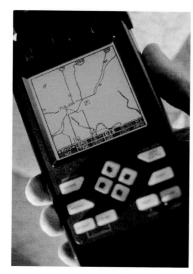

Screen from GPS unit

Language Arts

Voyager Hall of Fame

🧍 Singles	🕐 15 minutes
Objective	Write a nomination for a Voyager Hall of Fame.
Materials	Anthology

This theme is Voyagers, and its selections present many different kinds of voyagers. Suppose there was a Voyager Hall of Fame. Which voyager from this theme would you nominate to the Hall of Fame?

Write a letter to the chairman of the nominating committee. In your letter, explain

- who your candidate is
- what this person has done
- why this person deserves to be in the Voyager Hall of Fame

Connecting and Comparing Literature

Theme Wrap-Up

Check Your Progress

In this theme, you have taken voyages all over the world. The next two selections that you'll read and compare will take you to two new places. You will also practice your test-taking skills.

Before you set sail, take a look back at Sook Nyul Choi's letter on pages 150–152. Which characters in this theme best show the courage that she talks about?

Now you're ready to read about a voyage by boat across the Pacific Ocean and a voyage by horseback and car across America. As you read, think about the courage the voyagers show.

252

Read and Compare

The Island-below-the-Star

written and illustrated by James Rumford

Find out how five brothers discover Hawaii.

Try these strategies:
Monitor and Clarify
Predict and Infer

A Wild Ride
Boys' Life
KING OF THE HILL

by Thomas Fleming

Ride along as two young brothers face a challenging journey across America to meet their hero.

Try these strategies:
Evaluate
Question

Strategies in Action *Try using all your reading strategies while you read.*

253

Use Paired Selections: Check Your Progress

Have students read page 252. Discuss these questions:

- Why did the voyagers in this theme make their journeys? (to find a new home and religious freedom; to visit family; to cross the South Pole)

- Which journey did you think was the most exciting? Why? (Answers will vary.)

Have students read page 253. Ask this question:

- How might the voyagers in these stories be similar to the voyagers in the selections you have read? (Sample answers: They might be adventurous; their journeys might change them.)

Strategies in Action Remind students to use all their reading strategies, including the Predict/Infer strategy, to make predictions about story events as they read the Paired Selections.

TRANSPARENCY 5–29
TEACHER'S EDITION PAGE 253

VOYAGERS *The Island-below-the-Star*
Monitoring Student Progress
Key Vocabulary

ANNOTATED VERSION

Transparency 5–29

Voyage Words

The hunters had never seen such a huge whale. They stared at it in <u>awe</u>. When the whale was close enough, the hunters threw their <u>harpoons</u> at it. One of the spears pierced the whale's thick skin. The whale lashed its tail violently, and the water around it began <u>roiling</u> Smashing its tail against the boat, the whale made a small crack in the <u>hull</u>.

Afraid that the damaged boat might sink, the hunters sailed to the nearest island. There they fixed the boat to make it <u>seaworthy</u> again. On the island, the sailors found fresh water. They filled their <u>calabashes</u> with it so that they would have plenty to drink on the trip home.

Selection 1

The Island-below-the-Star

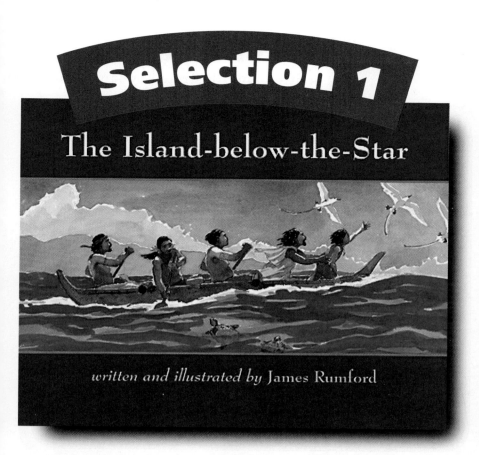

written and illustrated by James Rumford

Introducing Vocabulary

Key Vocabulary
These words appear in the selection.

harpoons spears used to hunt whales and large fish

seaworthy safe for sailing in

calabashes large, round bowls made from a gourd

awe a feeling of wonder and respect

hull the body of a boat

roiling moving roughly in many directions

e • Glossary
e • WordGame

See Vocabulary notes on pages 254, 256, 258, and 260 for additional words to preview.

Have students locate Key Vocabulary words in the story.

- Have volunteers read aloud each sentence containing a Key Vocabulary word.

Display Transparency 5–29.

- Model how to use context clues to find the meaning of *awe*.

- Ask students to use context clues to define each remaining Key Vocabulary word.

Practice/Homework Assign Practice Book page 135.

Introduce the Graphic Organizer.
Tell students to fill in **Practice Book** page 136 as they read the Paired Selections.

Practice Book page 135

Monitoring Student Progress
Key Vocabulary

Name _____

...ords for Ocean Voyagers

...the box above each word, draw a picture that shows the ...aning of the word. Then answer the questions below.

points)	(2)	(2)
harpoons	2. calabashes	3. hull

What might give you a feeling of **awe**?
Answers will vary. **(2)**

If the waves were **roiling**, would you want to go swimming? Why or why not?
Sample answer: no, because the waves would be rough and swimming
would be dangerous. **(2)**

Why would you want to make sure a boat was **seaworthy** before sailing on it?
Sample answer: Seaworthy means "safe for sailing," and I would only want
to sail on a safe boat. **(2)**

Practice Book page 136

Monitoring Student Progress
Graphic Organizer Making Inferences

Name _____

Inference Chart

Fill in the chart as you read the stories.
Answers will vary. Accept reasonable responses.
What are the voyagers in these stories like?

Characters	What the Characters Do	What I Know	My Inference
Manu in *The Island-below-the-Star*	He sneaks onto the boat when his brothers tell him not to come. **(1 point)**	The voyage will be dangerous. Very young brothers usually listen to their older brothers. **(1)**	Manu is independent and mischievous. **(1)**
Bud and Temple in *A Wild Ride*	They ride alone on horseback across the United States from Oklahoma to New York. **(1)**	These locations are over 1,000 miles apart. There is harsh weather and rough terrain between them. **(1)**	Bud and Temple are brave and resourceful. **(1)**
		Today kids are not allowed to buy and drive cars. **(1)**	

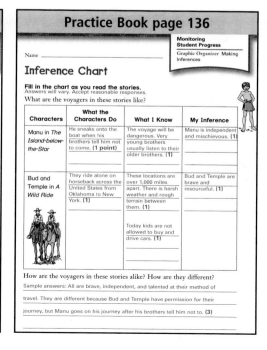

How are the voyagers in these stories alike? How are they different?
Sample answers: All are brave, independent, and talented at their method of
travel. They are different because Bud and Temple have permission for their
journey, but Manu goes on his journey after his brothers tell him not to. **(3)**

Reading the Paired Selections   253

CRITICAL THINKING
Guiding Comprehension

1 **MAKING JUDGMENTS** Is it fair for Manu's brothers to tell him he can't come on the trip? Explain. (Sample answers: yes, because he is young and the trip will be dangerous; no, because they are just his brothers, not his parents)

2 **MAKING INFERENCES** Manu sneaks onto the canoe, even though his brothers told him he could not come along. What does this action tell you about his personality? (Sample answer: Manu is adventurous, mischievous, and stubborn.)

COMPREHENSION STRATEGY
Predict/Infer

Teacher Modeling Remind students that making predictions about what will happen in a story can help them understand the story better. Read page 254 aloud and model making predictions about how the brothers will each help on a sailing trip.

Think Aloud *The first paragraph says that the stars are a map. Since Hōkū loves the stars, I think he will help find the island by using the stars as a map.*

Vocabulary

fashioned made or created

harpoons spears used to hunt whales and large fish

seaworthy safe for sailing in

calabashes large, round bowls made from a gourd

The Island-below-the-Star
written and illustrated by James Rumford

In the days when the stars were a map of the earth below, there lived on a tiny island in the South Pacific five brothers who loved adventure.

The first brother was Hōkū, and he loved the sun, the moon, and especially the stars.

The second was Nāʻale, and he loved the sea.
The third was ʻŌpua, and he loved clouds.
The fourth was Makani, and he loved the wind.
And the fifth was tiny Manu, and he loved birds.

One night, Hōkū said, "See, my brothers, that bright star there? There's an island below that star. Let us sail to it."

And as he spoke, the star sparkled with adventure.

Hōkū's four brothers looked up at the star over their own island and saw how very far away the other star was. No one had ever gone so far before.

254

Challenge

Additional Reading

Students might be interested in reading other books by James Rumford. Visit Education Place at **www.eduplace.com** to learn more about this author and illustrator.

Little Manu was first to speak. "I will go with you, Hōkū."

The other brothers, including Hōkū, laughed. Such a dangerous trip was out of the question for such a little boy.

"You might get washed overboard," said Nā'ale.

"Or frightened by the thunder and lightning," said 'Ōpua.

"Or blown away by the wind," said Makani. "Besides, you only care about birds."

The next morning, Manu stood watching as his four brothers prepared for their great trip without him to the Island-below-the-Star. **①**

Hōkū dried bananas, taro, and breadfruit in the hot sun, for they would need much food.

Nā'ale fashioned dozens of fishhooks and readied the harpoons, for they would live off the sea as well.

'Ōpua watched the clouds and gathered only the sweetest rainwater, for they would be thirsty on their long trip.

Makani repaired the sails, for they would need to catch even the tiniest breeze if they were ever to reach the Island-below-the-Star.

After several weeks, the canoe was seaworthy and the food and water were loaded on board. There was a great celebration for the four brothers.

Little Manu did not join in. No one noticed as he hid himself among the calabashes of food and baskets of coconuts. **②**

The brothers left just before dawn.

It was sunset before they discovered little Manu.

"Let's toss him overboard and let him swim back," said Nā'ale.

Connecting and Comparing

Making Inferences

- How would you describe Manu's relationship with his brothers? How do they treat him? (Manu's brothers think he is too little to help them; they laugh at him and tease him about tossing him overboard.)

- Reread page 198 of *Yunmi and Halmoni's Trip.* How would you describe Yunmi's relationship with Halmoni? (They are usually very close, but in Korea Halmoni seems to have little time to spend with Yunmi. Yunmi feels jealous.)

- How is Manu's relationship with his brothers like Yunmi's relationship with Halmoni? How are these relationships different? (Both are relationships between older and younger family members, and both Manu and Yunmi don't like the way they are being treated; they are different because Halmoni treats Yunmi better than Manu's brothers treat him.)

Extra Support/Intervention

Selection Preview

Pages 254–255 These five brothers live together on an island. They are looking at a star. One brother says there is another island far away below that star. What do you think the brothers might decide to do?

Pages 256–259 The brothers work together to sail through a terrible storm. What do you think it would be like to ride in a canoe through a storm like this one?

Pages 260–261 The brothers land on an island. Do you think they will stay there?

CRITICAL THINKING
Guiding Comprehension

❸ DRAWING CONCLUSIONS Why is Manu *in awe of his brothers*? (because each of them has a special talent, and they work together so well to sail the boat)

❹ WRITER'S CRAFT When the author says *the waves were mountains* and *the wind was a knife*, what does he mean? How does this language help readers picture the storm? (The waves were huge, and the sharp wind hurt the brothers' faces; these words help readers imagine how violent the storm was.)

"Let's throw him into the air and let the wind carry him home," said Makani.

Big 'Ōpua picked Manu up and held him over the side of the canoe.

"Hōkū!" cried Manu with his arms outstretched. "Hōkū!"

"All right! All right!" shouted 'Ōpua. "We were just kidding."

Hōkū began to laugh. "But you had better behave yourself," he told Manu.

Manu stood there, his head down.

"Make yourself useful," said Nā'ale. "We need fish."

Each day, as Manu sat with his fishing line, he was in awe of his brothers.

Hōkū used the sun, the moon, and the twinkling stars like a map to guide them.

When the clouds covered the heavenly map, they turned to Nā'ale, who kept the canoe on course as he felt the rhythms of the ocean waves.

256

Challenge

Navigation Posters

Ask students to find out more about how ancient sailors used the stars and other methods to guide their ships. Have students choose one navigation aid, such as a sextant or a Pacific Islander stick chart, and draw a picture of it. Students can then label the picture with facts about the navigation aid and how it was used.

Vocabulary

awe a feeling of wonder and respect

knotted mixed-up

hull body or frame of a boat

roiling moving roughly in all directions

'Ōpua was always there watching the clouds.

And when he predicted storms, Makani was at hand, disentangling the knotted wind as they sailed north to the Island-below-the-Star.

Several weeks later, it was Makani who first noticed a strange rush of warm air. He scanned the horizon.

The waves began to grow in strength as they slapped against the hull. Nā'ale alerted the others.

A thin palm frond of a cloud appeared above the horizon. 'Ōpua prepared his brothers for the worst.

By evening, the sky that Hōkū depended on was roiling with clouds. The waves were mountains. The wind was a knife.

④

The brothers tied a safety rope to Manu.

For five days and nights they hung on for dear life as they rode out the storm.

257

Connecting and Comparing

Making Inferences

- How do you think the brothers feel when the storm comes? (Sample answers: scared; confident that they can come through safely; excited)

- How do you think the brothers' feelings might be different from the feelings of the boy and his family during the storm on page 161 of *Across the Wide Dark Sea*? Why? (Sample answers: The brothers might not feel as afraid and helpless as the boy and his family; the brothers are experienced sailors, who have probably been through storms before.)

Fluency Practice

Rereading for Fluency Have pairs of students take turns rereading pages 256–257 aloud. Encourage them to use their voices to show the different moods in the story—the rowdy teasing, the nervous calm before the storm, and the terrifying storm itself.

English Language Learners

Supporting Comprehension

Use pantomime and paraphrasing to help students understand the figurative language on these pages. You might explain *the heavenly map* ("the map the stars make in the sky"), *palm frond of a cloud* ("a cloud with long, thin fingers"), *hung on for dear life* ("hung on as tightly as they could"), and *rode out the storm* ("sailed their ship through the storm").

Guiding Comprehension

5 **WRITER'S CRAFT** Why do you think the author tells what Manu did *not* do during the storm? (Sample answer: By telling what Manu did *not* do and what did *not* happen to him, the author emphasizes the bad things that could have happened during the storm.)

6 **COMPARE AND CONTRAST** How do Manu's brothers treat him differently now than they did at the beginning of the story? (At first, they thought he was too little to be any use, and they teased and laughed at him. Now they all listen to Manu and let him lead them to the island.)

7 **DRAWING CONCLUSIONS** How has Manu become "part of the team"? (He has proved that he can help with his own special talent, just like his brothers.)

COMPREHENSION STRATEGY
Predict/Infer

Teacher/Student Modeling Invite students to make predictions about how the brothers will find the island, and what they will do when they reach it.

Vocabulary

swirling whirling or spinning

predawn before sunrise

At last, the wind died down. The sea was calm, but the sky was still hidden behind a gray blanket of clouds. The canoe had been blown far off course. The brothers were lost.

Manu undid the safety rope. He had not cried when the thunder crashed through the sky. He had not been washed overboard or carried off by the wind.

Suddenly Manu stood very still. He could feel something coming.

He looked up and saw, perhaps on its way to the Island-below-the-Star, a tiny speck of a bird.

Manu called to his brothers, "Look, brothers, a bird! A bird on its way to land!"

"Where?" they cried. It was so high that they could not see it.

"Tell me where it is, Manu," said Hōkū. "Tell me which way to go."

258

Manu pointed in the direction the bird was flying, and Hōkū turned the canoe.

The bird stayed with the brothers all through the day, and Manu, proud Manu, told Hōkū of the bird's every turn.

That night, when the skies finally cleared, they all saw that they were beneath their star.

But where was the island?

Nāʻale showed them the waves crashing into one another, as though pushed back by something big.

ʻŌpua pointed to the moonlit clouds gathered in the north as though caught by a mountain.

Makani told them how the wind was swirling oddly, as though avoiding some huge shape.

No one slept.

Manu, now part of the team, spotted the first birds in the predawn light.

7

259

Connecting and Comparing

Making Inferences

- Why has the relationship between Manu and his brothers changed? (Manu's brothers respect him more now that he has used his knowledge of birds to find the island.)

- At the end of *Yunmi and Halmoni's Trip,* Yunmi and Halmoni's relationship has also changed. Why is that? (Yunmi has realized how much Halmoni loves her, and she is no longer worried that Halmoni will stay in Korea.)

- How do you think Manu and Yunmi feel about their journeys? (Sample answer: They are both glad to have taken their journeys, because traveling brought them closer to their families.)

CRITICAL THINKING
Guiding Comprehension

8 DRAWING CONCLUSIONS Why do you think the people sing about the brothers? (Sample answer: because they sailed farther than anyone had before and found a new land)

9 WRITER'S CRAFT In this story, the author imagines what the discovery of Hawaii by ancient explorers might have been like. Does he tell the story realistically or with elements of fantasy? Give some examples to show why you think so. (with elements of fantasy; the author uses phrases like *in the days when the stars were islands floating in a dark, heavenly sea* and he says the brothers are *a star, waves, clouds, the wind,* and *a bird* at the end.)

Summarize Have students use what they wrote on their Graphic Organizers to help them summarize *The-Island-below-the-Star.*

They were close — very close.

And then, at dawn, they saw the island. Its peaks towered above the waves and caught the first rays of the rising sun. The brothers shouted with joy and lifted Manu high on their shoulders.

At noon, they found a quiet bay for the canoe.

At sunset, they set foot on shore.

260

English Language Learners

Supporting Comprehension

You may want to help students understand the idioms *caught the first rays of* ("was lit by"), *set foot* ("walked onto"), and *called to them* ("led them on their trip").

Vocabulary

bay a part of the sea that extends into the land

That night, they gave thanks for their safe journey as they stood directly below the bright star that had called to them.

In the days when the stars were islands floating in a dark, heavenly sea and people were explorers living on specks of land surrounded by the vast ocean, they sang of

Hōkū, the star,

Nāʻale, the ocean waves,

ʻŌpua, the cloud bank,

Makani, the wind, and

Manu, the bird, who found the Island-below-the-Star. **9**

261

Connecting and Comparing

Predicting Outcomes

- Now that they have found the Island-below-the-Star, do you think the brothers will go exploring again? Why or why not? (Sample answers: yes, because they are so good at sailing and they love adventures; no, because they have found the island they were looking for)

- Will the brothers invite Manu to come along with them the next time they sail? Why or why not? (Sample answer: yes, because he took care of himself on the boat and found the island)

- Which character do you think is more likely to be a sailor when he grows up: Manu or the boy in *Across the Wide Dark Sea*? Use details from the stories to explain why you think so. (Sample answer: Manu, because he finds the island, helps catch fish, and is brave during the storm, and the boy in *Across the Wide Dark Sea* is afraid of storms, is not able to help the sailors, and grows tired of his journey)

Stop and Think

Critical Thinking Questions

1. **DRAWING CONCLUSIONS** How does this story show the valu[e] of teamwork? (The brothers work together to find the islan[d] and each one helps in his own way.)

2. **PREDICTING OUTCOMES** Do you think other people will con[e] to the island? Why or why not? (Sample answer: yes; now th[at] the brothers have found it, others will know how to get ther[e].)

3. **MAKING JUDGMENTS** Which ocean voyage do you think is more challenging: the brothers' journey to the island or the Pilgrims' journey in *Across the Wide Dark Sea*? Give reasons [for] your answer. (Sample answers: the brothers' journey, because they sail by themselves and become lost; the Pilgrims' journe[y] because many passengers die)

4. **COMPARE AND CONTRAST** In what ways are Manu's experienc[es] during the voyage like those of the boy in *Across the Wide Dark Sea*? How are these experiences different? (Both are bo[ys] traveling with family members on ocean voyages to new lan[ds.] Manu proves himself to his brothers by helping out, while th[e] boy has nothing to do and must stay out of the sailors' way.)

Strategies in Action Have students model how they used Predict/Infer and other strategies to help them understand this selection.

Connecting and Comparing

Predicting Outcomes

- Invite volunteers to imagine what Manu and his brothers migh[t] do now that they have reached the island. Encourage them to[?] back up their predictions with details from the story.

- Have students use **Practice Book** page 137 to make prediction[s] about events after the end of *The Island-below-the-Star* and another theme selection.

Practice Book page 137

Monitoring
Student Progress
Connecting and Comparing

Name _____

What Happens Next?

Make predictions about what will happen to Manu after the end of *The Island-below-the-Star*. Support each prediction with details from the story. Then choose another selection in Theme 5 to complete the chart. Predictions will vary. Story details should support each prediction. (**1 point** for each answer)

	Manu in *The Island-below-the-Star*	Character: _____ Story Title: _____
Will the character go back home, or stay at the trip's destination?		
What details make you think so?		
How will the character's life be different after this journey?		
What details make you think so?		
Will the character travel again, or not?		
What details make you think so?		

REACHING ALL LEARNERS

Extra Support/Intervention

Review Predictions

Have students discuss the predictions they made about how the brothers would find the island. How do their predictions compare to story events?

Monitoring Student Progress

If . . .	Then . . .
students had difficulty answering Guiding Comprehension questions,	guide them in reading aloud relevant portions of the text and discussing their answers.

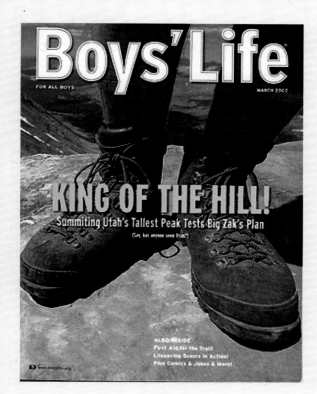

Selection 2

A Wild Ride

Boys' Life

FOR ALL BOYS | MARCH 2002

KING OF THE HILL!

Summiting Utah's Tallest Peak Tests Big Zak's Plan

(say, has anyone seen Pcak?)

ALSO INSIDE

First Aid for the Trail!
Lifesaving Scouts in Action!
Plus Comics & Jokes & More!

by Thomas Fleming

Introducing Vocabulary

Key Vocabulary

These words appear in the selection.

territory 1. land controlled by a certain group; 2. a part of the United States that is not a state

slogging moving slowly

newsreel a short movie about recent news

e • Glossary
e • WordGame

See Vocabulary note on page 264 for additional words to preview.

Have students locate Key Vocabulary words in the story.

- Have volunteers read aloud each sentence containing a Key Vocabulary word.

Display Transparency 5–30.

- Work with students to fill in the blanks with the correct Key Vocabulary words.

Practice/Homework Assign **Practice Book** page 138.

Transparency 5–30

Cross-Country Words

territory slogging newsreel

When my Grandma Liz was a little girl, she and her friend Polly got lost on a trip to a National Park. The park was government ____territory____ so they hoped to find a park ranger to help them. However, they could not find a ranger.

They spent a while ____slogging____ through mud as they tried to find their way out. Finally, after two whole days in the park, Liz and Polly found a ranger station. The park rangers were so impressed by their story that they told local reporters. A ____newsreel____ was made about their amazing hike. My Grandma says she didn't care about the attention—she was just glad to be out of the mud!

Practice Book page 138

Monitoring Student Progress
Key Vocabulary

Name _____

Safe at Last!

Use words from the box to complete the news article below.

Heroes Survive the Mountains

A group of climbers has survived being lost for a week in the wilderness. The group got lost during a snowstorm in Yellowstone National Park. This area of land is territory **(2 points)** controlled by the United States Park Service.
After six days of slogging **(2)** through heavy snow, the group was rescued by plane. For more details on this amazing story, watch the newsreel **(2)** that will soon be coming to a movie theater near you!

Vocabulary
territory
slogging
newsreel

Now write your own sentences using the Key Vocabulary words. Use one Vocabulary word in each sentence. Sentences will vary.

1. **(2 points)** _____

2. **(2)** _____

3. **(2)** _____

CRITICAL THINKING
Guiding Comprehension

1 MAKING JUDGMENTS Bud and Temple traveled across the country to meet Theodore Roosevelt. Would you travel many miles to meet one of your heroes? Why or why not? (Answers will vary.)

2 MAKING INFERENCES Based on Bud and Temple's actions, what inferences can you make about them? (They were determined and liked adventure, and they were good at horseback riding and finding their way.)

Continue the Graphic Organizer. Remind students to fill in their Graphic Organizers as they read *A Wild Ride*.

COMPREHENSION STRATEGY
Predict/Infer

Student Modeling Invite students to make predictions about Bud and Temple's adventures.

Vocabulary

territory 1. land controlled by a certain group; 2. a part of the United States that is not a state

slogging moving slowly

A Wild Ride
by Thomas Fleming

Boys' Li

KING OF THE HIL

Bud Abernathy was ten years old and Temple Abernathy six when the brothers from Cross Roads, Oklahoma, decided they wanted to take a trip to New York — by themselves, on horseback — to see ex-President Theodore Roosevelt. Armed with a checkbook and permission from Dad, the boys started their long journey when the school year ended on April 5, 1910. **1**

262

Extra Support/Intervention

Selection Preview

pages 262–263 Almost 100 years ago, these boys rode their horses across the United States, from Oklahoma to New York. Do you think their ride was easy or difficult?

page 264 In the bottom picture, the boys are sitting in an old-fashioned car. How do you think they traveled home?

Horse Down

Bud and Temple had been on the trail through Oklahoma's
ndian Territory about two days when they got lost. The boys used
sun as a guide. It worked. They reached Oklahoma
y and met their father for a day of sightseeing.

Their trip's first real trouble came a few days
r in the town of Hominy. Temple led his horse,
ronimo, from the stable. Geronimo was slow
stiff. They stayed until the next morning, but
ronimo had not improved.

Bud had to rope another horse and pay $85
he owner. That fee included the care of
ronimo until the boys could return.

gging Through Snow

Hard rain and mud slowed them from Hominy,
ough Coffeyville, Kansas, to the edge of the
rk Mountains at Joplin, Missouri.

The bad weather was just beginning. As they
e north of Springfield, Missouri, the wind
ame colder, and rain turned to snow. The boys got off their
ses and walked for miles to stay warm and get a break from the
d. At times, the snow was so thick they could see only a few feet
ront of them.

They reached Union, Missouri, on a Saturday night and sat in a
el room all day on Sunday.

On Monday morning, despite the storm, they decided to leave
St. Louis, Missouri. By that night, they reached St. Louis and
ed for a week.

Temple and Bud Abernathy ▲

263

Connecting
and Comparing

Text Organization

- How are the headings in this story
  different from the headings in
  Trapped by the Ice!? (The headings
  in *Trapped by the Ice!* tell the date
  when each section of the story
  occurred. The headings in this story
  describe what happens in each section
  but do not include the date.)

- Which story's headings did you find
  more useful in understanding the
  story? Why? (Sample answer: the
  headings in *A Wild Ride;* because these
  headings give me useful information
  about what happens instead of just
  the date when it happened)

Guiding Comprehension

❸ DRAWING CONCLUSIONS Why do you think people wanted to write newspaper articles and make newsreels about Bud and Temple? (Sample answers: The boys were young to be traveling alone; their adventures were interesting.)

❹ NOTING DETAILS What things are Bud and Temple allowed to do in the story that kids their age would not be allowed to do today? (travel so far alone; buy a car; drive)

❺ MAKING JUDGMENTS Do you think Bud and Temple's trip was a good idea, or a bad one? Explain why. (Sample answers: good, because they had adventures and became famous; bad, because it was very dangerous)

Fluency Practice

Rereading for Fluency Have students choose a favorite part of the story to reread to a partner. Remind students to read with expression.

Finish the Graphic Organizer. Have students share and discuss their completed Graphic Organizers.

Vocabulary

infection a disease or illness caused by bacteria or a virus

newsreel a short movie about recent news

persuaded caused to do or think something

Through Sickness and High Water

▼ Theodore Roosev[elt]

The boys quickly made it through Illinois and Indiana. In Dayton, Ohio, they met Wilbur Wright and took a tour of the Wright airplane factory. Shortly after that, Temple got sick. He fought through a fever and lung infection in Cambridge, Ohio, and had to rest. A few days later, Bud was nearly swept downstream on his horse just outside Wheeling, West Virginia.

The next stop was Washington, D.C., where the boys met President William Howard Taft before reaching New York City. In New York, people knew who they were because of newspaper articles, and they were paid to appear in newsreel films. And they got to greet Mr. Roosevelt.

On the Road Again

For the journey from New York to Oklahoma, Bud persuaded his father to let them use their newsreel money to buy a car. There were no laws against boys driving in 1910, and there were only a few cars on the road.

The boys paid $485 for a Brush Runabout with a top speed of 30 miles an hour. Their horse ride took two months, their return car trip three weeks. They traveled more than 5,000 miles.

◀ Bud and Temple in their brand-new ca[r]

264

Challenge

Wild Ride Map

Provide students with photocopied maps of the United States and have them use an atlas to trace the brothers' route. You might have students color in the states the brothers passed through, and find and connect specific stops such as Oklahoma City, St. Louis, Washington, D.C., and New York City.

Think and Compare

1. Compare Manu's experiences of his voyage in *Island-below-the-Star* with Bud and Temple's experiences of their voyage across America. Use details from the selections.

2. Compare the importance of teamwork among the travelers in *Island-below-the-Star* and in *Trapped by the Ice!*

3. Which of the voyages in this theme would you most like to go on? Give two or three reasons.

alone

4. Think of the characters in this theme. How do you think their experiences might change their lives?

Strategies in Action When did you use reading strategies in this theme? Tell how two or more of them helped you better understand the selections.

Persuading

Write a Radio Ad

Think about a place that you would like to travel to. Write a radio advertisement inviting people to go there. Tell why people should go, and what they will experience.

Tips

• Think about what visitors might see, hear, taste, smell, and touch.
• Use strong words, such as *certainly, really, of course*.

265

Think and Compare

Discuss or Write Have students discuss or write their answers. Sample answers are provided; accept reasonable responses.

1. In both stories, brothers travel long distances together. The brothers in both stories get lost and encounter terrible weather.

2. Teamwork is very important in both stories. The travelers in both stories survive dangerous situations by working together and staying together.

3. Answers will vary.

4. Answers will vary.

Strategies in Action Have students take turns modeling how and where they used Predict/Infer and other reading strategies.

REACHING ALL LEARNERS

Extra Support/ Intervention

Review Predictions

Have students discuss their predictions about Bud and Temple's adventures. How did their predictions help them understand the selection?

English Language Learners

Language Development

Beginning/Preproduction Work with students to create a word web of places they have been to on vacation or that they would like to visit. Help them to add words to the web that describe each place.

Early Production and Speech Emergence Ask students to give examples of words or phrases they would use in their radio advertisements to make people want to travel to the destination they chose.

Intermediate and Advanced Fluency Have partners describe their travel destinations to each other. Are their descriptions appealing?

Monitoring Student Progress

If . . .	Then . . .
students had difficulty answering Guiding Comprehension questions,	guide them in reading aloud relevant portions of the text and discussing their answers.

Reading the Paired Selections 265

THEME CONNECTIONS: Anthology Literature

Comprehension

Making Connections

Teach

Congratulate students on reaching the end of Theme 5: Voyagers. Point out that they will now participate in an activity to help them celebrate the theme.

- **Review with students the selections they have read in this theme.** *(Across the Wide Dark Sea, Yunmi and Halmoni's Trip, and Trapped by the Ice!)* Also remind students about this theme's Links, Monitoring Student Progress Paired Selections, and Leveled Books.

- **Create a list of the theme's main characters.** Have volunteers take turns adding names of characters to a list on the board.

- **Compare and contrast each voyage.** Then ask students how the individual voyagers are alike and different.

Practice/Apply

Next, choose one of these three activities to help students wrap up this theme. Note: Each activity can be divided into segments throughout the week.

 Portfolio Opportunity Suggest that students include copies of their lists, letters, or other material related to the theme wrap-up activity in their portfolios.

Practice Book

Suggest that students review Selection Connections on **Practice Book** pages 83–84.

Pack Your Bags

	Whole Class or Groups		60 minutes (can take place over 2–3 days)
Objective		Make a list of supplies needed for a theme voyage.	
Materials		Chalkboard and chalk, paper and pencil, markers or crayons	

Make a list of everything you would need to go on one of the voyages in this theme. Each list should include the special clothing and supplies needed for the journey.

1 Divide into small groups. Each group should choose one theme story. Imagine your group will go on the voyage described in that story.

2 Working together, review the story you chose to figure out what supplies are needed for that voyage. Think about the following:

- What do the characters take on their journey?

- What is the weather like where you are traveling? What clothing might you need?

- Will you encounter any dangers or hardships on your journey? What supplies might help you survive?

- Will you need to take food? What kinds of food will stay fresh during the trip?

3 Make a list of what you will pack for your voyage. Illustrate the list with pictures of the items.

4 Post your list on a bulletin board. Compare your list with your classmates'. Think about the following:

- What similarities and differences do you notice in the lists?

- Can you guess where each group is traveling just by looking at the things on its list?

- What else do the supplies needed for each trip tell you about that voyage?

Consider copying and laminating these activities for use in cent

Voyagers' Club

👤👤👤 **Whole Class or Groups**	🕐 60 minutes (can take place over 2–3 days)
Objective	Role-play a conversation among theme characters.

Role-play characters from this theme. Imagine that the theme characters joined a club for voyagers. What do you think they would say to each other in the clubhouse?

1 **Divide into groups** of four or five.

2 **Have each group member choose a different character** from this theme to role-play.

3 **Reread your character's story** and think about what the character's voyage was like.

4 **Decide what you want to tell others** about your adventure. You may want to tell:

- where you went and how you traveled there
- what happened on your voyage
- how the voyage made you feel
- how the voyage changed your life

5 **With your classmates, role-play the characters you chose.** Describe your journeys and ask each other questions. Use these questions to guide your discussion:

- How are your voyages different?
- What do they have in common?

Friendly Letters

👤👤👤 **Whole Class or Groups**	🕐 60 minutes (can take place over 2–3 days)
Objective	Create a scrapbook of letters from theme characters.
Materials	Paper and pencils, construction paper or other materials for binding into a book

Create a scrapbook of letters from voyagers in this theme. Compare and contrast the different characters' journeys.

1 **Choose a character from one of the stories in this theme.** Think about the voyage that the character goes on.

2 **Write a letter from the character** telling a friend about the journey. Imagine that the character is in the middle of the voyage. Include in your letter:

- descriptions of the place you are traveling to
- details that give the reader an idea of what the voyage is like
- feelings about the voyage
- wishes for how the voyage will end

3 **Read your letter to the class.** Then discuss the letters you and your classmates wrote. Talk about how the characters and their journeys are different, and what they have in common.

4 **Make copies of your letters** and create a class scrapbook.

Dear Aunt Mary,
Hello! How are you?
We have been
at sea for two
weeks now.

Independent Activities

While you work with small groups, students can choose from a wealth of books to complete these activities.

Leveled Readers . . .

for *Across the Wide Dark Sea*
  The Golden Land
  Chasing the Train
  Faith's Journey
  Going to America

for *Yunmi and Halmoni's Trip*
  Brothers are Forever
  South Pole Bound
  The Same, But Different
  Max Visits London

for *Trapped by the Ice!*
  Iceberg Rescue
  Racing Danger
  Voyage Across the Pacific
  Stuck in the Ice

Leveled Theme Paperbacks

  The Josefina Story Quilt
  A Child's Glacier Bay
  Balto and the Great Race

Leveled Bibliography

pages 148E–148F

Mixed-up Stories

👥 **Singles or Pairs**	🕐 **30 minutes**
Objective	Write a story taking a character from one book on a voyage from a different book.
Materials	Reference materials

Choose a character from any of the books you have read. Then choose a voyage from a different book. Imagine what it would be like if the character went on this new journey. How would the story be different?

Think about

- how the character you chose would react to the sights and events of this new journey
- what the character might do on this new journey
- how this new journey might make the character feel
- how this new journey might change the character

Write a story in which your character sets off on the new voyage. Then trade stories with a partner.

After you finish reading each other's stories, discuss them together. Use these questions to guide your discussion:

- How did different voyagers make the journeys different?
- How did the new journeys change the voyagers?

Consider copying and laminating these activities for use in centers.

THEME CONNECTIONS

Create a Picture Album

👥 Pairs	🕐 30 minutes
Objective	Draw pictures of places and events from a journey.
Materials	Paper, crayons or markers, stapler or other materials for binding pictures into an album, reference materials

Choose a character from any of the books you have read. Create an album of pictures showing what that character did and saw on his or her journey. You might include pictures showing

- what it is like to leave home
- how the character travels
- who travels with the character
- places the character visits
- people the character meets on the journey
- exciting things the character does

Share your picture album with the class or with a small group. Compare your character's journey with the journeys of other characters you have read about.

Use these questions to guide your discussion:

- What makes the journeys exciting?
- What problems do the characters face on their journeys?
- What do the characters learn on their journeys?

Your Own Journey

👤 Singles	🕐 30 minutes
Objective	Compare and contrast student's own journey (or imaginary journey) with a journey from a Leveled Reader.
Materials	Reference materials

Have you been on a journey to a place you had never visited before? Your journey could be anything from a trip to another country to a visit to a local skating rink.

Think about a journey you have taken. Write some notes about your journey. Think about

- where you went on your journey
- what you did and saw there
- how your journey made you feel

Now choose a journey from any of the books you have read. Write a paragraph comparing and contrasting your own journey with the journey from the book. How were the journeys different? How were they the same?

While you write your paragraph, think about these questions:

- How did you travel on your journey? How did the characters travel in the book?
- Did you travel as far as the characters did? Did your journey last as long?
- How did the characters' journey make them feel? Did you feel the same way on your journey?
- Did you and the characters learn similar things on your journeys?

Preparing for Tests

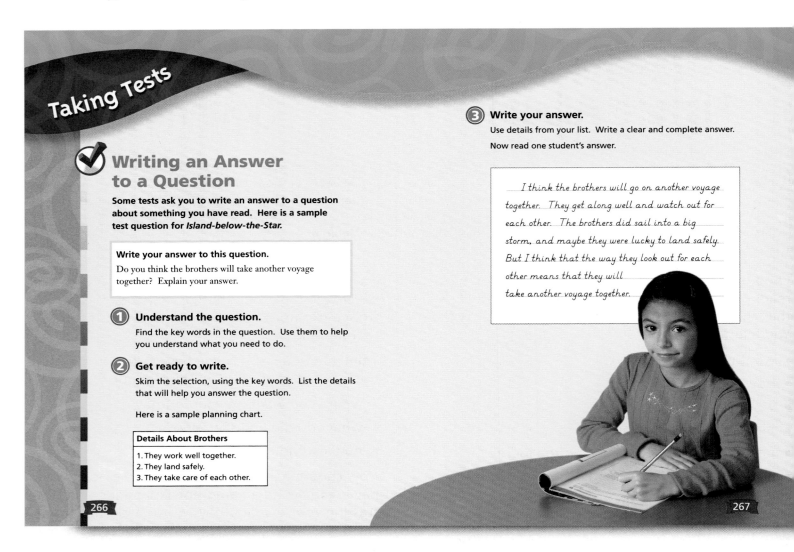

Taking Tests

✓ Writing an Answer to a Question

Some tests ask you to write an answer to a question about something you have read. Here is a sample test question for *Island-below-the-Star.*

Write your answer to this question.

Do you think the brothers will take another voyage together? Explain your answer.

1 Understand the question.

Find the key words in the question. Use them to help you understand what you need to do.

2 Get ready to write.

Skim the selection, using the key words. List the details that will help you answer the question.

Here is a sample planning chart.

Details About Brothers
1. They work well together.
2. They land safely.
3. They take care of each other.

266

3 Write your answer.

Use details from your list. Write a clear and complete answer.

Now read one student's answer.

> I think the brothers will go on another voyage together. They get along well and watch out for each other. The brothers did sail into a big storm, and maybe they were lucky to land safely. But I think that the way they look out for each other means that they will take another voyage together.

267

THEME	STRATEGY
1	**Choosing the Best Answer**
2	**Filling in the Blank**
3	**Writing a Personal Response**
4	**Vocabulary Items**
▶ **5**	**Writing an Answer to a Question**
6	**Writing a Story**

Introduce the Strategy

Taking Tests provides instruction and practice in different test formats. It will hel[p] you prepare your students for the **Theme Skills Test** and the **Integrated Theme Test,** as well as state and national standardized tests.

- Tell students that they will learn strategies that will help them do well on test[s]
- Explain that Anthology pages 266–267 show the steps for writing an answer t[o] a question.
- Emphasize that students will use details from what they have read to answer these questions.
- Have different volunteers read each step aloud. Explain that students will be learning more about each of these steps.
- Discuss the chart. Point out the details from the selection.

Teach the Strategy

1 Understand the Question.

Display Transparency 5–31 and model Step 1.

Have a volunteer read aloud Step 1. Tell students that they will learn more about this one step.

Explain that both questions are based on *The Island-Below-the-Star* on Anthology pages 254–261.

Model using the step to understand Question 1.

Think Aloud *First, I will circle the key words in Question 1 that tell whom or what the question is asking about. I will circle Manu's brothers, feelings and about Manu. Next, I will circle the key words that tell what the question is asking me to do. I will circle How and change. Finally, I will ask myself what I need to do. I need to write about details from the story that show how their feelings about Manu change during the story.*

Complete Transparency 5–31, using Step 1.

2 Get Ready to Write.

Display Transparency 5–32 and model Step 2.

Have a volunteer read aloud Step 2. Tell students that they will learn more about this one step.

Model using the step to get ready to write an answer to Question 1. Complete the chart at the top of the transparency.

Think Aloud *First, I will scan the selection for details that will help me describe how Manu's brothers' feelings about Manu change during the story. At the beginning, the brothers laugh at Manu when he says he wants to go with them. They think he's too young to help. They say he might be afraid of storms, washed overboard, or blown away by the wind. At the end, Manu sees a bird that no one else can see and guides the canoe to the island. The brothers shout with joy and lift Manu on their shoulders. They accept him as part of their team. I will add these details to the chart.*

Complete Transparency 5–32, using Step 2.

Have students save their charts.

Turn the page to teach the Strategy Step 3.

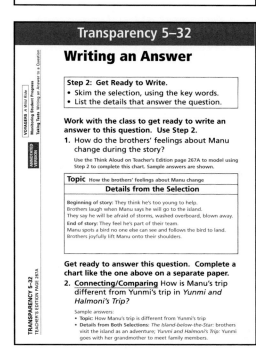

Transparency 5–33

Writing an Answer

Step 3: Write Your Answer.
• Use details from your list.
• Write a clear and complete answer.

Discuss the answer to this question.

1. How do the brothers' feelings about Manu change during the story?

Use the questions on Teacher's Edition page 267B to discuss this model.

The brothers' feelings about Manu change during the story. At the beginning, they think he is too young to help. At the end, they accept him as part of their team. When Manu offers to go to the island, his brothers laugh at him. They think he might be afraid of storms, washed overboard, or blown away by the wind. Later, when the boat is blown off course, Manu spots a bird that no one else can see. He follows the bird and leads the canoe to the island, and the brothers joyfully lift Manu onto their shoulders.

Write an answer to this question on a separate paper. Use the chart you made for Step 2.

2. **Connecting/Comparing** How is Manu's trip different from Yunmi's trip in *Yunmi and Halmoni's Trip*?

Sample answer: Manu's trip is different from Yunmi's trip. The story of *The Island-below-the-Star* is about five brothers who love adventures. They decide to visit the island beneath the star to have a great adventure. They will travel farther than anyone else has ever gone. In *Yunmi and Halmoni's Trip* Yunmi lives in New York and has never met many of her relatives who live in Korea. She goes with her grandmother to meet her aunts, uncles, and cousins for the first time. She doesn't take her trip just to have an adventure.

(sidebar: VOYAGERS A Wild Ride / Monitoring Student Progress / Taking Tests: Writing an Answer to a Question / ANNOTATED VERSION / TRANSPARENCY 5–33 / TEACHER'S EDITION PAGE 267B)

Teach the Strategy continued

STEP 3 Write Your Answer.

Display Transparency 5–33 and discuss Step 3.

• Have a volunteer read aloud Step 3.

• Tell students that they will learn more about writing an answer by studying a model of a written answer to a question.

Discuss the model. Ask these questions.

• Where does the writer repeat key words and phrases from the question? (in the first sentence)

• What details does the writer include from the selection? (See details with a single underscore in the Annotated Version.)

• What exact words does the writer use? (Sample answers: *accept* *part of their team; joyfully*)

Have students complete Transparency 5–33, using Step 3.

• When students have finished, ask them to share their answer with a partner and discuss places where they could add more details.

Extra Support/Intervention

Encourage students to be positive about answering open-response questions. Share these tips.

• If a question seems too hard, write what you know. Remember that writing something is better than writing nothing at all.

• Read each question at least twice. Read it slowly the second time to make sure you understand it. Underline or circle the key words.

• Use the key words in the first sentence of your answer. This will help you get started writing.

• Then write your thoughts about details from the passage. Be specific.

Apply the Strategy

Test Practice: Writing an Answer

Give students practice with timed writing.

Many writing assessments are timed.

If the writing assessment used in your state or district is timed, you might set a time limit for students as they work on their answer.

This will help students get used to pacing themselves.

Discuss how to check an answer to a question.

Take a short break before checking your answer. Stretch, stare out the window, or close your eyes and relax for a minute.

Reread your answer. Check to be sure that you repeated key words and phrases and answered all parts of the question.

Look for places where you need to add more details about the selection to support your answer.

Check for mistakes. Make sure you used clear handwriting.

Assign Practice Book pages 139 and 140.

Explain that both questions are based on *A Wild Ride* on Anthology pages 262–264.

Emphasize that students should use all three steps to write an answer to each question. Encourage them to use a chart to plan their answers.

Practice Book page 139

Monitoring Student Progress

Taking Tests Writing an Answer to a Question

Name _____

Test Practice

Use the three steps you've learned to write an answer to these questions about *A Wild Ride.* Make a chart on a separate piece of paper, and write your answer on the lines below. Use the checklist to revise your answer.

1. In what way does the title of the story *A Wild Ride* describe the trip that Bud and Temple Abernathy took?

To score each student's response, use the _____

Checklist for Writing an Answer to a Question.

_____
_____
_____
_____
_____
_____
_____
_____

Checklist For Writing an Answer to a Question
- ✔ Did I restate the question at the beginning? (2 points)
- ✔ Can I add more details from what I read to support my answer? (5)
- ✔ Do I need to delete extra details that do not help answer the question? (2)
- ✔ Did I write carefully? Did I make any mistakes? (2)

Continued on page 140.

Practice Book page 140

Monitoring Student Progress

Taking Tests Writing an Answer to a Question

Name _____

Test Practice continued

2. **Connecting/Comparing** Two brothers take a cross-country trip to meet Theodore Roosevelt in *A Wild Ride.* Five brothers sail to a distant island in *The Island-Below-the-Star.* How are the experiences alike?

To score each student's response, use the Checklist for Writing an

Answer to a Question.

_____
_____
_____
_____
_____
_____
_____
_____

Checklist for Writing an Answer to a Question
- ✔ Did I restate the question at the beginning? (2 points)
- ✔ Can I add more details from what I read to support my answer? (5)
- ✔ Do I need to delete extra details that do not help answer the question? (2)
- ✔ Did I write carefully? Did I make any mistakes? (2)

Read your answers to Questions 1 and 2 aloud to a partner. Then discuss the checklist. Make any changes that will make your answers better.

Additional Resources

Teacher's Assessment Handbook

Suggests more strategies for preparing students for standardized tests

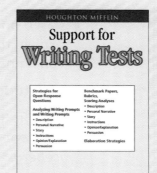

Support for Writing Tests

Provides strategy instruction and practice for open-response questions and writing to prompts at Grades 1–6

COMPREHENSION

OBJECTIVES

Students review how to
- make inferences about characters and events
- predict what characters might do in new situations
- identify the location and function of text features

Making Inferences

Review making inferences.

- Readers use story details and their own experiences to make inferences.
- Inferences can be adjusted, based on new story information.

Model how to make inferences.

- Read aloud the first paragraph on Anthology page 198.
- Explain that when Yunmi sees Halmoni spending all her time with the cousins, Yunmi very likely feels jealous. People sometimes feel jealous when someone they care about pays more attention to others than to them.

Have students make inferences.

- Assign **Practice Book** page 141.

Predicting Outcomes

Review predicting outcomes.

- Story details tell how characters talk, act, feel, and make choices.
- Readers can use these details and their own knowledge to predict what a character might do in a new situation.

Model how to predict outcomes.

- Remind students of details in *Trapped by the Ice!* that show Shackleton's resourcefulness in the face of extreme challenges.
- Based on these details and your own personal knowledge, explain that a good prediction would be that, faced with another challenge at sea, Shackleton would help his crew survive.

Have students predict outcomes.

- Present this situation: *Shackleton and his crew are sailing towards a harbor when he sees that the harbor entrance is blocked by icebergs.*
- Have partners predict what Shackleton might do in this situation. Ask them to write their predictions and list the story clues and personal knowledge that helped them.

Practice Book page 141

Name _____

Monitoring Student Progress

Comprehension Skill
Making Inferences

Guess How I Feel

Read the passage. Then answer the questions.

March 5

Today was cold and gray, the perfect match for my mood. Carlo, Tina, and I piled into Mom's car, and I turned to get one last look at our old neighborhood. Then I squeezed my eyes shut and tried to listen to what Mom was saying.

She told us our new house would be bigger than our apartment, and it even had a yard. Mom would make more money at her new job, and she knew we'd make new friends soon.

I heard all this, but none of it helped make the lump in my throat go away.

1. How does the writer feel about moving?

Story Clue	What I Know
The cold, gray day matches the writer's mood. **(1 point)**	Some people feel sad or scared when they move. **(1)**

My Inference The writer feels sad. **(2)**

2. How does Mom feel about moving?

Story Clue	What I Know
She talks about moving into a bigger home and making more money at a new job. **(1)**	Having a bigger home and more money can make life better. **(1)**

My Inference Mom feels happy about moving. **(2)**

Text Organization

Review text organization.

- Readers use the way a text is organized, including such features as titles, headings, and captions, to learn new information.
- Text features present information so it is easy to read and understand.

Model how to identify text features and their functions.

- Point out the introduction, section headings, and photo captions in *A Wild Ride*.
- Discuss how these features help to make the selection more enjoyable and understandable for readers.

Have students identify text features and their functions.

- Assign **Practice Book** page 142.

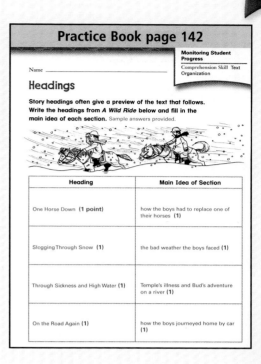

SKILL REVIEW:
Structural Analysis/Vocabulary

Students review how to

- decode words with the suffixes *-less* and *-ness*
- decode singular and plural possessives
- decode words with the VCCV pattern

Suffixes *-less* and *-ness*

Review the suffixes *-less* and *-ness*.

- A suffix is added to the end of a base word.
- A suffix adds meaning to a base word.
- The suffix *-less* adds the meaning "without."
- The suffix *-ness* changes an adjective into a noun and adds the meaning "state or condition of."

Model how to decode a word with *-ness*.

- Display this phrase: *the softness of the kitten's fur.*
- Model decoding *softness.*

Think Aloud *I see the base word* soft *and the ending* -ness. *Since* -ness *means "the state or condition of," I think* softness *means "the condition of being soft." That works here.*

Have students decode words.

- Display these words: *harmless, shyness, dampness, helpless.*
- Ask partners to underline the suffixes. Then have them decode each word and give its meaning.

Possessives

Review possessives.

- Add an apostrophe and *s* to a noun to show ownership.
- If a plural noun ends in *s*, add only an apostrophe to make the possessive.

Model how to decode a plural possessive.

- Display: *the boys' caps.* Model decoding *boys'.*

Think Aloud *I can read the word* boys, *but there is an apostrophe at the end of the word. Since it's a plural noun, and it ends in* s, *only an apostrophe is added to show ownership. I think* the boys' caps *means "the caps that belong to the boys."*

Have students decode possessives.

- Assign **Practice Book** page 143.

Practice Book page 143

Monitoring Student Progress
Structural Analysis
Possessives

Name _____

Whose Is It?

Replace each underlined phrase with a phrase containing a possessive noun. Rewrite the sentence. Remember that when a plural noun ends in *s*, you only need to add an apostrophe to make it possessive.

1. Tony passed <u>the house that belongs to the Jacksons.</u>
   Tony passed the Jacksons' house. **(1 point)**

2. <u>The coat that belongs to Emma</u> is red.
   Emma's coat is red. **(1)**

3. The wind blew <u>the nest of the birds</u> out of the tree.
   The wind blew the birds' nest out of the tree. **(1)**

4. We bought <u>the birthday present for Mom</u> yesterday.
   We bought Mom's birthday present yesterday. **(1)**

5. <u>The face of the teacher</u> was kind.
   The teacher's face was kind. **(1)**

6. <u>The favorite food of the twins</u> is pizza.
   The twins' favorite food is pizza. **(1)**

7. The kids listened to <u>the CD that belongs to Katy.</u>
   The kids listened to Katy's CD. **(1)**

8. <u>The shoes that belong to the dancers</u> were worn out.
   The dancers' shoes were worn out. **(1)**

VCCV Pattern

Review the VCCV pattern.

- Words with the VCCV pattern can usually be divided into syllables between the two consonants.
- A syllable that ends in a consonant is a closed syllable and has a short vowel sound.

Model how to decode a VCCV word.

- Display this phrase: *until we go to bed*.
- Model decoding *until*.

Think Aloud *I see a VCCV pattern, so I'll divide the word between* n *and* t. *The first syllable ends in a consonant, so the* u *has a short vowel sound. The second syllable also ends with a consonant, so the* i *will have a short sound, too. Blending the sounds together, I get* uhn TIHL. *It means "up to the time."*

Have students decode words.

- Display these words: *mitten, nutmeg, admit, upset, window*.
- Have partners work together to divide the words into syllables, and say each word aloud.

Options

SKILL REVIEW:
Vocabulary

OBJECTIVES

Students review how to

- identify syllabication in a dictionary entry
- solve analogies
- use context to identify the correct homophone
- use a thesaurus

Syllables in a Dictionary

Review the features of a dictionary entry.

- A dictionary entry shows the base form of a word, its part of speech, one or more definitions, and its pronunciation.
- A dictionary entry also shows how a word is divided into syllables.
- Large dots usually show where the syllables break.

Model how to use the dictionary syllabication feature.

- Display this phrase: *chocolate milk*.
- Circle the three inside vowels in the word *chocolate*. Then tell students that the word should have three syllables.
- Display *choc•o•late,* and pronounce the three syllables with students.

Have students use the dictionary syllabication feature.

- Display *chisel, event, nickel, solid,* and *promising*.
- Have partners break the words into syllables and then check their work, using a dictionary.

Practice Book page 144

Name _____

Monitoring Student Progress
Vocabulary Skill Analogies

Find the Analogy

Read the first part of each analogy below. Decide how the words in dark print are related. Then write the word that best completes the analogy.

1. **Kitten** is to **cat** as **puppy** is to <u>dog (1 point)</u>.
2. **Leaf** is to **green** as **snow** is to <u>white (1)</u>.
3. **Day** is to **night** as **up** is to <u>down (1)</u>.
4. **Scale** is to **fish** as **feather** is to <u>bird (1)</u>.
5. **Uncle** is to **aunt** as **father** is to <u>mother (1)</u>.
6. **Coach** is to **athlete** as **teacher** is to <u>student (1)</u>.
7. **Water** is to **swim** as **ground** is to <u>walk (1)</u>.
8. **Air** is to **breathing** as **food** is to <u>eating (1)</u>.

Analogies

Review analogies.

- An analogy is a kind of comparison, in which one pair of words is compared to a second pair.
- The words in the second pair are related to each other in the same way as the words in the first pair are.

Model how to solve an analogy.

- Display this analogy: *Toe* is to *foot* as *finger* is to _____.
- Point out the relationship in the first pair of words: A *toe* is part of a *foot*.
- Explain that a *finger* is part of a *hand*, so the completed analogy must be *Toe* is to *foot* as *finger* is to *hand*.

Have students solve analogies.

- Assign **Practice Book** page 144.

Homophones

Review homophones.

- Homophones are words that sound alike but have different spellings and meanings.
- Readers use sentence context to figure out the correct homophone.

Model how to choose the correct homophone.

- Display this sentence: *I ____ the boats floating on the ____.*
- Explain that the first missing word has to be a verb, so *see* is the correct homophone.
- Explain that the second missing word has to be a noun that names something boats float on, so *sea* fits there. Write the homophones in the blanks.

Have students use homophones.

- Display *sale/sail, plain/plane, right/write.*
- Have partners write sentences using each pair of homophones.

Options

SKILL REVIEW: Spelling

OBJECTIVES

Students review

- words with the vowel sounds in *tooth* and *cook*
- words with the vowel sound in bought
- words with the VCCV pattern
- words with added endings

SPELLING WORDS

Basic

grew	brought
daughter	hello
until	tooth
cook	Monday
ought	pretty
forget	chew
balloon	sudden
caught	order
dollar	spoon
boot	thought
window	happen
taught	bought
flew	

Challenge

brook

expect

loose

stubborn

granddaughter

DAY 1 · VOWEL SOUNDS IN *tooth/cook*

Pretest Use the Day 5 sentences.

Review the vowel sounds in *tooth* and *cook*.

- Display *tooth* and *drew*. Read the words aloud. Ask students to name the vowel sound in each word. (/o͞o/)

- Underline *oo* and *ew*. Remind students that these are two spellings for the /o͞o/ sound.

- Next, display *cook* and repeat the procedure for the /o͝o/ sound spelled *oo*.

Have students identify vowel sounds.

- Have students make a two-column chart with the headings *tooth* and *cook*.

- Display *grew, balloon, flew, boot, brook, chew, spoon*.

- Have students write each word in the appropriate column and underline the letters that stand for the /o͞o/ or /o͝o/ sound.

Practice/Homework Assign **Practice Book** page 243.

DAY 2 · VOWEL SOUND IN *bough[t]*

Review the vowel sound in *bought*.

- Display *bought* and *caught*. Read the words. Have students repeat.

- Have students name the vowel sound in these words. (/ô/)

- Underline *ough* and *augh*. These are two spellings for the /ô/ sound

- Explain that *ough* and *augh* do n[ot] always stand for this sound. Help students to think of examples, su[ch] as *dough, through, laugh*.

Have students identify words with the vowel sound in *bough[t]

- Display *daughter, ought, enough, taught, brought, rough, thought.*

- Have students write down only tho[se] words containing the /ô/ sound. A[sk] them to underline the letters in ea[ch] word that stand for the /ô/ sound

Practice/Homework Assign **Practice Book** page 145.

Practice Book page 243

Take-Home Word List	Take-Home Word List	Take-Home Word List
Smart Solutions Reading-Writing Workshop	**Pepita Talks Twice**	**Voyagers Spelling Review**
Look for familiar spelling patterns in these words to help you remember their spellings.	**Words That End with er or le** /ər/ → summer /əl/ → little	**Spelling Words**
Spelling Words	**Spelling Words**	1. grew 14. brought
1. his	1. summer	2. daughter 15. hello
2. I'd	2. winter	3. until 16. tooth
3. I'm	3. little	4. cook 17. Monday
4. that's	4. October	5. ought 18. pretty
5. didn't	5. travel	6. forget 19. chew
6. don't	6. color	7. balloon 20. sudden
7. know	7. apple	8. caught 21. order
8. outside	8. able	9. dollar 22. spoon
9. been	9. November	10. boot 23. thought
10. we're	10. ever	11. window 24. happen
11. anyone	11. later	12. taught 25. bought
12. anyway	12. purple	13. flew
Challenge Words	**Challenge Words**	
1. lose	1. thermometer	**See the back for Challenge Words**
2. finally	2. mumble	
3. different		
4. happily		
My Study List Add your own spelling words on the back. →	**My Study List** Add your own spelling words on the back. →	**My Study List** Add your own spelling words on the back. →

Practice Book page 145

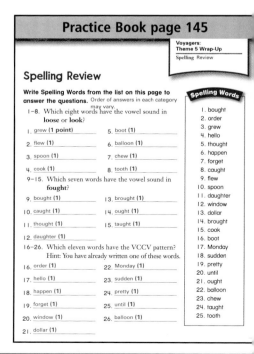

Voyagers: Theme 5 Wrap-Up Spelling Review

Spelling Review

Write Spelling Words from the list on this page to answer the questions. Order of answers in each category may vary.

Spelling Words

1. bought
2. order
3. grew
4. hello
5. thought
6. happen
7. forget
8. caught
9. flew
10. spoon
11. daughter
12. window
13. dollar
14. brought
15. cook
16. boot
17. Monday
18. sudden
19. pretty
20. until
21. ought
22. balloon
23. chew
24. taught
25. tooth

1–8. Which eight words have the vowel sound in **loose** or **look**?

1. grew **(1 point)**   5. boot **(1)**

2. flew **(1)**   6. balloon **(1)**

3. spoon **(1)**   7. chew **(1)**

4. cook **(1)**   8. tooth **(1)**

9–15. Which seven words have the vowel sound in **fought**?

9. bought **(1)**   13. brought **(1)**

10. caught **(1)**   14. ought **(1)**

11. thought **(1)**   15. taught **(1)**

12. daughter **(1)**

16–26. Which eleven words have the VCCV pattern?
Hint: You have already written one of these words.

16. order **(1)**   22. Monday **(1)**

17. hello **(1)**   23. sudden **(1)**

18. happen **(1)**   24. pretty **(1)**

19. forget **(1)**   25. until **(1)**

20. window **(1)**   26. balloon **(1)**

21. dollar **(1)**

DAY 3 — VCCV PATTERN

Review the VCCV pattern.

Display *market* and *follow*.

Explain that both words have two syllables. Then point out the VCCV pattern in each one. (*arke, ollo*)

Tell students that dividing words with this pattern into syllables can help them spell the words correctly.

Draw lines to divide each word into syllables. (*mar | ket, fol | low*)

Remind students that words with the VCCV pattern are often divided between the two consonants, whether the consonants are the same or different.

Have students write words with the VCCV pattern.

Display these words: *Monday, until, window, forget, sudden, happen, order, dollar, hello.*

Ask students to copy the words, underline the VCCV pattern in each one, and draw lines showing how to break each word into syllables.

Practice/Homework Assign **Practice Book** page 146.

Practice Book page 146

Name _____

Voyagers:
Theme 5 Wrap-Up
Spelling Review

Spelling Spree

New TV Shows! Write the Spelling Word that best completes each title of a new TV show. Remember to use capital letters.

Spelling Words
1. brought
2. cook
3. until
4. flew
5. tooth
6. chew
7. happen
8. ought
9. boot
10. sudden
11. order
12. spoon
13. window
14. Monday

1. *Sook Can _____, Bake, and Roast*
2. *Look Out the _____: What Do You See?*
3. *The Superhero Who _____ Too High*
4. *Alphabetical _____: A Game Show for the Very Young*
5. *I _____ to Have Brought My Camera*
6. *A _____ Storm Springs Up in Egypt*
7. *Always _____ Your Food Well*
8. *Tongue, _____, and Throat: Have a Healthy Mouth*

1. Cook (1 point)   5. Ought (1)
2. Window (1)   6. Sudden (1)
3. Flew (1)   7. Chew (1)
4. Order (1)   8. Tooth (1)

A Strange Hike A few words are missing from this paragraph. Use a Spelling Word to fill in each blank.

We went hiking on 9. Monday (1) . It had to 10. happen (1) that the laces on my left 11. boot (1) broke. Then we found out that no one had 12. brought (1) any food. However, we did find one plastic 13. spoon (1) . The weather was warm 14. until (1) the afternoon. That's when we went home.

DAY 4 — ADDED ENDINGS

Review words with added endings.

- Display these word equations:
  grin + n + ing = grinning; care − e + ed = cared; baby − y + ies = babies.

- Remind students that
  – when a base word ends with a vowel and a consonant, double the consonant and add *-ed* or *-ing*.
  – when a base word ends with *e*, drop the final *e* and add *-ed* or *-ing*.
  – when a base word ends with a consonant and *y*, change the *y* to *i* and add *-es* or *-ed*.

Have students write words with added endings.

- Display these words: *smiled, moving, wrapped, hurries, saving, stopped.*

- Have partners copy the words and write word equations that show how the inflected forms are made from the base words.

Practice/Homework Assign **Practice Book** page 147.

Practice Book page 147

Voyagers:
Theme 5 Wrap-Up
Spelling Review

Proofreading and Writing

Proofreading Circle the five misspelled Spelling Words below. Then write each word correctly.

Spelling Words
1. balloon
2. thought
3. grew
4. caught
5. forget
6. bought
7. pretty
8. dollar
9. until
10. taught
11. daughter
12. hello

I flew in a hot-air ~~baloon~~. My uncle ~~bot~~ it from his friend. I never ~~thoght~~ it could go so high. The city looked ~~pritty~~ from up high. I will never ~~fourget~~ the ride.

1. balloon (1 point)   4. pretty (1)
2. bought (1)   5. forget (1)
3. thought (1)

Today's News Fix this speech. Write the Spelling Word that is the opposite of each underlined word.

Who 6. <u>learned</u> that we all should travel by car? Last year, the number of cars 7. <u>shrank</u>. Even my 8. <u>son</u> has her own car. Say good-bye to cars and 9. <u>good-bye</u> to trains! People have 10. <u>let go</u> of the excitement of train travel. If everyone gave one 11. <u>coin</u>, we could have a train tomorrow, but 12. <u>after</u> then, we won't!

6. taught (1)   9. hello (1)   12. until (1)
7. grew (1)   10. caught (1)
8. daughter (1)   11. dollar (1)

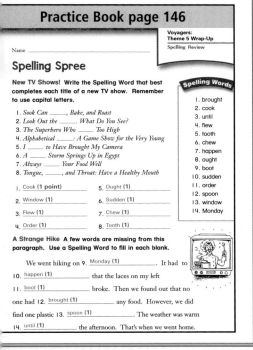

Write a Story On another sheet of paper, write about a trip you would like to take. Use the Spelling Review Words. *Responses will vary.* (3)

DAY 5 — TEST

Say each underlined word, read the sentence, and then repeat the word. Have students write only the underlined words.

Basic Words

1. The clown made a lobster out of a red **balloon**!
2. The bird **flew** in through the **window**.
3. You **ought** to **chew** your food more carefully.
4. I wasn't careful with my **spoon** and hit a **tooth**.
5. Her **daughter** **grew** two inches last year.
6. The recipe says to **cook** the broccoli **until** it is soft.
7. Don't **forget** to go to the dentist on **Monday**.
8. I **bought** a new shirt to wear to my recital.
9. I **taught** my bird to say **hello**.
10. Did you ever **order** that **pretty** dress?
11. I **brought** your other **boot** from the basement.
12. Did it **happen** all of a **sudden**?
13. People once **thought** the earth was flat.
14. My aunt gives me a **dollar** whenever she visits.
15. The boy **caught** the ball right in front of the fence.

Challenge Words

16. I **expect** you to do your homework before supper.
17. The boy saw fish swimming in the **brook**.
18. His **granddaughter** turned six last month.
19. The **stubborn** horse would not move.
20. These pants are much too **loose** on me.

Spelling 267K

SKILL REVIEW: Grammar

Review subject pronouns and display the examples.

- A pronoun takes the place of one or more nouns: *Manu loved birds.* → *He loved birds.*
- The pronouns *I, you, he, she, it, we,* and *they* are subject pronouns. Pronouns can be singular or plural.
- Add *-s* or *-es* to a verb when the subject *is he, she,* or *it: She enjoys folktales.*
- Do not add *-s* or *-es* to a verb when the subject is *I, you, we,* or *they: We enjoy folktales.*

Have students identify subject pronouns.

- Assign **Practice Book** page 148.

Review object pronouns and display the examples.

- The pronouns *me, you, him, it, us,* and *them* are object pronouns: *Manu's brothers did not notice hi* in the boat.
- *It* and *you* are both subject and object pronouns.
- Use *I* as the subject of a sentence. Use *me* as an object pronoun: *I ar a skillful sailor. Father taught me.*
- Always capitalize the word *I.*
- Name yourself last when you talk about another person and yourse *Manu and I are brothers. A bird guided him and me.*

Have students identify object pronouns.

- Assign **Practice Book** page 149.

OBJECTIVES

Students review how to
- identify and use subject pronouns
- identify and use object pronouns
- identify and use possessive pronouns
- identify correct present and past forms of the irregular verb *be*
- identify correct forms of helping verbs

Practice Book page 148

Monitoring Student Progress
Grammar Skill Subject Pronouns

Name _____

Working with Subject Pronouns

Circle each subject pronoun in the following paragraph. Then write each pronoun and the verb it matches on the lines below the paragraph.

(I) fill my backpack with books and games. Mother packs a suitcase with clothes. (We) wait a long time for the van. Finally, (it) arrives. Mother gathers our things. (We) climb into the van. The driver shuts the door. Then (he) sits in the driver's seat and starts the engine.

1. I fill **(1 point)**   4. We climb **(1)**
2. We wait **(1)**   5. he sits **(1)**
3. it arrives **(1)**

Write the correct verb to complete each sentence.

6. I ask **(1)** Mother if we will be late. (ask, asks)
7. She checks **(1)** the time of our flight. (check, checks)
8. We arrive **(1)** in plenty of time. (arrive, arrives)
9. I hop **(1)** off, and Mother takes the suitcase from the van. (hop, hops)
10. It rolls **(1)** away. (roll, rolls)

Practice Book page 149

Monitoring Student Progress
Grammar Skill Object Pronouns

Name _____

Working with Object Pronouns

Circle each object pronoun in the paragraph below. Then write the object pronouns on the lines below the paragraph.

Sometimes Father cooks special foods outdoors for the family. Sis always asks (him) for a scallop dinner. Sis puts the scallops on little sticks called skewers. Then Father places (them) on the grill. Because Sis helps, the first scallops go to (her). The next ones go to (me). Mother makes (us) salad and rice to have with the scallops.

1. him **(1 point)**   4. me **(1)**
2. them **(1)**   5. us **(1)**
3. her **(1)**

Write the correct word or phrase in parentheses to complete each sentence.

6. Sometimes Grandmother and Grandfather eat with us **(1)** . (we, us)
7. Mother makes special place mats for them **(1)** . (they, them)
8. They usually bring her **(1)** a small gift. (she, her)
9. Grandfather gave me **(1)** a fishing pole last week. (I, me)
10. He told Sis and me **(1)** about his childhood in Japan. (me and Sis, Sis and me)

DAY 3 — POSSESSIVE PRONOUNS

Review possessive pronouns.

A possessive pronoun shows ownership.

The pronouns *my, your, her, his, its, our,* and *their* are possessive pronouns.

Identify possessive pronouns.

Display these sentences: *Bud and Temple let the sun be their guide. Its path goes from east to west.*

Underline *their* and *its*. Point out that these are possessive pronouns.

Explain that *their* refers to *Bud and Temple.*

Explain that *its* refers to *the sun.*

Have students identify possessive pronouns.

Display these sentences: *Temple left his horse in the town of Hominy. The boys walked beside their horses.*

Have students copy the sentences and underline the possessive pronouns. (*his, their*)

Then have students circle the words the possessive pronouns take the place of. (*Temple, The boys*)

DAY 4 — THE VERB *be*

Review the verb *be*.

- The verb *be* does not show action. It tells what something is or was.
- This verb has special forms: *am, is,* and *are* show present time; *was* and *were* show past time.

Identify forms of the verb *be*.

- Display these sentences: *The ocean is calm today. It was rough last week.*
- Underline *is* and explain that it shows present time.
- Underline *was* and explain that it shows past time.

Have students identify forms of *be*.

- Display these sentences: *The stars are very bright tonight. Yesterday, they were covered with clouds.*
- Have students find the form of *be* that shows present time, (*are*) and the form that shows past time. (*were*)

DAY 5 — HELPING VERBS

Review helping verbs.

- Sometimes the words *has* and *have* help other verbs show past time. *Has* and *have* are called helping verbs.
- Use *has* with a singular noun in the subject and with *he, she,* or *it.*
- Use have with a plural noun in the subject and with *I, you, we,* or *they.*

Identify helping verbs.

- Display these sentences: *The boys have stopped in Dayton, Ohio. Wilbur Wright has given them a tour of his airplane factory.*
- Identify the verb in each sentence. (*have stopped, has given*)
- Point out that each has a main verb (*stopped, given*) and a helping verb. (*have, has*)
- Show that *has* is used with a singular noun (*Wilbur Wright*) and *have* is used with a plural noun. (*boys*)

Have students choose helping verbs.

- Display these incomplete sentences: *Temple ___ recovered from his fever. The riders ___ reached Washington, D.C.*
- Have students write each sentence, filling the blank with *has* or *have.* (*has, have*)

GRAMMAR

SKILL REVIEW:
Prompts for Writing

WRITING

Play Scene

👤 Singles	🕐 45 minutes
Objective	Write a scene for a play.

Many of the selections in this theme would make good plays. Imagine watching the five brothers in *The Island-below-the-Star* on their journey across the sea. Think how exciting it would be to see Shackleton and his crew overcome one obstacle after another in *Trapped by the Ice!*

Write a scene based on a passage from one of the selections you have read.

- Below the title, be sure to list the setting and the characters in the scene.
- To show who is speaking, write the character's name (in capitals), a colon, and then the words the character says.
- Write stage directions in parentheses.
- Use the characters' words and actions to tell the story.

Remember to use exclamation points to show strong feeling, such as at the end of a command or a warning.

Title:_____

Setting: _____

Characters: _____

_____

_____

_____

Message

👤 Singles	🕐 30 minutes
Objective	Write a message.

In *Yunmi and Halmoni's Trip,* the two main characters visit relatives in Korea. If Yunmi's parents had called her while she was at Grandfather's burial site, whoever was at home would have had to take a message.

Imagine you're at home when someone calls to speak to a member of your family who is not home. Write a message for that person, telling about the call. Be sure the message includes

- the name of the person the message is for
- the caller's name
- the time and date of the call
- the caller's phone number
- the message
- the name of the person who took the message

Remember to include all the information necessary for the phone message to make sense.

Consider copying and laminating these activities for use in centers.

Learning Log

👤 Singles	🕐 30 minutes
Objective	Write a learning log entry.

...yagers like the Pilgrims and ...ackleton and his crew sometimes ...ote down what they learned on ...eir voyages. You, too, can track ...at you have learned in a learning ...g. A learning log is also a good ...ace to write the goals you plan ...work toward.

...oose two different examples of ...ur writing, and use them to write ...earning log entry.

...Write the title or description of each writing sample, and the date when it was written.

...Read each writing sample carefully.

...Under the heading *What I Learned,* list what you learned from writing these pieces.

...Under the heading *My Goals,* list areas in which you can improve.

...**member** that there are two ...mmon ways to write dates: using ...umerals, as in 10/23/05, and using ...word for the month and numbers ...r the day and year, as in October ...3, 2005.

News Article

👤 Singles	🕐 30 minutes
Objective	Write a news article.

Many of the trips in this theme, such as Shackleton's journey in Antarctica or Bud and Temple's wild ride, would make interesting news articles.

Choose one of the trips from this theme, and write a news article about it. The article should only include facts, not opinions. Be sure that your news article answers the following questions:

- Who went on the trip?
- Where did they go?
- Why did they go?
- How did they get there?
- When did the trip take place?
- What happened on the trip?

Remember to keep your audience in mind as you write.

Description

👤 Singles	🕐 30 minutes
Objective	Write a description.

There are many descriptions in *Across the Wide Dark Sea* that make the reader feel he or she is experiencing what is happening in the story.

Write a description of a trip you have taken. Your description should help a reader see, hear, smell, feel, or taste what you have experienced.

- Introduce the topic.
- Use descriptive words to describe the trip.
- Include meaningful details in an order that makes sense.
- Write a conclusion that wraps up the description.

Remember to use complete sentences. A complete sentence expresses a complete thought and has a subject and a predicate.

Assessing Student Progress

Monitoring Student Progress

Preparing for Testing

Throughout the theme, your students have had opportunities to read and think critically, to connect and compare, and to practice and apply new and reviewed skills and reading strategies.

Monitoring Student Progress

For Theme 5, *Voyagers,* students have read the paired selections—*The Island-below-the-Star* and *A Wild Ride*—and made connections between these and other selections in the theme. They have practiced strategies for writing an answer to a question, and they have reviewed all the tested skills taught in this theme, as well as some tested skills taught in earlier themes. Your students are now ready to have their progress formally assessed in both theme assessments and standardized tests.

Testing Options

The **Integrated Theme Test** and the **Theme Skills Test** are formal group assessments used to evaluate student performance on theme objectives. In addition to administering one or both of these tests, you may wish to assess students' oral reading fluency.

Integrated Theme Test

- Assesses students' progress as readers and writers in a format that reflects instruction
- Integrates reading and writing skills: comprehension strategies and skills, high-frequency words, spelling, grammar, and writing
- Includes authentic literary passages to test students' reading skills in context

Theme Skills Test

- May be used as a pretest or administered following the theme
- Assesses students' mastery of discrete reading and language arts skills taught in the theme: comprehension skills, high-frequency words, spelling, grammar, writing and information and study skills
- Consists of individual skill subtests, which can be administered separately

Fluency Assessment

l reading fluency is a useful measure of a student's development of rapid automatic rd recognition. Students who are on level in Grade 3 should be able to read, urately and with expression, an appropriate level text at the approximate rates wn in the table below.

Early Grade 3	Mid-Grade 3	Late Grade 3
79–110 words correct per minute	93–123 words correct per minute	114–142 words correct per minute

You can use the **Leveled Reading Passages Assessment Kit** to assess fluency or a eveled Reader from this theme at the appropriate level for each student.

or some students, you may check their oral fluency rate three times during the ear. If students are working below level, you might want to check their fluency ate more often. Students can also check their own fluency by timing themselves eading easier text.

Consider decoding and comprehension, as well as reading rate, when evaluating tudents' reading development.

or information on how to select appropriate text, administer fluency checks, and nterpret results, see the **Teacher's Assessment Handbook,** pp. 25–28.

Using Multiple Measures

addition to the tests mentioned on page 267P, multiple measures might include e following:

Observation Checklist from this theme

Description from the Reading-Writing Workshop

Other writing, projects, or artwork

One or more items selected by the student

udent progress is best evaluated through multiple measures. Multiple measures of sessment can be collected in a portfolio. The portfolio provides a record of student ogress over time and can be useful when conferencing with the student, parents, other educators.

Technology

Managing Assessment

The **Learner Profile CD-ROM** lets you record, manage, and report your assessment of student progress electronically.

You can

● record student progress on objectives in Theme 5.

● add or import additional objectives, including your state standards, and track your students' progress against these.

● record and manage results from the **Integrated Theme Test** and the **Theme Skills Test** for Theme 5, as well as results from other reading assessments.

● organize information about student progress and generate a variety of student assessment reports.

● use **Learner Profile To Go** to record student progress throughout the day on a handheld computer device, and then upload the information to a desktop computer.

rn the page to continue.

Using Assessment to Plan Instruction

You can use the results of theme assessments to determine individual students' need for additional skill instruction and to modify instruction during the next theme. For more detail, see the test manuals or the **Teacher's Assessment Handbook.**

This chart shows Theme 5 resources for differentiating additional instruction. As you look ahead to Theme 6, you can plan to use the corresponding Theme 6 resources.

Differentiating Instruction

Assessment Shows	Use These Resources	
Difficulty with Comprehension **Emphasize** Oral comprehension, strategy development, story comprehension, vocabulary development	• **Get Set for Reading CD-ROM** • Reteaching: Comprehension, *Teacher's Edition,* pp. R8; R10; R12 • Selection Summaries in **Teachers' Resource Blackline Masters,** pp. 37–39	• Below Level **Leveled Readers** • *Extra Support Handbook,* pp. 164–165, 170–171; 174–175, 180–181; 184–185, 190–191
Difficulty with Word Skills Structural Analysis Phonics Vocabulary **Emphasize** Word skills, phonics, reading for fluency, phonemic awareness	• **Get Set for Reading CD-ROM** • Reteaching: Structural Analysis, *Teacher's Edition,* pp. R14; R16; R18 • *Extra Support Handbook,* pp. 162–163, 166–167; 172–173, 176–177; 182–183, 186–187	• *Handbook for English Language Learners,* pp. 166–167, 168, 170–171, 172, 174; 176–177, 178, 180–181, 182, 184; 186–187, 188, 189–190, 192, 194 • **Lexia Quick Phonics Assessment CD-ROM** • **Lexia Phonics CD-ROM: Intermediate Intervention**
Difficulty with Fluency **Emphasize** Reading and rereading of independent level text, vocabulary development	• Leveled Bibliography, *Teacher's Edition,* pp. 148E–148F • Below Level **Theme Paperback** • Below Level **Leveled Readers**	• Leveled Readers: Below Level lesson, *Teacher's Edition,* pp. 183O; 213O; 251O
Difficulty with Writing **Emphasize** Complete sentences, combining sentences, choosing exact words	• *Handbook for English Language Learners,* pp. 175; 185; 195 • Reteaching: Grammar Skills, *Teacher's Edition,* pp. R20–R22	• Improving Writing, *Teacher's Edition,* pp. 183J, 183L; 185E; 213J, 213L; 251J 251L
Overall High Performance **Emphasize** Independent reading and writing, vocabulary development, critical thinking	• Challenge/Extension Activities: Comprehension, *Teacher's Edition,* pp. R9; R11; R13 • Challenge/Extension Activities: Vocabulary, *Teacher's Edition,* pp. R15; R17; R19 • Reading Assignment Cards, **Teachers' Resource Blackline Masters,** pp. 79–84	• Above Level **Theme Paperback** • Above Level **Leveled Readers** • Leveled Readers: Above Level lesson, *Teacher's Edition,* pp. 183Q; 213Q; 251Q • Challenge Activity Masters, **Challenge Handbook,** CH5–1 to CH5–6

FAIRY TALES

Literature

FAIRY TALES

❶ Background and Genre Vocabulary

❷ Main Selections

❸ Write a Fairy Tale

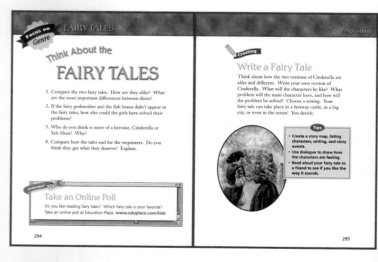

Instructional Support

Planning and Practice

- Planning and classroom management
- Reading instruction
- Skill lessons
- Materials for reaching all learners

- Independent practice for skills, Level 3.2

- Transparencies
- Strategy Posters
- Blackline Masters

Technology

Audio Selections

Cinderella

Yeh-Shen: A Cinderella Story from China

www.eduplace.com

Log on to Education Place for vocabulary support—
- e • **Glossary**
- e • **WordGame**

Leveled Books for Reaching All Learners

Leveled Readers and Leveled Practice

- Independent reading for building fluency

- Topic, comprehension strategy, and comprehension skill linked to selections

- Lessons in Teacher's Edition, pages 295O–295R

- Leveled practice for every book

Technology

Leveled Readers
Audio available

● BELOW LEVEL

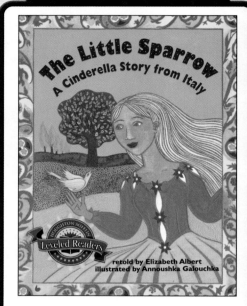

Smudge-Face
A Native American Cinderella Tale

retold by Alexandra Behr
illustrated by Arvis Stewart

Houghton Mifflin
Leveled Readers

▲ ON LEVEL

The Little Sparrow
A Cinderella Story from Italy

Houghton Mifflin
Leveled Readers

retold by Elizabeth Albert
illustrated by Annoushka Galouchka

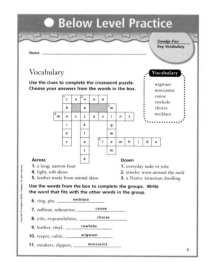

● Below Level Practice

Smudge-Face
Key Vocabulary

Name _____

Vocabulary

Use the clues to complete the crossword puzzle.
Choose your answers from the words in the box.

Vocabulary
wigwam
moccasins
canoe
rawhide
chores
necklace

Across
1. a long, narrow boat
4. light, soft shoes
5. leather made from animal skins

Down
1. everyday tasks or jobs
2. jewelry worn around the neck
3. a Native American dwelling

Use the words from the box to complete the groups. Write
the word that fits with the other words in the group.

6. ring, pin, _____ necklace
7. sailboat, submarine, _____ canoe
8. jobs, responsibilities, _____ chores
9. leather, vinyl, _____ rawhide
10. teepee, cabin, _____ wigwam
11. sneakers, slippers, _____ moccasins

5

▲ On Level Practice

The Little Sparrow
Key Vocabulary

Name _____

Vocabulary

Many fairy tales contain a series of three similar events.
Therefore, here are three similar puzzles!

Vocabulary
announced
glittering
purse
glaring
greedy
disappointed

Read the clues for each puzzle. Use words from
the box to complete each puzzle.

Puzzle 1 Clues:
Across: feeling sad or let down
Down: declared or made known

Puzzle 2 Clues:
Across: a small handbag
Down: selfish, too fond of
money or other valuables

Puzzle 3 Clues:
Across: staring
unpleasantly at
someone
Down: shiny and
sparkling

5

● Below Level Practice

Smudge-Face
Writing Skill
Writing a Fairy Tale

Name _____

Writing

Check your writing. Make sure you have included all the
parts of a good fairy tale. Read each sentence in this checklist
for help. Can you say yes to each question? If so, put a
checkmark in the box. If not, make a few changes. By
revising your fairy tale, you will make it even better! Responses will vary.

☐ Do you include details like those in the original fairy tale?

☐ Do you base your new fairy tale on those details?

☐ Is your main character a good person?

☐ Do you have at least one bad character?

☐ Do you write the events in the plot in the right order?

☐ Does the very good character win in the end?

☐ Did you use the original title or a clever new title?

7

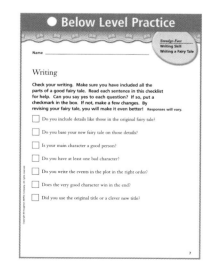

▲ On Level Practice

The Little Sparrow
Writing Skill
Writing a Fairy Tale

Name _____

Writing

Check your writing. Make sure you have included all the
parts of a good fairy tale. Read each sentence in this
checklist for help. Can you say yes to each question? If so,
put a checkmark in the box. If not, make a few changes.
By revising your fairy tale, you will make it even better!
Responses will vary.

☐ Do you include details like those in the original fairy tale?

☐ Do you base your new fairy tale on those details?

☐ Is your main character a very good person?

☐ Do you have at least one mean character?

☐ Do you make it clear when and where the story takes place?

☐ Do you write the events in the plot in the right order?

☐ Do you add any characters or events that couldn't happen in real life?

☐ Does the very good character win in the end?

☐ Did you use the original title or a clever new title?

7

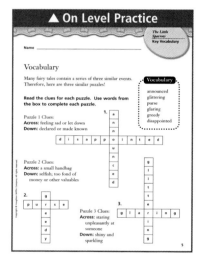

■ ABOVE LEVEL

Rella's Wish
by Sarah Golland
illustrated by Ann Boyajian

Houghton Mifflin
Leveled Readers

■ Above Level Practice

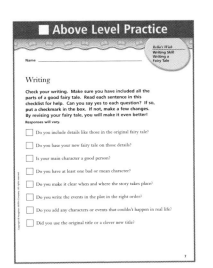

Rella's Wish
Key Vocabulary

Name

Vocabulary

Use the words in the box to solve the clues.

Vocabulary

expensive
gowns
longing
fulfill
coincidence
dazed

1. to satisfy or complete f u l f i l l
2. costing a lot of money e x p e n s i v e
3. very surprised or stunned d a z e d
4. an unexpected surprise c o i n c i d e n c e
5. strongly wishing or hoping for l o n g i n g
6. fancy, formal dresses g o w n s

Write the letters above the numbers to answer this question.

QUESTION: What adventure will Rella and Prince Alfred try next?

ANSWER: s a i l i n g

■ Above Level Practice

Rella's Wish
Writing Skill
Writing a Fairy Tale

Name

Writing

Check your writing. Make sure you have included all the parts of a good fairy tale. Read each sentence in this checklist for help. Can you say yes to each question? If so, put a checkmark in the box. If not, make a few changes. By revising your fairy tale, you will make it even better!
Responses will vary.

☐ Do you include details like those in the original fairy tale?
☐ Do you base your new fairy tale on those details?
☐ Is your main character a good person?
☐ Do you have at least one bad or mean character?
☐ Do you make it clear when and where the story takes place?
☐ Do you write the events in the plot in the right order?
☐ Do you add any characters or events that couldn't happen in real life?
☐ Did you use the original title or a clever new title?

◆ LANGUAGE SUPPORT

To Tell the Truth
A Native American Cinderella Tale

retold by Alexandra Behr
illustrated by Arvis Stewart

Houghton Mifflin
Leveled Readers

◆ Language Support Practice

To Tell the Truth
Build Background

Name

Build Background

Match each picture to the correct caption.

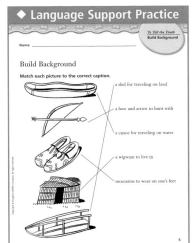

a sled for traveling on land

a bow and arrow to hunt with

a canoe for traveling on water

a wigwam to live in

moccasins to wear on one's feet

◆ Language Support Practice

To Tell the Truth
Key Vocabulary

Name

Vocabulary

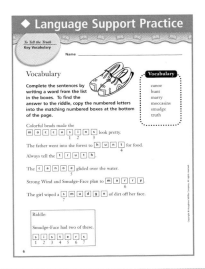

Vocabulary

canoe
hunt
marry
moccasins
smudge
truth

Complete the sentences by writing a word from the list in the boxes. To find the answer to the riddle, copy the numbered letters into the matching numbered boxes at the bottom of the page.

Colorful beads made the m o c c a s i n s look pretty.

The father went into the forest to h u n t for food.

Always tell the t r u t h.

The c a n o e glided over the water.

Strong Wind and Smudge-Face plan to m a r r y.

The girl wiped a s m u d g e of dirt off her face.

Riddle:

Smudge-Face had two of these.

s i s t e r s

Suggestions for Independent Reading

- Recommended trade books for independent reading in the genre

The Dragon Prince: A Chinese Beauty and the Beast Tale

(HarperCollins)
by Laurence Yep

The Fabrics of Fairy Tale: Stories Spun from Far and Wide

(Barefoot Books)
retold by Tanya Robyn Batt

The Random House Book of Fairy Tales

(Random House)
adapted by Amy Ehrlich

Joe Cinders

(Henry Holt and Company)
by Marianne Mitchell

Daily Lesson Plans

Technology

Lesson Planner CD-ROM allows you to customize the chart below to develop your own lesson plans.

 50–60 minutes

Reading
Comprehension

Leveled Readers
- Fluency Practice
- Independent Reading

DAY 1

Teacher Read Aloud, 267CC–267DD
"Billy Beg and the Dragon"

Building Background, 268

Genre Vocabulary, 269

folktale	hero	culture
fairy	heroine	

Reading the Selection, 270–281
Cinderella

 Comprehension Skill, 270
Understanding Fairy Tales

Comprehension Strategy, 270
Monitor/Clarify

Leveled Readers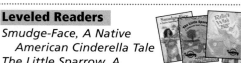

*Smudge-Face, A Native
   American Cinderella Tale*
*The Little Sparrow, A
   Cinderella Story from Italy*
Rella's Wish
*To Tell the Truth, A Native American
   Cinderella Tale*

Lessons and Leveled Practice, 295O–295R

DAY 2

Reading the Selection, 282–293
*Yeh-Shen: A Cinderella Story
from China*

Comprehension Check, 293

Responding, 294
Think About the Selections

Comprehension Strategy, 286
Monitor/Clarify

Leveled Readers

*Smudge-Face, A Native
   American Cinderella Tale*
*The Little Sparrow, A
   Cinderella Story from Italy*
Rella's Wish
*To Tell the Truth, A Native American
   Cinderella Tale*

Lessons and Leveled Practice, 295O–295R

 20–30 minutes

Word Work

Phonics/Decoding
Vocabulary
Spelling

DAY 1

Phonics/Decoding, 271
Phonics/Decoding Strategy

Vocabulary, 270–281
Selection Vocabulary

Spelling, 295E
The /s/ Sound in *face*

DAY 2

Structural Analysis, 295C
Prefixes and Suffixes

Vocabulary, 282–293
Selection Vocabulary

Spelling, 295E
The /s/ Sound in *face* Review and Practice

20–30 minutes

Writing and Oral Language

Writing
Grammar
Listening/Speaking/Viewing

DAY 1

Writing, 295, 295K
Prewriting a Fairy Tale

Grammar, 295I
Using Pronouns

Daily Language Practice
1. cinderella wishhed to danse at a ball. (Cinderella; wished; dance)
2. Cinderella's stepsisters was not nise. (were; nice.)

Listening/Speaking/Viewing,
267CC–267DD, 281
Teacher Read Aloud, Stop and Think

DAY 2

Writing, 295K
Drafting a Fairy Tale

Grammar, 295I
Using Pronouns Practice

Daily Language Practice
3. An old man noticed Yeh-Shens sad fase (Yeh-Shen's; face.)
4. yeh-Shen walkked like a prinsess. (Yeh-Shen; walked; princess.)

Listening/Speaking/Viewing, 293, 294

Wrapping Up, Responding

Target Skills of the Week

Comprehension	Monitor/Clarify; Understanding Fairy Tales
Vocabulary	Connotations
Phonics/Decoding	Prefixes and Suffixes
Fluency	Leveled Readers

DAY 3

Rereading the Selections
Rereading for Writer's Craft, 273
Varying Sentence Structure

Responding, 294
Preparing for Literature Discussion

Comprehension Skill, 295A–295B
Understanding Fairy Tales

Leveled Readers

Smudge-Face, A Native American Cinderella Tale
The Little Sparrow, A Cinderella Story from Italy
Rella's Wish
To Tell the Truth, A Native American Cinderella Tale

Lessons and Leveled Practice, 295O–295R

Phonics Review, 295D
Two Sounds of c

Vocabulary, 295G
Connotations

Spelling, 295F
Vocabulary: Idioms; The /s/ Sound in *face* Practice

Writing, 149L
Revising a Fairy Tale
Using Similes

Grammar, 149J
Pronoun Game

Daily Language Practice
5. A big fish were in the senter of the pond (was; center; pond.)
6. The king walked in a sircle and waited for Yeh-Shens' answer. (circle; Yeh-Shen's)

DAY 4

Rereading the Selections
Rereading for Writer's Craft, 285
Avoiding Repetition

Responding, 294
Literature Discussion

Comprehension Skill, 279
Visualizing

Leveled Readers

Smudge-Face, A Native American Cinderella Tale
The Little Sparrow, A Cinderella Story from Italy
Rella's Wish
To Tell the Truth, A Native American Cinderella Tale

Lessons and Leveled Practice, 295O–295R

Phonics, 295M
Language Center: Cinderella Says

Vocabulary, 295M
Language Center: Building Vocabulary

Spelling, 295F
Spelling Game, Proofreading

Writing, 295L
Proofreading a Fairy Tale

Grammar, 295J
Using Pronouns Practice

Daily Language Practice
7. Yeh-Shen had to rase home and she lost a slipper from one of her foots. (race; home,; feet.)
8. onse at home, her fell asleep under an apple tree. (Once; she)

Listening/Speaking/Viewing, 294
Literature Discussion

DAY 5

Rereading for Fluency, 277

Rereading for Writer's Craft, 291
Time Words and Phrases

Responding, 294
Internet Activity

Information and Study Skills, 295H
Using an Almanac

Leveled Readers
Smudge-Face, A Native American Cinderella Tale
The Little Sparrow, A Cinderella Story from Italy
Rella's Wish
To Tell the Truth, A Native American Cinderella Tale

Lessons and Leveled Practice, 295O–295R

Phonics, 295N
Language Center: Spelling Collage

Vocabulary, 295M
Language Center: Vocabulary Game

Spelling, 295F
Test: The /s/ Sound in *face*

Writing, 295L
Publishing a Fairy Tale

Grammar, 295J
Correct Pronouns

Daily Language Practice
9. The King lived in a large sity (king; city.)
10. Yeh-Shen kept her pet in a secret plase? (place.)

Listening/Speaking/Viewing, 295N
Language Center: Comparing Stories in Print and Movies

Managing Flexible Groups

	DAY 1	**DAY 2**
WHOLE CLASS	• Teacher Read Aloud (TE pp. 267CC–267DD) • Building Background, Introducing Vocabulary (TE pp. 268–269) • Comprehension Strategy: Introduce (TE p. 270) • Comprehension Skill: Introduce (TE p. 270) • Purpose Setting (TE p. 271) **After reading "Cinderella"** • Stop and Think (TE p. 281)	• Building Background (TE p. 268) • Comprehension Strategy: Reinforce (TE pp. 274, 283, 286, 288) **After reading "Yeh–Shen"** • Wrapping Up (TE p. 293) • Responding: Think About the Selections (TE p. 294)
SMALL GROUPS **Extra Support**	**TEACHER-LED** • Preview "Cinderella" (TE pp. 270–281). • Support reading with Extra Support/Intervention notes (TE pp. 271, 279).	**Partner or Individual Work** • Reread "Cinderella" (TE pp. 270–281). • Preview, read "Yeh–Shen" (TE pp. 282–293). • Support reading with Extra Support/Intervention notes (TE pp. 280, 282, 290, 292). • Comprehension Check (Practice Book p. 152)
Challenge	**Individual Work** • Extend reading with Challenge note (TE pp. 277, 289). • See Independent Activities below and Classroom Management (TE pp. 267AA–267BB).	**Individual Work** • See Independent Activities below and Classroom Management (TE pp. 267AA–267BB).
English Language Learners	**TEACHER-LED** • Preview vocabulary and "Cinderella" to Stop and Think (TE pp. 269–281). • Support reading with English Language Learners notes (TE pp. 268, 272, 280).	**TEACHER-LED** • Review "Cinderella" (TE pp. 270–281). ✔ • Preview, read "Yeh–Shen" (TE pp. 282–293). • Support reading with English Language Learners notes (TE pp. 283, 286, 287). • Begin Comprehension Check together (Practice Book p. 152).

Independent Activities

- Journals: selection notes, questions
- Complete, review Practice Book (pp. 150–154) and Leveled Readers Practice Blackline Masters (TE pp. 295O–295R).
- Leveled Readers (TE pp. 295O–295R) or Suggestions for Independent Reading (TE p. 267V)
- Responding activities (TE pp. 294–295)

✔ Opportunity to informally assess oral reading rate

DAY 3

- Rereading: Lesson on Writer's Craft (TE p. 273)
- Comprehension Skill: Main lesson (TE pp. 295A–295B)
- Responding: Preparing for Literature Discussion (Practice Book p. 153)

TEACHER-LED

- Review Comprehension Check (Practice Book p. 152).
- Preview Leveled Reader: Below Level (TE p. 295O), or read book from Suggestions for Independent Reading (TE p. 267V). ✔

TEACHER-LED

- Preview Leveled Reader: Above Level (TE p. 295Q), or read book from Suggestions for Independent Reading (TE p. 267V). ✔

Partner or Individual Work

- Complete Comprehension Check (Practice Book p. 152).
- Begin Leveled Reader: Language Support (TE p. 295R), or read book from Suggestions for Independent Reading (TE p. 267V).

DAY 4

- Rereading: Comprehension Skill lesson (TE p. 279)
- Responding: Literature Discussion (TE p. 294)

Partner or Individual Work

- Complete Leveled Reader: Below Level (TE p. 295O), or read book from Suggestions for Independent Reading (TE p. 267V).

Individual Work

- Complete Leveled Reader: Above Level (TE p. 295Q), or read book from Suggestions for Independent Reading (TE p. 267V).

TEACHER-LED

- Complete Leveled Reader: Language Support (TE p. 295R), or continue book from Suggestions for Independent Reading (TE p. 267V). ✔

DAY 5

- Rereading: Lesson on Writer's Craft (TE p. 291)
- Responding: Select from Activities (TE pp. 294–295)
- Information and Study Skills (TE p. 295H)

TEACHER-LED

- Read or reread book from Suggestions for Independent Reading (TE p. 267V). ✔

TEACHER-LED

- Read or reread book from Suggestions for Independent Reading (TE p. 267V). ✔

Partner or Individual Work

- Read or reread book from Suggestions for Independent Reading (TE p. 267V).

- Language Center activities (TE pp. 295M–295N)
- **Fluency Practice:** Reread "Cinderella;" "Yeh–Shen" ✔
- Activities relating to "Cinderella;" "Yeh–Shen" at Education Place www.eduplace.com

Turn the page for more independent activities.

Classroom Management

Independent Activities

Assign these activities while you work with small groups.

Differentiated Instruction for Small Groups

- **Leveled Readers**
  Below Level, On Level, Above Level, Language Support

- **Lessons and Leveled Practice,** pp. 295O–295R

Independent Activities

- Language Center, pp. 295M–295N

Look for more activities in the Classroom Management Kit.

Folktale

What Happens Next?

👤 **Singles**	🕐 30 minutes
Objective	Write what happens after a fairy tale ends.

What happens to Cinderella after she gets married? Does Yeh-Shen take her fish bones to her new home?

- Write a short sequel, or continuation, for one of these fairly tales.
- Include the characters from the original fairy tale in your sequel, and you can add some new characters if you wish.
- Share your sequel with your classmates. Compare the sequels to find out how they are alike and different.

Technology

Cinderella's Future Ride

👥 **Pairs**	🕐 30 minutes
Objective	Design a new vehicle for Cinderella.
Materials	Drawing paper, markers, colored pencils

Cinderella's fairy godmother turns a pumpkin into a beautiful coach. Suppose Cinderella lives hundreds of years in the future. What kind of vehicle will she ride in?

- Fold a piece of drawing paper in half.
- On one side draw a pumpkin.
- On the other side draw a picture of a futuristic vehicle that Cinderella can ride in to the ball.
- Pretend you are Cinderella's godmother or godfather and explain to your partner where and what everything is in the vehicle.

Consider copying and laminating these activities for use in centers.

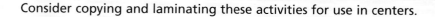

Language Arts
Character Sketch

👤 Singles	🕐 30 minutes
Objective	Write a character sketch.

Think about the different characters in *Yeh-Shen*.

- Choose a character to write about.
- Think about the different characteristics of that person. How would you describe the person? What makes him or her happy? What does that person like to do?
- Write a short description of the character. Tell whether or not you like him or her. Explain why.

Share your character sketch with the class.

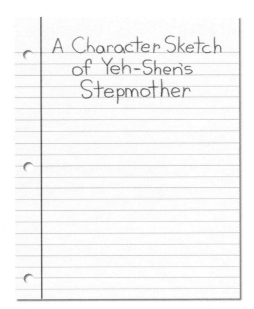

A Character Sketch of Yeh-Shen's Stepmother

Dance
Fairy Tale Dance

👥 Groups	🕐 45 minutes
Objective	Perform a dance about a fairy tale.

Make up a dance that tells the story of Cinderella or Yeh-Shen.

- Divide the story into parts and give a part to each member of your group.
- Make up motions and steps that tell what is happening in the story.
- Practice performing all of the parts together before you perform in front of another group.

Language
My Special Friend

👤 Singles	🕐 30 minutes
Objective	Describe an imaginary friend.
Materials	drawing paper, colored pencils

Cinderella has a fairy godmother. Yeh-Shen had a fish. Pretend you have a special friend that only you can see.

- Draw a picture of your friend. It can be an object, an animal, or a person.
- Give your special friend a name.
- Display your picture as you tell your classmates about how you met your friend, what your friend has already done for you, and the wishes that you hope your friend will help you with in the future.

My Special Friend

Louie

Listening Comprehension

Building Background

Tell students that they will read two fairy tales in this section. They will learn about the characteristics of fairy tales, and try writing a fairy tale of their own.

Explain that you will begin by reading aloud a fairy tale about a young man and a dragon.

Fluency Modeling

Explain that as you read aloud, you will be modeling fluent oral reading. Ask students to listen carefully to your phrasing and your expression, or tone of voice and emphasis.

COMPREHENSION SKILL

Understanding Fairy Tales

Ask students what elements are usually present in a fairy tale. (Sample answer: the setting is "long ago"; make-believe events can happen; some characters are make-believe and may have special powers; after a problem is solved the main character lives happily ever after)

Purpose Setting Read the story aloud, asking students to note the elements of a fairy tale as they listen. Then use the Guiding Comprehension questions to assess students' understanding. Reread the story for clarification as needed.

Teacher Read Aloud

Billy Beg and the Dragon

retold by Reba Wayne

1 Long ago, in a peaceful land, a young man named Billy Beg worked on a farm. Billy seemed very ordinary. But he had two magic tools that no one else knew about. One was a stick with special powers. The other was a belt that protected him from harm.

One day the farmer said, "Come to town with me, Billy! Today Sir Fairweather, the bravest knight in the **2** kingdom, will battle a dragon. If Sir Fairweather wins, the princess will marry him."

"No thanks," said Billy. "I think I'll have plenty to keep me busy." But when everyone else had gone, Billy picked up his magic stick and tied the magic belt around his waist. With the stick he changed a shaggy goat into a fine horse and his ragged work clothes into a colorful suit. Then he rode to town.

All the villagers were gathered in the town square. On a high platform sat the king, the queen, and their daughter. Sir Fairweather strode up and down in front of them, sword at the ready.

Suddenly a huge shadow blocked out the sun. With a great hiss of flames and a flap of wings, the dragon swooped into view. Its scales shone like green diamonds, and its red eyes glittered with evil. Sir Fairweather took one look and leaped into the nearest well to hide.

Now the dragon stalked up and down, breathing fire at the people, who scrambled away. "Please," called the king, "is no one else willing to battle this dragon?"

Billy held up his magic stick, and it changed into a gleaming sword. "Over here, fire worm!" he shouted. The villagers gasped with admiration. Who was this new hero?

The dragon blew fire at Billy, but the flames bounced off his sword and belt and disappeared. Billy galloped toward the dragon, his sword flashing in the sun.

❸ The battle raged fiercely, Billy's sword sending sparks off the dragon's scales and the dragon's foul breath scorching the ground but never touching Billy or his horse. Then Billy turned his sword into a heavy cudgel. He hit the dragon on its head and knocked it out cold. From the platform, the princess sprinkled water on the dragon. Immediately the beast disappeared in a cloud of smoke. (Swords can't kill sleeping dragons, but water will put out their fire forever.)

The townsfolk shouted and cheered. In the confusion, Billy galloped away, but the princess grabbed his shoe as he rode past.

When the farmer came home, Billy was in the pasture as usual. "You should've seen the fight, Billy!" the farmer said.

"Oh, I've had plenty to keep me busy," said Billy.

The next day the princess announced that she would marry the hero whose shoe she had snatched. Young men and old, weak men and strong, handsome men and homely lined up to try on the shoe, but it fit no one.

Billy walked to the castle wearing his ragged work clothes. The crowd laughed at him. "This stable boy wants to marry the princess!" The palace guards came to throw Billy out.

"Wait," said the princess. "He has a fine face despite the ragged clothes. Let him try on the shoe for size."

Billy put the shoe on, and the onlookers gasped. It fit him perfectly. "Will you marry me?" the princess asked.

"If you'll marry me," Billy answered.

For the rest of their days, Billy and the princess ruled the kingdom well. And because a new dragon came along every once in a while, they always had plenty to keep them busy.

CRITICAL THINKING
Guiding Comprehension

❶ **UNDERSTANDING FAIRY TALES** When and where does this fairy tale take place? (long ago, in a peaceful land)

❷ **UNDERSTANDING FAIRY TALES** What make-believe character is in this fairy tale? What character has special powers? (The dragon is make-believe; Billy has special powers: a magic stick and a magic belt.)

❸ **UNDERSTANDING FAIRY TALES** What problem has to be solved? How is the problem solved? (An evil dragon must be defeated. Billy and the princess together slay the dragon.)

Discussion Options

Personal Response Ask students to tell what kind of a person they think Billy Beg is and why they think he kept his magic stick and magic belt a secret.

⭐ **Connecting/Comparing** Have students discuss which elements in this fairy tale are realistic and which are make-believe.

English Language Learners

Supporting Comprehension

Discuss with students the elements of make-believe in this fairy tale. Invite volunteers to tell a fairy tale from their native land. List on the board similarities and differences between the tales.

Building Background

Key Concept: Fairy Tales

Connecting to the Genre Ask a volunteer to read aloud the text on page 269. Review the key elements of fairy tales. Remind students that a fairy tale is a kind of folktale that usually contains the following elements:

- Fairies or other make-believe characters appear.
- A hero or heroine has a problem to solve.
- Events happen that cannot happen in real life.
- There is a happy ending.

Then ask students to name some fairy tales that they have read or seen dramatized in the movies or on television. List the titles, and have students tell about the principal characters and events of the tales.

Focus on Genre

FAIRY TALES

268

Supporting Comprehension

Beginning/Preproduction Have students listen as you reread the text on page 269. Ask students what makes the illustration on pages 268–269 seem like a fairy tale.

Early Production and Speech Emergence Have students draw a scene from a fairy tale they know. Ask them to explain their drawings.

Intermediate and Advanced Fluency Ask students to name the characters in a favorite fairy tale and tell what problem the characters solve.

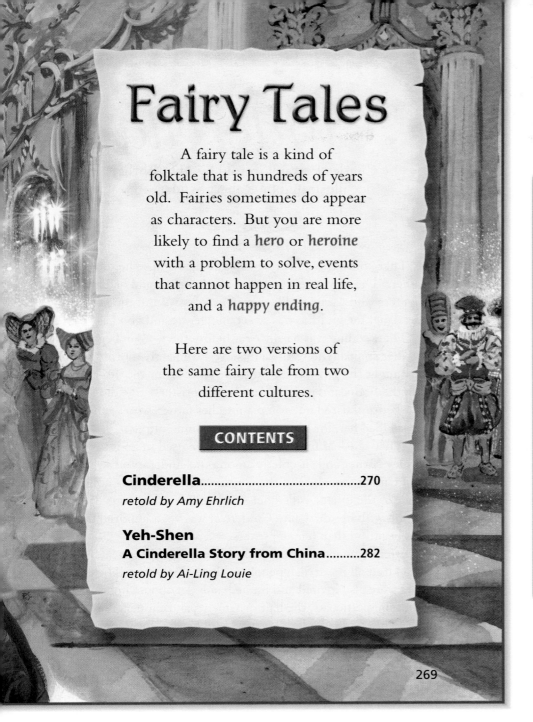

Fairy Tales

A fairy tale is a kind of folktale that is hundreds of years old. Fairies sometimes do appear as characters. But you are more likely to find a **hero** or **heroine** with a problem to solve, events that cannot happen in real life, and a **happy ending**.

Here are two versions of the same fairy tale from two different cultures.

CONTENTS

269

Introducing Vocabulary

Genre Vocabulary
These words support the Key Concept.

folktale a traditional story handed down by the people of a country or region from one generation to the next

fairy a tiny imaginary being in human form who has magical powers

hero the main male character in a story, poem, or play

heroine the main female character in a story, poem, or play

culture the customs, beliefs, and ways of living that belong to a people

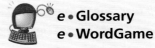

e • **Glossary**
e • **WordGame**

See Vocabulary Notes on pages 272, 274, 276, 278, 284, 286, 288, 290, and 292 for additional words to preview.

Display Transparency F5–1.

- Model how to use the process of elimination to choose the correct Genre Vocabulary word from the list to complete the first sentence.

- For each remaining sentence, ask students to use context clues to choose the correct Vocabulary word. Then have them define each Vocabulary word.

- Ask students to use these words as they discuss fairy tales.

Practice/Homework Assign **Practice Book** page 150.

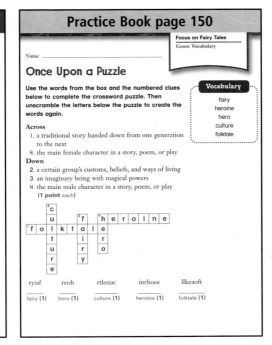

Transparency F5–1

Genre Vocabulary

| heroine | fairy | hero | cultures | folktale |

1. The story of "Pecos Bill" is an American ___folktale___
2. The ___hero___ of that story is Pecos Bill.
3. A little girl is the ___heroine___ of "Little Red Riding Hood."
4. Similar stories can be found in many different ___cultures___ around the world.
5. When a character has a problem, a ___fairy___ can use special powers to help out.

Practice Book page 150

Focus on Fairy Tales
Genre Vocabulary

Name _____

Once Upon a Puzzle

Use the words from the box and the numbered clues below to complete the crossword puzzle. Then unscramble the letters below the puzzle to create the words again.

Vocabulary
fairy
heroine
hero
culture
folktale

Across
1. a traditional story handed down from one generation to the next
4. the main female character in a story, poem, or play

Down
2. a certain group's customs, beliefs, and ways of living
3. an imaginary being with magical powers
4. the main male character in a story, poem, or play
(**1 point** each)

ryiaf ___fairy (1)___
reoh ___hero (1)___
rtleuuc ___culture (1)___
inrhoee ___heroine (1)___
llkeaoft ___folktale (1)___

Cinderella

COMPREHENSION STRATEGY
Monitor/Clarify

Teacher Modeling Remind students that they can clear up any parts of a story that they don't understand by rereading or reading ahead. Have a volunteer read the title and the first two paragraphs of the story on page 270. Then model the strategy:

Think Aloud *The title of this story is "Cinderella," and on this page I read about a sweet, gentle girl who is mistreated by her father's new wife. I wonder if this girl is Cinderella. I'll read ahead to see whether I can find out the answer. If it is still not clear, I'll read the pages again.*

Remind students to use Monitor/Clarify and other strategies as they read.

COMPREHENSION SKILL
Understanding Fairy Tales

Display **Transparency F5–2** and direct students to the chart on **Practice Book** page 151.

- Discuss the chart, and tell students to fill it in as they read.
- Work with students as needed to fill in the chart for "Cinderella." Tell students that they will complete the rest of the chart later.

Focus on Genre / FAIRY TALES

Cinderella

by Charles Perrault, retold by Amy Ehrlich
illustrated by Robert Sauder

There once was a man whose wife died and so he took another. The new wife was proud and haughty, and had two daughters who were just like her in every way. But the man also had a daughter, and she was sweet and gentle and good as gold. **1**

The wedding was hardly over before the woman began to make her stepdaughter's life a misery. From early morning until late at night the girl was forced to work, to scour the dishes and scrub the floors and pick up after her stepsisters. She did all she was asked and dared not complain to her father, who would only have scolded her, for his new wife ruled him entirely.

When she had finished her work, she used to go into the chimney corner and sit quietly among the cinders, and so she was called Cinder-wench. But the younger sister, who was not quite as rude as the others, called her Cinderella. In her ragged clothing with her dirty face Cinderella was yet a hundred times more beautiful than her stepsisters.

After some months had passed, the king's son gave a ball and invited to it all the stylish people in the countryside. The two sisters were also invited and immediately set about choosing the gowns and petticoats, the hair ornaments and slippers they would wear. This made Cinderella's work still harder, for it was she

270

Transparency F5–2
Fairy Tale Chart

	"Cinderella"	"Yeh-Shen"
Characters	Cinderella, her stepmother, her stepsisters, the king's son, the godmother	Yeh-Shen, her stepmother, her stepsister, the king, a fish, an old man
Setting (time and place)	a long time ago; somewhere in Europe	China; before the Ch'in and Han dynasties
Problem	Cinderella is treated badly and can't go to the ball.	Yeh-Shen is treated badly and can't go to the festival.
Events Beginning	1. Before the ball Stepsisters get ready for ball, leaving Cinderella behind. Godmother prepares Cinderella for the ball.	1. Before the festival Stepmother kills Yeh-Shen's fish, but its bones provide for Yeh-Shen, including clothes for the festival.
Middle	2. At the ball, first night The king's son spends all his time with Cinderella. Guests say how beautiful she is. She gets home safely.	2. At the festival People notice Yeh-Shen's beauty. When her stepsister seems to recognize her, she flees, losing her golden shoe.
	3. At the ball, second night Cinderella forgets to leave on time. She runs, leaving behind her glass slipper.	3. After the festival The bones of the fish no longer speak to Yeh-Shen. The shoe is presented to a king.
End	4. Ending The king's son searches for Cinderella. Her foot fits the slipper. Cinderella marries the prince and is kind to her stepsisters.	4. Ending Yeh-Shen takes the shoe. The king follows her, and the shoe fits her. She marries the king, but the stepmother and stepsister are left to die.

THEME 5 Focus on Fairy Tales
Graphic Organizer

ANNOTATED VERSION

TRANSPARENCY F5–2
TEACHER'S EDITION PAGES 270 AND 295A

Practice Book page 151

Focus on Fairy Tales
Graphic Organizer Fairy Tale Chart

Name _____

Fairy Tale Chart
Some answers may vary. Examples are given.

	"Cinderella"	"Yeh-Shen"
Characters	Cinderella, her stepmother, her stepsisters, the king's son, the godmother **(1 point)**	Yeh-Shen, her stepmother, her stepsister, the king, a fish, an old man **(1)**
Setting (time and place)	a long time ago; somewhere in Europe **(1)**	China; before the Ch'in and Han dynasties **(1)**
Problem	Cinderella is treated badly and can't go to the ball. **(1)**	Yeh-Shen is treated badly and can't go to the festival. **(1)**
Events Beginning	1. Before the ball Stepsisters get ready for ball, leaving Cinderella behind. Godmother prepares Cinderella for the ball. **(1)**	1. Before the festival Stepmother kills Yeh-Shen's fish, but its bones provide for Yeh-Shen, including clothes for the festival. **(1)**
Middle	2. At the ball, first night The king's son spends all his time with Cinderella. Guests say how beautiful she is. She gets home safely. **(1)**	2. At the festival People notice Yeh-Shen's beauty. When her stepsister seems to recognize her, she flees, losing her golden shoe. **(1)**
	3. At the ball, second night Cinderella forgets to leave on time. She runs, leaving behind her glass slipper. **(1)**	3. After the festival The bones of the fish no longer speak to Yeh-Shen. The shoe is presented to a king. **(1)**
End	4. Ending The king's son searches for Cinderella. Her foot fits the slipper. Cinderella marries the prince and is kind to her stepsisters. **(1)**	4. Ending Yeh-Shen takes the shoe. The king follows her, and the shoe fits her. She marries the king, but the stepmother and stepsister are left to die.

who ironed their linen and pleated their ruffles. All day long the sisters talked of nothing but how they should be dressed.

One night, as Cinderella was helping them, they said to her, "Cinderella, would you not like to go to the ball?"

"Please, sisters, do not mock me," she said. "How could I ever dream of such a thing?"

"You are right," they answered. "People would surely laugh to see a Cinderwench at the ball."

For two days the sisters could hardly eat for excitement. So tightly did they lace themselves that they broke a dozen laces, and they were always at their looking glasses, trying on their gowns.

271

Building Background

- Discuss the name *Cinderella* with students. Ask a volunteer to define *cinders*. (bits of partly burned coal or wood) Ask students why they think a person might be named *Cinderella*.

- Ask what is likely to happen in a fairy tale to someone like Cinderella. (She is likely to receive help from a fairy.)

Purpose Setting

Have students read to identify the fairy tale elements in "Cinderella."

Journal ▶ Students can write a list of the powers that a fairy might have. They can use this list when writing their own fairy tale.

STRATEGY REVIEW

Phonics/Decoding

Remind students to use the Phonics/Decoding Strategy as they read.

Extra Support/Intervention

Selection Preview

Pages 270–271: What differences do you see in the picture between the young girl and the three women?

Pages 272–273: Why do you think Cinderella looks so happy?

Pages 274–279: What happens at the ball?

Pages 280–281: Why is Cinderella trying on a shoe?

CRITICAL THINKING
Guiding Comprehension

❶ COMPARE AND CONTRAST How is Cinderella different from her step-mother and her stepsisters? (She is sweet and good, and they are haughty and nasty.)

❷ DRAWING CONCLUSIONS Why do you think the fairy godmother comes to help Cinderella? (She is responsible for protecting Cinderella and wants to make her happy.)

❸ MAKING INFERENCES What can the fairy godmother do? (She can change whatever her wand touches into something else.)

At last the evening of the ball came. Cinderella watched the sisters leave for the court, and when she had lost sight of them, she began to weep.

Her godmother, who was a fairy, saw her tears and asked what was the matter.

"I wish I could — I wish I could — go to the ball," stammered Cinderella, but she could say no more for crying.

"Well, then, go you shall," said her godmother. Then she ❷ told the girl to go into the garden for a pumpkin. Cinderella picked the finest she could find and carried it indoors. Her godmother scooped it out and struck it with her wand. Instantly the pumpkin turned into a fine gilded coach.

272

Vocabulary

godmother a woman who acts as a sponsor at a child's christening

wand a slender rod or stick

gilded covered with a thin layer of gold

coachman the driver of a coach

footmen male servants

English Language Learners

Language Development

Explain that *stepsister* means "the daughter of one's mother's husband (or father's wife) by another marriage." Explain the meanings of related words such as *stepbrother, stepmother, stepfather,* and *stepparent.* Point out that a person may also have a *half sister* or a *half brother* (a sister or brother related through only one parent).

Next her godmother went to look in the mousetrap, where she found six mice, all alive. She tapped each one with her wand and they were turned into white horses, a fine set of them to draw the coach.

But they would still need a coachman, so Cinderella brought the rat trap to her godmother. Inside there were three rats. The godmother chose the one with the longest whiskers, and as soon as she touched him with her wand, he became a fat coachman with a most imposing beard.

After that the godmother turned six lizards into footmen, who jumped up behind the coach and held on as if they had done nothing else their whole lives.

273

Varying Sentence Structure

Teach

- Remind students that good writers make their writing more interesting by varying sentence structure.

- List these ways to vary sentences:

  – Mix long and short sentences in a paragraph.

  – Vary the pattern by beginning some sentences with a phrase or a word such as *when, in, after,* or *next.*

  – Combine short sentences to make longer sentences.

Practice/Apply

- Have a volunteer read aloud the second paragraph on page 273 and ask students to describe the length of each sentence in the paragraph. (long sentence; short sentence; long sentence)

- Rephrase the paragraph as short simple sentences and compare with the original. Have students discuss how using different sentence lengths makes the writing more interesting.

- Ask students to look for varying words or phrases that begin sentences on page 273. (*Next, Inside, After that*)

CRITICAL THINKING
Guiding Comprehension

4 **CAUSE AND EFFECT** What will happen if Cinderella does not return home by midnight? (Her coach and horses will turn back into a pumpkin and mice, her coachman and footmen will turn back into a rat and lizards, and her clothing will turn back into rags.)

5 **MAKING INFERENCES** Is Cinderella accepted at the ball? How do you know? (Yes, the prince himself greets her, and the people say she is lovely.)

COMPREHENSION STRATEGY
Monitor/Clarify

Teacher/Student Modeling Model using the Monitor/Clarify strategy.

- Ask, How does Cinderella get a coach to go to the ball?

- Have students reread page 272 to clarify the question above. (Her fairy godmother creates a coach by striking a pumpkin with her wand.)

Then her godmother said to Cinderella, "Well, my dear, here is your carriage. I hope it pleases you."

"Oh, yes!" the girl cried. "But am I to wear these rags to the ball?"

Her godmother simply touched Cinderella with her wand and at once her clothes were turned into a gown of silver. Then she gave Cinderella a pair of glass slippers, the most beautiful imaginable. But as the girl was making ready to leave, her godmother warned her that she must return home by midnight. If she stayed one moment longer, her coach would be a pumpkin again, her horses mice, her coachman a rat, her footmen lizards, and her clothing would turn back into rags. **4**

Cinderella promised she would not be late and then she went off to the ball, her heart pounding for joy.

The king's son had been told that a great princess, unknown to all the company, would soon arrive, and he ran out to receive her himself. He gave her his hand as she sprang from the coach and led her into the hall where everyone was assembled. At once there was silence. So awed were the guests by the mysterious princess that they left off dancing and the musicians ceased to play. Then a hushed murmur swept the room: **5**

"Ah, how lovely she is! How lovely!"

274

Vocabulary

gown formal woman's dress

receive to greet or welcome

275

CRITICAL THINKING

Guiding Comprehension

6 **MAKING INFERENCES** Why do you think the prince cannot eat a bite of food at the banquet? (He is falling in love with Cinderella.)

7 **WRITER'S CRAFT** Why does the author tell us that Cinderella's stepsisters are pleased to sit with her at the ball? (to show that they do not recognize Cinderella)

The king's son led her across the floor and they danced together again and again. A fine banquet was served, but the young prince only gazed at her and could not eat a bite.

6

After a time she left his side and went to sit by her sisters. She treated them with kindness and offered them sections of oranges that the prince had given to her. It very much pleased them to be singled out in this way.

7

Then Cinderella heard the clock strike a quarter to twelve. Quickly she wished the company good night and ran from the hall and down the palace steps to her coach.

276

Vocabulary

banquet large, formal meal for many people

When she was home again, she found her godmother and thanked her and asked if she might go to the ball again the next day. As Cinderella was telling her godmother all that had happened, her two sisters came into the room.

"If you had only been there," said her sisters. "There was an unknown princess, the most beautiful ever seen in this world. She sat with us and gave us oranges."

"Was she really so very beautiful? And do you not know her name?" Then Cinderella turned to the elder one. "Ah, dear sister, won't you give me your plainest dress so that I might see the princess for myself?"

"What? Lend my clothing to a dirty Cinderwench? I should be out of my mind!" cried the sister.

277

TARGET SKILL
Fluency Practice

Rereading for Fluency Have students choose a favorite part of the story to reread to a partner or in small groups. Encourage students to read expressively.

Challenge

Comparing Fairy Tale Characters

Challenge students to look in the library for other fairy tales, such as "Sleeping Beauty" or "Rumplestiltskin." Ask them to compare the fairies and the human characters in these stories with the ones in "Cinderella."

CRITICAL THINKING

Guiding Comprehension

8 MAKING INFERENCES Why do you think Cinderella asks if the unknown princess had again appeared at the ball? (She probably wants to find out if anyone saw her flee at midnight.)

9 WRITER'S CRAFT Why does the author list all the women who tried on the glass slipper? (to show that no other woman in the country is a match for Cinderella)

TARGET SKILL

COMPREHENSION STRATEGY

Monitor/Clarify

Student Modeling Have students model the strategy by monitoring their comprehension and clarifying the events on page 279.

278

Vocabulary

exquisitely beautifully

entranced filled with great pleasure and wonder

vanished disappeared

proclaimed announced publicly

couriers messengers

Cinderella had expected such an answer and she was very glad of the refusal. The next evening the two sisters went to the ball and she went too, dressed even more exquisitely than the first time. The king's son was always with her and spoke to her with words of praise. So entranced was Cinderella that she forgot her godmother's warning and heard the chimes of midnight striking when she thought it could be no more than eleven o'clock.

At once she arose and fled, nimble as a deer. Though the prince rushed after her, he could not catch her. In her haste she left behind one of the glass slippers, which he picked up and carried with him.

Cinderella's coach had vanished and she had to run home in the dark. Of her finery nothing remained but the other glass slipper. The guards at the palace gates were asked if they had seen a princess, but they replied that no one had come there but a poor country girl dressed in rags.

When the two sisters returned from the ball, Cinderella asked whether the unknown princess had again appeared. They told her yes but said she had hurried away the moment the clock struck midnight. And now the king's son had only the glass slipper she had left behind. They said he was brokenhearted and would do anything to find her once more. **8**

All this was true. A few days afterward the king's son proclaimed that he would marry the woman for whom the glass slipper had been made. The couriers began by trying the slipper on all the princesses. They tried it on the duchesses and then on the ladies of the court. But nowhere in the land could they find a woman whose foot was small enough to fit the slipper. At last it was brought to the two sisters. **9**

279

Visualizing

Teach

- Remind students that when you visualize, you use a writer's words to "see" a picture in your mind.

- Explain that visualizing a scene or event in a fairy tale helps you to understand the characters and the sometimes surprising events that take place in this type of story.

Practice/Apply

- Have students read the first three paragraphs on page 279. Then have them close their eyes and visualize the scene in which Cinderella hears the clock strike midnight.

- Ask students to describe their mental images. Guide them with questions:

  – What is Cinderella wearing when she hears the clock strike? What expression is on her face?

  – How does she move and where does she go?

  – What expression is on the prince's face as he picks up the glass slipper?

  – What is Cinderella wearing when she arrives home? What expression is on her face?

- Have students share their ideas; then have them draw or write a description of their images.

CRITICAL THINKING
Guiding Comprehension

10 WRITER'S CRAFT Why do you think the author mentions that the courier thought Cinderella was lovely? (to show why the courier allows Cinderella to try on the glass slipper)

11 CAUSE AND EFFECT Why does the fairy godmother change Cinderella's clothes into a beautiful ball gown? (She wants to prove to everyone that Cinderella is the unknown princess.)

They pushed and pushed, trying to squeeze their feet inside, but they were not able to manage it.

Cinderella was in the room and recognized her slipper at once. "Let me see if it will fit my foot," she said.

Her sisters began to laugh and tease her. But the courier who'd been sent with the slipper looked at Cinderella and saw that she was lovely. He said his orders were that every woman in the land must try it on. **10**

Cinderella sat down and he held the slipper up to her little foot. It went on at once, as easily as if it had been made of wax.

280

Extra Support/ Intervention

Review (pages 270–281)

Before students who need extra support join the whole class for Stop and Think on page 281, have them

- review the fairy tale elements in "Cinderella"
- complete the chart for "Cinderella" on **Transparency F5–2** with you
- check and revise their Fairy Tale Chart on **Practice Book** page 151 and use it to summarize the story

English Language Learners

Supporting Comprehension

Point out to students the phrase *squeeze their feet inside.* Ask them to tell you what they think it means. Have students act out trying to get a small slipper on large feet.

Then, while the two sisters watched, Cinderella drew from her pocket the other glass slipper and put it on too. Suddenly her godmother was there and she touched the girl's ragged clothes with her wand and they became a gown even more beautiful than the ones she had worn to the ball. **11**

And now her two sisters knew she had been the unknown princess they had so admired. They threw themselves at her feet to beg her forgiveness for all their ill treatment. Cinderella bid them to rise and said that she forgave them with all her heart.

Then Cinderella was taken before the prince. He was overwhelmed with love for her and sometime later they were married. Cinderella, who was as good as she was beautiful, gave her two sisters a home in the palace, and that very same day they were married to two lords of the court.

Stop and Think

Focus On Genre

Critical Thinking Questions

1. **MAKING INFERENCES** What does the king's son assume to be true about the glass slipper? (It will fit only the foot of the unknown princess.)

2. **COMPARE AND CONTRAST** How is the stepsisters' attitude toward Cinderella different at the end of the story from what it was at the beginning? (At the beginning they mock and scorn her, and at the end they respect her and ask for forgiveness.)

3. **WRITER'S CRAFT** Why do you think the author mentions that Cinderella gives her sisters a home in the palace? (to show how good and forgiving Cinderella is)

4. **NOTING DETAILS** What is special about Cinderella's godmother? (She is a fairy with the power to change one thing into another by touching it with her wand.)

Strategies in Action

Have students take turns modeling the Monitor/Clarify strategy and ask what other strategies they found helpful.

REACHING ALL LEARNERS

Extra Support/Intervention

Phonics/Decoding

Model the strategy for the word *forgiveness*.

I recognize two words I know: for *and* give. *I'll pronounce them just as if they were the base words, and I'll run them together to make one word. Oh—that's the word* forgive, *meaning "to stop being angry at someone." The suffix* -ness *has been added to the word. That suffix means "the condition of" or "the act of." So adding it to* forgive *makes a word that means "the condition of no longer being angry at someone," and that makes sense in the sentence.*

Monitoring Student Progress

If . . .	Then . . .
students have successfully completed the Extra Support activities on page 280,	have them read the next selection cooperatively or independently.

Yeh-Shen

retold by Ai-Ling Louie, illustrated by Ed Young

Building Background

- Tell students that stories similar to "Cinderella" exist in many different cultures all around the world. Discuss why people everywhere appreciate Cinderella stories.

- Ask students what is likely to happen in other fairy tales to characters who are like Cinderella. (They are likely to receive help from a fairy or another imaginary being.)

Purpose Setting

As students read, ask them to look for the fairy tale elements in "Yeh-Shen."

Extra Support/Intervention

Selection Preview

Pages 282–285: What can you tell about Yeh-Shen from these pictures?

Pages 286–287: What is strange about this picture of the huge fish?

Pages 288–289: What is happening to the fish?

Pages 290–291: What is the small golden object at the center of this picture?

Pages 292–293: Where have you seen Yeh-Shen dressed like this before?

Monitor/Clarify

Teacher Modeling Read aloud page 283. Then model the strategy.

Think Aloud *To make sure I understand this page, I ask myself questions such as:* Who is the main character? *and* What do I know about her? *If I don't know the answers, I go back and reread to find them.*

In the dim past, even before the Ch'in and the Han dynasties, there lived a cave chief of southern China by the name of Wu. As was the custom in those days, Chief Wu had taken two wives. Each wife in her turn had presented Wu with a baby daughter. But one of the wives sickened and died, and not too many days after that Chief Wu took to his bed and died too.

Yeh-Shen, the little orphan, grew to girlhood in her stepmother's home. She was a bright child and lovely too, with skin as smooth as ivory and dark pools for eyes. Her stepmother was jealous of all this beauty and goodness, for her own daughter was not pretty at all. So in her displeasure, she gave poor Yeh-Shen the heaviest and most unpleasant chores.

283

REACHING ALL LEARNERS

English Language Learners

Supporting Comprehension

Point out the idioms *took to his bed* (page 283) and *the only friend Yeh-Shen had to her name* (page 285). Explain that these are expressions in which the words *took* and *name* have meanings that are slightly different than usual. Explain that *took to his bed* means "got into his bed and stayed there." Explain that the phrase *to her name* means "belonging to her." In other words, the only friend that belonged to Yeh-Shen was the fish. Offer other examples, such as *He didn't have a nickel to his name.*

CRITICAL THINKING
Guiding Comprehension

12 **NOTING DETAILS** Why does the author tell us that Yeh-Shen always shared her food with her pet fish? (to show that Yeh-Shen is kind and generous, even though she is poor and mistreated)

13 **DRAWING CONCLUSIONS** Why does Yeh-Shen's stepmother wear the girl's coat? (She wants to disguise herself as Yeh-Shen to fool the fish.)

14 **DRAWING CONCLUSIONS** Why do you think the old man will not say who he is? (The old man is not a real person. He is the spirit of the fish and has come to help Yeh-Shen.)

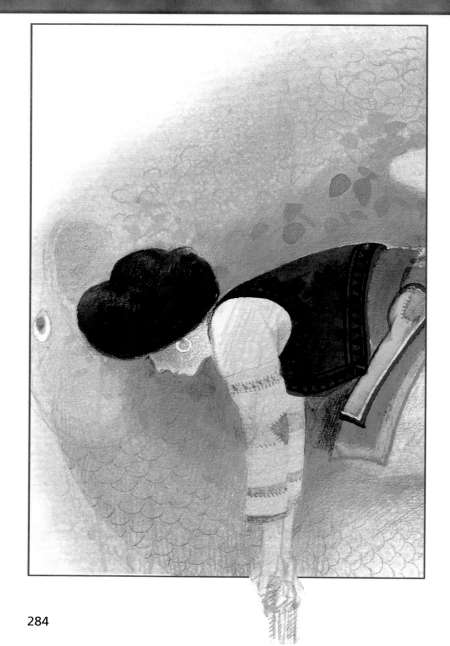

284

Vocabulary

crafty skilled at deceiving others

filthy very dirty

garments articles of clothing

coarsest lowest and poorest quality

THEME 5: Focus on Fairy Tales

The only friend that Yeh-Shen had to her name was a fish she had caught and raised. It was a beautiful fish with golden eyes, and every day it would come out of the water and rest its head on the bank of the pond, waiting for Yeh-Shen to feed it. Stepmother gave Yeh-Shen little enough food for herself, but the orphan child always found something to share with her fish, which grew to enormous size.

Somehow the stepmother heard of this. She was terribly angry to discover that Yeh-Shen had kept a secret from her. She hurried down to the pond, but she was unable to see the fish, for Yeh-Shen's pet wisely hid itself. The stepmother, however, was a crafty woman, and she soon thought of a plan. She walked home and called out, "Yeh-Shen, go and collect some firewood. But wait! The neighbors might see you. Leave your filthy coat here!" The minute the girl was out of sight, her stepmother slipped on the coat herself and went down

again to the pond. This time the big fish saw Yeh-Shen's familiar jacket and heaved itself onto the bank, expecting to be fed. But the stepmother, having hidden a dagger in her sleeve, stabbed the fish, wrapped it in her garments, and took it home to cook for dinner.

When Yeh-Shen came to the pond that evening, she found her pet had disappeared. Overcome with grief, the girl collapsed on the ground and dropped her tears into the still waters of the pond.

"Ah, poor child!" a voice said.

Yeh-Shen sat up to find a very old man looking down at her. He wore the coarsest of clothes, and his hair flowed down over his shoulders. "Kind uncle, who may you be?" Yeh-Shen asked.

"That is not important, my child. All you must know is that I have been sent to tell you of the wondrous powers of your fish."

"My fish, but sir . . ." The girl's eyes filled with tears, and she could not go on.

285

Writer's Craft

Focus On Genre

Teach

- Remind students that using the same word to name something every time it is mentioned can make writing dull and repetitive.
- Explain that good writers try not to use the same words over and over. Instead, they substitute other words that mean the same thing.

Practice

- Display this sentence: *She hurried down to the pond, but she was unable to see the fish, for Yeh-Shen's fish wisely hid itself.*
- Ask students to suggest words that can substitute for the second *fish*. (*pet, friend*)
- Point out that on page 285, the author uses *pet* instead of repeating the word *fish*.
- Reread both versions and discuss the effect of the substitution.

Apply

- Have students search page 285 for another example of a word substitution to avoid repetition. (*Jacket* is substituted for *coat*.)
- As students read page 286, have them note another example. (*old man/old sage*)
- Have students discuss how each example makes the writing more interesting.

Focus on Fairy Tales

Reading the Selection 285

CRITICAL THINKING
Guiding Comprehension

15 MAKING INFERENCES What does the old man mean when he says of the fish bones, *But do not waste their gifts*? (He is telling Yeh-Shen to take advantage of the good fortune the bones can bring to her.)

16 MAKING INFERENCES Why does Yeh-Shen have a heavy heart? (She is sad over the loss of her pet fish.)

17 PREDICTING OUTCOMES What other plans do you think the stepmother has for Yeh-Shen? (The stepmother probably plans to prevent Yeh-Shen from attending the spring festival.)

COMPREHENSION STRATEGY
Monitor/Clarify

Teacher/Student Modeling Model using the Monitor/Clarify strategy to identify important story elements.

- What is Yeh-Shen's problem?
- Who is the fairy in this story?

Ask students to read the first column of page 286 and to summarize what the old man tells Yeh-Shen.

The old man sighed and said, "Yes, my child, your fish is no longer alive, and I must tell you that your stepmother is once more the cause of your sorrow." Yeh-Shen gasped in horror, but the old man went on. "Let us not dwell on things that are past," he said, "for I have come bringing you a gift. Now you must listen carefully to this: The bones of your fish are filled with a powerful spirit. Whenever you are in serious need, you must kneel before them and let them know your heart's desire. But do not waste their gifts."

15

Yeh-Shen wanted to ask the old sage many more questions, but he rose to the sky before she could utter another word. With heavy heart, Yeh-Shen made her way to the dung heap to gather the remains of her friend.

16

Time went by, and Yeh-Shen, who was often left alone, took comfort in speaking to the bones of her fish. When she was hungry, which happened quite often, Yeh-Shen asked the bones for food. In this way, Yeh-Shen managed to live from day to day, but she lived in dread that her stepmother would discover her secret and take even that away from her.

So the time passed and spring came. Festival time was approaching: It was the busiest time of the year. Such cooking and cleaning and sewing there was to be done! Yeh-Shen had hardly a moment's rest. At the spring festival young men and young women from the village hoped to meet and choose whom they would marry. How Yeh-Shen longed to go! But her stepmother had other plans. She hoped to find a husband for her own daughter and did not want any man to see the beauteous Yeh-Shen first. When finally the holiday arrived, the stepmother and her daughter dressed themselves in their finery and filled their baskets with sweetmeats. "You must remain at home now, and watch to see that no one steals fruit from our trees," her stepmother told Yeh-Shen, and then she departed for the banquet with her own daughter.

17

286

REACHING ALL LEARNERS
English Language Learners

Supporting Comprehension

Yeh-Shen's actions and words in the story show what kind of person she is. Ask students to think of words to describe her. Show their ideas in a word web. Have students copy the word web and add more words to it as they continue to read.

Vocabulary

sage a very wise person

dung heap trash pile

 English Language Learners

Supporting Comprehension

Ask students to summarize the story so far. Prompt with questions such as: Where does Yeh-Shen live? Who was her only friend? What happened to her friend? Who is the old man who speaks to her? What does he tell her about the bones of the fish?

CRITICAL THINKING
Guiding Comprehension

18 MAKING INFERENCES Why do you think Yeh-Shen's new slippers are woven in a pattern that looks like fish scales? (They are a gift from the spirit of the fish.)

19 DRAWING CONCLUSIONS Why does Yeh-Shen run away from the feast? (She is afraid that her stepsister will recognize her.)

20 CAUSE AND EFFECT Why do Yeh-Shen's clothes turn back into rags as soon as she loses one of her golden slippers? (There was magic in the slippers, and the magic disappeared when one slipper was lost.)

TARGET SKILL
COMPREHENSION STRATEGY
Monitor/Clarify

Student Modeling Have students model the strategy by reading page 288 and explaining in their own words how the old sage helps Yeh-Shen.

As soon as she was alone, Yeh-Shen went to speak to the bones of her fish. "Oh, dear friend," she said, kneeling before the precious bones, "I long to go to the festival, but I cannot show myself in these rags. Is there somewhere I could borrow clothes fit to wear to the feast?" At once she found herself dressed in a gown of azure blue, with a cloak of kingfisher feathers draped around her shoulders. Best of all, on her tiny feet were the most beautiful slippers she had ever seen. They were woven of golden threads, in a pattern like the scales of a fish, and the glistening soles were made of solid gold. There was magic in the shoes, for they should have been quite heavy, yet when Yeh-Shen walked, her feet felt as light as air.

18

"Be sure you do not lose your golden shoes," said the spirit of the bones. Yeh-Shen promised to be careful. Delighted with her transformation, she bid a fond farewell to the bones of her fish as she slipped off to join in the merrymaking.

That day Yeh-Shen turned many a head as she appeared at the feast. All around her people whispered, "Look at that beautiful girl! Who can she be?"

But above this, Stepsister was heard to say, "Mother, does she not resemble our Yeh-Shen?"

Upon hearing this, Yeh-Shen jumped up and ran off before her stepsister could look closely at her. She raced down the mountainside, and in doing so, she lost one of her golden slippers. No sooner had the shoe fallen from her foot than all her fine clothes turned back to rags. Only one thing remained — a tiny golden shoe. Yeh-Shen hurried to the bones of her fish and returned the slipper, promising to find its mate. But now the bones were silent.

19

20

288

Vocabulary

kingfisher bird that has brightly colored feathers

glistening shining

transformation the act of changing in form or appearance

resemble to be similar to in looks

289

Challenge

Fairy Tale Cartoons

Have students create cartoons to illustrate scenes from their own fairy tale story or a favorite classic fairy tale. Display student cartoons on a classroom bulletin board.

Guiding Comprehension

21 **CAUSE AND EFFECT** Why do you think the fish bones no longer speak to Yeh-Shen? (She had promised to be careful with the golden slippers, but by losing one, she broke her promise.)

22 **WRITER'S CRAFT** What is the author telling us about the character of the stepmother and stepsister by saying that they tried on the slipper? (Neither of them was the rightful owner, so by trying on the slipper they were being dishonest.)

21 Sadly Yeh-Shen realized that she had lost her only friend. She hid the little shoe in her bedstraw, and went outside to cry. Leaning against a fruit tree, she sobbed and sobbed until she fell asleep.

The stepmother left the gathering to check on Yeh-Shen, but when she returned home she found the girl sound asleep, with her arms wrapped around a fruit tree. So thinking no more of her, the stepmother rejoined the party. Meantime, a villager had found the shoe. Recognizing its worth, he sold it to a merchant, who presented it in turn to the king of the island kingdom of T'o Han.

The king was more than happy to accept the slipper as a gift. He was entranced by the tiny thing, which was shaped of the most precious of metals, yet which made no sound when touched to stone. The more he marveled at its beauty, the more determined he became to find the woman to whom the shoe belonged.

A search was begun among the ladies of his own kingdom, but all who tried on the sandal found it impossibly small. Undaunted, the king ordered the search widened to include the cave women from the countryside where the slipper had been found. Since he realized it would take many years for every woman to come to his island and test her foot in the slipper, the king thought of a way to get the right woman to come forward. He ordered the sandal placed in a pavilion by the side of the road near where it had been found, and his herald announced that the shoe was to be returned to its original owner. Then from a nearby hiding place, the king and his men settled down to watch and wait for a woman with tiny feet to come and claim her slipper.

All that day the pavilion was crowded with cave women who had come to test a foot in the shoe. Yeh-Shen's stepmother and stepsister were among them, but not Yeh-Shen — they had told her to stay home. By day's end, although many women had eagerly tried to put on the slipper, it still had not been worn. Wearily, the king continued his vigil into the night. **22**

290

Extra Support/Intervention

Phonics/Decoding

Model the strategy for *wearily*.

This contains a base word I know, the word wear, *meaning "to have on." It also includes the suffix* -ly, *meaning "in a certain way." I'll pronounce* wear *to sound like* ear, *a word that I know. Maybe the* i *before* -ly *was a* y *before the suffix was added. I'll try pronouncing it as* WEER-ee. *Oh, that word means "tired," so* wearily *must mean "in a tired way." That makes sense in the sentence.*

Vocabulary

undaunted not discouraged

pavilion a large tent

herald a person who makes announcements, as for a king

291

Time Words and Phrases

Teach

- Tell students that authors often use special words and phrases that help readers understand the sequence and time frame of events in a story.

Practice/Apply

- Read aloud the second paragraph on page 290.

- Ask students to identify the different events described in the paragraph. (The stepmother leaves the party; she finds Yeh-Shen asleep; she rejoins the party; a villager finds the shoe; he sells it to a merchant; the merchant presents the shoe to the king.)

- Guide students to identify the time words and phrases that explain when things happened. (*When she returned home* indicates the time when the stepmother found Yeh-Shen asleep; *meantime* indicates that the villager found the shoe at the same time as the stepmother rejoined the party.)

- As students read, have them note other examples of words and phrases used to indicate time. Have students share their examples and discuss how each one clarifies the sequence of events.

CRITICAL THINKING

Guiding Comprehension

23 **MAKING INFERENCES** Why does the king at first think that Yeh-Shen is a thief? (Because she is wearing rags, he thinks it is unlikely that she could be the owner of a golden slipper.)

24 **CAUSE AND EFFECT** Why are Yeh-Shen's stepmother and stepsister not permitted to go to the palace? (The king would not allow it because they had been unkind to Yeh-Shen.)

It wasn't until the blackest part of night, while the moon hid behind a cloud, that Yeh-Shen dared to show her face at the pavilion, and even then she tiptoed timidly across the wide floor. Sinking down to her knees, the girl in rags examined the tiny shoe.

Only when she was sure that this was the missing mate to her own golden slipper did she dare pick it up. At last she could return both little shoes to the fish bones. Surely then her beloved spirit would speak to her again.

Now the king's first thought, on seeing Yeh-Shen take the precious

slipper, was to throw the girl into prison as a thief. But when she turned to leave, he caught a glimpse of her face. At once the king was struck by the sweet harmony of her features, which seemed so out of keeping with the rags she wore. It was then that he took a closer look and noticed that she walked upon the tiniest feet he had ever seen.

With a wave of his hand, the king signaled that this tattered creature was to be allowed to depart with the golden slipper. Quietly, the king's men slipped off and followed her home.

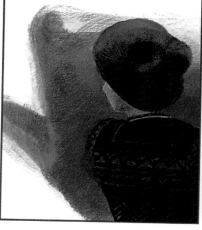
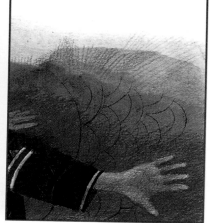

292

Extra Support/Intervention

Review (pages 282–293)

Before students who need extra support join the whole class for Wrapping Up on page 293, have them

- review the fairy tale elements in "Yeh-Shen"
- help you complete **Transparency F5–2**
- finish their own Fairy Tale Charts
- summarize "Yeh-Shen"

Vocabulary

fate the invisible force or power that is believed to determine events

All this time, Yeh-Shen was unaware of the excitement she had caused. She had made her way home and was about to hide both sandals in her bedding when there was a pounding at the door. Yeh-Shen went to see who it was — and found a king at her doorstep. She was very frightened at first, but the king spoke to her in a kind voice and asked her to try the golden slippers on her feet. The maiden did as she was told, and as she stood in her golden shoes, her rags were transformed once more into the feathered cloak and beautiful azure gown.

Her loveliness made her seem a heavenly being, and the king suddenly knew in his heart that he had found his true love.

Not long after this, Yeh-Shen was married to the king. But fate was not so gentle with her stepmother and stepsister. Since they had been unkind to his beloved, the king would not permit Yeh-Shen to bring them to his palace. They remained in their cave home, where one day, it is said, they were crushed to death in a shower of flying stones.

24

293

Wrapping Up

Critical Thinking Questions

1. **MAKING INFERENCES** What kind of person is Yeh-Shen? (She is good and kind. She is also very loyal to her one friend, the spirit of the fish.)

2. **MAKING INFERENCES** Why do you think the spirit of the fish helps Yeh-Shen? (The spirit is grateful for the affection and friendship that Yeh-Shen showed when the fish was alive.)

3. **MAKING JUDGMENTS** Do you think that Yeh-Shen deserves what happens to her at the end of the story? Why or why not? (Sample answer: Yes, because she is good, kind, and unselfish.)

4. **MAKING JUDGMENTS** Do you think that Yeh-Shen's stepmother deserves what happens to her at the end of the story? Why or why not? (Sample answer: Yes, because she was mean to Yeh-Shen and killed her pet fish.)

Strategies in Action

Ask students to tell how they used the Monitor/Clarify strategy and have them take turns modeling it. Ask what other strategies they found helpful.

Comprehension Check

Use **Practice Book** page 152 to assess students' comprehension of the selection.

REACHING ALL LEARNERS

English Language Learners

Supporting Comprehension

Have students draw pictures to illustrate the resolution of Yeh-Shen's problem.

Practice Book page 152

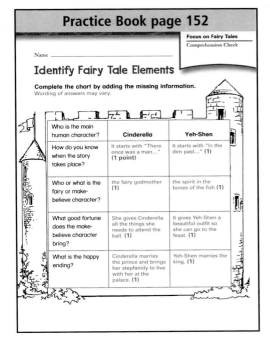

Focus on Fairy Tales
Comprehension Check

Name _____

Identify Fairy Tale Elements

Complete the chart by adding the missing information.
Wording of answers may vary.

	Cinderella	Yeh-Shen
Who is the main human character?		
How do you know when the story takes place?	It starts with "There once was a man…" (1 point)	It starts with "In the dim past…" (1)
Who or what is the fairy or make-believe character?	the fairy godmother (1)	the spirit in the bones of the fish (1)
What good fortune does the make-believe character bring?	She gives Cinderella all the things she needs to attend the ball. (1)	It gives Yeh-Shen a beautiful outfit so she can go to the feast. (1)
What is the happy ending?	Cinderella marries the prince and brings her stepfamily to live with her at the palace. (1)	Yeh-Shen marries the king. (1)

Monitoring Student Progress

If . . .	Then . . .
students score 6 or below on **Practice Book** page 152,	have partners review the story for details that support their answers.

Responding

Think About the Selections

1. **COMPARE AND CONTRAST** (In both fairy tales, a girl who is kind and good is mistreated by a stepmother; a fairy or magical character gives the girl fine clothes; she loses a slipper; she marries royalty. A difference is that Cinderella has two mean stepsisters, but Yeh-Shen has only one. Also, in Cinderella, the magical character is her fairy godmother; in Yeh-Shen, it is an old man who is the spirit of her dead pet fish. Another difference is that Cinderella forgives her sisters and they come to live in the palace, but Yeh-Shen's stepsister and stepmother are banned from the palace and die.)

2. **PROBLEM SOLVING** (Answers will vary.)

3. **MAKING JUDGMENTS** (Answers will vary.)

4. **MAKING JUDGMENTS** (Answers will vary. Sample answer: No, Cinderella's sisters didn't really deserve to be forgiven.)

Literature Discussion

To help students prepare for the discussion, assign **Practice Book** page 153. Students may also refer to **Practice Book** page 152.

1. **STORY STRUCTURE** Explain the pattern that most fairy tales follow. Review the elements of a fairy tale for ideas. (A fairy or similar imaginary being brings sudden good fortune to an unhappy human character; there is a happy ending; the story takes place at some indefinite time long ago.)

2. **DRAWING CONCLUSIONS** What message or moral can you take from "Cinderella" and "Yeh-Shen"? (Answers will vary.)

Think About the

FAIRY TALES

1. Compare the two fairy tales. How are they alike? What are the most important differences between them?

2. If the fairy godmother and the fish bones didn't appear in the fairy tales, how else could the girls have solved their problems?

3. Who do you think is more of a heroine, Cinderella or Yeh-Shen? Why?

4. Compare how the tales end for the stepsisters. Do you think they get what they deserve? Explain.

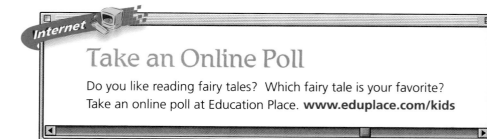

Take an Online Poll

Do you like reading fairy tales? Which fairy tale is your favorite? Take an online poll at Education Place. **www.eduplace.com/kids**

294

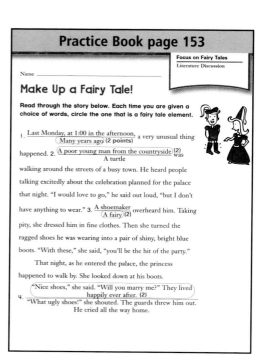

Practice Book page 153

Focus on Fairy Tales
Literature Discussion

Name _____

Make Up a Fairy Tale!

Read through the story below. Each time you are given a choice of words, circle the one that is a fairy tale element.

1. Last Monday, at 1:00 in the afternoon, / Many years ago (2 points) a very unusual thing happened. 2. A poor young man from the countryside (2) / A turtle was walking around the streets of a busy town. He heard people talking excitedly about the celebration planned for the palace that night. "I would love to go," he said out loud, "but I don't have anything to wear." 3. A shoemaker / A fairy (2) overheard him. Taking pity, she dressed him in fine clothes. Then she turned the ragged shoes he was wearing into a pair of shiny, bright blue boots. "With these," she said, "you'll be the hit of the party."

That night, as he entered the palace, the princess happened to walk by. She looked down at his boots.

4. "Nice shoes," she said. "Will you marry me?" They lived happily ever after. (2) / "What ugly shoes!" she shouted. The guards threw him out. He cried all the way home.

Creating

Write a Fairy Tale

Think about how the two versions of Cinderella are alike and different. Write your own version of Cinderella. What will the characters be like? What problem will the main character have, and how will the problem be solved? Choose a setting. Your fairy tale can take place in a faraway castle, in a big city, or even in the ocean! You decide.

Tips

- **Create a story map, listing characters, setting, and story events.**
- **Use dialogue to show how the characters are feeling.**
- **Read aloud your fairy tale to a friend to see if you like the way it sounds.**

295

Write a Fairy Tale

Have students read and briefly discuss the writing assignment on page 295 of the Anthology. Before students begin writing their own fairy tales, present the writing lesson on pages 295K–295L.

Extra Support/Intervention

Avoiding Repetition

Remind students of the importance of avoiding repetition in their writing. Have them check a recent piece of their writing to see whether they need to revise for this point.

Monitoring Student Progress

End-of-Selection Assessment

Student Self-Assessment Have students assess their reading and writing with questions such as

- Which parts of the selections were challenging to read? Why?
- Which strategies helped me understand the fairy tales?
- Would I recommend these fairy tales to my friends? Why or why not?

- Identify the elements of a fairy tale.
- Compare and contrast two versions of the Cinderella tale.

Target Skill Trace

| Preview; Teach | p. 267CC, p. 270; pp. 295A–295B |

Transparency F5–2

Fairy Tale Chart

	"Cinderella"	"Yeh-Shen"
Characters	Cinderella, her stepmother, her stepsisters, the king's son, the godmother	Yeh-Shen, her stepmother, her stepsister, the king, a fish, and old man
Setting (time and place)	a long time ago; somewhere in Europe	China; before the Ch'in and Han dynasties
Problem	Cinderella is treated badly and can't go to the ball.	Yeh-Shen is treated badly and can't go to the festival.
Events Beginning	1. Before the ball Stepsisters get ready for ball, leaving Cinderella behind. Godmother prepares Cinderella for the ball.	1. Before the festival Stepmother kills Yeh-Shen's fish, but its bones provide for Yeh-Shen, including clothes for the festival.
Middle	2. At the ball, first night The king's son spends all his time with Cinderella. Guests say how beautiful she is. She gets home safely.	2. At the festival People notice Yeh-Shen's beauty. When her step-sister seems to recognize her, she flees, losing her golden shoe.
	3. At the ball, second night Cinderella forgets to leave on time. She runs, leaving behind her glass slipper.	3. After the festival The bones of the fish no longer speak to Yeh-Shen. The shoe is presented to a king.
End	4. Ending The king's son searches for Cinderella. Her foot fits the slipper. Cinderella marries the prince and is kind to her stepsisters.	4. Ending Yeh-Shen takes the shoe. The king follows her, and the shoe fits her. She marries the king, but the stepmother and stepsister are left to die.

TRANSPARENCY F5–2 TEACHER'S EDITION PAGES 270 AND 295A

Practice Book page 151

Focus on Fairy Tales
Graphic Organizer Fairy Tale Chart

Name _____

Fairy Tale Chart
Some answers may vary. Examples are given.

	"Cinderella"	"Yeh-Shen"
Characters	Cinderella, her stepmother, her stepsisters, the king's son, the godmother (1 point)	Yeh-Shen, her stepmother, her stepsister, the king, a fish, an old man (1)
Setting (time and place)	a long time ago; somewhere in Europe (1)	China; before the Ch'in and Han dynasties (1)
Problem	Cinderella is treated badly and can't go to the ball. (1)	Yeh-Shen is treated badly and can't go to the festival. (1)
Events Beginning	1. Before the ball Stepsisters get ready for ball, leaving Cinderella behind. Godmother prepares Cinderella for the ball. (1)	1. Before the festival Stepmother kills Yeh-Shen's fish, but its bones provide for Yeh-Shen, including clothes for the festival. (1)
Middle	2. At the ball, first night The king's son spends all his time with Cinderella. Guests say how beautiful she is. She gets home safely. (1)	2. At the festival People notice Yeh-Shen's beauty. When her stepsister seems to recognize her, she flees, losing her golden shoe. (1)
	3. At the ball, second night Cinderella forgets to leave on time. She runs, leaving behind her glass slipper. (1)	3. After the festival The bones of the fish no longer speak to Yeh-Shen. The shoe is presented to a king. (1)
End	4. Ending The king's son searches for Cinderella. Her foot fits the slipper. Cinderella marries the prince and is kind to her stepsisters. (1)	4. Ending Yeh-Shen takes the shoe. The king follows her, and the shoe fits her. She marries the king, but the stepmother and stepsister are left to die. (1)

TARGET SKILL — COMPREHENSION: Understanding a Fairy Tale

❶ Teach

Review the elements of a fairy tale. Fairy tales

- take place long ago and far away
- include some fantasy events that could not happen in reality
- have some make-believe characters with special powers
- have a happy ending for the main character

Display and discuss Transparency F5–2. Students may refer to the selection and to **Practice Book** page 151.

- Who are the main characters in "Cinderella"? (Cinderella, her stepsisters, her godmother, the king's son)
- Where and when does the story take place? (a long time ago; somewhere in Europe)
- Who is the make-believe character in "Cinderella"? (her godmother)
- What special power does the make-believe character have? (the ability to change animals into other kinds of animals and into people, to change rags into nice clothing)

Explain how make-believe characters solve problems. Make-believe characters can solve the main character's problems by using special powers, such as

- transforming things into other things
- making things appear or disappear
- granting special powers to the main character

Explain that often the make-believe character requires the main character to make a promise, such as getting home by midnight. If the promise is broken, the special powers will be lost.

Model reading a fairy tale to understand the make-believe character. Ask a volunteer to read aloud the top half of page 274. Think aloud to understand the fantasy.

Think Aloud *Cinderella's godmother seems kind and she wants to help. I know she has special powers because she uses her wand to change Cinderella's rags into a beautiful gown. She also gives Cinderella something unusual—glass slippers. Then she warns Cinderella that her clothing will turn back into rags by midnight. It's too bad that Cinderella can't keep the clothes, but make-believe characters know things and usually have reasons for setting rules.*

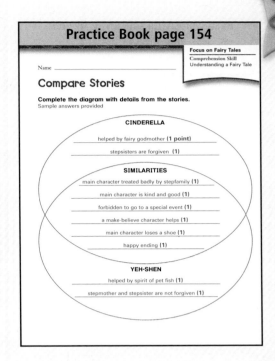

Focus on Fairy Tales
Comprehension Skill
Understanding a Fairy Tale

Name _____

Compare Stories

Complete the diagram with details from the stories.
Sample answers provided

CINDERELLA
helped by fairy godmother **(1 point)**
stepsisters are forgiven **(1)**

SIMILARITIES
main character treated badly by stepfamily **(1)**
main character is kind and good **(1)**
forbidden to go to a special event **(1)**
a make-believe character helps **(1)**
main character loses a shoe **(1)**
happy ending **(1)**

YEH-SHEN
helped by spirit of pet fish **(1)**
stepmother and stepsister are not forgiven **(1)**

❷ Guided Practice

Have students practice identifying elements of fairy tales.
Have partners review their completed Fairy Tale Charts for
"Yeh-Shen." Then discuss their results as a class, guiding students
to discover any elements they may have missed.

❸ Apply

Assign Practice Book page 154. Also have students apply this
skill as they read their **Leveled Readers** for this week. You may
also select books from Suggestions for Independent Reading on
the Lesson Overview (page 267V).

Test Prep Tell students that reading tests will sometimes ask them to
identify the genre of a passage they have read. Emphasize that students can identify
a fairy tale by looking for a setting that is long-ago and faraway, a make-believe
character, a problem that is solved by special powers, and a happy ending.

Leveled Readers

Students at all levels apply the comprehension skill
as they read their Leveled Readers.

● BELOW LEVEL   ▲ ON LEVEL   ■ ABOVE LEVEL   ◆ LANGUAGE SUPPORT

Smudge-Face A Native American Cinderella Tale — retold by Alexandra Behr, illustrated by Arvis Stewart

The Little Sparrow A Cinderella Story from Italy — retold by Elizabeth Albert, illustrated by Annouchka Galouchko

Rella's Wish by Sarah Golland, illustrated by Ann Boyajian

To Tell the Truth A Native American Cinderella Tale — retold by Alexandra Behr, illustrated by Arvis Stewart

Reading Traits

Teaching students to think about genre
is one way of encouraging them to
"read the lines" of a selection. This
comprehension skill supports the reading
trait **Decoding Conventions.**

Monitoring Student Progress

If . . .	Then . . .
students score 7 or below on **Practice Book** page 154,	have them work with partners to correct the items they missed.

Focus On Genre

COMPREHENSION SKILLS

Focus on Fairy Tales

- Read words with prefixes *un-*, *dis-*, *re-*, and *non-*.
- Read words with suffixes *-y, -ly, -ful, -er, -less,* and *-ness*.
- Apply the Phonics/Decoding Strategy.

 STRUCTURAL ANALYSIS/ VOCABULARY: Prefixes and Suffixes

❶ Teach

Review the prefixes *un-*, *dis-*, *re-*, and *non-* and the suffixes *-y, -ly, -ful, -er, -less,* and *-ness*. Write: *There was an <u>unknown</u> princess, the most <u>beautiful</u> ever seen in this world.*

- Guide students to locate the prefix and base word in the first underlined word and read the word aloud. (un-; known)
- Ask students to locate the suffix and base word in the second underlined word and read the word aloud. (-ful; beauty)
- Point out the spelling change in *beautiful*: *y* changes to *i* before the suffix is added.
- Remind students that they can decode unfamiliar words by looking for prefixes and suffixes that are attached to base words they know.

Model the Phonics/Decoding Strategy. Display: *She was <u>unable</u> to see the fish, for it <u>wisely</u> hid itself.* Model how to decode the underlined words.

> **Think Aloud** *I recognize the prefix un- in the first word. If I separate it from the base word, I get* un- *plus* able. *So the word is* unable, *or "not able." In the second word, I see the suffix* -ly. *It has been added to the base word* wise. *Wise* plus *-ly is* wisely, *which means "in a wise way."*

❷ Guided Practice

Have students identify prefixes and suffixes. Display the sentences below. Have students copy the underlined words and draw a line to separate each prefix or suffix from its base word.

Yeh-Shen was a bright child and <u>lovely</u> too.

The <u>crafty</u> stepmother was <u>unkind</u> to Yeh-Shen.

Yeh-Shen was a hard <u>worker</u>.

She worked <u>nonstop</u> from morning till night.

Her pet had <u>disappeared</u>, and she was filled with <u>sadness</u>.

The bones had a <u>powerful</u> spirit.

Her <u>kindness</u> to the fish was <u>repaid</u>.

❸ Apply

Assign Practice Book page 155.

Practice Book page 155

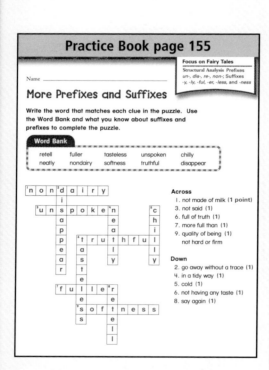

Focus on Fairy Tales
Structural Analysis Prefixes
un-, dis-, re-, non-; Suffixes
-y, -ly, -ful, -er, -less, and *-ness*

Name _____

More Prefixes and Suffixes

Write the word that matches each clue in the puzzle. Use the Word Bank and what you know about suffixes and prefixes to complete the puzzle.

Word Bank

| retell | fuller | tasteless | unspoken | chilly |
| neatly | nondairy | softness | truthful | disappear |

Across
1. not made of milk (1 point)
3. not said (1)
6. full of truth (1)
7. more full than (1)
9. quality of being (1) not hard or firm

Down
2. go away without a trace (1)
4. in a tidy way (1)
5. cold (1)
6. not having any taste (1)
8. say again (1)

Monitoring Student Progress

If . . .	Then . . .
students score 7 or below on **Practice Book** page 155,	have them work with partners to decode the whole word before identifying the prefixes and suffixes.

PHONICS REVIEW:
Two Sounds of *c*

❶ Teach

Review the sounds of *c*. Review these guidelines:

- The spelling patterns *c* and *ck* can have the /k/ sound.
- The spelling patterns *ci* and *ce* can have the /s/ sound.

Modeling Write *She went to the <u>corner</u> and sat among the <u>cinders</u>.* Then model decoding the *c* sounds in the underlined words:

Think Aloud *The first word has the word* corn *in it, and I know that* corn *has the* /k/ *sound. So that word is pronounced with a hard* c: KOR-nur. *The second word has a* ci *spelling pattern, which should mean that the* c *is soft. I'll pronounce it as* /s/: SIHN-durz. *I know I'm right, because* Cinderella *has the same soft* c.

❷ Guided Practice

Have students identify sounds of *c*. Have students sort these words into two sets according to the sound of the initial *c*. Then have volunteers model the use of the Phonics/Decoding Strategy to decode the words.

city	certain	cuff	cellar
ceiling	circle	center	circus
correct	captain	cotton	creek

❸ Apply

Have students practice decoding. Have partners decode the following words.

century	ceramic	citizen	cistern
clumsy	college	crevice	curdle

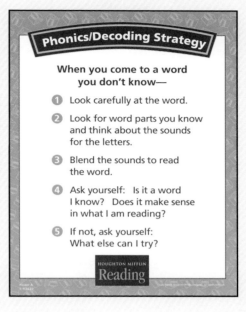

SPELLING: The /s/ Sound in *face*

OBJECTIVE

- Write Spelling Words in which the /s/ sound is spelled *c*.

SPELLING WORDS

Basic

face*	race*
city	circle
pencil	nice
place*	once*
center	princess*
dance*	circus

Review†	**Challenge**
chase	silence*
size*	excitement*

Forms of these words appear in the literature.

†*Because this lesson presents these spelling patterns for the first time, the Review Words do not contain the lesson's patterns.*

Extra Support/ Intervention

Basic Word List Consider using only the left column of Basic Words with students who need extra support.

Challenge

Challenge Word Practice Have students write an ad, using the Challenge Words.

DAY 1 — INSTRUCTION

The /s/ Sound in *face*

Pretest Use the Day 5 Test sentences.

Teach Review that the /s/ sound is often spelled *s*. Explain that it can also be spelled *c*.

- Write *nice* and *city*. Read the words and have students repeat them.
- Ask these questions:
  Which letter spells the /s/ sound? (*c*)
  Which letter follows the *c* in *nice*? (*e*) Underline *ce*.
  Which letter follows the *c* in *city*? (*i*) Underline *ci*.
- Help students summarize that the /s/ sound may be spelled *c* when the *c* is followed by *e* or *i*.
- List the remaining Basic Words. Have volunteers underline the vowel that follows *c* in each word.

Practice/Homework Assign **Practice Book** page 247.

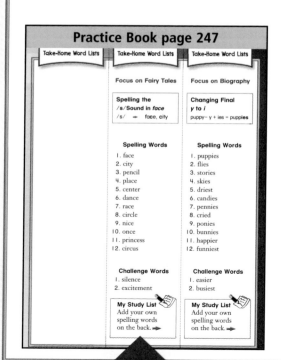

Practice Book page 247

DAY 2 — REVIEW & PRACTICE

Reviewing the Principle

Go over the spelling principle that the /s/ sound may be spelled *c* when *c* is followed by *e* or *i*.

Practice/Homework Assign **Practice Book** page 156.

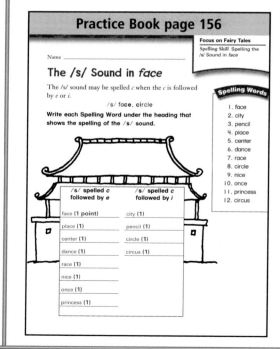

Practice Book page 156

Take-Home Word List

DAY 3 VOCABULARY

Idioms

Tell students that an **idiom** is an expression whose meaning is different from the meanings of its separate words.

- Write *face the music*. Explain that this expression doesn't really mean "to look at music." It means "to deal with the results of bad actions," as in *You will have to face the music if you don't do your homework.*

- Write the underlined idioms below and read aloud the sentences. Discuss the meanings with students.

  That whistle is sold <u>all over the place</u>. (in many places at one time)

  My mother told my uncle that he had to <u>show his face</u> at her picnic. (put in an appearance)

  Put away your games <u>at once</u>. (immediately)

- Next, list the Basic Words. Have students use each Basic Word orally in a sentence. (Sentences will vary.)

Practice/Homework For spelling practice, assign **Practice Book** page 157.

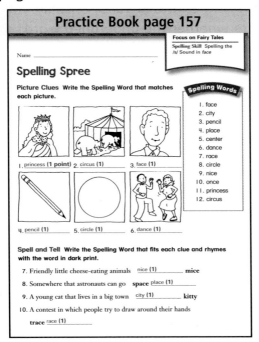

Practice Book page 157

Focus on Fairy Tales
Spelling Skill Spelling the /s/ Sound in *face*

Name _____

Spelling Spree

Picture Clues Write the Spelling Word that matches each picture.

Spelling Words
1. face
2. city
3. pencil
4. place
5. center
6. dance
7. race
8. circle
9. nice
10. once
11. princess
12. circus

1. princess **(1 point)** 2. circus **(1)** 3. face **(1)**
4. pencil **(1)** 5. circle **(1)** 6. dance **(1)**

Spell and Tell Write the Spelling Word that fits each clue and rhymes with the word in dark print.

7. Friendly little cheese-eating animals nice **(1)** mice
8. Somewhere that astronauts can go **space** place **(1)**
9. A young cat that lives in a big town city **(1)** kitty
10. A contest in which people try to draw around their hands trace race **(1)**

DAY 4 PROOFREADING

Game: Charades

Write each Basic Word on a slip of paper and put it in a bag or a box.

- Have students take turns drawing a word card and pantomiming the word for the class to guess.

- If you have a large class, you may want to divide the class into two groups so that each student has a chance to pantomime a word. In that case, you will need two sets of word cards.

Practice/Homework For proofreading and writing practice, assign **Practice Book** page 158.

Practice Book page 158

Focus on Fairy Tales
Spelling Skill Spelling the /s/ Sound in *face*

Name _____

Proofreading and Writing

Proofreading Circle the four misspelled Spelling Words in the paragraphs below. Then write each word correctly. Order of answers may vary.

Spelling Words
1. face
2. city
3. pencil
4. place
5. center
6. dance
7. race
8. circle
9. nice
10. once
11. princess
12. circus

There was (onse) a princess who lived at the top of a tower. One morning a colorful bird flew in her window and landed in the (senter) of her room. It looked around and then began to (danse), hopping from one foot to the other.

The princess was very surprised. "What a strange bird!" she said.

"I'm not strange," said the bird. "I'm quite talented, and I've just escaped from a (sercus). Please help me!"

1. once **(2 points)** 3. dance **(2)**
2. center **(2)** 4. circus **(2)**

Write a TV News Report Think of a fairy tale you know. How would a TV reporter describe the events in the fairy tale to people watching at home?

On a separate sheet of paper, write a short TV report about the main events in the fairy tale. Use Spelling Words from the list.

Responses will vary. **(2 points)**

DAY 5 ASSESSMENT

Spelling Test

Say each underlined word, read the sentence, and then repeat the word. Have students write only the underlined word.

Basic Words

1. He had a smile on his <u>face</u>. 4
2. Many people live in that <u>city</u>. 3
3. Please write with a <u>pencil</u>. 2
4. I am moving to a new <u>place</u>. 1
5. He sat in the <u>center</u> of the room. 12
6. Will you <u>dance</u> with me? 11
7. It was a very fast <u>race</u>. 10
8. Draw a <u>circle</u> on your paper. 9
9. Your teacher is <u>nice</u>. 8
10. I caught a fish <u>once</u>. 7
11. The beautiful <u>princess</u> lives in a castle. 6
12. She is a clown in the <u>circus</u>. 5

Challenge Words

13. There was <u>silence</u> when the music stopped. 14
14. We are looking for fun and <u>excitement</u>. 13

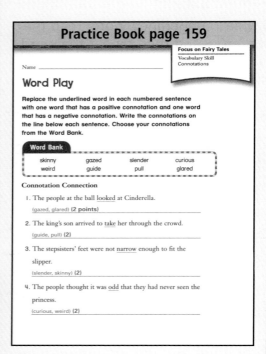

Practice Book page 159

Focus on Fairy Tales

Vocabulary Skill
Connotations

Name _____

Word Play

Replace the underlined word in each numbered sentence with one word that has a positive connotation and one word that has a negative connotation. Write the connotations on the line below each sentence. Choose your connotations from the Word Bank.

Word Bank

| skinny | gazed | slender | curious |
| weird | guide | pull | glared |

Connotation Connection

1. The people at the ball looked at Cinderella.
   (gazed, glared) **(2 points)**

2. The king's son arrived to take her through the crowd.
   (guide, pull) **(2)**

3. The stepsisters' feet were not narrow enough to fit the slipper.
   (slender, skinny) **(2)**

4. The people thought it was odd that they had never seen the princess.
   (curious, weird) **(2)**

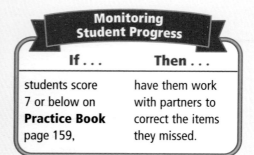

English Language Learners

Language Development

Have students list different words that name character traits. Some words that name character traits taken from the stories are *crafty*, *haughty*, and *gentle*. Use a separate list for each character. Then have students identify character traits with positive and negative connotations.

Monitoring Student Progress

If . . .	Then . . .
students score 7 or below on **Practice Book** page 159,	have them work with partners to correct the items they missed.

VOCABULARY SKILLS: Connotations

❶ Teach

Explain connotations. Write these sentences:

Yeh-Shen's <u>crafty</u> stepmother wanted to catch the fish.

Yeh-Shen's <u>wise</u> stepmother wanted to catch the fish.

- Explain that both *crafty* and *wise* have the dictionary meaning of "clever," but *crafty* communicates a negative feeling (one who may try to trick or mislead others), while *wise* communicates a positive feeling (one who does what is right).

- Tell students that some words communicate ideas or feelings beyond their simple dictionary meanings. These feelings are called *connotations*.

- Writers use words with positive or negative connotations to show how they feel about what they are describing.

Model identifying connotations. Write *Yeh-Shen worked outside in the <u>cold</u> rain. Yeh-Shen worked outside in the <u>freezing</u> rain.*

Think Aloud *The underlined word* cold *has the dictionary meaning "being at a low temperature." That doesn't tell me very much, so* cold *doesn't have a strong positive or negative connotation. The underlined word* freezing *means more than just cold. It means "very cold and uncomfortable." To me, this word has a strong negative connotation.*

❷ Guided Practice

Give students practice in identifying connotations. Display these sentences. Have students state whether the underlined word in each B sentence has a more positive or negative connotation than the underlined word in the A sentence.

1A. The <u>crowd</u> watched Cinderella dance.

1B. The <u>mob</u> watched Cinderella dance. (negative)

2A. She looked <u>nice</u> in her gown.

2B. She looked <u>beautiful</u> in her gown. (positive)

3A. The stepmother had a <u>plan</u> to catch the fish.

3B. The stepmother had a <u>scheme</u> to catch the fish. (negative)

❸ Apply

Assign Practice Book page 159.

STUDY SKILL:
Using an Almanac

❶ Teach

Display an almanac and introduce its features.

- An almanac is a book of facts on many topics, such as countries around the world. Almanacs are updated yearly.

- Features of an almanac include the table of contents, charts, illustrations, graphs, and text that presents facts. Most almanacs include an index that can be used to locate specific subjects.

Model using an almanac.

- Tell students that you would like to find information about China, the setting of "Yeh-Shen."

- Demonstrate finding a specific fact, such as the population of China, by using the table of contents or the index and then locating the fact on the page.

❷ Practice/Apply

Provide practice in using an almanac to find information.

- Ask volunteers to use the almanac table of contents or index to find other information about China, such as

    – a picture of the flag

    – names of major cities

    – languages spoken

    – names of geographic features, such as mountains or rivers

    – important crops or products

    – a map of the country

- Have small groups of students use an almanac to find six important facts about a particular country.

- Have students share their findings in class and explain how to find information about countries in the almanac.

GRAMMAR: Using Pronouns

OBJECTIVES

- Identify subject, object, and possessive pronouns.
- Correctly use pronouns to replace nouns and prevent repetition of nouns.
- Recognize and correct unclear pronoun referents.
- Proofread for correct pronoun usage.

DAY 1 INSTRUCTION

Using Pronouns

Teach Tell students that when they write, they should be careful not to repeat the same nouns too often.

- Display **Transparency F5–4**. Read aloud the sentences at the top. Point out the pronouns that replace *Cinderella* and *The stepsisters*. Explain that good writers balance pronouns and nouns.
- Ask volunteers to replace nouns with pronouns to avoid repetition in Items 1–3.
- Explain that good writers also make sure that there is no confusion about which word a pronoun is replacing.
- Read aloud the examples below Items 1–3. Point out that the second pair of sentences clears up the confusion in the first pair.
- Ask volunteers to rewrite Items 4–5 to make the meanings clear.

Daily Language Practice

Have students correct Sentences 1 and 2 on **Transparency F5–3**.

Transparency F5–4

Using Pronouns

Repetitive: Cinderella worked all day. The stepsisters made fun of Cinderella. The stepsisters were cruel.
Better: Cinderella worked all day. The stepsisters made fun of **her**. **They** were cruel.

1. Cinderella scoured the dishes and scrubbed the floor. Cinderella didn't complain.
   Cinderella scoured the dishes and scrubbed the floor. She didn't complain.

2. The prince gave a ball and invited many stylish people to the ball.
   The prince gave a ball and invited many stylish people to it.

3. The sisters were invited. Cinderella ironed clothes for the sisters.
   The sisters were invited. Cinderella ironed clothes for them.

Confusing: The fairy godmother asked Cinderella what was wrong. She stammered.
Clear: The fairy godmother asked Cinderella what was wrong. Cinderella stammered.

4. The stepmother met Cinderella. She was mean.
   The stepmother met Cinderella. The stepmother was mean.

5. The prince sent the slipper with a courier. He asked to see Cinderella.
   The prince sent the slipper with a courier. The courier asked to see Cinderella.

TRANSPARENCY F5–4
TEACHER'S EDITION PAGE 295I

THEME 5 Focus on Fairy Tales
Grammar Skill Using Pronouns

DAY 2 PRACTICE

Independent Work

Practice/Homework Assign **Practice Book** page 160.

Daily Language Practice

Have students correct Sentences 3 and 4 on **Transparency F5–3**.

Practice Book page 160

Focus on Fairy Tales
Grammar Skill Using Pronouns

Name _____

Replacing Nouns with Pronouns

These sentences repeat the same nouns too often. Choose the correct pronoun to replace the underlined word or phrase. Then rewrite each sentence with the pronoun.

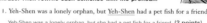

1. Yeh-Shen was a lonely orphan, but <u>Yeh-Shen</u> had a pet fish for a friend.
   Yeh-Shen was a lonely orphan, but she had a pet fish for a friend. (2 points)

2. Yeh-Shen had caught and raised the fish, and the <u>fish</u> lived in a nearby pond.
   Yeh-Shen had caught and raised the fish, and it lived in a nearby pond. (2)

3. Yeh-Shen got some food and shared the <u>food</u> with the fish.
   Yeh-Shen got some food and shared it with the fish. (2)

4. Yeh-Shen asked the old man who <u>the old man</u> was.
   Yeh-Shen asked the old man who he was. (2)

5. The old man disappeared before Yeh-Shen could ask <u>the old man</u> another question.
   The old man disappeared before Yeh-Shen could ask him another question. (2)

6. The king saw Yeh-Shen take the slipper, and he followed <u>Yeh-Shen</u> home.
   The king saw Yeh-Shen take the slipper, and he followed her home. (2)

Transparency F5–3

Daily Language Practice

Correct two sentences each day.

1. cinderella wishhed to danse at a ball.
   Cinderella wished to dance at a ball.

2. Cinderella's stepsisters was not nise.
   Cinderella's stepsisters were not nice.

3. An old man noticed Yeh-Shens sad fase
   An old man noticed Yeh-Shen's sad face.

4. yeh-Shen walkked like a prinsess.
   Yeh-Shen walked like a princess.

5. A big fish were in the senter of the pond
   A big fish was in the center of the pond.

6. The king walked in a sircle and waited for Yeh-Shens' answer.
   The king walked in a circle and waited for Yeh-Shen's answer.

7. Yeh-Shen had to rase home and she lost a slipper from one of her foots.
   Yeh-Shen had to race home, and she lost a slipper from one of her feet.

8. onse at home her fell asleep under an apple tree. Once at home she fell asleep under an apple tree.

9. The King lived in a large sity.
   The king lived in a large city.

10. Yeh-Shen kept her pet in a secret plase?
    Yeh-Shen kept her pet in a secret place.

TRANSPARENCY F5–3
TEACHER'S EDITION PAGE 295I

THEME 5 Focus on Fairy Tales
Grammar Skill Using Pronouns
Spelling Skill Spelling the /k/ sound in *face*

ANNOTATED VERSION

Monitoring Student Progress

If . . .	Then . . .
students score 7 or below on **Practice Book** page 161,	have them work with partners to revise their incorrect sentences.

DAY 3 — PRONOUN GAME

Pronoun Pros

Ask students to form groups of four. Provide pencils and paper for each group.

- One student in each group writes a sentence that includes nouns but no pronouns.

- That student passes the paper to the second student, who writes a sentence related to the first but uses at least one pronoun.

- The second student passes the paper to the third student, who writes a sentence related to the other two, using at least one pronoun.

- The fourth student reads the three sentences and writes the noun that each pronoun is replacing. If there is confusion over which word is being replaced, students should work together to rewrite the sentences.

- Students may take turns being the first one to write a sentence.

Daily Language Practice
Have students correct Sentences 5 and 6 on **Transparency F5–3**.

Practice Book page 161

Name _____

Focus on Fairy Tales
Grammar Skill Using Pronouns

Clear References

Each sentence contains an unclear pronoun. Underline each confusing pronoun. Then rewrite the sentence to make the meaning clear.

Example: Cinderella's stepmother told the family that she would clean the house.

Cinderella's stepmother told the family that Cinderella would clean the house
Sentences may vary. Sample answers are shown.

1. The sisters asked their parents if they were invited to the ball.

   The sisters asked their parents if the sisters were invited to the ball. **(2 points)**

2. Cinderella's godmother promised that she would attend the ball.

   Cinderella's godmother promised that Cinderella would attend the ball. **(2)**

3. Cinderella asked her godmother when she could help.

   Cinderella asked her godmother when the godmother could help. **(2)**

4. The prince told the courier that he would marry the owner of the slipper.

   The prince told the courier that the prince would marry the owner of the slipper. **(2)**

5. The courier told the prince that he must meet Cinderella.

   The courier told the prince that the prince must meet Cinderella. **(2)**

DAY 4 — PRACTICE

Independent Work

Practice/Homework Assign **Practice Book** page 161.

Daily Language Practice
Have students correct Sentences 7 and 8 on **Transparency F5–3**.

Transparency F5–5

THEME 5 Focus on Fairy Tales
Grammar Skill Improving Writing

ANNOTATED VERSION

Correct Pronouns

1. Yeh-Shen grew up in she stepmother's house.
   Yeh-Shen grew up in her stepmother's house.

2. Her only friend was a beautiful fish.
   correct

3. Her and the fish met every day.
   She and the fish met every day.

4. Yeh-Shen's stepmother tricked she and the fish.
   Yeh-Shen's stepmother tricked her and the fish.

5. An old man helped Yeh-Shen, but him left very quickly.
   An old man helped Yeh-Shen, but he left very quickly.

TRANSPARENCY F5–5
TEACHER'S EDITION PAGE 295J

DAY 5 — IMPROVING WRITING

Correct Pronouns

Teach Remind students that good writers take care to choose the correct form of a pronoun to replace a noun:

- *I, she, he, we,* and *they* are subject pronouns; *me, him, her, us,* and *them* are object pronouns; *it* and *you* are both subject and object pronouns; *my, your, his, her, its, our,* and *their* are possessive pronouns.

- Display **Transparency F5–5.** Ask volunteers to read the sentences. Have them write *correct* if the pronoun in the sentence is used correctly. Have them rewrite and correct the sentence if it is not.

- Have students proofread a piece of their own writing for correct pronoun usage.

Practice/Homework Assign **Practice Book** page 162.

Daily Language Practice
Have students correct Sentences 9 and 10 on **Transparency F5–3**.

Practice Book page 162

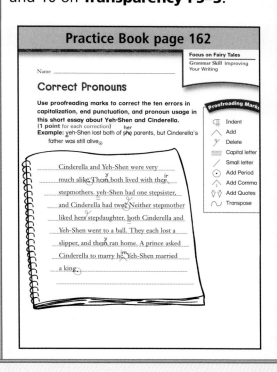

Name _____

Focus on Fairy Tales
Grammar Skill Improving Your Writing

Correct Pronouns

Use proofreading marks to correct the ten errors in capitalization, end punctuation, and pronoun usage in this short essay about Yeh-Shen and Cinderella. **(1 point** for each correction)
Example: yeh-Shen lost both of she parents, but Cinderella's father was still alive

Cinderella and Yeh-Shen were very much alike. Them both lived with their stepmothers. yeh-Shen had one stepsister, and Cinderella had two. Neither stepmother liked her stepdaughter. both Cinderella and Yeh-Shen went to a ball. They each lost a slipper, and them ran home. A prince asked Cinderella to marry him. Yeh-Shen married a king.

Proofreading Marks
¶ Indent
∧ Add
✄ Delete
≡ Capital letter
/ Small letter
⊙ Add Period
∧ Add Comma
⌄⌄ Add Quotes
∼ Transpose

WRITING: Fairy Tale

OBJECTIVES

- Plan a fairy tale.
- Write a fairy tale.
- Use similes to improve writing.

DAY 1 — PREWRITING

Introducing the Format

Review the characteristics of a fairy tale:

- a setting that is long-ago and faraway
- a main character with a problem to overcome
- a make-believe character with special powers
- a happy ending

Start students thinking about writing their own fairy tale version of "Cinderella." Ask:

- What changes can you make to the "Cinderella" plot without completely changing the story?
- Where will the story take place?
- What will the characters be like?
- Who will the make-believe character or characters be?
- What problem will the main character have, and how will the problem be solved?

Have students brainstorm and list ideas for their fairy tales.

- Tell them to save their notes.

Transparency F5–6

Guidelines for Writing a Fairy Tale

- Make creative changes to the story, but keep some traditional elements.
- Organize events in time order. Use order words such as *after that, the next day,* and *later* to help readers follow the story.
- Include a make-believe character who uses special powers to help the main character.
- Give details to show what the characters, setting, and events are like.
- Use your voice. Make your writing sound serious, funny, lively, or thoughtful—whatever suits your retelling.
- Mix short and long sentences. Add some dialogue, too.

THEME 5 Focus on Fairy Tales
Writing Skill
Guidelines for Writing a Fairy Tale

ANNOTATED VERSION

TRANSPARENCY F5–6
TEACHER'S EDITION PAGES 295K AND 295L

DAY 2 — DRAFTING

Discussing the Model

Use the Anthology to discuss how writers use make-believe characters in fairy tales.

- Make-believe characters may be fairies, trolls, giants, dragons, or animals with special powers.
- The make-believe character helps the main character solve a problem.
- The make-believe character may set some rules for the main character to follow. If the rules are broken, things will not go as the main character hopes.

Display Transparency F5–6, and discuss the guidelines.

Have students draft a fairy tale.

- Have students use their prewriting notes from Day 1.
- Assign **Practice Book** page 163 to help students plan characters, setting, and plot.
- Provide support as needed.

Practice Book page 163

Focus on Fairy Tales
Writing Skill

Name _____

Write a Fairy Tale!

Fairy Tale Chart: Your Own Cinderella Tale

Human characters	Answers will vary.
Make-believe characters and their powers	
Setting (time and place)	
Problem	
Plot Events	
Beginning	
Middle	
Ending	

Writing Traits

Word Choice Explain to students that using exact words will help their readers to better understand what they are saying. Provide these examples:

Without exact words: The prince <u>went</u> after Cinderella, but he could not catch her.

With exact words: The prince <u>dashed</u> after Cinderella, but he could not catch her.

DAY 3	**REVISING**

Improving Writing: Using Similes

Explain similes.

- A simile is a comparison using *like* or *as*.

- Writers use similes to add interesting details and to help readers picture what is being described.

- *The horse galloped* can be improved with a simile: *The horse galloped as fast as a shooting star.*

Display Transparency F5–7.

- Ask what is being compared in Item 1.

- Have students identify the similes in Items 2–8.

- Ask students to read the last sentence of column 1 on page 288.

- Have them identify the simile. (*her feet felt as light as air*)

Assign Practice Book page 164.

Have students revise their drafts.

- Display **Transparency F5–6** again. Have students use it to revise their fairy tales.

- Have partners hold writing conferences.

- Ask students to further revise their fairy tales and to add some similes.

Transparency F5–7

Making Comparisons with Similes

Identify the two items compared in each simile.

1. Cinderella's dress was as brilliant as peacock feathers.
2. She moved quickly like a hummingbird to get ready.
3. Her jewels were as colorful as a rainbow.
4. The dancers at the ball were as graceful as swans.
5. Cinderella ran swiftly like a deer to leave the ball.
6. The glass slipper was as clear as water.
7. The stepmother's heart was as prickly as a thorn bush.
8. The stepsister groaned like a creaking door.

DAY 4	**PROOFREADING**

Checking for Errors

Have students proofread for errors in grammar, spelling, punctuation, and usage.

- Students can use the proofreading checklist on **Practice Book** page 250 to help them proofread their fairy tales.

- Students can also use the chart of proofreading marks on **Practice Book** page 251.

- See Writing Traits on the preceding page.

Practice Book page 164

Name _____

Adding Similes

Read the paragraph. Fill in each blank to create a simile. Write the answers on the lines below.

At the ball, lights shone as brightly as (1) _____. The music flowed like (2) _____. As the dancers moved across the floor, they twirled like (3) _____. A long table was piled with food, and a bowl of punch as big as a (4) _____ sparkled at one end of the table. The prince sat on his throne, and Cinderella sat near him. They looked as contented as (5) _____ as they enjoyed the evening.

Answers will vary but should reflect an understanding of similes.

1. _____ (2 points)
2. _____ (2)
3. _____ (2)
4. _____ (2)
5. _____ (2)

DAY 5	**PUBLISHING**

Sharing a Fairy Tale

Consider these publishing options.

- Ask students to read their fairy tale or some other piece of writing from the Author's Chair.

- Encourage students to present their fairy tales as a puppet show.

Portfolio Opportunity

Save students' fairy tales as samples of their writing development.

Monitoring Student Progress

If . . .	Then . . .
students' writing does not follow the guidelines on **Transparency F5–6,**	work with students to improve specific parts of their writing.

Language Center

VOCABULARY

Building Vocabulary

👥👥👥 Groups	🕐 20 minutes
Objective	Brainstorm words that name character traits.

Traits are the qualities that a character has. For example, you could describe Cinderella as hard-working and kind. Think of traits that would describe other characters in *Focus on Fairy Tales*.

- List the names of two characters from the selections.

- Brainstorm words that describe the qualities that each of these characters has.

- Make a word web of character traits for each character.

- Meet with other groups and compare your traits.

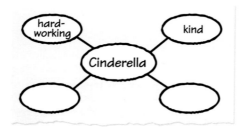

VOCABULARY

Connotation Connection

👥👥 Pairs	🕐 20 minutes
Objective	Identify positive and negative connotations.
Materials	Activity Master 5–4 on page R26

Some words communicate positive feelings. Some words communicate negative feelings. These feelings are called connotations. Find positive and negative connotations.

- With a partner, read the sentences on Activity Master 5–4.

- Look at each underlined word. Find a positive and a negative connotation for each underlined word in the word box at the top of the page.

- Write the appropriate words on the lines next to each sentence.

PHONICS

Cinderella Says

👥👥👥 Groups	🕐 20 minutes
Objective	Play a phonics game.
Materials	Index cards or small pieces of paper

Play a game of *Cinderella Says* to distinguish between the two sounds of the letter *c*.

- Write the words below on index cards or small pieces of paper. Mix up the cards.

- Have one person be the reader and choose a card. The reader says "Cinderella says *ceiling*." If the listeners hear a soft *c* they stand up. If they hear a hard *c*, they stay sitting.

Remember: The reader must say "Cinderella says."

- If a player makes a mistake or stands up without the reader saying "Cinderella says," he or she is out. Play until there is one player left. This player becomes the new reader.

Soft *c*	Hard *c*
city	cotton
ceiling	captain
cellar	correct
certain	cuff
center	creek
century	clumsy
ceramic	college
citizen	crevice

Consider copying and laminating these activities for use in centers.

LISTENING/SPEAKING/VIEWING

Comparing Stories in Print and Movies

👤👤👤 Groups	⏱ 45 minutes	
Objective	Compare and contrast the film version of *Cinderella* with the written version.	
Materials	*Cinderella* (the movie)	

Many fairy tales that you are familiar with were made into animated movies. As the stories were remade in movie form, certain elements were added, and others were taken away. Look for the similarities and differences between the story and the movie.

- Watch the first twenty-five minutes of the animated film *Cinderella*.

- Then skim through the pages of *Cinderella* in *Focus on Fairy Tales*.

- Afterward, work in a small group to complete a chart showing how the two versions are alike and different.

	Cinderella	
	The Movie	The Story
Characters		
Setting		
Plot		
Details		

PHONICS/SPELLING

A Spelling Collage

👤👤 Pairs	⏱ 30 minutes	
Objective	Make collages of pictures that represent Basic Words.	
Materials	Old magazines, scissors, glue, drawing paper, markers	

Yeh-Shen's fish bones and Cinderella's godmother turned ordinary objects into beautiful things. Create a collage using spelling words.

- Each partner makes his or her own collage.

- Choose as many words as possible from the Basic Word list to represent in the collage.

- Draw your own pictures or cut out pictures from magazines that you think will make others think of the spelling words.

- Exchange your collage with your partner. Write the spelling words that are represented in the collage you are viewing on a separate sheet of paper. Pass the paper back and check the spelling of the words.

- Discuss which words were easy to represent and which words were more difficult.

Leveled Readers

Smudge-Face, A Native American Cinderella Tale

Summary *In this Native American version of Cinderella, a father and his three daughters do all the chores. Across the lake lives a powerful man named Strong Wind. One morning, Strong Wind's sister announces that the first woman who answers her questions truthfully will become Strong Wind's bride. When it is Smudge-Face's turn, she tells the truth. They marry and live happily ever after.*

Vocabulary

Introduce the Key Vocabulary and ask students to complete the BLM.

wigwam a dome or triangular-shaped Native American dwelling, *p. 4*

moccasins light, soft shoes made from leather, *p. 5*

canoe a long, narrow boat, *p. 7*

rawhide leather made from the skins of deer or cattle, *p. 7*

chores everyday tasks, such as cooking and cleaning, *p. 10*

necklace a piece of jewelry worn around the neck, *p. 14*

Building Background and Vocabulary

Ask students to summarize the main events in *Cinderella*. Then explain that they will be reading a different version of the same fairy tale, *Smudge-Face, A Native American Cinderella Tale*. Preview the story with students, using the story vocabulary when possible.

⌾ Writing Skill: Writing a Fairy Tale

Have students read the Strategy Focus on the book flap. Remind students to use the strategy and to think about elements of fairy tales as they read the book. (See the Leveled Readers Teacher's Guide for **Vocabulary and Comprehension Practice Masters.**)

Responding

Have partners discuss how to answer the questions on the inside back cover.

Think About the Selection Sample answers:

1. Ashes from the fire made her face dirty, so her sisters called her Smudge-Face.

2. He wants to be able to trust the woman who will become his wife.

3. Possible response: She can see Strong Wind because she is true and honest.

Making Connections Responses will vary.

⌾ Building Fluency

Model Read aloud pages 7–9, changing your voice slightly when reading the conversation among Strong Wind's sister, Oldest Sister, and Middle Sister. Explain that your voice changes to show that a different character is speaking.

Practice Have students read aloud to a partner the dialogue of Strong Wind's sister and Smudge-Face on pages 11–12. Encourage them to use a slightly different voice when a different character is speaking.

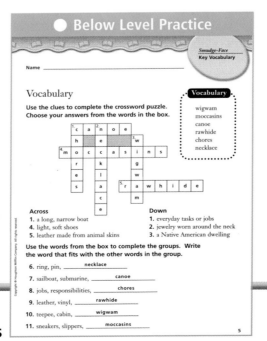

The Little Sparrow, A Cinderella Story from Italy

Summary *Cinderella's father gives her a little yellow sparrow. He announces that the King has invited them to go to three balls. Cinderella doesn't have a gown to wear, so she stays behind as the others go off to the first ball. Suddenly, her sparrow begins to sing, and Cinderella's normal clothes are transformed into beautiful clothes. She meets the prince, and they fall in love.*

Vocabulary

Introduce the Key Vocabulary and ask students to complete the BLM.

announced declared, *p. 4*

glittering shiny, sparkling, *p. 5*

purse a small handbag, *p. 5*

glaring staring unpleasantly at someone, *p. 6*

greedy selfish; too fond of money or other valuables, *p. 7*

disappointed feeling sad or let down, *p. 15*

*Forms of these words are Anthology Key Vocabulary words.

▲ ON LEVEL

Building Background and Vocabulary

Point out that this is an Italian version of the fairy tale *Cinderella*. Ask students to summarize the main event in *Cinderella*. Preview the story with students, using the story vocabulary when possible.

Writing Skill: Writing a Fairy Tale

Have students read the Strategy Focus on the book flap. Remind students to use the strategy and to think about elements of fairy tales as they read the book. (See the Leveled Readers Teacher's Guide for **Vocabulary and Comprehension Practice Masters.**)

Responding

Have partners discuss how to answer the questions on the inside back cover.

Think About the Selection Sample answers:

1. The older sisters are interested in dresses and jewelry. Cinderella does not care as much about these things.

2. The sparrow gives Cinderella beautiful dresses and jewelry to wear at the balls.

3. The guards dive for the gold coins that Cinderella tosses. She throws the sand at them to keep them from seeing her escape.

4. Responses will vary.

Making Connections Responses will vary.

Building Fluency

Model Read aloud pages 9 and 12, modeling changing the rate of reading. The passage on page 9 should be read more slowly than the one on page 12. Explain how a reader chooses to read faster or slower based on the action in the story.

Practice Have volunteers read to the class the two passages at the appropriate speed.

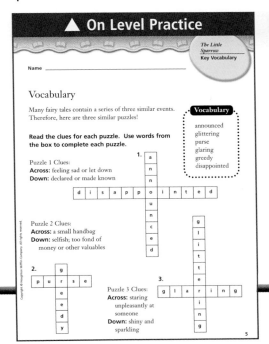

LEVELED READERS

Rella's Wish

Summary *In this version of Cinderella, Rella lives with her father, stepmother, and two stepsisters. When Priscilla the fairy godmother offers to give her a beautiful gown for Prince Alfred's ball, Rella asks for seven adventures instead. On each adventure, she is amazed to meet the same friendly man, Fred. Rella attends the ball as promised. Finding it dull, she steps outside for a breath of fresh air and is stunned to find Prince Alfred there.*

Vocabulary

Introduce the Key Vocabulary and ask students to complete the BLM.

expensive costing a lot of money, *p. 2*

gowns fancy, formal dresses, *p. 2*

longing strongly wishing or hoping for, *p. 6*

fulfill to satisfy or complete, *p. 7*

coincidence an unexpected surprise, *p. 8*

dazed very surprised; stunned, *p. 15*

■ ABOVE LEVEL

Building Background and Vocabulary

Point out that this a modern, funny version of the fairy tale *Cinderella*. Ask students to summarize the main events in *Cinderella*. Preview the story with students, using the story vocabulary when possible.

Writing Skill: Writing a Fairy Tale

Have students read the Strategy Focus on the book flap. Remind students to use the strategy and to think about elements of fairy tales as they read the book. (See the Leveled Readers Teacher's Guide for **Vocabulary and Comprehension Practice Masters.**)

Responding

Have partners discuss how to answer the questions on the inside back cover.

Think About the Selection   Sample answers:

1. Possible responses might include that the basic characters are the same, that the fairy godmother grants wishes, or that there is a fancy ball.

2. Possible responses might include that Rella's sisters and stepmother aren't mean, just different; the fairy godmother grants very different wishes.

3. Possible response: I wasn't very surprised. I guessed that since Rella kept meeting Fred on her adventures, he would be a part of the story later too.

4. Possible response: I think they will be very happy because they both like adventures.

Making Connections   Responses will vary.

Building Fluency

Model   Explain that the sentences around dialogue often give us clues about how the dialogue should be read. Then read aloud the dialogue on page 9 appropriately.

Practice   Have students read page 10 with a partner, looking for clues on how to read Rella's dialogue.

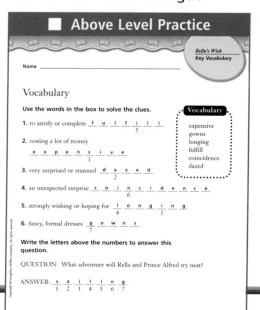

◆ **LANGUAGE SUPPORT**

To Tell the Truth, A Native American Cinderella Tale

Summary *Smudge-Face lives with her father and two older sisters, who force her to do all the work. An important man, Strong Wind, lives on the other side of the lake. Strong Wind wants to marry a girl who tells the truth. Smudge-Face's sisters both lie and do not pass the test. But Smudge-Face demonstrates her truthfulness and marries Strong Wind in a Cinderella ending.*

Vocabulary

Introduce the Key Vocabulary and ask students to complete the BLM.

hunt to search for game for food, *p. 2*

smudge a smear of dirt, *p. 3*

moccasins shoes made of soft leather, *p. 5*

marry to wed, become husband and wife, *p. 6*

truth what is fact, real, honest, *p. 6*

canoe light, narrow boat with paddles, *p. 7*

Building Background and Vocabulary

Ask students if they know the stories *Cinderella, Snow White,* or other fairy tales. Discuss what the good characters do, and who the mean or scary characters are. Then distribute the **Build Background Practice Master** and discuss the pictures. Have partners complete the page together. (See the Leveled Readers Teacher's Guide for **Build Background and Vocabulary Masters.**)

Reading Strategy: Summarize

Have students read the Strategy Focus on the book flap. Remind students to look for the parts of the story that will help them summarize the story after they read.

Responding

Have partners discuss how to answer the questions on the inside back cover.

Think About the Selection Sample answers:

1. She told the truth.

2. Possible response: They probably thought Strong Wind couldn't tell the difference, so they said what they thought he wanted to hear.

3. Responses will vary.

Making Connections Responses will vary.

Building Fluency

Model Have students follow along on pages 2–3 as they listen to the recording on audio CD.

Practice Have students read along with the recording until they can read on their own with accuracy and expression.

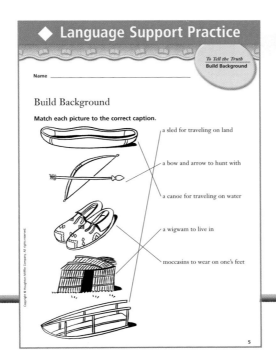

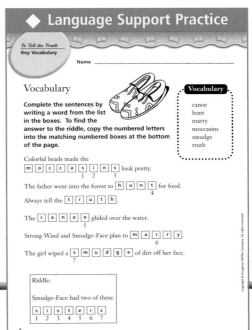

295R

Resources for Theme 5

Contents

● **BELOW LEVEL**

An I Can Read Book

The Josefina Story Quilt

Eleanor Coerr

Pictures by Bruce Degen

The Josefina Story Quilt

Summary *Set in the 1850s, this historical fiction book tells the story of Faith and her pet hen, Josefina, as they travel with Faith's family to California by wagon train. Only because of Faith's pleading has Josefina, an old and useless hen, been allowed to come along. But she proves valuable during the long, hard journey. Furthermore, she gives Faith memories that will endure through her story quilt.*

Vocabulary

calico brightly patterned cotton cloth, *p. 27*

bellowed gave a loud roar, *p. 33*

pesky troublesome; annoying, *p. 33*

stampede a sudden rush of startled animals, *p. 34*

current a mass of liquid in motion, *p. 41*

Preparing to Read

Building Background Briefly discuss the historical setting with students. Begin by reading the author's note on pages 63–64. Ask students about different ways people keep memories alive for future generations. Explain that quilts, with their patchwork squares, began as a way to tell and preserve stories. Remind students to use their strategies as they read *The Josefina Story Quilt.*

Developing Key Vocabulary Before students read the book or book part, preview with them the Key Vocabulary words. Have volunteers read and define the words. Ask students how these words might be used in a book about settling the West.

Previewing the Text

Read *The Josefina Story Quilt* in its entirety or in two segments, pages 5–36 and pages 37–62. Have students preview the book by reading the chapter titles and looking at the illustrations. Then have students view the cover. What is the square that Faith is holding? Have students predict what will happen to Josefina. Will she be allowed to go on the trip?

Supporting the Reading

pages 5–36

- Why won't Pa let Faith bring Josefina? (There isn't much room, and Josefina is old and useless.)

- Does Pa have good reasons for telling Faith that her hen can't go West? Explain why or why not. (Answers will vary. Some students may think Pa doesn't realize that just being a pet is an important use for an animal.)

- Based on what you've read about Faith so far, what inferences can you make about her character? (She is loyal and very persistent. She is also smart to realize the stampede was the dog's fault, and brave for saying so.)

- What does the author mean when she says, *They understood one another as true friends do?* (Answers will vary.)

THEME PAPERBACKS

37–62

volunteers to share how they used reading strategies to figure out
meaning of *humdinger* on page 54. (Since Josefina has just saved the
ily from robbers, Pa must think she is a great "watchdog." So *humdinger*
t mean "very good" or "fantastic.")

er Josefina dies, what finally makes Faith begin to feel better? (She
des to make a pine tree patch for her quilt so she can remember her hen.)

you think Faith will continue to make quilts in the future? Why or
not? (Answers will vary. Some students may think Faith will make many
ts because her experience has shown her how important they are.)

y does the author end the story by saying, *And every night Faith felt
m and happy under the Josefina story quilt?* (The quilt keeps Faith
sically warm, while the memories the quilt brings about give her
otional warmth.)

ponding

students summarize the main events in *The Josefina Story Quilt.* Ask
to share their latest predictions and discuss which were accurate.
have them make a paper quilt by first brainstorming class memories
ries, and then representing each in a pattern drawn in a large
e. Help students cut out the squares and tape them together to
a class story quilt.

**English Language
Learners**

Some students may not know that the
buffalo (page 48) was crucial to the Plains
Indians' survival in many ways, providing
meat for food, hide for clothes and tents,
and bone for tools and weapons.

▲ **ON LEVEL**

A Child's Glacier Bay

Summary *This nonfiction narrative presents the wild habitat of Alaska's Glacier Bay through the eyes of young Hannah Corral. During a three-week family trip along the coastline, Hannah learns to take on the challenges of the wilderness and appreciate its beauty.*

Vocabulary

kayaks Eskimo canoes made of skins stretched over wooden frames, *p. 12*

molting shedding outer skin, feathers, or hair, and replacing with new growth, *p. 13*

flukes flaps of a whale's tail, *p. 13*

endangered faced with extinction, *p. 14*

swells long, rolling waves, *p. 17*

wake the track or path of waves, ripples, or foam left by a moving boat, *p. 25*

dramatically with a striking or forceful effect, *p. 31*

Preparing to Read

Building Background Ask students to share what they know about Alaska, inviting volunteers to indicate this state on a map. Explain that *A Child's Glacier Bay* tells the real story of one family's trip through the Alaskan wilderness. Note that a *glacier* is a huge mass of ice, and the more familiar *iceberg* is a piece that has broken off a glacier. Tell students that this book is a narrative told through the eyes of Hannah, a young girl, but that it also contains many facts about the environment. Ask what reading strategies might be helpful for this type of book. Remind students to use these strategies as they read *A Child's Glacier Bay*.

Developing Key Vocabulary Before students read the book or book part, preview with them the Key Vocabulary words. Have volunteers read and define the words. Ask students which words might help describe certain animals. Which might describe an ocean or bay?

Previewing the Text

Read *A Child's Glacier Bay* in its entirety or in two segments, pages 9–21 and pages 22–36. Have students preview the book by looking at the cover and inside photographs. Point out the map on page 7, indicating Bartlett Cove, where the Corrals begin and end their trip. Then have students predict what the family might encounter during their journey. What animals will they see? What dangers will they face?

Supporting the Reading

pages 9–21

- Is the kayak trip up the West Arm too dangerous for small children? Explain. (Answers will vary. Some students may think that the children are safe because they're with their parents, who seem to be experienced kayakers.)

- Use what you've learned so far about Hannah's dad to make inferences about what he's like. (Since he's already been to Glacier Bay, he must love the wilderness. He seems to know a lot about the animals. And he's a good photographer.)

- Have students share and evaluate the predictions they made before reading. Then have them make new predictions about what the family will encounter in the next section. Will they complete their trip safely?

...at challenge does Hannah face while crossing the West Arm? (She
...to help land her kayak in big crashing waves.)

...y have Ben and his dad fallen behind? (Ben is only six and can't paddle
... fast.)

...o students pronounce *lichens* (LI-kens) on page 28, and explain that
...se plants are made up of fungus and algae growing together.
...ens look like scaly growths on rocks or tree trunks.

... Hannah go on future wilderness trips? Explain. (Answers will vary.
...t students may think that Hannah will go on future trips because she
...yed her experience at Glacier Bay.)

...at does the author mean when she writes, *It's clear to me that
...derness is the real treasure at Glacier Bay*? (Since so many places have
...ome overcrowded, a place that is still in its natural state is very valuable.)

...ponding

...udents to share their use of strategies while reading *A Child's Glacier
...sk for examples of how they used the Monitor/Clarify strategy to
...hem follow the narrative and understand the information presented
... the story. Then have them share and evaluate their latest predictions.
..., have students share their reactions to *A Child's Glacier Bay*.

English Language Learners

Some students may not understand why Hannah believes that seeing a bald eagle on July 4 before a treacherous journey might be a good sign (pages 24–25). Explain that the bald eagle is the national symbol of the United States and that July 4 is the country's Independence Day.

THEME PAPERBACKS

Balto and the Great Race

Summary *This nonfiction narrative presents the story of Balto, a sled dog that led his team through the harsh Alaskan winter to bring desperately needed serum to Nome during an outbreak of diphtheria. Balto's courage and tenacity saved many lives and made him famous.*

Vocabulary

endurance the ability to withstand pain and hardship, *p. 2*

fidelity devotion or loyalty, *p. 2*

diphtheria an easily spread disease marked by high fever, breathing difficulty, and weakness, *p. 10*

serum medicine used to fight a disease, *p. 12*

relay to pass or send along; a race in which each team member goes partway, *p. 15*

plateau a flat area that is higher than the land around it, *p. 39*

flawless perfect, without mistakes, *p. 48*

Preparing to Read

Building Background Ask students to share what they know about mushers or sled dogs. Tell them that the book they are about to read tells the true story of a famous sled dog and the race that made him so well known. Explain that the race is not a competition but a race against time to save lives. Be sure students are aware of the harsh weather conditions and isolation experienced by people living in Alaska. Ask what reading strategies might be helpful to use with this type of book. Remind students to use these strategies as they read *Balto and the Great Race*.

Developing Key Vocabulary Before students read the book or book part, preview with them the Key Vocabulary words. Have volunteers read and define the words. Ask students how the words might relate to a sled dog race.

Previewing the Text

Balto and the Great Race may be read in its entirety or in three segments, pages 1–26, pages 27–62, and pages 63–97. Have students preview the book by looking at the cover, the chapter titles, and the illustrations. Point out the map of Alaska at the front of the book, indicating Nome, Bluff, and Nenana. Then have students predict what dangers a musher and a team of sled dogs might encounter during their journey.

Supporting the Reading

pages 1–26

- What does the author mean when she says that a musher *could look at a dog and know in an instant if he was a natural for a team*? (The author means that an experienced musher can easily recognize the qualities that make a good sled dog.)

- Why are the workers for the Northern Commercial mail system so willing to try to get the serum to Nome? (They want to try to help save lives. They understand that people who live in such an unforgiving climate have to help each other as much as possible.)

- Have students share and evaluate the predictions they made before reading.

Then have them make new predictions about what Balto's role will be in delivering the serum.

27–62

y are mushers concerned about the effect of ice on the dogs' feet?
e bitter cold can make the ice crystals as sharp as glass; the ice can cut the
s' feet, and the cuts can become infected.)

nt out the word *anchor* on page 52 and explain that it refers to the
y the musher positions himself on the sled. Discuss the other meaning
anchor: a weight used to hold a ship in place.

y does the author write that Balto *remembered what they had left
ind in [Nome] and why they needed to return*? (The author wants to
w that Balto seems to understand the importance of the journey they are
ut to begin.)

63–97

v does Kassen's team become lost? (The lead dog can't tell where the
is because of the high winds and blowing snow of the blizzard.)

v is Balto able to follow the trail? (He relies on his sense of smell and
memory of the feel of the land.)

at information is given in the afterword on pages 96–97? Why is this
ormation in a separate section? (The section explains that the Iditarod is
in memory of the efforts that brought the serum to Nome. This separate
ion gives information that is not central to Balto's story.)

ponding

udents to share their use of strategies while reading *Balto and the
Race.* Have them give examples of how they used the Predict/Infer
gy to help them understand story events. Then have them share
valuate their latest predictions. Finally, ask students to define the
cteristics of a hero and explain whether Balto fits that definition.

English Language Learners

Be sure students understand that the
sentence "*Seppala had not made the
decision to cross the sound lightly*" on
page 47 means that Seppala had thought
carefully about his decision. Point out the
multiple-meaning words *sound* and *light*
in the sentence and discuss the meanings with which students are familiar.

RETEACHING: Comprehension Skills

Making Inferences

OBJECTIVE

- Use personal knowledge and understanding to make inferences.

Target Skill Trace

- Making Inferences, pp. 183A–183B

Teach

Read the following story:

Jake stood on the riverbank. He cast his fishing line into the deep water. He had been trying to catch a fish for many hours. Alexandra and Zachary laughed as they watched Jake throw the line into the water one more time.

Ask, What kind of person is Jake? (patient, hard-working) How do you think Alexandra and Zachary feel about Jake's efforts to catch a fish? (They think he is wasting his time and will not catch anything.)

Explain that authors don't tell readers everything. Readers must fill in the information by using word clues and what they already know, along with picture clues when they are present. Readers make inferences about the characters and events in the story.

Practice

Ask students, What are the three types of clues you can use to make inferences? (picture clues, word clues, and what we know clues) Make a three-column chart like the one below.

Picture clues	Word clues	What we know clues

Use the following examples from *Across the Wide Dark Sea* to fill in the chart.

page 120 *Tears streamed down my mother's face, yet she was smiling.*

How was mother feeling? (happy)

Word clues: *Land had been sighted. The trip was over. It had been difficult.*

What I know: *People sometimes cry when they are happy.*

Apply

Have students make inferences, with an eye to using picture clues, word clues, and what they know as they read their **Leveled Readers** for this week. Ask students to complete the questions and the activity on the Responding page.

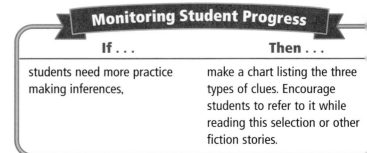

Monitoring Student Progress

If . . .	Then . . .
students need more practice making inferences,	make a chart listing the three types of clues. Encourage students to refer to it while reading this selection or other fiction stories.

ALLENGE/EXTENSION:
king Inferences

Plan a Trip

Think about a place that you would like to visit. Make a list of items you would need to e, taking into account the weather, the kinds of vities you would want to do, and the length of e you would be there. Beneath your packing list, ne the types of transportation you would need to ch your destination, such as plane, car, bus, boat, or seback. Exchange papers with a partner and read r partner's list. Try to guess where your partner uld like to go, based on what you know and the d clues on the paper.

Plan a Trip
Packing List
• goggles
• swimsuit
• sunscreen
• flippers
• underwater camera
transportation: boat

Design an Experiment

In the story, the settlers are planting seeds and crops that they have brought with them he ship. Design an experiment to find out which ve plants can be eaten and which might be poison-
Write a paragraph explaining how you would find

out which plants are not poisonous. Remember that the settler cannot test the plants by eating them, because the colony needs every member and cannot afford any more sick members. You can work alone, with a partner, or in a small group.

Tell About a Voyage

Bring pictures or other souvenirs from a trip, family visit, or vacation you have taken. te a short paragraph that tells what you liked best

about the trip, and what you liked the least. Read your paragraph to a partner and ask him or her to think about the trip being described.

RETEACHING: Comprehension Skills

Predicting Outcomes

> ### OBJECTIVE
> - Use details and personal knowledge to predict outcomes.
>
> ### Target Skill Trace
> - Predicting Outcomes, pp. 213A–213B

Teach

Ask students to think about the fable *The Tortoise and the Hare.* Ask, What was the outcome of the story? How did it end? (The tortoise won the race.) Ask, Did any clues in the story lead you to think the tortoise would win the race? (The tortoise kept going, and the hare took a nap.) Ask, If the hare were to race against the tortoise again, what might happen? Accept all reasonable suggestions, making sure one of the suggestions involves the hare acting in a way that is different from the original tale.

Use a Think Aloud to model predicting outcomes:

Think Aloud *I use the details and events from the story and my prior knowledge to predict what will happen next or at the end of the story.*

Explain to students that guessing what will happen next in a story and guessing how the story will end is called predicting outcomes. Tell students they can use story clues and their own knowledge to predict what will happen.

Practice

Ask, What was the problem in the story *Yunmi and Halmoni's Trip*? (Yunmi was afraid her grandmother would not return to New York.) Say, What was the outcome of the story? How did it end? (Halmoni said she would go back with Yunmi.)

Direct students to turn to page 153. Ask a student volunteer to read the text aloud. Ask, How did Yunmi feel? (worried and scared) Ask, What was Yunmi worried about? (She thought Halmoni might not want to leave Korea.) Tell students to look for story clues to help them predict what will happen.

Direct students to turn to page 159 and ask them to read the text. Ask, What does Yunmi find out? (Halmoni will go back to New York with her for another year.) Point out that the word *"suddenly"* in the last paragraph shows that a change is taking place. Ask, How does Yunmi feel now? (ashamed and selfish) Tell students to turn to pages 160–161. Ask them to look for clues in the text and picture that show how Yunmi's behavior changed. Call on volunteers to point out clues. (Yunmi is smiling; she is thinking about others instead of herself.)

Apply

Have students predict outcomes, with an eye to using story clues and their own knowledge, as they read their **Leveled Readers** for the week. Ask students to complete the questions and activity on the Responding page.

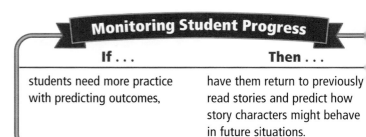

Monitoring Student Progress

If . . .	Then . . .
students need more practice with predicting outcomes,	have them return to previously read stories and predict how story characters might behave in future situations.

ALLENGE/EXTENSION:
edicting Outcomes

Use story clues and personal knowledge to predict outcomes for characters you have read about. Discuss the following questions n a partner:

Vhat might Mulan say or do if the Emperor asked er to fight in another war?

Vhat do you think the Giant of Barletta would do the townspeople asked him for help again?

Vhat might the little girl in *Raising Dragons* do if one of her eggs hatched a mean dragon instead of a nice one?

- Do you think Alan, from *The Garden of Abdul Gasazi*, would take Fritz for another walk? What might he do differently?

- What did Sonia learn about wildlife in the story *Two Days in May*? What might she do if some different animals wandered into her garden?

Predicting outcomes is often used in mathematics. This concept is called probability, and mathematicians use their prior knowledge facts to predict how likely it is that an event will pen. Test this by flipping a coin 100 times. First, dict together how many times the coin will land on ds, and how many times the coin will land on tails.

Then take turns flipping the coin. Make a simple chart and use hatch marks to record your results. When they are finished, discuss the results as a whole group. Ask, Did your results match your prediction? Why or why not? Discuss.

CHALLENGE

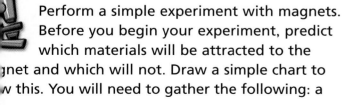

Perform a simple experiment with magnets. Before you begin your experiment, predict which materials will be attracted to the net and which will not. Draw a simple chart to v this. You will need to gather the following: a

magnet, an iron nail, a thumb tack, a cork, a crayon, an aluminum washer, and an eraser. Test your predictions and note what happens. When you finish, share what you have found with the rest of the class.

RETEACHING: Comprehension Skills

Text Organization

OBJECTIVE

- Identify how text is organized in a book or story.

Target Skill Trace

- Text Organization, pp. 251A–251B

Teach

Have chapter books on hand, including one that has numbers as chapter heads and one that has chapter titles. Have a newspaper on hand as well. Show students the chapter book that is separated into sections by numbers. Explain that dividing a book into chapters is one way of organizing the text in the story. Show them the chapter book with chapter titles. Explain that another way of organizing text is to label each chapter with a short title that tells something about that chapter.

Show students the newspaper. Ask, How is the text organized in the newspaper? (by subject) Ask, What sections is this newspaper organized into? (Answers will vary but may include world news, local news, sports, classifieds, and life or variety.)

Hold up the first section of the newspaper. Ask, What kind of stories would you expect to find in this section? (major news, world news) Repeat this procedure with the other sections of the newspaper. Explain that text organization can help us to locate specific information in a newspaper. Inform students that authors organize text to make information clear. Text headings help readers make sense of the information in a story.

Practice

Direct students back to page 172 of the story *Trapped by the Ice!*

Ask students to identify how the text is organized this page. (by date) List the date heading on the boar (October 27, 1915) Page through the story and loca some of the headings. List them on the board.

Discuss what is important about each heading. Ask students to tell how the headings help them understa what they read. Explain that text can be organized by dates, events, or main ideas.

Apply

Have students note how text is organized, with an eye to identifying chapters, heads, dates, and even as they read their **Leveled Readers** for the week. Ask students to complete the questions and activity on the Responding page.

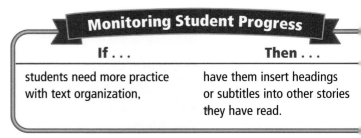

Monitoring Student Progress

If . . .	Then . . .
students need more practice with text organization,	have them insert headings or subtitles into other stories they have read.

ALLENGE/EXTENSION:
xt Organization

Work with a partner. Use the date headings and other information in the story *Trapped by the Ice!* to write and solve time problems. e the problem and solution on your papers. You need to use an old calendar as a counting tool. e: 1916 was a leap year, so remember to count 29.) Answer the following questions:

ow many days passed between the day the *ndurance* was trapped by the ice and the day e sank?

- How many days passed between the day the *Endurance* was trapped by the ice and the day Shackleton reached the whaling station?
- How many days passed between the day the men got the lifeboats to open water and the day they spotted Elephant Island?

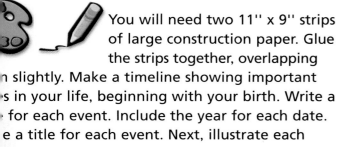

You will need two 11'' x 9'' strips of large construction paper. Glue the strips together, overlapping slightly. Make a timeline showing important s in your life, beginning with your birth. Write a for each event. Include the year for each date. e a title for each event. Next, illustrate each

event or write a brief description about the event's importance. You could show such milestones as birthdays, holidays, and trips. Include activities such as learning to ride a bike, winning a ball game, and learning to play a musical instrument.

CHALLENGE

Work in small groups to map out a voyage from your hometown to Antarctica. You may need an atlas or a world map. Travel ugh major or capital cities whenever possible. el by land and sea only. Think about what types

of transportation you will use, and make a list of the major cities and countries you will pass through on your journey.

RETEACHING: Structural Analysis

Suffixes *-less* and *-ness*

OBJECTIVES

- Identify words that contain the suffixes *-less* and *-ness*.
- Define meanings for words containing the suffixes *-less* and *-ness*.

Target Skill Trace

- Suffixes, p. 183E

Teach

Remind students that suffixes are word parts that are added to a base word. Give each student two index cards containing the suffixes *-less* or *-ness*. Tell students that they are going to use these suffixes to make new words from base words. Direct them to hold up their card (or cards) when they see a base word to which they can add their suffix and create a new word.

Write *hope*. Ask, What word part can combine with *hope* to make a new word? Wait for students holding the *-less* suffix to hold up their cards. Add the suffix *-less* to the base word *hope*. Ask, What is this word?

Continue this procedure using the following words:

> *help* (*helpless*)
> *end* (*endless*)
> *sick* (*sickness*)
> *fearful* (*fearfulness*)
> *hopeful* (*hopefulness*)

Explain to students that the suffix *-less* means "without," and the suffix *-ness* means "the state of being." Have students define the words above, helping them as necessary.

Remind students that when we add suffixes, we change the meanings of the base words. Tell students they are going to use what they know to decode words with the suffixes *-less* and *-ness*.

Practice

Go back to the story *Across the Wide Dark Sea*. Rere the list of words in the left column. Have the students find an example of when the people in the story might have experienced the feeling of helple ness. (during the storms) Continue through the oth words in the list, having students locate one or mo examples for each word.

Ask, What does the suffix *-less* mean? (*without*) Sa Tell me some words containing *-less*. Write the wo on chart paper. Repeat the procedure with the meani for *-ness* (the state of being) and words containing that suffix. Return to the word list in the left colum Point to a specific word and call on a volunteer to give a definition for that word. Continue until each student has had the opportunity to share an answe

Apply

Have students write sentences using words with *-le* and *-ness*. Direct them to use words from the list y created together. Remind them to think about the meanings of the words as they write them. Have th exchange papers and underline the words with the suffixes *-less* and *-ness*.

Monitoring Student Progress

If . . .	Then . . .
students need more practice with suffixes,	have them identify words with suffixes from stories they have read. Then have them work in pairs to use the words to write a paragraph, using as many words with suffixes as possibl

ay a Word Game

e as many words as you can from the letters in the
d *thoughtlessness*. The letters you use do not have
e in the same order as they are in the word
ughtlessness, but you can only use as many letters
here are in the original word. For example, there is
one *o* in *thoughtlessness*, so you can only use one
any word you make. You can reuse letters when
begin a new word.

thoughtlessness

ought

guess

nest

cabulary Expansion

will need these words to complete this activity:
ness, clueless, peacefulness, weightless, senseless.

e down the meaning of each word. You can use
onaries to identify each word's meaning. Choose a

word and write it in the center of a word web. Use as
many words as you can to describe the center word,
without using the center word in any form.

CHALLENGE

tonyms

a piece of paper in half lengthwise. Next, fold the
er in half, widthwise, three times. When the paper
folded, you will have two columns, each with
t boxes. Write a word containing the suffix *-less*
ness in each box in the left column. In the right

column, write a word that is opposite in meaning of
the word in the left column. You may use a dictionary
or thesaurus to do the activity.

RETEACHING

Possessives

OBJECTIVES

- Identify examples of possessives in a story.
- Use possessives in writing, including *'s* and *s'*.

Target Skill Trace

- Possessives, p. 183C

Teach

Write the following phrases:

> One boy's jacket
> The students' jackets

Point out the apostrophes in both examples. Ask, What does the apostrophe show us in these phrases? (possession, belonging) Read the phrases aloud. Explain to students that we add an apostrophe and the letter *s* to singular nouns to show possession. Explain that when a plural noun ends in *s*, we just add the apostrophe.

Write the following phrases:

> Dads jacket (Dad's)
> two girls lunches (girls')
> teachers desk (teacher's)
> Glorias pencil (Gloria's)
> dogs tail (dog's)
> elephants trunks (elephants')

Have students add the apostrophe in each phrase. Help them to see that the apostrophe indicates possession—whether it precedes or follows the *s*.

Practice

Point out to students the apostrophe in the story title *Yunmi and Halmoni's Trip*. Invite students to explain the use of the apostrophe. Then work with them to find examples of possessives in the story. Include some of the following examples:

> page 145 Grandfather's birthday celebration
>   Yunmi's grandfather
>
> page 146 foreigners' line
>
> page 149 Halmoni's house
>   Yunmi's cousins

Circle the *'s* or *s'* in each example. For each example ask, Who is showing possession? To whom does the object belong? Encourage students to respond together.

Review these rules once more:

- If a noun is single, add *'s* to the end of the noun.
- If a noun is plural and ends in *s*, just add an apostrophe.

Apply

Have students look at the illustrations from the story. For each picture, have students list a possessive phrase about an object they see. For example, on page 149 students could list Halmoni's house, Yunmi's cousins, or the house's steps. Have students share their work.

Monitoring Student Progress

If . . .	Then . . .
students need more practice with possessives,	have them make a list of the items in a classmate's desk, using possessives. Then have them change it to indicate that the same items were in several students' desks.

ssessives

...ke a list of your classmates on a piece of paper.
...each person, identify something the person is
...aring, or an object the person owns, or a positive
...aracteristic of that person and write the word on
...paper next to the person's name. Remember to
...'s to describe possession. Use the following examples
... model:

> Ross's red shirt
> Teresa's markers
> The teacher's stamp

ocabulary Expansion

...his story, Yunmi experiences many feelings during
...trip. Use the story to make a list of words related
...eelings. Look for examples of a variety of feelings
...he story and, once you find them, write them on a
...e of paper. Then fold a piece of paper into eight

squares. In each square, write a feeling word and draw
a picture to express that word. Draw something that
word makes you think of, or a person's face expressing
that feeling.

CHALLENGE

...nonyms

...will need to use the following words from the
...y for this activity: *died, promise, foreigner, broad,*
...fy, sweet, roam, crowded, press, hurry. With a part-
...use a dictionary or thesaurus to find synonyms for
...se words. Write each word and its synonym on a
...e of paper. Identify both familiar and unfamiliar

synonyms for your list. Describe an object or person
from the story. Do not list the object or person's name.
Write the correct answer upside down on the back of
your paper, at the bottom. Hang the descriptions on
the board for other classmates to guess, or compile
them together in a book.

RETEACHING: Structural Analysis

VCCV Pattern and Syllabication

OBJECTIVES

- Decode words with a VCCV pattern.
- Divide words with a VCCV pattern into syllables.

Target Skill Trace

- VCCV Pattern and Syllabication, p. 213C

Teach

Write the word *happen*. Under the word, write the letters VCCV, so the word appears like this:

> **happen**
> **V C C V**

Circle the letters *appe* in *happen* and print out that they are in a vowel-consonant-consonant-vowel pattern (VCCV). Explain that the letter patterns in words can help us to know how to pronounce the word, divide it into syllables, and spell it.

Draw a vertical line between the two *p*'s in *happen*. Tell students that when we divide this word into syllables, we divide it between the two consonants.

Say the word *happen* slowly, clapping each syllable. Explain that words with a VCCV pattern are usually divided between the two consonants. Ask, What vowel sound do you hear in the beginning of *happen*? (ă) Ask, Is this a long or short vowel sound? (short) What vowel sound do you hear in the second syllable of happen? (ə) Is this a short or long vowel sound? (short) Explain that a syllable that ends in a consonant is a closed syllable. Closed syllables have short vowel sounds. Words with a VCCV pattern often have short vowel sounds because each vowel is followed by a consonant.

Display the following words: *summer, winter, suffix, basket, market, target*. Have students read the words with you. Explain that all of these words have VCCV patterns. Ask a student to mark *summer* with the VCCV pattern. Have the students clap the syllables the word while saying it aloud. Repeat with the other five words.

Practice

Go back to the story *Trapped by the Ice!* Have students help you find and list words that have the VCCV pattern. Some examples of words are: *person, lumber, skipper, concern, danger, after*.

Call on students to circle the letters forming the VCCV pattern. Then divide the word into syllables.

Apply

Have students continue to look in the story for words with the VCCV pattern. Have each student make a list of words. Have students swap papers and label vowels with *V* and consonants with *C*. Have students exchange papers again and divide the words into syllables. When finished, ask each student to read aloud the list of words.

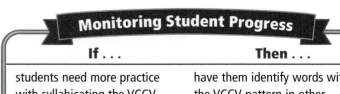

Monitoring Student Progress	
If . . .	**Then . . .**
students need more practice with syllabicating the VCCV pattern,	have them identify words with the VCCV pattern in other stories they have read, write them on a list, and divide them into syllables.

ALLENGE/EXTENSION: Vocabulary

rd Mix-Up

will need between 6 and 12 pieces of 3" X 3" es of construction paper. Make a list of -syllable words that contain a VCCV pattern. Write first syllable of the word on one piece of paper the second syllable on another piece. Mix up your papers when you have finished writing. Exchange papers with a partner. Take your new group of papers and make words out of the syllables. When you have matched all the syllables, read the words aloud to your partner.

cabulary Expansion

the word Antarctica in a center circle for a word . Brainstorm as many words and phrases as possi-to describe Antarctica. You may want to refer to the story to look for descriptive words. After ing a word web, write a cinquain. A cinquain is a m in which every stanza has five lines. See the owing example:

Antarctica
Far away
Cold, colder, coldest
Ice, snow, frost, wind
Seals, penguins, birds, walrus, fish

CHALLENGE

tion Verb Game

k with a partner. Look through the story *Trapped he Ice!* and make a list of action verbs. Some n verbs used in the story are *skiing, burst, lunged, stalking, hunt, tripped, springing, cried, rushed, ped.* Fold a blank piece of paper in half length-twice, and then fold it in half widthwise, three es. The paper will show a total of 32 squares. ose 16 action verbs and write them on the paper, to a square, scattering them around the squares. words do not need to be in any kind of order or ern. Fill in the remaining 16 squares with nouns.

Now you will need a number cube. One player rolls the cube and moves that number of spaces, from the top left to right. If the player lands on an action verb, he or she can roll again. If he or she lands on a noun, the other player takes a turn. Move from left to right until the end of a row, then drop down one square and continue from right to left. The game ends when one player has traveled to the bottom right corner of the paper. If time allows, switch papers with another pair of classmates and play again.

RETEACHING: Grammar

Subject Pronouns

OBJECTIVES

- Replace subject nouns with subject pronouns in the story.
- Write sentences with subject pronouns.

Target Skill Trace

- Subject Pronouns, pp. 183I–183J

Teach

Write the following sentences:

> The girls play soccer.
> They play soccer.

Read each sentence aloud. Underline the word *they* in the second sentence. Explain to students that the word *they* is a pronoun that takes the place of the subject noun in the first sentence. Identify for students other pronouns that can be used as subjects, for example, *I, you, she, he, it,* and *we.*

Have students work in pairs. Give each pair five index cards on which to write the subject pronouns *she, he, it, they,* and *we.* Tell students that you will say some sentences aloud. Ask them to listen carefully and identify the subject of the sentence. Tell each pair to hold up the index card that has the pronoun that can replace the subject. Read the following sentences aloud, or make up your own.

> The boys rode bikes. (They)
> Hope and I watched TV. (We)
> The bird caught a worm. (It)
> Antonio wrote a poem. (He)
> Yolanda ate pizza. (She)
> The bug has green wings. (It)

Practice

Repeat the activity above, using sentences from the story *Across the Wide Dark Sea*. Have the students follow along in the story with you. After each sentence you read, ask student pairs to hold up the index card with the pronoun that can replace the subject of the sentence. Some examples from the story include the following:

page 113 *My father was waving to friends on shore.* (He)

Our family was luckier than most. (We were)

page 115 *My mother and brother were seasick down below.* (They)

page 119 *Could our ship survive another storm?* (It)

page 120 *Our long journey was over.* (It)

Summarize with students by asking the following questions: What words are subject pronouns? (*I, you, he, she, they, we,* and *it*) What does a subject pronoun do? (replaces the subject noun in a sentence)

Apply

Have students write sentences of their own that contain the subject pronouns *I, he, she, we, they, it,* and *you.* When they are done, have students exchange papers. Students can then underline the subject pronouns in their partners' sentences. Then have them give the papers back so that each partner can check to see if the underlining is correct.

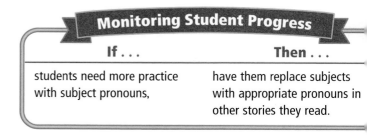

Monitoring Student Progress	
If . . .	**Then . . .**
students need more practice with subject pronouns,	have them replace subjects with appropriate pronouns in other stories they read.

TEACHING: Grammar

Object Pronouns

OBJECTIVES

- Identify object pronouns.
- Write sentences with object pronouns.

Target Skill Trace

- Object Pronouns, pp. 213I–213J

Teach

Write the following sentences:

Mary plays basketball with Lucy and Simon.

Mary plays basketball with them.

Read each sentence aloud. Circle *Lucy* and *Simon* in the first sentence. Underline *them* in the second sentence. Explain that *them* is a pronoun that replaces the proper nouns *Lucy* and *Simon*. Explain that examples of object pronouns are: *me, you, us, them, him, her,* and *it*.

List the object pronouns. Then give each pair of students five blank index cards. Tell them to write *us, them, him, her,* and *it* on their index cards. Explain that these can be used to replace a noun or nouns. Write the following sentences and underline words

I like <u>Carla</u>. (her)

I went inline skating with <u>Luisa and Sheryl</u>. (them)

My mother danced with <u>my friend and me</u>. (us)

I bought <u>the comic book</u> for <u>Jared</u>. (it, him)

Josh loves to play cards with <u>Serena</u>. (her)

My big brother gave <u>his old TV</u> to <u>my sister and me</u>. (it, us)

The children read <u>a story</u>. (it)

as shown:

Ask students to read the first sentence together. As you reread the sentence, have them hold up and say the object pronoun that can replace the underlined word. Follow the same procedure with each of the other sentences.

Practice

Tell students that you are going to work together to identify object pronouns in *Yunmi and Halmoni's Trip*. After you read each of the following sentences, ask, What noun or nouns did this pronoun replace?

page 145 *She pulled out a thick bundle of photos of Yunmi's many relatives, and began to tell her about each of them.* (Yunmi, Yunmi's relatives)

page 148 *Suddenly a huge crowd of people rushed toward them, waving and bowing.* (Yunmi and Halmoni)

page 149 *A cat and a dog with a fluffy tail ran behind her.* (Halmoni's sister) *"Oh, I missed you, too," she said to him.* (the dog)

When finished, review with students by asking: What words are object pronouns? (*them, us, me, you, him, her, it*)

Apply

Have students make up sentences containing the pronouns *them, us, me, you, him, her,* and *it*. Then have students exchange papers and underline the object pronouns.

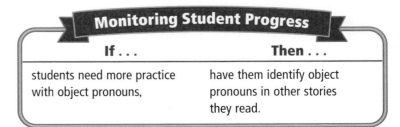

Monitoring Student Progress	
If . . .	**Then . . .**
students need more practice with object pronouns,	have them identify object pronouns in other stories they read.

RETEACHING

Possessive Pronouns

OBJECTIVES

- Identify possessive pronouns.
- Form sentences with possessive pronouns.

Target Skill Trace

- Pronouns, pp. 251I–251J

Teach

Write the following sentences:

Jamal took out Jamal's notebook.

Jamal took out his notebook.

Read each sentence aloud. Circle *Jamal's* in the first sentence. Underline *his* in the second sentence. Explain that *his* is a pronoun that shows possession and that it replaces *Jamal's* in the first sentence. Offer other examples of possessive pronouns such as *my, your, his, her, our, their,* and *its.*

Give each student an index card with a possessive pronoun written on it, excluding *my* and *your.* Explain that you will be saying some sentences aloud. Ask them to listen carefully to each sentence. Tell them that if they have a card with the pronoun that can replace the possessive noun, they should hold it up. Read the following sentences aloud:

Gina brought <u>Gina's</u> ball for the soccer game. (her)

Stan brings <u>Stan's</u> lunch every day. (his)

Jeff and Chantal forgot <u>Jeff and Chantal's</u> homework. (their)

The cat licked <u>the cat's</u> paw. (its)

Practice

Tell students you are going to work together to identify possessive pronouns in *Trapped by the Ice!* After you read each sentence, ask students to tell how the sentence would read if a possessive pronoun were not used.

> **page 172** *Giant blocks of ice were slowly crushing <u>her</u> sides.* (the ship's) *Now <u>his</u> only concern was for <u>his</u> men.* (Shackleton's) *The* Endurance *was a sad sight now, a useless hulk lying on <u>its</u> side.* (*Endurance's* or hulk's)

> **page 174** *Turning toward the ship's wreckage, they saw <u>her</u> stern rise slowly in the air, tremble, and slip quickly beneath the ice.* (the ship's)

> **page 176** *Executing <u>their</u> plan would be difficult* (the men's)

> **page 180** *During <u>their</u> five and a half months on the ice they hadn't had a bath.* (the men's)

Ask, What words are possessive pronouns? (*my, your, his, her, our, their,* and *its*) What does a possessive pronoun do? (replaces a possessive noun)

Apply

Have students write sentences that contain the possessives *my, your, his, her our, their,* and *its.* Then, have them exchange papers and underline the possessive pronouns.

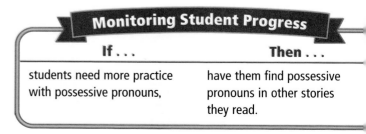

Monitoring Student Progress	
If . . .	**Then . . .**
students need more practice with possessive pronouns,	have them find possessive pronouns in other stories they read.

Name_____

Does It Have an *e?*

anchor	**settlement**
cramped	**survive**
journey	**weary**
seeping	

Theme 5: **Voyagers**

Name_____

Crossword Creation

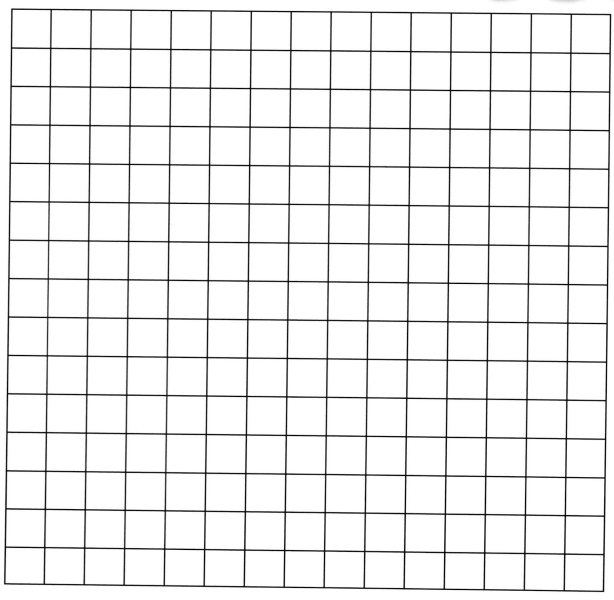

Clues

1. _____

2. _____

3. _____

4. _____

Theme 5: **Voyagers**

Name _____

Key Vocabulary
Concentration

large sheets of floating ice	very tiring	very dangerous	land, ground, or earth
perilous	terrain	having little plant or animal life	deep hole or crack
barren	crevasse	floes	grueling

Theme 5: **Voyagers**

Connotation Connection

Look at the underlined word in each sentence. Find a positive and negative connotation for each word in the word box. Write the connotations on the lines next to each sentence.

pull	weird	relaxed	modest	gazed	
slender	lazy	mousy	glared	skinny	
grin	confident	guide	curious	smirk	conceited

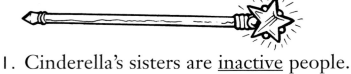

	Positive	Negative
1. Cinderella's sisters are <u>inactive</u> people.	_____	_____
2. Her godmother made Cinderella <u>smile</u>.	_____	_____
3. Before she met her, Cinderella was <u>shy</u>.	_____	_____
4. In her beautiful clothes, she felt <u>proud</u>.	_____	_____
5. The people at the ball <u>looked</u> at Cinderella.	_____	_____
6. The king's son arrived to <u>take</u> her through the crowd.	_____	_____
7. The sisters' feet were not <u>narrow</u> enough to fit in the slipper.	_____	_____
8. The people though it was <u>odd</u> that they had never seen the princess.	_____	_____

Theme 5: **Voyagers**

1. relaxed   lazy   glared
2. grin   smirk   pull
5. gazed
6. guide

Writer _____   Listener _____

Writing Conference:

What Should I Say?

In a writing conference, a writer reads a draft to a partner or a small group. A listener can help the writer by discussing the draft and asking questions such as these.

If you're thinking . . .

- I can't really picture what the writer is describing.
- The writer uses the same words over and over.
- I can't follow this description.

You could say . . .

- Could you tell more details about how _____ looked? smelled? felt? tasted? sounded?
- What sensory words could you add?
- Could you group together details that belong together?

More Questions a Listener Might Ask

Read these questions before you listen. Take notes on the other side of this paper. Then discuss your thoughts with the writer.

1. What do you like about the writer's description?

2. What is the writer describing? Retell what you heard.

3. What details help paint a clear picture?

4. Where does the writer need to add more details?

Theme 5: **Voyagers**

TECHNOLOGY RESOURCES

American Melody
P.O. Box 270
Guilford, CT 06437
800-220-5557
www.americanmelody.com

Audio Bookshelf
174 Prescott Hill Road
Northport, ME 04849
800-234-1713
www.audiobookshelf.com

Baker & Taylor
100 Business Center Drive
Pittsburgh, PA 15205
800-775-2600
www.btal.com

BDD Audio/Random House
400 Hohn Road
Westminster, MD 21157
800-733-3000

Big Kids Productions
1606 Dywer Ave.
Austin, TX 78704
800-477-7811
www.bigkidsvideo.com

Books on Tape
P.O. Box 25122
Santa Ana, CA 92799
800-541-5525
www.booksontape.com

Broderbund Company
1 Martha's Way
Hiawatha, IA 52233
www.broderbund.com

Filmic Archives
The Cinema Center
Botsford, CT 06404
800-366-1920
www.filmicarchives.com

Great White Dog Picture Company
10 Toon Lane
Lee, NH 03824
800-397-7641
www.greatwhitedog.com

HarperAudio
10 E. 53rd St.
New York, NY 10022
800-242-7737
www.harperaudio.com

Houghton Mifflin Company
222 Berkeley St.
Boston, MA 02116
800-225-3362

Informed Democracy
P.O. Box 67
Santa Cruz, CA 95063
800-827-0949

JEF Films
143 Hickory Hill Circle
Osterville, MA 02655
508-428-7198

Kimbo Educational
P.O. Box 477
Long Branch, NJ 07740
800-631-2187
www.kimboed.com

Library Video Co.
P.O. Box 580
Wynnewood, PA 19096
800-843-3620
www.libraryvideo.com

Listening Library
P.O. Box 25122
Santa Ana, CA 92799
800-541-5525
www.listeninglibrary.com

Live Oak Media
P.O. Box 652
Pine Plains, NY 12567
800-788-1121
www.liveoakmedia.com

Media Basics
Lighthouse Square
P.O. Box 449
Guilford, CT 06437
800-542-2505
www.mediabasicsvideo.com

Microsoft Corp.
One Microsoft Way
Redmond, WA 98052
800-426-9400
www.microsoft.com

National Geographic School Publishing
P.O. Box 10597
Des Moines, IA 50340
800-368-2728
www.nationalgeographic.com

New Kid Home Video
P.O. Box 10443
Beverly Hills, CA 90213
800-309-2392
www.NewKidhomevideo.com

Puffin Books
345 Hudson Street
New York, NY 10014
800-233-7364

Rainbow Educational Media
4540 Preslyn Drive
Raleigh, NC 27616
800-331-4047
www.rainbowedumedia.com

Recorded Books
270 Skipjack Road
Prince Frederick, MD 20678
800-638-1304
www.recordedbooks.com

Sony Wonder
Dist. by Professional Media Service
19122 S. Vermont Ave.
Gardena, CA 90248
800-223-7672
www.sonywonder.com

Spoken Arts
195 South White Rock Road
Holmes, NY 12531
800-326-4090
www.spokenartsmedia.com

SRA Media
220 E. Danieldale Rd.
DeSoto, TX 75115
800-843-8855
www.sra4kids.com

Sunburst Technology
1550 Executive Drive
Elgin, IL 60123
800-321-7511
www.sunburst.com

SVE & Churchill Media
6677 North Northwest Highway
Chicago, IL 60631
800-829-1900
www.svemedia.com

Tom Snyder Products
80 Coolidge Hill Road
Watertown, MA 02472
800-342-0236
www.tomsnyder.com

Troll Communications
100 Corporate Drive
Mahwah, NJ 07430
800-526-5289
www.troll.com

Weston Woods
143 Main St.
Norwalk, CT 06851-1318
800-243-5020
www.scholastic.com/west

PRONUNCIATION GUIDE

s book some unfamiliar or hard-to-pronounce words are followed by respellings to
you say the words correctly. Use the key below to find examples of various sounds and
respellings. Note that in the respelled word, the syllable in capital letters is the one
ving the most stress.

ictionary letter or mark	Respelled as	Example	Respelled word
(pat)	a	basket	BAS-kiht
(pay)	ay	came	kaym
(care)	air	share	shair
(father)	ah	barter	BAHR-tur
(church)	ch	channel	CHAN-uhl
(pet)	eh	test	tehst
(bee)	ee	heap	heep
(gag)	g	goulash	GOO-lahsh
(pit)	ih	liver	LIHV-ur
(pie, by)	y	alive	uh-LYV
	eye	island	EYE-luhnd
(hear)	eer	year	yeer
(judge)	j	germ	jurm
(kick, cat, pique)	k	liquid	LIHK-wihd
(pot)	ah	otter	AHT-ur
(toe)	oh	solo	SOH-loh
(caught, paw)	aw	always	AWL-wayz
(for)	or	normal	NOR-muhl
(noise)	oy	boiling	BOYL-ihng
(took)	u	pull, wool	pul, wul
(boot)	oo	bruise	brooz
(out)	ow	pound	pownd
(sauce)	s	center	SEHN-tur
(ship, dish)	sh	chagrin	shuh-GRIHN
(cut)	uh	flood	fluhd
(urge, term, firm, word, heard)	ur	earth bird	urth burd
(zebra, xylem)	z	cows	kowz
(vision, pleasure, garage)	zh	decision	dih-SIHZH-uhn
(about)	uh	around	uh-ROWND
(item)	uh	broken	BROH-kuhn
(edible)	uh	pencil	PEHN-suhl
(gallop)	uh	connect	kuh-NEHKT
(circus)	uh	focus	FOH-kuhs
(butter)	ur	liter	LEE-tur

Glossary

This glossary contains meanings and pronunciations for some of the words in this book. The Full Pronunciation Key shows how to pronounce each consonant and vowel in a special spelling. At the bottom of the glossary pages is a shortened form of the full key.

Full Pronunciation Key

Consonant Sounds

b	**bib**, ca**bb**age	kw	**ch**oir, **qu**ick	t	**t**igh**t**, stop**ped**
ch	**ch**urch, sti**tch**	l	**l**id, need**le**, ta**ll**	th	**b**a**th**, **th**in
d	**d**ee**d**, mai**led**, pu**ddle**	m	a**m**, **m**an, du**mb**	th	**b**a**the**, **th**is
f	**f**ast, **fife**, o**ff**, **ph**rase, rou**gh**	n	**n**o, su**dden**	v	ca**ve**, **v**alve, **v**ine
		ng	thi**ng**, i**nk**	w	**w**ith, **w**olf
g	**g**a**g**, **g**et, fin**ger**	p	**p**o**p**, ha**pp**y	y	**y**es, **y**olk, on**i**on
h	**h**at, **wh**o	r	**r**oar, **rh**yme	z	**r**o**se**, **s**i**z**e, **x**ylophone, **z**ebra
hw	**wh**ich, **wh**ere	s	mi**ss**, **s**auce, **sc**ene, **s**ee	zh	gara**ge**, plea**s**ure, vi**s**ion
j	**j**udge, **g**em	sh	**d**i**sh**, **sh**ip, **s**ugar, ti**ss**ue		
k	**c**at, **k**ick, **sch**ool				

Vowel Sounds

ă	p**a**t, l**au**gh	ŏ	h**o**rrible, p**o**t	ŭ	c**u**t, fl**oo**d, r**ou**gh, s**o**me
ā	**a**pe, **ai**d, p**ay**	ō	g**o**, r**ow**, t**oe**, th**ou**gh	û	c**i**rcle, f**u**r, h**ea**rd, t**er**m, t**ur**n, **ur**ge, w**or**d
â	**ai**r, c**a**re, w**ea**r	ô	**a**ll, c**au**ght, f**o**r, p**aw**		
ä	f**a**ther, k**oa**la, y**a**rd	oi	b**oy**, n**oi**se, **oi**l		
ĕ	p**e**t, pl**ea**sure, an**y**	ou	c**ow**, **ou**t	yōō	c**u**re
ē	b**e**, b**ee**, **ea**sy, p**ia**no	ōō	f**u**ll, b**oo**k, w**o**lf	yōō	**a**b**u**se, **u**se
ĭ	**i**f, p**i**t, b**u**sy	ōō	b**oo**t, r**u**de, fr**ui**t, fl**ew**	ə	**a**go, sil**e**nt, penc**i**l, lem**o**n, circ**u**s
ī	r**i**de, b**y**, p**ie**, h**igh**				
î	d**ea**r, d**ee**r, f**ie**rce, m**e**re				

Stress Marks

Primary Stress ´: bi·ol·o·gy [bī ŏl´ ə jē]
Secondary Stress ´: bi·o·log·i·cal [bī ə lŏj´ ĭ kəl]

Pronunciation key and definitions © 1998 by Houghton Mifflin Company. Adapted and reprinted by permission from *The American Heritage Children's Dictionary*.

414

A

an·chor (ăng´ kər) *noun* A heavy metal object, attached to a ship, that is dropped overboard to keep the ship in place: *We dropped the anchor so that our sailboat wouldn't crash onto the rocky shore.*

ap·pre·ci·ate (ə prē´ shē āt´) *verb* To enjoy and understand: *Max could appreciate that having a dog was a big responsibility.*

a·shore (ə shôr´) *adverb* On or to the shore: *The seal came ashore and then went back into the water.*

B

bar·ren (băr´ ən) *adjective* Not able to produce growing plants or crops: *Because the country's land was barren, food had to be shipped in from other places.*

bask (băsk) *verb* To rest in a pleasant warmth: *Rochelle enjoyed the summer weather as she basked in the warm sun.*

buf·fet (bŭf´ it) *verb* To strike against powerfully: *Luis held his kite tightly as it was buffeted by the strong wind.*

bur·row (bûr´ ō) *noun* A hole or tunnel small animals use as an underground nest.

bus·tling (bŭs´ ling) *adjective* Full of activity; busy: *The bustling mall was full of people shopping for holiday gifts.*

C

cease·less (sēs´ lĭs) *adjective* Continuing without end: *Kim played indoors all day because of the ceaseless rain.*

com·pan·ion·a·ble (kəm păn´ yən ə bəl) *adjective* Friendly: *Maria talked to a companionable girl who was sitting next to her on the train.*

cramped (krămpt) *adjective* So small as to prevent free movement: *The travelers could not stretch out their legs in the plane's cramped space.*

cre·vasse (krĭ văs´) *noun* A deep opening or crack: *A crevasse appeared in the iceberg before it broke apart.*

cus·tom (kŭs´ təm) *noun* Something that the members of a group usually do: *It is an American custom to eat turkey on Thanksgiving.*

burrow

Companionable
Companionable comes from the Latin word *companio*. *Com-* means "together," and *panis* means "food." Friends who share activities and sometimes eat together are companions.

crevasse

ōō **boot** / ou **out** / ŭ **cut** / û **fur** / hw **which** / th **thin** / th **this** / zh **vision** /
ə **ago, silent, pencil, lemon, circus**

415

D

de·sert·ed (dĭ zûrt´ ĕd) *adjective* Not lived in; having few or no people: *No one has lived in the deserted house for many years.*

dis·cour·aged (dĭ skûr´ ĭjd) *adjective* Less hopeful or enthusiastic: *Instead of being discouraged by his poor grade on the test, Matt decided to study more for the next one.*

dis·mal (dĭz´ məl) *adjective* Causing, feeling, or showing gloom or sadness: *It was a dismal day for Yoshiko when her best friend moved away.*

drape (drāp) *verb* To hang in loose folds: *Ellie's long skirt draped to the floor.*

drear·y (drîr´ ē) *adjective* Gloomy; dismal; without cheer: *We decided not to let the dreary weather ruin our vacation.*

E

en·chi·la·da (ĕn´ chə lä´ də) *noun* A tortilla that is folded around a meat filling and covered with a spicy tomato sauce: *Greg learned to make delicious chicken enchiladas in cooking class.*

ex·haust·ed (ĭg zôst´ əd) *adjective* Worn out; tired: *Tina was exhausted after carrying the heavy boxes.*

floe

graze

F

fab·ric (făb´ rĭk) *noun* Material that is produced by weaving threads, or fibers, together; cloth: *Kelly's shirt was made of a cotton fabric.*

floe (flō) *noun* A large, flat mass of floating ice: *The polar bear dove off the ice floe into the freezing water.*

for·eign·er (fôr´ ə nər) *noun* A person from a different country or place: *Americans are foreigners in Europe.*

G

graze (grāz) *verb* To feed on growing plants: *The cows were grazing on grass near the barn.*

gru·el·ing (grōō´ ə lĭng) *adjective* Extremely tiring: *Hannah went to sleep early after running the grueling ten-mile race.*

H

hem (hĕm) *verb* To fold back and sew down the edge of: *I will have to hem my new skirt because it is too long.*

ă **rat** / ā **care** / ä **father** / ĕ **pet** / ē **be** / ĭ **pit** / ī **pie** / î **fierce** / ŏ **pot** /
ō **go** / ô **paw, for** / oi **oil** / ōō **book**

416

---

ho·ri·zon (hə rī´ zən) *noun* The line along which the earth and the sky appear to meet: *Jack watched the setting sun until it disappeared below the horizon.*

I

im·pass·a·ble (ĭm păs´ ə bəl) *adjective* Impossible to travel across or through: *The mountains were impassable, so we had to drive around them.*

in·stinc·tive·ly (ĭn stĭngk´ tĭv lē) *adverb* Acting on an inner feeling that is not learned: *Most dogs instinctively try to protect their owners.*

J

jour·ney (jûr´ nē) *noun* Movement from one place to another; a trip: *The astronauts traveled in a spaceship during their journey to the moon.*

L

lan·guage (lăng´ gwĭj) *noun* Spoken or written human speech: *Jessica took a class to learn the Russian language.*

M

launch (lônch) *verb* To send forcefully upwards like a rocket: *The swimmer pushed off the diving board before launching into the air high above the pool.*

mend (mĕnd) *verb* To put back into good condition; repair: *Koji couldn't wear the shirt until the rip on the sleeve was mended.*

P

pass·port (păs´ pôrt) *noun* A government document that gives a person permission to travel in foreign countries: *Alicia needed a passport to travel to Brazil.*

pat·tern (păt´ ərn) *noun* An artistic design used for decoration: *The curtains have a blue striped pattern.*

pelt (pĕlt) *verb* To strike or beat against again and again: *During the storm, Tomás listened to the rain pelting down on the roof.*

per·il·ous (pĕr´ ə ləs) *adjective* Dangerous: *The icy steps were perilous to walk on.*

horizon

Language
Language comes from the Latin word *lingua*, which means "tongue."

Mend
Mend is a shortened form of the word *amend*, which means "to improve."

ōō **boot** / ou **out** / ŭ **cut** / û **fur** / hw **which** / th **thin** / th **this** / zh **vision** /
ə **ago, silent, pencil, lemon, circus**

417

quay

Skyscraper
The highest sails on a ship used to be called skyscrapers. When the world's first ten-story building was built, writers called it a skyscraper, naming it after those high sails.

skyscraper

Strand
Strand comes from an Old English word that meant "seashore."

plaid (plăd) *adjective* Having a pattern formed by stripes of different widths and colors that cross each other at right angles: *Gus put on his **plaid** scarf before he went out into the cold.*

pop·u·la·tion (pŏp´ yə lā´ shən) *noun* The total number of plants, animals, or people living in a certain place: *Our class did a **population** survey to learn about the people who live in our town.*

Q

quay (kē) *noun* A dock where ships are loaded or unloaded: *The boy stood on the **quay** watching supplies being loaded onto the ships.*

R

rus·tling (rŭs´ lĭng) *noun* A soft fluttering sound: *Deb heard the **rustling** of the leaves in the wind.*

S

sal·sa (säl´ sə) *noun* A spicy sauce made of tomatoes, onions, and peppers: *We dipped our chips in the spicy **salsa**.*

seep (sēp) *verb* To pass slowly through small openings; ooze: *We stuffed a towel in the crack under the door to keep the cold air from **seeping** in.*

set·tle·ment (sĕt´l mənt) *noun* A small community in a new place: *When they reached the new land, the pioneers built a **settlement** to live in.*

sight·see·ing (sīt´ sē´ ĭng) *verb* The act of touring interesting places: *When Marc took his visitors **sightseeing** in Washington, D.C., they went to the Washington Monument.*

sky·scra·per (skī´ skrā pər) *noun* A very tall building: *The Empire State Building is one of the tallest **skyscrapers** in New York City.*

Span·ish (spăn´ ĭsh) *noun* The language of Spain, Mexico, and most of Central America and South America: *My cousin grew up in Mexico and speaks **Spanish**.*

starve (stärv) *verb* To suffer or die from lack of food: *We put seeds in the feeder so the birds wouldn't **starve** in the winter.*

strand·ed (strănd´ əd) *adjective* In a difficult or helpless position: *When our car ran out of gas, we were **stranded** on the side of the road.*

ă rat / ā **pay** / â **care** / ä **father** / ĕ **pet** / ē **be** / ĭ **pit** / ī **pie** / î **fierce** / ŏ **pot** /
ō **go** / ô **paw, for** / oi **oil** / ōō **book**

418

sul·len·ly (sŭl´ ən lē) *adverb* Angrily or unhappily: *When his parents wouldn't let him have a cookie, the little boy **sullenly** refused to eat dinner.*

surf (sûrf) *verb* To ride on waves, often on a surfboard: *During summer vacation, Doug **surfed** at the beach.*
—*noun* The waves of the sea as they break on a shore or reef: *Lucy swam in the **surf**.*

sur·round·ing (sə round´ dĭng) *adjective* On all sides of: *The **surrounding** trees shaded the house from the sun.*

sur·vive (sər vīv´) *verb* To stay alive or continue to exist: *A whale cannot **survive** out of water.*

swell (swĕl) *noun* A long rolling wave in open water: *The swimmer was lifted gently by the ocean **swell**.*

swoop (swōōp) *verb* To move with a sudden sweeping motion: *The seagull **swooped** down to catch a fish.*

T

ta·co (tä´ kō) *noun* A tortilla that is folded around a filling, such as ground meat or cheese: *We added lettuce and tomato to our **tacos**.*

ta·ma·le (tə mä´ lē) *noun* A steamed cornhusk that is wrapped around a meat filling made with red peppers and cornmeal: *When I go to my favorite Mexican restaurant, I love to order **tamales**.*

ter·rain (tə rān´) *noun* Any piece of land; ground, soil, earth: *It was difficult to hike across the rocky **terrain**.*

ter·ri·to·ry (tĕr´ ĭ tôr´ ē) *noun* An area of land; region: *Bears roam their **territory** in search of food.*

tor·til·la (tôr tē´ yə) *noun* A round, flat bread made from cornmeal and water and baked on a grill: *My grandmother showed me how to make a **tortilla**.*

U

un·in·hab·i·ted (ŭn´ ĭn hăb´ ə tĭd) *adjective* Having no people living there: *The explorer was the first person to visit the **uninhabited** island.*

V

vend·or (vĕn´ dər) *noun* A person who sells something: *In Chicago, Carl bought a hot dog from a street **vendor**.*

surf

Terrain
Terrain comes from the Latin word *terra*, which means "earth." Other words that come from *terra* are *territory*, *terrace*, and *terrier*.

vendor

ōō **boot** / ou **out** / ŭ **cut** / û **fur** / hw **which** / th **thin** / *th* **this** / zh **vision** /
ə **ago**, sil**e**nt, penc**i**l, lem**o**n, circ**u**s

419

venture

ven·ture (vĕn´ chər) *verb* To do something in spite of risk: *We decided to **venture** out to the edge of the cliff.*

W

wan·der (wŏn´ dər) *verb* To move from place to place without a special purpose or goal: *People in shopping malls often **wander** from store to store.*

wea·ry (wîr´ ē) *adjective* Needing rest; tired: *After climbing the mountain, the **weary** hikers took a nap.*

ă rat / ā **pay** / â **care** / ä **father** / ĕ **pet** / ē **be** / ĭ **pit** / ī **pie** / î **fierce** / ŏ **pot** /
ō **go** / ô **paw, for** / oi **oil** / ōō **book**

420

Acknowledgments

Pronunciation key and definitions © 1998 by Houghton Mifflin Company. Adapted and reprinted by permission from The American Heritage Children's Dictionary.

Main Literature Selections
Across the Wide Dark Sea: The Mayflower Journey, by Jean Van Leeuwen, illustrated by Thomas B. Allen. Text copyright © 1995 by Jean Van Leeuwen. Illustrations copyright © 1995 by Thomas B. Allen. Reprinted by permission of Dial Books for Young Readers, a division of Penguin Books Inc.
Alejandro's Gift, by Richard E. Albert, illustrated by Sylvia Long. Text copyright © 1994 by Richard E. Albert. Illustrations copyright © 1994 by Sylvia Long. Reprinted by permission of the publisher, Chronicle Books LLC, San Francisco. Visit http://www.chroniclebooks.com.
"Helen Keller" from *Sisters in Strength*, by Yona Zeldis McDonough, illustrated by Malcah Zeldis. Text copyright © 2000 by Yona Zeldis McDonough. Reprinted by permission of Henry Holt and Company, LLC.
The Island-Below-the-Star, written and illustrated by James Rumford. Copyright © 1998 by James Rumford. Reprinted by permission of Houghton Mifflin Company. All rights reserved.
Nights of the Pufflings, by Bruce McMillan. Copyright © 1995 by Bruce McMillan. Reprinted by permission of Houghton Mifflin Company. All rights reserved.
Pepita Talks Twice/Pepita habla dos veces, by Ofelia Dumas Lachtman. Copyright © 1995 by Ofelia Dumas Lachtman. Reprinted with permission from the publisher Arte Publico Press/University of Houston.
Poppa's New Pants, by Angela Shelf Medearis, illustrated by John Ward. Text copyright © 1995 by Angela Shelf Medearis. Illustrations copyright © 1995 by John Ward. Reprinted by permission of Holiday House, Inc.
Selection from *Prairie School*, by Avi. Text copyright © 2001 by Avi. Reprinted by permission of HarperCollins Publishers.

Selection from *Ramona Quimby, Age 8*, by Beverly Cleary, illustrated by Alan Tiegreen. Copyright © 1981 by Beverly Cleary. Reprinted by permission of HarperCollins Publishers.
Seal Surfer, by Michael Foreman. Copyright © 1996 by Michael Foreman. Reprinted by permission of Harcourt Inc.
Trapped by the Ice!: Shackleton's Amazing Antarctic Adventure, by Michael McCurdy. Copyright © 1997 by Michael McCurdy. Reprinted by arrangement with Walker & Co.
Two Days in May, by Harriet Peck Taylor, pictures by Leyla Torres. Text copyright © 1999 by Harriet Peck Taylor. Illustrations copyright © 1999 by Leyla Torres. Reprinted by permission of Farrar, Straus and Giroux, LLC.
"A Wild Ride," by Thomas Fleming, from the March 2002 issue of *Boy's Life* magazine. Text copyright © 2002 by Thomas Fleming. Cover copyright © 2002 by the Boy Scouts of America. Reprinted by permission of the author and Boy's Life, published by the Boy Scouts of America.
Yunmi and Halmoni's Trip, by Sook Nyul Choi, illustrated by Karen Dugan. Text copyright © 1997 by Sook Nyul Choi. Illustrations copyright © 1997 by Karen Dugan. Reprinted by permission of Houghton Mifflin Company. All rights reserved.

Focus Selections
Cinderella, by Charles Perrault, retold by Amy Ehrlich. Text copyright © 1985 by Amy E. Ehrlich. Published by arrangement with Dial Books for Young Readers, a member of Penguin Putnam Inc.
Selection from *Yeh-Shen: A Cinderella Story from China*, retold by Ai-Ling Louie, illustrated by Ed Young. Text copyright © 1982 by Ai-Ling Louie. Illustrations copyright © 1982 by Ed Young. Reprinted by permission of Philomel Books, a division of Penguin Young Readers Group, a member of Penguin Group (USA) Inc. Electronic rights granted by the author for the text and by McIntosh and Otis, Inc. for the illustrations. All rights reserved.

421

Glossary G2

Glossary continued

422

423

424

Index